THE FIRST TOTAL WAR

Books by David A. Bell

LAWYERS AND CITIZENS

*The Making of a Political Elite in
Old Regime France*

THE CULT OF THE NATION
IN FRANCE

Inventing Nationalism, 1680–1800

THE FIRST TOTAL WAR

*Napoleon's Europe and the
Birth of Warfare as We Know It*

The First
TOTAL WAR

Napoleon's Europe and the
Birth of Warfare as We Know It

David A. Bell

HOUGHTON MIFFLIN COMPANY

BOSTON · NEW YORK

2007

Visit our Web site: www.houghtonmifflinbooks.com.

Library of Congress Cataloging-in-Publication Data
Bell, David Avrom.
The first total war : Napoleon's Europe and the birth of
warfare as we know it / David A. Bell.
p. cm.
Includes bibliographical references and index.
ISBN-13: 978-0-618-34965-4
ISBN-10: 0-618-34965-0
1. Napoleon 1, Emperor of the French, 1769–1821 — Military
leadership. 2. Napoleonic Wars, 1800–1815. 3. France — History,
Military — 1789–1815. 4. Europe — History, Military — 1789–1815.
5. Military history, Modern. 6. War and society —
History. I. Title.
DC202.1.B39 2007
940.27 — dc22   2006023077

Printed in the United States of America

Book design by Robert Overholtzer

MP 10 9 8 7 6 5 4 3 2 1

ILLUSTRATIONS: Page 22: from *Memoires Secrets de Beau Lauzun* (Editions Colbert, 1943); page 33: courtesy of Universite Paris-Sorbonne; pages 38, 55, 135, 142,
226, 229, 248: courtesy of Réunion des Musées Nationaux/Art Resource, NY; page
60: courtesy of Johns Hopkins University Special Collections and Archives; page
91: courtesy of Giraudon/Art Resource, NY; page 141: courtesy of Bibliothèque Nationale de France; page 200: courtesy of Erich Lessing/Art Resource, NY; page 246:
courtesy of Saint Louis Art Museum. Gift of Mr. and Mrs. R. Crosby Kemper
through the Crosby Kemper Foundations; page 255: courtesy of Cornell University,
Division of Rare and Manuscript Collections; page 277: courtesy of Scala/Art Resource, NY; pages 283, 292: copyright The Trustees of The British Museum.

To Elana Kathleen Bell and Joseph Nathaniel Bell

Contents

Maps and Illustrations

Acknowledgments

To give adequate thanks to everyone who helped me with this project would probably take the equivalent of an additional chapter. I doubt that my editor would approve, even though several pages would go to singing her praises. But I do want to acknowledge my most important debts.

The idea for the project first gelled in a memorable conversation with Darrin McMahon in the spring of 2000. My agent, Elyse Cheney, encouraged me to write a book for a general audience and gave me invaluable assistance throughout.

The American Council of Learned Societies Frederick Burkhardt Residential Fellowship Program for Recently Tenured Scholars and the John Simon Guggenheim Memorial Foundation generously granted me fellowships, and the Johns Hopkins University not only allowed me to take two years' leave but also provided additional financial assistance. At Hopkins, I am grateful to Deans Daniel Weiss and Adam Falk and to two chairs and friends, Gabrielle Spiegel and Richard Kagan, for their incredibly generous support. Over the years, I have benefited in too many ways to mention from the wonderful atmosphere provided at Johns Hopkins by my colleagues, graduate students, and the History Department staff. My students Jason Kuznicki and Mary Ashburn-Miller tracked down stray items in Paris for me. Rebecca Pekron and Jeremy Caradonna provided invaluable assistance with the book's illustrations and Katie Jorgensen-Gray with editing.

Away from Baltimore, Leon Wieseltier at the *New Republic* and Paul Laity at the *London Review of Books* kindly kept sending me books about Napoleon and the French Revolution to review, gave me a chance to try out some of my ideas in print, and provided expert editing. I received helpful bibliographical suggestions from David Armitage and Sophia Rosenfeld. Dena Goodman did me a great favor by prodding me to think about the phenomenon of soldier-poets.

I inflicted draft chapters and articles on Mary Ashburn-Miller, Doron Ben-Atar, Claire Cage, Jane Dailey, Dan Edelstein, Eddie Kolla, Darrin McMahon, David Nirenberg, John Pocock, Eran Shalev, Donald Suther-land, Dror Wahrman, and David Woodworth and the whole manuscript on Rafe Blaufarb, Michael Broers, and Steven Englund. I am grateful for all the resulting corrections, suggestions, and criticisms, which in some cases forced me to rethink critical aspects of the project. I am also grate-ful to the audiences to which I presented portions of the work at Berkeley, the United States Naval Academy, the Sorbonne conference "La Révolu-tion à l'oeuvre," Rice University, the Johns Hopkins conference "Napo-leon and His Legend," the University of Delaware, Florida State Univer-sity, George Mason University, the Yale conference "Napoleon's Legacies," the Baltimore-Washington Old Regime France Group, the Consortium on the Revolutionary Era, the University of Buffalo, the University of Chicago, New York University, Johns Hopkins University, the Indiana University Eighteenth-Century Seminar, and my spring 2006 graduate seminar. I have a particular debt to audiences at the École Normale Su-périeure de la rue d'Ulm, where I spent a highly stimulating month in 2005, and to my generous and thoughtful host there, Antoine Lilti.

At Houghton Mifflin, I want to thank Amanda Cook for her brilliant editing, her toleration of delays, her support, and her good cheer. Thanks as well to her assistant Will Vincent and to manuscript editor Beth Bur-leigh Fuller.

To my parents, Daniel and Pearl Kazin Bell, I am profoundly grateful, as always. The way my father cared for my mother during the years I wrote this book means more to me than I can say. Unlike many of the sto-ries I tell here, it is a case of true heroism.

To my wife, Donna Lynn Farber, I owe, well, everything. She and our children, Elana and Joseph Bell, have made these years unreasonably happy ones for me. The book is dedicated to Elana and Joseph, with the hope that its subject will remain forever academic to them. *L'dor va-dor.*

THE FIRST TOTAL WAR

Introduction

This war will be the last war.

— CHARLES-FRANÇOIS DUMOURIEZ, 1792

T HE YEARS '89 AND '90 were years of elation and hope. A powerful and much-loathed regime not only collapsed unexpectedly but did so with surprisingly little violence. Amid its ruins, a new international order seemed to be taking shape, built on a respect for peace, democracy, and human rights. So transformative did the moment appear that many advanced thinkers predicted nothing less than the coming end of warfare. But disillusion followed with cruel speed. The years that followed brought not peace but unremitting violence, which the dominant powers found frustratingly difficult to contain. Soon, the widespread expectation of an end to war gave way to the equally widespread conviction that an era of apocalyptic conflict had begun. Indeed, it was widely argued that to defeat evil adversaries, war now needed to be waged on a sustained and massive scale, and with measures once condemned as barbaric.

The strange thing about this description is that it applies equally well to two different centuries. Most obviously for us, it applies to the period that began in 1989–90. Even before the rotten timbers of the Soviet

Union finished crashing to the ground, prominent political scientists were claiming that an end to war was at hand. Some thought that the world had simply begun to outgrow large-scale conflict. Others believed that peace would follow the spread of democracy, since democracies supposedly do not fight one another. Francis Fukuyama, in a famous and unjustly mocked article, linked the end of war to "the end of history" — by which he meant an end to conflicts over the proper form of society.

Instead of an end to war, of course, there followed an intensification of conflict and danger: in the Gulf War, the wars in the Balkans, and then the global upheaval that began on September 11, 2001. In the wake of that day's horrific terrorist attacks, U.S. president George W. Bush began to describe the struggle between the West and its adversaries as one between the forces of freedom and the forces of evil. Prominent supporters of his administration likened it to World War II and warned that the very survival of the West hung in the balance. Some insisted that to prevail, the West would even have to flout established restraints on military behavior. "Among ourselves, we keep the law but when we are operating in the jungle, we must also use the laws of the jungle," wrote the British diplomat Robert Cooper in an influential 2002 essay. Soon afterward, the United States and its allies began a preemptive war in Iraq, starting with an open attempt to assassinate its head of state. Since then, American military operations have involved a number of well-publicized lapses into the "laws of the jungle." At this writing, it is difficult to see how or when the current period of violent instability and danger might come to an end.

So far, so familiar. Yet, surprisingly, the description applies just as well to the years 1789–90, when the collapse of the Old Regime and the beginning of the French Revolution untethered hopeful imaginations around the world. Even before these events, advanced opinion in the West was already beginning to think of war as a rapidly vanishing anachronism. As an optimistic English clergyman wrote in 1784: "The time is approaching, when *the sound of the trumpet,* and the alarm of war, will be heard no more throughout the earth." On May 22, 1790, France's new revolutionary government went so far as to issue a formal renunciation of "wars of conquest," in what has been called a "declaration of peace to the world." It promised that France would henceforth use its armed forces only in self-defense. But just twenty-three months later, France invaded Austrian-ruled Belgium, starting a conflict that would drag in all of Europe's major powers and continue, with only short interruptions, for more than twenty-three years, until France's final defeat in 1815. From early on, both sides saw this long struggle in apocalyptic terms: "a war to the death," as one of its early French advocates declared, "which we will fight . . . so as to destroy and annihilate all who attack us, or to be destroyed ourselves." Neither side went so far as to practice assassination openly. But desperate guerrilla warfare and savage attempts to repress it spawned atrocities across the Continent on a scale not matched again until World War II. As Napoleon Bonaparte himself explained, foreshadowing Cooper: "It has cost us dearly to return . . . to the principles that characterized the barbarism of the early ages of nations, but we have been constrained . . . to deploy against the common enemy the arms he has used against us."

Needless to say, the parallels are hardly exact. The sheer scale of bloodshed and destruction in Napoleon's Europe — by which I mean both the Europe he lived through as a young officer and the one he came to dominate as ruler of France — greatly exceeded anything yet seen since 1989. Yet neither are the parallels coincidental. The late eighteenth and early nineteenth centuries saw fundamental changes in Western attitudes toward war and the start of a recurrent historical pattern, of which events since 1989 provide only the most recent, if also a particularly clear, example. In this pattern, the dream of perpetual peace and the nightmare of total war have been bound together in complex and disturbing ways, each sustaining the other. On the one hand, a large and sustained current of public opinion has continued to see war as a fundamentally barbaric phenomenon that should soon disappear from a civilized world. On the other hand, there has been a recurrent and powerful tendency to characterize the conflicts that do arise as apocalyptic struggles that must be fought until the complete destruction of the enemy and that might have a purifying, even redemptive, effect on the participants. Today, these twin languages of war and peace define the extremes of Western, and particularly American, thinking on the subject, with "speakers" of each dismissing their opponents as a species of reality-denying mental patients: the "delusional" doves versus the "paranoid" or "war-mongering" hawks.

Some sophisticated commentators have interpreted these languages as reflections of recent historical circumstances. Robert Kagan, for instance, contrasts a Western Europe, which has allegedly enjoyed peace without responsibility, thanks to American protection, since World War II, and therefore shuns military action, with an America that has grindingly confronted one lethal opponent after another. "Americans are from Mars and Europeans are from Venus," he concludes.

But, in fact, these languages took shape long before World War II. And they have more in common with each other than either side likes to admit, for in each case, war figures as something wholly exceptional, wholly outside the established social order. Not surprisingly, intellectuals and statesmen have often braided them together in the idea that one final, all-consuming war might paradoxically inaugurate the reign of perpetual peace. To quote the single most famous expression of this idea, H. G. Wells's 1914 tract *The War That Will End War:* "This is now a war for peace . . . This, the greatest of all wars, is not just another war — it is the last war!" A hundred and twenty-two years before, the French politician-general Charles-François Dumouriez had likewise promised: "this war will be the last war."

The fact that we see war through conceptual lenses that were largely ground and polished two centuries ago in Europe does not mean that our vision is necessarily distorted. Obviously, there *are* occasions on which the West has faced apocalyptic danger. Nonetheless, we need to recognize the power and persistence of these lenses and the distorting effects they can often give rise to. In the 1990s, a reluctance to use military force, grounded in part in a perception of war as an anachronistic folly, led to massive suffering and death in the Balkans and Rwanda while Western statesmen sat learnedly discussing sanctions and political pressure. Only in the former case did they finally remember that there *are* barbarians in the world and that they respond only to force.

But consider this as well. Since September 2001, the United States has been involved in a War on Terror that has, to date, cost the same number of American civilian lives that are lost every two and a half weeks in road accidents on American highways. It is the same number of lives that the Soviet Union lost *every six hours,* for four agonizing years, during World War II. Our opponents in this new conflict, for all their stated desire to acquire weapons of mass destruction, have so far demonstrated no ability to wield anything more powerful than knives, guns, and conventional explosives. A war it may be, but does it really deserve comparison to World War II and its 50 million dead? Not every adversary is an apocalyptic threat. Yet the languages in which we are used to discussing war and peace make it difficult for this point to emerge. Put simply, it has become very difficult to discuss war in nonapocalyptic terms.

Why is this the case? Why has the West returned again and again to the twin visions of an end to war and apocalyptic war? I don't pretend to be offering an answer to this entire, vast question. But in this book, I explore how and why the pattern began.

At the heart of the story is an astonishing transformation. During the eighteenth century, as in previous centuries, most Western cultures accepted war as an inevitable, and ordinary, facet of human existence. Western rulers saw war as their principal purpose and fought continually — during the 1700s, no more than six or seven years passed without at least one major European power at war. But since the end of the terrible religious conflicts of the Reformation, war had also become relatively easy to control and to restrain. Armies were relatively small, major battles relatively infrequent (though devastating when they occurred), and civilians relatively well treated. Military leaders saw their adversaries largely as honorable equals. This is not to say that war was not horrific. War is horrific by definition. But historians need to be able to make distinctions between shades of horror, and if the eighteenth century did not exactly reduce the slavering dogs of war to "performing poodles" (as Sir Michael Howard once jokingly put it), its conflicts still ranked among the *least* horrific in European history.

This state of virtually permanent but restrained warfare seemed entirely natural and proper to the noblemen who led Europe's armies under the Old Regime, for it allowed the aristocratic values of honor and service to find full expression without serious threats to social stability and prosperity. Indeed, war operated as a sort of theater of the aristocracy, just as the royal courts of the period did. In war, aristocratic lives and values were put on display, amid splendor, polish, gallantry, and shows of utter self-assurance. European elites of the eighteenth century assumed that this world would last indefinitely. They did not realize that it was on the edge of total eclipse.

The transformation had its origins in the realm of the intellect. During the great movement of ideas we now call the Enlightenment, influential thinkers began to argue that permanent warfare might not, in fact, be the permanent fate of mankind. Human societies, they wrote, followed a common path of historical evolution from savage beginnings toward ever-greater levels of peaceful civilization, politeness, and commercial exchange. From this point of view, the prevailing state of restrained warfare did not represent a natural equilibrium but rather a stage on the way to war's eventual complete disappearance. In modern times, war would soon become an abhorrent, exceptional state of affairs, a grotesque remnant of mankind's violent infancy.

These thinkers were by no means the first prophets of perpetual peace: philosophical and religious pacifists had long preceded them. But for devout Christians in particular, the inescapable fact of original sin implied that a reign of peace could come about only as the result of a providential change in human nature. By contrast, the secular eighteenth-century writers described peace as the culmination of entirely natural social changes that were already visible and taking place according to scientifically observable laws. This difference made them the most convincing, and the most apparently realistic, pacifists the world had ever known, and their ideas rapidly became conventional wisdom among educated Europeans, including even many nobles and military officers.

Yet even as these beliefs gained in popularity, other Europeans began to stare into the abyss of war and see not only something terrible but also something that held a terrible fascination, even a terrible sublimity. They began to see in it the ultimate test of a society and of an individual self. They began to imagine it as an elemental, cleansing, even redemptive experience — and therefore, perhaps, as a desirable one. War might be fundamentally alien to a civilized way of life — but was "civilization" necessarily such a blessing? Could not war serve as a corrective to the corruption and pettiness of civilized existence? "War is one of the healthiest phenomena for the cultivation of the human race," the German polymath Wilhelm von Humboldt would write. "It is the admittedly fearful extreme." This new glorification of war did not, however, mark a return to the earlier, aristocratic understandings. Quite the contrary. War remained seen as an exceptional, extreme state of affairs, not as an ordinary facet of human existence. For the enthusiasts, it was no longer a matter of aristocratic self-control, of establishing a reputation by emulating an impersonal model of glory. It was becoming a matter of Romantic self-expression. In fact, the very concept and experience of the "self" in war was changing.

Before the French Revolution, ideas of this sort had little effect on Europe's rulers, still less on the conduct of war. But during the first three years of the French Revolution (1789–92), one of the greatest moments of political and cultural fermentation in all history, they burst into the mainstream of political debate in Europe's largest and most powerful state. During the same period, the French aristocracy lost its predominant position in the French state and armed forces and found itself the target of visceral revolutionary hostility. As a result of these changes, when France took up arms in 1792, it was not to fight anything like the limited wars familiar to the powers of the Old Regime.

What followed deserves the adjective "apocalyptic." The conflicts of 1792 to 1815 did not witness any great leaps ahead in military technology, but Europe nevertheless experienced an astonishing transformation in the scope and intensity of warfare. The figures speak for themselves. More than a fifth of all the major battles fought in Europe between 1490 and 1815 took place just in the twenty-five years after 1790. Before 1790, only a handful of battles had involved more than 100,000 combatants; in 1809, the battle of Wagram, the largest yet seen in the gunpowder age, involved 300,000. Four years later, the battle of Leipzig drew 500,000, with fully 150,000 of them killed or wounded. During the Napoleonic period, France alone counted close to a million war deaths, possibly including a higher proportion of its young men than died in World War I. The toll across Europe may have reached as high as 5 million. In a development without precedent, the wars brought about significant alterations in the territory or the political system of every single European state. Guerrilla fighting left livid scars in regions of Spain, Italy, Austria, Switzerland, and France itself. This, then, was the first total war.

The concept of "total war" deserves some explanation. It has enormous resonance, and many historians have used it to describe the wars of 1792–1815. But it is also one of those concepts that seems to get blurrier the closer you come to it. It is often defined as a war involving the complete mobilization of a society's resources to achieve the absolute destruction of an enemy, with all distinction erased between combatants and noncombatants. This formulation seems, at first, clear enough. But can any real war live up to this ideal standard? (Even a massive thermonuclear exchange would not involve the mobilization of all of a society's resources!) And if not, what determines which wars come sufficiently close to the ideal to qualify? The ambiguities are such that one leading scholar, Roger Chickering, has come close to concluding that the concept should simply be scrapped.

I believe that "total war" remains a useful term but only when applied to war in a broad political and cultural context. What marked the conflicts that began in 1792 was not simply their radically new scope and intensity but also the political dynamic that drove the participants relentlessly *toward* a condition of total engagement and the abandonment of restraints. Even before France attacked Austria, much of the French political leadership had come to see war in the new manner, as an unfathomable extreme, set outside the ordinary bounds of social existence, that could end only in total victory or total defeat. This vision drove France into declaring war even though it lacked clear, practical strategic goals. It produced the widespread conviction that France's enemies were themselves bent on a "war of extermination." It helped demonize enemy populations and made it almost impossible to see enemy soldiers as honorable adversaries or enemy noncombatants as innocent bystanders. It drove France to conquer ever more territories as a buffer against these enemies and to impose revolutionary reforms there, even at the cost of provoking massive uprisings. These actions drove France's enemies, particularly rebels against French occupations, to adopt an equally radical vision of the conflict. In short, the French advocates of war set up a race into the abyss that could not easily be reversed, even after they themselves had largely vanished from the scene. Napoleon Bonaparte, despite his taste for conquest, was no conscious advocate of total war (still less was he the bloodthirsty megalomaniac of legend). But it was the radical intensification of war that brought him to prominence and power, and in the end, he could not contain it. He was, in turn, the product, master, and victim of total war.

As the French scholar Jean-Yves Guiomar has compellingly argued, it is this fusion of politics and war that distinguishes modern "total war" from earlier incidents of unrestrained or even exterminatory warfare. Needless to say, humanity had a long and sorry record of such conflicts before the eighteenth century. It did not, however, except in a few, geographically confined arenas (e.g., city-states), see concerted political attempts to harness entire societies — every human being, every resource — to a single, military purpose. This factor is what brings the continent-wide conflicts of 1792–1815 closer to the world wars of the twentieth century. Tellingly, the term "total war" itself first appeared in France and Germany at the end of the First World War, not only to describe the fighting but also to help envisage even more violent conflicts, in which nations would concentrate all available strength for one, great, convulsive blow. In the World War II speech that gave the term particular notoriety — Joseph Goebbels shrieking at a crowd of Nazis at the Berlin Sports Palace just weeks after the German surrender at Stalingrad, *"Wollt ihr den totalen Krieg?"* ("Do you want total war?") — it again referred to an as yet unrealized future, not the past or the present. Calls for total engagement, Guiomar observes, have tended to come from civilian political leaders far more than from military professionals.

Here, then, is the essential argument of *The First Total War.* The intellectual transformations of the Enlightenment, followed by the political fermentation of 1789–92, produced new understandings of war that made possible the cataclysmic intensification of the fighting over the next twenty-three years. Ever since, the same developments have shaped the way Western societies have seen and engaged in military conflict.

This is a new argument. Among historians, conventional wisdom has long attributed the intensification of war after 1792 to two different factors. First, they cite revolutionary ideology, suggesting that the wars grew out of a conflict between fundamentally incompatible belief systems: one radically egalitarian and the other conservative and hierarchical. Second, they invoke nationalism, arguing that even though earlier wars had pitted dynastic houses against each other, these new conflicts took place between entire nations that were coming to new states of self-consciousness.

Ideology and nationalism both played hugely important roles in the history of this period. But were they the principal factors driving the intensification of war? Both explanations date back to the period itself and echo rather too neatly the justifications for war given at the time. For example, the British conservative Edmund Burke, in 1796: "It is with an armed doctrine that we are at war . . . if it can at all exist, it must finally prevail." Or the future military strategist Carl von Clausewitz, in 1812: "It is not [now] the king who wages war on the king, not an army against another army, but a people against another people." Furthermore, both explanations reduce war to little more than an instrument of changing political goals. Neither allows any scope for treating war as a meaningful and dynamic activity in its own right, exerting profound and complex effects on politics and culture in its turn (not surprisingly, the famous definition of war as "the continuation of political intercourse, carried on with other means" derives from the period — from Clausewitz himself).

Both explanations also suffer from more specific, chronological problems. Consider that even during the most radical period of the French Revolution (which ended in 1794), not all French leaders advocated the spread of revolutionary ideology by force. Under Napoleon, there followed a return to naked dynastic politics: he put three of his brothers and a brother-in-law on foreign thrones, and himself married the daughter of the Austrian emperor. Yet it was precisely during the later, least revolutionary years of his rule that the wars grew largest in scope and most vicious in the suppression of rebellions against French rule.

Nationalism certainly contributed to the wars. The concepts of forging nations anew and mobilizing entire populations helped inspire everything from France's 1793 "*levée en masse*" (mass levy of soldiers) to Spain's 1808 rising against Napoleon to the German "war of liberation" of 1813. Yet the slogan of a "war of nations" had appeared in France and Britain decades *before* the Revolutionary war, while Napoleon's regime ended up downplaying nationalist language, in keeping with its revival of dynastic politics and its transformation into a multinational empire. Nor did the spectacle of the "people in arms," so loudly hailed as a world-changing event at the time, ever entirely live up to its reputation. The ill-trained and ill-equipped soldiers of the *levée en masse* did matter because of their sheer numbers, but they helped the French war effort much less than contemporaries claimed. Similar attempts at general levies in Austria and Prussia also had only partial success. Napoleon depended on professional soldiers as much as possible. As for the Spanish war against Napoleon, which still generally has the reputation of being a spontaneous rising of the entire Spanish people, much of the popula-

tion in fact remained aloof from the war, while the activities of the rebels sometimes resembled organized crime as much as national liberation.

In this book, then, I look less at nationalism and ideology than at
transformations in what I would call the "culture of war" between the
mid-eighteenth century and the first decades of the nineteenth — in
other words, roughly across the lifetime of Napoleon Bonaparte (1769–
1821). I have already mentioned the single most important transformation: the way war ceased to be seen as an ordinary part of the social order and began to appear as something entirely apart from the proper
course of history. But two other, related shifts took place at the same
time, and *The First Total War* discusses them as well.

First, there came new perceptions of the armed forces. It was in this
period, I argue, that the "military" came enduringly to be defined as a
separate sphere of society, largely distinct from the "civilian" one. The
distinction was not unknown in Europe but had previously appeared
primarily in societies that relied on mercenary armies, such as the city-
states of Renaissance Italy. In most of Europe, common soldiers had often lived apart from nonsoldiers and had a distinct set of experiences,
but the idea of "military" and "civilian" as opposites did not yet form
part of the social vocabulary. Indeed, the word "civilian" itself, in the
sense of "nonmilitary," did not yet appear in English or French dictio-
naries. Before the 1790s, a "civilian" in English meant an expert in civil
(i.e., Roman) law. The distinction did not exist, because the men who
dominated Old Regime societies did not draw sharp lines between their
professional role as military officers and their social identity as aristocrats. Only in the new era of war did the notion of the "military" as a
world unto itself, with its own distinct rules and values, run by men
whose experiences cut them off from civilian peers, take shape for the
first time. Only then did the noun "civilian" — in French, *"civil"* — take
on its familiar, modern meaning.

True, this redefinition of the "military" coincided with the appearance of citizen armies, fed by conscription. As early as 1793, the French
Revolutionaries proclaimed every male citizen a soldier, an action that
in one sense lowered the barriers between "military" and "civilians,"
rather than the reverse. But conscription and universal military training
did not mean that every male citizen should always behave as a soldier.

It meant, rather, that every male citizen should stand prepared to give up "civilian" life in times of national emergency and cross the boundary into the distinct realm of the "military." Indeed, the military leaders of the Revolutionary and Napoleonic wars explicitly sought to break their conscripts' links to civilian life and provide them with a new, military ethos. In this sense, the rise of conscript armies actually reinforced the distinction between military and civilian.

This new separation of realms gave rise in turn to a second phenomenon that had not truly existed before 1789: namely, militarism. Militarism, as I would define it, relies precisely on the assumption of a sharp, clear divide between "military" and "civilian" society, for it involves the imposition of the values and customs of the former on the latter. Militarists believe in the moral superiority of the armed forces, which they praise as disciplined, self-sacrificing, and tested by adversity, to civilian society, which they usually deride as weak, corrupt, and self-absorbed. In the Europe of the Old Regime, the subordination of the armed forces to the aristocracy and the princes made such a doctrine virtually unthinkable, except perhaps in the Prussia of Frederick the Great. And even there, the notion that an autonomous military might seize political power for itself would have seemed utterly absurd. The whole purpose of the army was service to the monarch. Modern militarism first arose, rather, in Revolutionary France and helped bring about the first military coup d'état of modern times: by Napoleon Bonaparte in 1799. The word "militarism" appeared about the same time. Of course, it has since become a familiar element of modern Western politics and culture. In the United States today, the historian Andrew Bacevich has described a "new American militarism" that expresses itself in everything from such films as *Top Gun* to the widespread idea that military service constitutes a principal qualification for high political office (think of the presidential candidacies of John Kerry and Wesley Clark in 2004).

As a result of these shifts, a culture of war that seems quite alien to us had given way, by the early 1800s, to one that remains highly recognizable today across the Western world and especially in the United States. In fact, current American attitudes sometimes seem particularly, eerily close to those of Napoleon's Europe. On the one hand, Americans today generally see war as an exceptional state of affairs — despite the fact that American forces have engaged in five major military operations in the last fifteen years and maintain bases in scores of countries. Americans frequently describe war as something civilized nations have outgrown. American politicians automatically denounce the country's adversaries as criminal malefactors, threaten them with prosecution or even assassination, and never do them the courtesy of a formal declaration of war. But many Americans, as Bacevich observes, also have an unabated fascination with war, considering it a test of their society's worth. They treat members of the armed forces with respect verging on reverence and take for granted that no one who has not been in combat can ever really understand "what it is like" or how it changes a person. These attitudes, which seem timeless and natural to us, only came into being in late eighteenth- and early nineteenth-century Europe, from where they subsequently spread across the world.

It is for this reason that if we want to understand the place of war in the modern imagination, we need to travel back in time, strange as it may seem, to the era of muskets, cannon, and sailing ships. The technology of war has since changed beyond recognition. Strategy, tactics, and logistics have changed to nearly as great a degree. But the place war holds in Western culture has changed much less, even taking into account the vast changes wrought by the two world wars.

Yet surprisingly, the cultural history of war in Napoleon's Europe remained largely unexplored territory until quite recently and still lacks a systematic overview. True, many aspects of the story told here have featured in history books before — it could hardly be otherwise, since by some estimates more than 220,000 books and articles had appeared on Napoleon and his empire alone by 1980! But historians and social scientists have attempted far less often to examine the place of war in Western society and culture, particularly for periods before the twentieth century. Before plunging into the story itself, it's worth briefly discussing why they have not done so, because this context will help show where *The First Total War* is coming from and how the book has taken shape.

We can begin with the fact that the modern social sciences have in fact never done a very good job of understanding war. Indeed, they have often preferred not to deal with the subject at all. This is mostly not because many academics have pacifist tendencies, and few have military experience — although these things are true. More fundamentally, as sociologists such as Hans Joas and Michael Mann have perceptively observed, it is because, broadly speaking, the social sciences descend from precisely the liberal, Enlightenment-era thinking that dismissed war as primitive, irrational, and alien to modern civilization. Even Marxism, which had such vast intellectual influence from the mid-nineteenth to the late twentieth centuries, did not fundamentally depart from this thinking. Although Marx saw class conflict (which is conflict within societies, not between them) as the motor of historical change, he still believed it would eventually lead to a condition of social harmony and perpetual peace. Nor did he ever exalt violence as cleansing and redemptive, the way some of his followers would do in the twentieth century. One strain of nineteenth-century philosophers and social scientists did take war more seriously, arguing that without it, societies would weaken and wither. But they lived mostly in Germany and largely disappeared from view after World War I.

Among leading twentieth-century thinkers, one of the few to set war at the center of his reflections was a man whose reactionary politics put him entirely at odds with the liberal social scientific tradition. The German jurist Carl Schmitt went so far as to place his formidable intellect at the service of Adolf Hitler and to embrace the Nazi persecution of the Jews. Yet the hatred he felt toward liberal thought gave him disturbingly keen insights into its paradoxical consequences for war, and no serious student of the subject can afford to ignore them, however repugnant their author. What happens, Schmitt asked, when a war was fought for the sake of perpetual peace, when it was "considered to constitute the absolute last war of humanity"? He responded: "Such a war is necessarily unusually intense and inhuman because, by transcending the limits of the political framework, it simultaneously degrades the enemy into moral and other categories and is forced to make of him a monster that must not only be defeated but utterly destroyed." Writing these lines in 1932, Schmitt had in mind particularly World War I and the Versailles peace settlement that imposed punitive reparations on Germany, but the passage has relevance for the earlier period as well — one that Schmitt himself singled out for attention in later works. In his *Theory of the Partisan,* which begins with Spain's struggle against Napoleon, Schmitt usefully proposed the concept of "absolute enmity" to describe a condition in which each side denies the very humanity of the other.

For a time, the historical profession differed from the social scientists. In the nineteenth century, history was still preeminently a literary, narrative art, and the past offered no more dramatic or compelling subject than war. Such masters as Ranke, Macaulay, Michelet, and Parkman all gave it a major place in their works, took military science seriously, and put climactic battles at the heart of their stories. In the twentieth century, however, history turned in a more explicitly scientific, academic direction, and so, many historians followed the social scientists' lead away from the battlefield. The leaders of the influential *"Annales* school" of social history, which developed in France in the early twentieth century, explicitly downplayed "event history" — by which they particularly meant military history — in favor of "deeper" geological, social, and economic factors. The most important *Annaliste,* Fernand Braudel, held to this principle so strongly that he managed to draft much of his masterpiece, *The Mediterranean,* while in a World War II German prisoner-of-war camp. Historians of the twentieth century resisted these tendencies better than others (not surprisingly, given the cataclysmic impact of the world wars), but in accounts of earlier periods, war lost its formerly commanding position.

Since the 1980s, many historians have turned toward literary criticism and postmodern philosophy for inspiration, but these disciplines share the social sciences' aversion to war. One of the contemporary philosophers most important for historians, Michel Foucault, did have a certain fascination with war — but mostly because he saw modern society waging a "silent war" on itself, through a broad spectrum of repressive practices (inverting Clausewitz's remark, Foucault quipped that "politics is the continuation of war by other means"). Mainstream historians, meanwhile, remain surprisingly uninterested in and ignorant of pre–twentieth century military history. The *American Historical Review,* flagship journal of the profession in the United States, has not published an article on Napoleonic military history for more than thirty years.

Military history itself has by no means died out, but it has become remarkably segregated from other branches of history — virtually a discipline of its own. It attracts many talented and original practitioners, but for the most part, they have not asked the same sorts of questions as their colleagues in nonmilitary fields. They have concentrated on the development of technology, tactics and strategy, on motivation and combat effectiveness, on the social makeup of armed forces, and on the way common soldiers experienced combat. John Keegan, one of the most brilliant and prolific of them, once complained that "not even the beginnings of an attempt have been made by military historians to plot the intellectual landmarks and boundaries of their own field of operations." For a very long time, military historians did regrettably little to place war within a larger cultural context.

In recent years, though, the situation has finally begun to change. In Britain and the United States, historians of ideas have rediscovered the central place held by war and diplomacy in premodern political thought. In France, a new generation of experts in the Revolutionary era have finally begun to exorcise the ghost of the fin-de-siècle diplomatic historian Albert Sorel, whose grandly intimidating history of the Revolutionary period's foreign relations was driven by a reductive insistence on the primacy of French national interests. In Germany, cultural historians, such as Michael Jeismann and Karen Hagemann, have devoted renewed attention to the origins of modern forms of militarism and bellicosity. In much of this work, Carl Schmitt has stood as a prominent — and hotly disputed — point of reference.

It is no coincidence that this new work has begun to appear since the end of the cold war and that reflection on the subject has intensified since September 11, 2001. The competition between NATO and the Warsaw Pact, with its basso continuo of proxy war in the third world and the threat of mutual assured destruction supposedly preventing open superpower conflict, made the utopian hopes and apocalyptic struggles of early modernity feel far away. Since 1989, the parallels and connections have come to seem much more pressing and important. It has become a much more vital task to understand how the modern culture of war and peace first took shape.

The First Total War addresses this task, drawing on both military history as it has traditionally been practiced and the forms of cultural history that have developed over the past generation. I try to establish some connections between these unjustly separated fields, emphasizing the centrality of war to a period in which it has recently been ignored by mainstream historians, and the centrality of culture to military transformations that have been studied mostly from an operational viewpoint.

Because I am dealing with such a broad subject, there are a number of things that I have necessarily *not* done in the pages that follow, and for the sake of clarity, it may be worth saying what these are. To begin with, readers will not find here a systematic survey of the Revolutionary and Napoleonic wars. As the people who lived through the period often remarked, it sometimes seemed as if time itself had become impossibly compressed — "this quarter-century equalled many centuries," to quote Chateaubriand. Merely recounting the major battles would have made this book twice as long. In any case, readers can turn to many other places for such a history, starting with Timothy Blanning's superb histories of the Revolutionary wars, David Chandler's magisterial survey of Napoleon's campaigns, and Jean-Paul Bertaud's and John Lynn's incisive studies of the armies of the French Revolution.

Two other important subjects are relatively tangential to the changing place of war within the European imagination at the time, and so they get short shrift as well. One of these is economics. I have no desire to deny the importance of economic competition in starting wars or the importance of economic resources and systems of taxation and expenditure in the waging of them, not to mention the way Napoleon's France raised the practice of pillage to a fine art. But except where economics impinged on fantasies, myths, and representations of war — for instance, in the way Enlightenment thinkers linked commerce to peace — I do not give it systematic attention. The second of these subjects — painful as it is for a devotee of C. S. Forester and Patrick O'Brian to admit — is naval warfare. Again, I have no desire to downplay the importance of navies in the course of the Revolutionary and Napoleonic wars. British dominance of the seas in general, and Britain's victories at Aboukir and Trafalgar in particular, determined the outcome of the wars as much as any other factor did. But naval warfare changed much less than land warfare during this period, and outside of Great Britain had relatively little to do either with the developments of total war or with the beliefs, stories, and myths that arose around it.

This mention of Great Britain leads to another caveat. Although the changes I am examining flowed across Europe, I have necessarily con-

centrated on France more than on any other country. France stood at
the crossroads of the European Enlightenment; its Revolution and the
rise of Napoleon were the decisive events of the period. The phenomenon of total war reached a hideous peak in 1793–94, in the French region of the Vendée. Modern militarism, as I have defined it, first took
shape in France in the late 1790s. And, of course, France largely drove
the period's wars forward, both under the Revolutionary governments
of 1792–99 and then under Napoleon. Napoleon's conquests went further toward creating a Europe-wide empire than anything else since the
time of Charlemagne, perhaps even the Caesars.

With many of my historian colleagues currently embracing the cause
of "world history," one last omission may strike readers as problematic:
I deal only rarely with the world beyond Europe. Can this decision be
justified on grounds other than, again, wanting to keep this book a
manageable size? As I was writing it, colleagues often suggested to me
that the origins of modern total war are surely to be found on the early
modern imperial frontiers. Surely it was here, long before the French
Revolution, that Europeans first dispensed with notions of chivalric restraint and waged brutal wars of extermination against supposed "savages." Did not Europeans learn their worst behavior from imperial encounters in Asia, Africa, and the Americas?

In fact, I think that the answer to this question is no. To begin with,
Europeans hardly needed colonial empires to learn the art of mass murder. The horrendous slaughters of the Reformation-era wars of religion
began well before most European empires had developed much beyond
trading posts, and the worst examples occurred in the German states,
which had no colonies. The development of the French and British
overseas empires coincided with the introduction of relative moderation and restraint into European warfare, not with their disappearance.

European forces often committed terrible atrocities on their colonial
frontiers, but it is simply wrong to think that they usually behaved in a
systematically exterminatory manner toward indigenous populations.
Most European empires in this period were still surprisingly weak and
thinly spread. Europeans *depended* on the indigenous populations: as
trading partners, as guides, and as military allies. European powers were
continually negotiating with indigenous authorities and, indeed, attempting to instruct them in the peculiar rites of European warfare. Episodes like the Fox Wars — in which the French helped exterminate an

Indian tribe in present-day Wisconsin — tended to take place not as a result of planned aggression but when these fragile networks and alliances broke down or when Europeans found themselves dragged into wars between indigenous entities. Even in the nineteenth century, as Isabel Hull has suggested in a recent study of German East Africa, the colonial setting mostly offered Europeans a laboratory for testing their own preexisting ideas about war. "The Germans," she concludes, ". . . learned nothing from colonial warfare that did not confirm their prejudices about the correct way to fight wars."

This point applies even more strongly to eighteenth-century France, for one simple reason. A few years ago, the French historian Jean-Clément Martin confessed his bafflement at the sheer incompetence of the French Revolutionaries who tried to suppress the bloody insurgency in the Vendée region in 1793–94. Surely, he speculated, French soldiers had gained considerable experience with irregular, guerrilla warfare of this sort outside of Europe. But had they? Although many French military personnel had fought in the Americas, India, and Africa in the 1770s and 1780s, the turmoil of the Revolution cut this living skein of experience clean through. Even before the Vendée rebellion began, almost all the officers from the Old Regime had either resigned or been dismissed, and pre-1789 veterans made up a distinct minority of the rank and file. In fact, the Revolutionary armies initially lacked colonial experience almost entirely. They would soon gain it, however — especially, as we will see soon, in Egypt and Haiti. And so they would begin to export Europe's new culture of war to the rest of the world, to its cost.

One final word of introduction. I have written *The First Total War* for general readers, not only my fellow historians. I have therefore tried, as much as possible, to embed my arguments in sketches and stories — at times, rather impressionistic ones — rather than in analysis alone. In taking this approach, I have been fortunate in one respect, for few periods offer such a rich concentration of vivid, gripping events — all too often, horrifyingly gripping ones. Few periods offer such astonishing characters, starting with Napoleon Bonaparte himself. In describing these events and characters, I have drawn not only on my own original research but also, naturally, on the rich veins of expertise to be found in the scholarly literature. If these qualities make the book something other than a definitive, exhaustive pronouncement on the subject, and if specialists find some of the stories familiar, so be it. The book is a voyage of exploration, not an exhaustive survey of unplowed archival terrain. But we are living in a moment that needs accessible essays at least as much as weighty monographs. For as Americans have been discovering in recent years, few subjects are more dangerous than war to discuss in a dry, abstract manner, without a sense of the human costs involved — without hearing the screams, seeing the bodies, and smelling the powder and the blood.

1

Officers, Gentlemen, and Poets

As I ponder'd in silence,
Returning upon my poems, considering, lingering long,
A Phantom arose before me with distrustful aspect,
Terrible in beauty, age, and power,
The genius of poets of old lands . . .
What singest thou? it said,
Know'st thou not there is but one theme for ever-enduring bards?
And that is the theme of War . . .

— WALT WHITMAN

orsica, 1768. He is twenty-one years old, and beautiful. He has soft, fair skin, delicate red lips, seductively lidded eyes, and a trim, lithe figure. He wears an expensive, exquisitely tailored uniform, with a large white feather stuck rakishly in his hat. His name is Armand-Louis de Gontaut, but he is known by his title, as the duc de Lauzun. He is heir to another dukedom as well and to one of the largest fortunes in France.

France is fighting a nasty little war here in this wild, rocky Mediterranean island, and Lauzun is part of it. Earlier in the year, King Louis XV acquired Corsica from its nominal Genoese overlords, but the islanders, who have lived in a state of effective independence for decades, have no intention of resubmitting meekly to foreign rule. Their charismatic leader, Pasquale Paoli, is waging a struggle for independence, and France will need 25,000 soldiers to subdue him. (Among Paoli's followers are a young couple named Carlo and Letitzia Buonaparte, who will

Louis-Auguste Brun: *The Duc de Lauzun*

soon have a second son, Napoleone.) Lauzun, who holds the rank of colonel, is serving as aide to the French commander, the Marquis de Chauvelin. It is Lauzun's first taste of active service, and he wants to prove himself in battle.

He would seem to be behaving rather oddly, though, for an ambitious young officer. So eager is he to see action that he disobeys direct orders to wait for Chauvelin in France, and makes his way to Corsica surreptitiously by fishing boat — a feat that earns him several days under arrest. Afterward, he devotes less attention to his duties than to a flirtatious, doll-like, eighteen-year-old named Marie-Anne-Adélaïde Chardon. She has a husband — France's civil administrator in Corsica — a dour lawyer twice her age. But then, Lauzun has a wife, back in France. After Paoli inflicts a major defeat on the French in October, Lauzun rushes back to the French-held port of Bastia because Marie-Anne has hinted, in a note, that she is ready to surrender to his charms. And she does. Later that day, her distrustful husband arrives and tries to fool her into revealing her feelings by claiming that Lauzun has died on the battlefield. Disdainfully, she admits the affair: "Then I've brought him back to life, for he's in the next room, rather tired in fact, but I'm quite sure he's still alive." The happy couple continues to see each other openly through the winter of 1768–69, indifferent to Monsieur Chardon's reaction (although according to some sources, he finally agrees to a *ménage à trois*). Marie-Anne even follows her lover to the siege of Barbaggio in January, and the two dash across the battlefield together on horseback under Corsican fire, as if the war were nothing more than a glorious game.

It hardly seems like the start of a serious military career. Indeed, Lauzun will soon leave Corsica to return to the social whirl of Paris and the gleam of the court of Versailles (the unstable Marie-Anne will eventually find God and return to a conventional marriage). For many years, Lauzun will continue philandering on a grand scale, squander his fortune, and gain a reputation as an outrageous rake — something that, I cannot stress enough, takes considerable effort for eighteenth-century French aristocrats. Rumors, which he himself does nothing to stifle, will even link him romantically to Queen Marie-Antoinette. Along the way, he will consult sorcerers, befriend famous authors, attend the literary *salon* of Madame Du Deffand, and dabble in intellectual fads of all sorts.

Yet in the same years, Lauzun will also become one of France's most famous soldiers. His courage under fire in Corsica will lead to the command of a prestigious regiment. In 1779, he will command an expedition that briefly captures Senegal for France. In 1780, he will raise a regiment of his own and take it across the Atlantic, following in Lafayette's footsteps to fight in the American Revolution. He will serve with particular distinction at Yorktown, risking his life to save a wounded man. Lauzun will go on to play a significant role in the politics of the French Revolution and in the French Revolutionary wars — indeed, as we will see, his life illustrates the shift to total war as well as anyone's.

To modern eyes, these two sides of Lauzun's career — the seducer and the soldier — sit uneasily with each other, to say the least. Yet in eighteenth-century France, the boudoir did not seem anywhere near as far from the battlefield as it does today. One of Lauzun's companions, the novelist and military officer Pierre-Ambroise Choderlos de Laclos, repeatedly likened the art of seduction to the art of war. In his novel *Les liaisons dangereuses,* the callous seducer Valmont (who bears more than a passing resemblance to Lauzun) compares his own amorous conquests to the battles of Frederick the Great, recounting how he carefully prepared the terrain and left nothing to chance before closing with "the enemy." One of France's most famous eighteenth-century generals, the duc de Richelieu (great-nephew of the more famous Cardinal), had almost as great a sexual reputation as Lauzun and was admired for his ability to overcome the most concerted feminine resistance. The great *philosophe* Voltaire, a school friend of Richelieu's, hailed him in verse as the favorite of Venus and Mars alike. Those famous nineteenth-century aesthetes the Goncourt brothers would claim that eighteenth-century men approached seduction the way soldiers approached siege warfare: "It was in this war and this game of love that this century perhaps revealed its most profound qualities."

It is precisely because Lauzun strikes our own sensibilities so strangely that he provides a good introduction to the military culture of his time. It was an aristocratic culture, very different from the one we know today in the West, for the idea of a sharp separation between "military" and "civilian" spheres of life did not as yet exist. (As I have already noted, the English and French languages did not even recognize the words "military" and "civilian" as opposites until the nineteenth century.) Men like Lauzun would have found the very idea of such a separation quite odd. They passed easily from the theater of the aristocracy that was the royal court, with its intrigues and scandals and seductions, to the theater of the aristocracy that was the military campaign, where they could find more of the same. In each arena, they were expected to show the same grace, coolness, and splendor. War was less a profession, in the modern sense of the word, than an integral part of their social identity. And this fact, in turn, had enormous consequences for the way wars were fought.

It is worth taking a moment to look at some of the principal differences between the military culture of Lauzun's Europe and our own. Today, military personnel are, to a very large extent, literally segregated from the rest of society: they have their own communities (military bases), complete with special forms of housing (barracks), a separate educational system (military academies and other specialized schools), and even a separate legal system. They are conspicuously marked off from civilians by their uniforms. Soldiering is a demanding, full-time occupation. But in eighteenth-century Europe, this infrastructure of difference was only beginning to develop — even in Prussia, the state usually cited as an example of precocious "militarism." Before 1750, virtually no peacetime European soldiers lived in barracks but instead were quartered on the general population (much to its displeasure). Only in the mid-eighteenth century did European monarchies begin creating specialized military schools, and even then, high-ranking officers, such as Lauzun, often failed to attend them and disdained the formal study of military science. Ordinary soldiers wore uniforms, but officers often did not. In France, for an officer to appear at court in military dress actually constituted a grievous breach of etiquette, and as late as 1758, the minister of war had to scold generals for not wearing their uniforms while on campaign.

Even during military campaigns, soldiers and civilians mixed promiscuously together. A 26,500-man Swedish army that tramped through Ukraine during the Great Northern War of 1700–21 brought along with it 1,100 nonmilitary administrators, 4,000 male servants, and 1,700 wives, children, and serving girls. As for the British army, during the Seven Years' War of 1756–63, as many as a quarter of the persons in its encampments were women (who had, by definition, no military status). In addition to wives, servants, and the inevitable prostitutes, women served as sutlers, nurses, clerks, wagoners, and laborers. Some critics blamed British general John ("Gentleman Johnny") Burgoyne's defeat at Saratoga, in the American Revolution, on the 2,000 women who accompanied his 4,700-man army. As late as 1812, the Duke of Wellington allegedly complained of his army in Spain: "We are a marching brothel."

Soldiering was also much less a full-time occupation than it is today. Campaigns generally took place between May and October, and when not in the field, soldiers and officers alike devoted relatively little time to drill and training. Lauzun, when not on active service, generally returned to court or to the pursuit of a new mistress, and less well-born officers found their vocations scarcely more time consuming. While posted in Belfort in 1777, the future Revolutionary Théodore de Lameth whiled away his days drawing, playing music, and studying German. He reserved an hour a day for paying social calls "so as not to be seen as a savage." The young Napoleon Bonaparte, after gaining his commission in 1785, paid no such calls and devoted most of his copious free time to intensive reading: "I lived like a bear . . . always alone in my small room with my books . . . my only friends!" Napoleon also taxed the patience of his superiors by spending over half the period 1785–90 at home, on leave, but then, *most* French officers spent at least four months a year away from their regiments. And the army was delighted to see them go, because, like many of its European counterparts, it suffered from an absurd level of overmanning at the higher ranks. In 1789, the French state could provide full-time employment for less than a third of its 35,000 active officers.

One consequence of the overmanning was that it left officers free to pursue other vocations without resigning their commissions. Most strikingly, perhaps, many tried their hands at literature. Take the example of Napoleon before the French Revolution — a time when his opportunities for promotion remained distinctly limited. Serving in a series of dull provincial postings, he not only read obsessively through the great works of the Enlightenment but also took copious notes and even kept a file of obscure expressions to sprinkle ostentatiously through his own writings (*rhizophage, cacique, tomogun*). He tried writing everything from histories of Corsica to an essay on suicide, a dialogue on love, and short stories that betrayed an unfortunate taste for the grotesque: "having awoken, she saw — O God! — she saw a ghost that approached her bed . . . He drew her hand to his neck. O horror! The countess's fingers sank into his broad wounds, and came out covered with blood." Chateaubriand would scathingly comment on these works: "Destiny was mute, and Napoleon should have been."

Napoleon's biographers have taken these ambitions mostly as yet another sign of this extraordinary man's extraordinary nature, but in fact, they were quite commonplace. Lauzun's companion Laclos, like Napoleon an artillery officer, started publishing poetry while posted in Grenoble in the early 1770s. A few years later, he turned a popular novel into a comic opera, but the audience booed the first and only performance, and the queen's presence in the theater only added to the humiliation. Laclos packed up his resentments and took them off to the Atlantic coast, where he helped construct France's naval defenses and in his spare time wrote *Les liaisons dangereuses,* arguably the greatest French novel of the century (and, in its savage portrayal of high society, a most satisfying act of revenge). The ranks of French soldier-authors also included that famous scion of an ancient noble family who fought bravely in the Seven Years' War (1756–63), rose to the rank of captain, and then retired to start exploring the outer limits of human experience: the Marquis de Sade. As for Louis de Fénelon, a French cavalry captain, he not only wrote poetry but also tried to ensure good reviews by challenging to a duel anyone who disliked it. And the long-serving officer Jean-François de Saint-Lambert was a true literary polymath, who published poetry, "oriental fables," short stories about American Indians and African slaves, dense treatises on human nature, and satirical verse on the quarrels of Catholic theologians. In 1785, no fewer than seven men with military backgrounds, including Saint-Lambert, numbered among the forty "immortals" of the French Academy, the royal institution charged with overseeing the French language and French letters.

Outside France, those crossing the military-literary divide included many other famous names. There was Frederick the Great of Prussia, who wrote philosophical treatises and verse (in French); the great British essayist Richard Steele; and General Burgoyne, who moonlighted as a playwright (his successes included *The Heiress, The Maid of the Oaks,* and a comic opera called *The Lord of the Manor*). Imagine, by way of comparison, a Norman Schwarzkopf or a Colin Powell taking time off from Middle Eastern combat to compose poetry or engage in philosophical correspondence.

Today, a sign of the existence of a distinct military sphere is the fact that soldiers, no matter how rich or well connected, can attain high rank only by working their way up the military ladder, according to professional criteria of merit. Not so in eighteenth-century Europe, where high birth and money trumped talent and seniority. Lauzun had a typical career in this regard, entering the army at age twelve and becoming a colonel at nineteen. Maurice of Saxony, one of France's best-known eighteenth-century generals, reached high rank at fifteen, yet even he was a grizzled old-timer next to George, Lord Ettrick, who, in 1688, took titular command of a company in the Royal Scots at the tender age of eighteen months! Although most officers in the British and French armies started at the rank of ensign (just below lieutenant), advancement often required hard cash. The most prestigious French commissions could go for as much as half a million pounds — a vast sum for the day, thousands of times larger than a laborer's annual wages. France abolished "purchase" in the 1770s, but a grandee, such as Lauzun, could still create his own, "proprietary" regiment. In Britain, the system lasted well into the nineteenth century.

Perhaps the most powerful factor that today sets military service aside as an exceptional, quasi-sacred vocation is the idea of patriotic sacrifice. Soldiers, unlike the rest of us, stand ready to give their lives for a cause, for their country. Patriotism had a powerful place in eighteenth-century culture as well. But inside the military, the persistence of a powerful mercenary ethos did much to dilute its importance. Foreign soldiers, for instance, made up roughly 20 percent of France's wartime army — including most of Lauzun's regiment. Maurice of Saxony was German and would not have won his most famous victory, against the British at Fontenoy in 1745, during the War of the Austrian Succession, without the soldiers of the Clare Regiment, who charged into battle screaming the Irish war cry *Cuimnidh ar luimneach agus ar feall na Sasanach* ("Remember Limerick and the deceit of the English"). Lauzun seriously considered enrolling in the Russian army; the young Napoleon, in the Turkish. Consider also the well-traveled *comte* de Saint-Germain. Forced to leave the French army after killing a fellow officer in a duel, he went into the service first of the German prince Palatine, then of the Holy Roman Emperor, and then of the Elector of Bavaria. He returned to France during the Seven Years' War, only to leave soon afterward for Denmark, where he became a field marshal and commander-in-chief in the 1760s. The moves entirely failed to raise patriotic eyebrows back home, and Saint-Germain crowned his career in old age by becoming French war minister. Aristocratic officers generally did not fight *against* their native countries, but apart from this stricture, their code of honor mattered more than the particular sovereign they served.

Eighteenth-century soldiers also mixed warfare with private enterprise — i.e., pillage. Blatant theft was frowned on, but spoils taken directly from enemy forces were a different matter. The Swedish army in the early eighteenth century even applied a set scale to enemy loot: a wounded captain, for instance, received twenty times the share of spoils doled out to a wounded private. While campaigning through Poland, Swedish captain Magnus Steinbock managed to send home cash, jewels, silver cups, icons, weapons, bedspreads — even a whole bed. A few years earlier, critics complained to King Louis XIV of France (1638–

1715) that his commander in Germany was doing very well for himself out of the fighting. "Yes," the king replied, "but he is doing very well for me, too." Naval captains benefited particularly from the spoils system, with a few victories often providing the basis for a considerable private fortune.

It would be wrong to conclude that a distinct sense of military identity did not exist at all in the eighteenth century. The development of standing armies a hundred years earlier, with standardized ranks and uniforms, had gone some distance toward creating one. Military units could inspire intense loyalty in their soldiers, as they do today — the regiment was "a society, a family, where friendship, bravery and honor dwelled," to quote the memoirs of one French officer. The experience of a battle, with its stresses and fears, created an enduring sense of fellowship then as now — although eighteenth-century military authors devoted far less discussion to the matter than do their modern counterparts.

Common soldiers felt a stronger sense of separation from nonmilitary life than the officers did. Few soldiers possessed the wherewithal to return home between campaigns or the education to devote idle hours to literary composition (the Prussian army, though, sent its infantry back home to their farms for several months each year). Recent research has emphasized that European common soldiers generally had relatively stable, long-lasting careers, which further contributed to a sense of collective identity (such a sense flourished even more in European navies, thanks to the crews' isolation during long months at sea). True, common soldiers also had a reputation as the "filth of the nation" (as Saint-Germain charmingly put it), "recruited" out of poorhouses and prisons, and the populations on which they were quartered often treated them as pariahs. A character in Sheridan's play *Saint Patrick's Day, or the Scheming Lieutenant* insisted that he would rather have his daughter catch scarlet fever than marry a man in uniform, and French tavern keepers posted signs reading "No Dogs, Whores or Soldiers." Yet these attitudes, too, fostered solidarity in the ranks.

Nonetheless, the eighteenth century remained fundamentally different from our own age on this score, and when a leading military historian like Sir John Keegan insists that early modern European militaries possessed a radically distinct "warrior culture," he is projecting contemporary experience back on the past. A separate military culture certainly exists today at places like Sandhurst, Saint-Cyr, and West Point or on military bases. The interesting thing about eighteenth-century Europe is precisely how *little* it was then in evidence, particularly in the officer corps.

This was the case because of two characteristics of eighteenth-century European society that mainstream historians of the past fifty years have usually done their best to ignore. First, warfare was an utterly normal, unexceptional state of affairs and was treated as such by nearly all concerned. In the seventeenth century, the continent as a whole enjoyed peace for perhaps two years out of a hundred, and the eighteenth century did only a little better. In the book of world history, claimed Edmund Burke in 1756, the story of peace would fill barely ten pages: "War is the Matter which fills all History." For Luc de Clapiers de Vauvenargues, a French officer and essayist: "Everything in the universe comes down to violence; this order of things . . . is in fact the most general, immutable and important law of nature." Second, by many obvious measures — money, manpower, elite education, and occupations — European societies seemed to have war as their primary purpose. In 1752, the Prussian state spent fully 90 percent of its budget on the military, whereas in France, in 1784, the proportion probably amounted to two-thirds — and both years were ones of peace. Although no European state yet had a universal draft, many had limited forms of conscription. During the War of the Spanish Succession (1701–13), at least one French adult male in six spent time in uniform.

Most important, war is what the rulers did. Frederick the Great of Prussia commanded his armies in person and led them to their greatest victories. So did the extravagantly ambitious Charles XII of Sweden, who also led his countrymen to their greatest military catastrophe, at Poltava in 1709, at the hands of Tsar Peter the Great. Thereafter, as if in penance for this loss, he recklessly exposed his life in battle after battle and finally, in 1718, succeeded in dying a glorious death. Although other monarchs did little real commanding, they still knew that it was important to appear on the battlefield. What passed for a royal education in early modern Europe tended to concentrate heavily on horsemanship, swordsmanship, and military studies. Royal playtime was even more warlike. The European upper classes knew as well as any present-day, peace-loving parent that toy weapons can stimulate aggressive behavior.

The difference is, they liked the idea, and so, when still a little boy, France's Louis XIII (1601–43) could count among his playthings a miniature pike, musket, bow, and cannon. His son, Louis XIV, built the palace at Versailles as a temple of French military glory, lining its grand galleries with depictions of his victories. In its gardens, Louis staged mock battles costing as much as 16 million French pounds each, with scale-model warships firing miniature cannons as they maneuvered on the Grand Canal.

What was true of kings was equally true of nobles, a class that had originally defined itself, in the Middle Ages, as the *bellatori:* "those who fought." It is true that eighteenth-century nobilities had little in common with their medieval predecessors. Wealthy commoners routinely and openly purchased noble rank for themselves with the full connivance of perennially strapped royal treasuries. And even the scions of ancient lineages often proved surprisingly forward looking: managing their estates parsimoniously and investing heavily in trade and in the early stirrings of industrialism. Nonetheless, in law, nobles throughout Europe remained a distinct, separate order of the state, and they still controlled a hugely disproportionate share of the continent's wealth and political offices. The eighteenth century was still very much an aristocratic century, and nobles had not forgotten the vocation of their predecessors. "The proper, the only, the essential form of nobility in France is the military profession," the essayist Montaigne had written in the sixteenth century. "The nobility knows no station, and no profession other than that of arms," a French noble echoed in 1781.

Throughout most of Europe, noble families still took such injunctions literally. In the Prussian province of Pomerania, virtually all male nobles spent at least some time in the army. In Sweden, 80 percent did so. Elsewhere, the proportion was smaller but still enough to ensure that most noble families had at least one son in arms. In the 1789 elections to the Estates General, France's national representative body, more than four-fifths of the nobles chosen had military backgrounds. Nobles made up the majority of all major European officer corps. Moreover, the highest social ranks tended to monopolize the highest military ones and to exercise a correspondingly disproportionate influence. During the Seven Years' War, France's 181 generals included 8 princes, 11 dukes, 44 counts, 38 marquis, and 6 barons.

Nobles shaped the relationship between society and the military by the fact that their behavior and values remained much the same, whether at home or on campaign. Certainly, as Lauzun's experience suggests, going to war did not mean giving up the frills and pleasures of the court or the manor. Noble officers devoted enormous attention and expense to their costume. "Dear me," remarked the susceptible heroine of Sheridan's *Saint Patrick's Day*, "to think how the sweet fellows sleep on the ground, and fight in silk stockings and lace ruffles." She was quite correct, except for the fact that high-ranking officers did precious little sleeping on the ground. French colonels on campaign generally took along camp beds, as well as enough china and silver to give elegant three-course dinners for twelve, along with the domestic staff to prepare and serve them. Generals had several carriages, thirty to forty horses, and almost as many footmen. As for Britain's cumbersome Duke of Cumberland, he dragged no less than 145 *tons* of baggage along with him in the field. Even a humble Prussian first lieutenant needed a servant to curl his hair, clean his uniforms, and prepare his meals.

It was no coincidence that one of the most famous French generals of the century, the duc de Richelieu, was also one of the most accomplished courtiers. He was famous for his primping, using so much perfume that fellow courtiers claimed that they could detect his fragrance on people who had done no more than sit on a chair he had occupied hours earlier. Despite several terms of imprisonment for everything from gambling debts to conspiring against the throne, he eventually became King Louis XV's intimate companion and rose to the post, entirely appropriate for this noted seducer, of First Gentleman of the Bedchamber. Incidentally, although not an author himself (some called him barely literate), Richelieu participated in literary salons, became a governor of France's principal theater, and engineered his election to the French Academy. Yet, like Lauzun, the duke also had a serious, successful military career. In 1745, he helped Maurice of Saxony beat Cumberland at Fontenoy, and in 1756, he led the forces that captured Minorca from the British, which was one of the few French victories in the otherwise disastrous Seven Years' War.

To modern readers, the idea of silk-stockinged courtiers charging into battle trailing clouds of wig powder may well seem entirely ridiculous. Surely, these effeminate fops were simply begging to be knocked into the dustbin of history by real soldiers who didn't stop to take out their curling irons before drawing their swords. But this reaction,

Alexandre Roslin: *The Duc de Richelieu*

although natural enough, is unfair and anachronistic. Soldiers like Richelieu were indeed an endangered species by the time he died, at the age of ninety-two, in 1788. But it was not because of any lack of military acumen, still less because of any lack of personal courage. Indeed, eighteenth-century European officers collectively strove to maintain a reputation for reckless, if not suicidal, courage. French officers occasionally made a point of dressing for battle in red so as to make themselves clearer targets. Lauzun, during the Corsican campaign, insisted on keeping his large white feather (a gift from Marie-Anne) in his hat, even though "it singled me out so that I became a preferred target." Commanders like Richelieu ostentatiously rode at the head of their troops, as did Charles XII of Sweden and Frederick the Great, who was wounded at the battle of Torgau in 1760. "Dogs!" Frederick would call to his men. "Do you want to live forever?"

These stories conceal a more serious point. As the German sociologist Norbert Elias observed many years ago, during the seventeenth and eighteenth centuries, European aristocracies developed remarkable forms of daily behavior, based on astonishingly difficult standards of self-control. Aristocrats at court were expected to make their public personas conform to carefully developed models and to make use of a rigorously defined and limited repertory of acceptable movements, gestures, language, and even facial expressions, not to mention clothes. Emotional responses had to be suppressed, or channeled into well-defined, acceptable forms. Reputation depended on it, and a single mistake could, in extreme cases, invite a lifetime of ridicule, as in the case of a French officer who, on slipping and falling at a ball, cried out, "Jésus Maria!" The words became his unshakeable nickname. Eighteenth-century noble life often deviated from the ideal standard Elias later described, but the ideal was visible in hundreds of primers and memoirs.

Aristocratic culture therefore depended on close and sure control over aristocratic bodies. If male aristocratic education emphasized such activities as sword fighting, horseback riding, dancing, and hunting, it was not simply to prepare young rakes for a lifetime of leisurely debauchery. There was a more serious purpose. And the same coolness and grace that was expected of aristocrats at court was, naturally, expected of them on the battlefield as well. So we should not laugh when we read in a German officer's manual from 1787 that "dancing is most necessary for the man of good education or the officer" or discover that at the royal Military School established in Paris in 1751, instructors set aside forty-five minutes a day for dancing lessons. What might seem superficial to a modern West Point cadet was, to the eighteenth century warrior, an integral part of his identity. It would not have seemed to him a wasteful distraction to go into battle properly and elegantly dressed or to entertain in the proper manner while on campaign. The same qualities that made him a graceful and well-mannered noble — not to mention an able seducer — would also, he believed, make him an able warrior.

Aristocratic ritual and *politesse* could even extend onto the battle-

field. The story is told that at Fontenoy, in 1745, the British captain
Charles Hay had a brief exchange with the French *comte* d'Anterroches,
in which each invited the other side to fire first. *"Messieurs les Anglais,
tirez les premiers,"* are the words attributed to the Frenchman. An exchange of this sort probably did take place (not all great historical
lines are apocryphal), but modern military historians take delight in
debunking the lace-and-ruffles image it conjures up. In eighteenth-
century battles, they dutifully observe, the side that fired second often
had the advantage. True enough, but they are missing the point. The
very ability to exchange polite remarks under battlefield conditions
should not be underestimated, and the fact that the story was widely repeated at the time speaks volumes about how contemporaries understood the warfare of their day.

   Not surprisingly, early modern authors often compared the wars they
knew to that quintessentially aristocratic ritual, the duel. Both followed
intricate sets of rules and involved scrupulous attention to appearance,
gesture, movement, and expression. Both demanded a high degree of
physical courage. Both, of course, were socially acceptable arenas for
the taking of human life. By the early eighteenth century, most European states were doing their best to stamp out dueling, but it remained
common in European armies. Many French generals, including the
duc de Richelieu, fought duels on several occasions. Two captains in
France's *Champagne* regiment, La Fenestre and d'Agaÿ, fought each
other repeatedly over a period of twenty-eight years. In 1761, a cannonball took off La Fenestre's head, but a piece of his skull blinded d'Agaÿ
in the right eye, and the regiment agreed that honor had been satisfied.
Dueling and warfare came together in the (originally medieval) practice
of single combat: officers from the opposing sides fighting while their
men looked on, as spectators. Lauzun claimed that he nearly managed a
duel of this sort with British colonel Banastre Tarleton during the
Yorktown campaign, only for Tarleton's horse to founder at the last
minute.

   As the survival of dueling suggests, at the heart of aristocratic military culture lay an obsession with honor. "The point of honor," a Saxon
service handbook of 1753 explained succinctly, "commands us to prefer
duty to life, and honor to duty." Codes of honor long predated the
elaborate systems of aristocratic etiquette and ritual that had developed
at the European courts of the sixteenth and seventeenth centuries, but

they fit in seamlessly with them. Like systems of etiquette, honor was grounded in a stiletto-sharp sense of social standing. Like them, it demanded strict mastery of the self and prescribed inviolable rules of acceptable behavior. Like them, it was also curiously amoral, more concerned with form, process, and appearance than with cause and right. One could fight honorably for a bad cause or dishonorably for a good one. A sixteenth-century noble officer had expressed the point in a particularly striking way: "Our lives and possessions are the king's. Our soul is God's. Our honor is our own." Eighteenth-century noble officers would have agreed. They certainly had little, if any, sense that they were fighting for a transcendent moral cause. For their king and country, perhaps. For money, quite possibly. But also, above all, for honor.

It is worth mentioning that officers usually failed to credit their social inferiors with the same values. They might express affection and admiration for individual soldiers or even individual regiments, but they saw soldiers in general as beneath contempt. Just as the *comte* de Saint-Germain called them "filth," the British officer Campbell Dalrymple complained that "the ranks are filled with the scum of every country, the refuse of mankind." To forge these men into reliable professional soldiers, armies relied on monotonous drill and savage discipline, especially in Prussia (where punishment notoriously involved not only whipping but also blows with the flat of a sword). The average European soldier did not, in fact, come from the lowest strata of society, and a few "soldiers of fortune" even managed to rise out of the ranks into the officer corps. But officers still usually had more in common with their counterparts on the other side of the battlefield than they did with their own troops. For one thing, in an age of French cultural hegemony, they most likely both spoke French. The armies remained fundamentally aristocratic in character.

During the course of the eighteenth century, European governments began to take steps toward changing this character and making their armed forces more professional — more distinct from civil society. They began to house soldiers in barracks, separate from the general population. They founded the specialized military schools to give officers extensive training (Napoleon was the most famous French graduate). They sought to instill a professional ethos among officers and to create impersonal standards for measuring talent and accomplishment —

although the extent to which they achieved these goals has been exaggerated, and traditional forms of patronage and fidelity continued to flourish. For many Europeans, the Prussia of Frederick the Great offered a glimpse of this future: a state where the military as a whole not only had a more distinct identity than elsewhere but also where it served as a model for civilian society. As the great French revolutionary orator Mirabeau famously quipped: "Most states have armies; Prussia is an army which has a state." Because of its military successes, Prussia stirred much jealousy and emulation. But Mirabeau's remark reflects the extent to which other Europeans still considered Prussia as something of a freak. Frederick himself cast aside many of his innovations as he grew older. At the end of his reign, in 1786, most Europeans still lived in a world in which the military and civilian spheres flowed easily into each other.

This discussion may have given the impression that despite the undoubted dangers, eighteenth-century European warfare amounted to an elaborate form of play-acting. It did not. Indeed, it had grown far more murderous since the time of the heavily armored medieval knights, of whose battles Machiavelli famously joked that they "offered no danger." Machiavelli was exaggerating outrageously, but since the Middle Ages, European armies' capacity for slaughter had indeed grown exponentially, thanks to a "military revolution" variously dated to different periods between 1450 and 1700. This revolution involved new techniques of fortification, a capacity to raise larger armies, and, above all, the effective use of firearms. Artillery became a fixture on the battlefield, firing solid balls, explosive shells, or canister: metal containers filled with bullets and scrap metal. Muskets appeared and, despite atrocious accuracy and cumbersome reloading procedures, gained effectiveness through such techniques as the infantry volley (in which a long line of infantry fired together and then moved back to reload, its place taken by another line, allowing for a continuous barrage). The ringlock bayonet allowed soldiers to use their muskets both as firearms and as short, deadly pikes. As a result, by the eighteenth century, battles frequently involved the death or wounding of 40 percent of the participants and, occasionally, much more. In the Swedish attack on the Russian lines at Poltava in 1709, several regiments had over 90 percent of their men killed, and overall, the Swedish army sustained a casualty rate

Horace Vernet: *The Battle of Fontenoy*

of 49 percent. The dead and the dying produced such powerfully mephitic odors that they managed what the living had not and forced the
victorious Russians from the battlefield.

Less extreme than Poltava but still quite deadly enough, Fontenoy
provides a good example of a typical eighteenth-century battle. It was
fought between the French and a British-Dutch alliance in the flat
fields of Flanders (in modern Belgium) on a cool and wet spring morning in 1745. France, then allied with Prussia and several other powers,
was attempting to wrest the region from Austria (which was allied with
Britain and the Netherlands) in the context of a larger war over the succession to the Austrian throne. The French won the battle and went on
to occupy much of present-day Belgium, although King Louis XV later
ended up giving back most of the conquered territory at the negotiating
table in return for dubious gains elsewhere.

Anyone who likes parades and pageantry would certainly have adored
Fontenoy's opening stages, which might have briefly reinforced the
impression of play-acting. Some 55,000 British, Dutch, and German
troops marched south toward where 40,000 French troops were dug in
near the Escaut River, not far from the French border. Trumpets, fifes,
and drums played; elaborate regimental flags rippled in the wind; and
brightly colored uniforms enlivened the gray morning. Particularly gor-

geous were the officers, with their powdered wigs, sashes, epaulettes, and silk stockings. One French officer had seven extra pairs of silk stockings carefully folded away in his luggage. In a last, symbolic vestige of medieval armor, shiny metal gorgets gleamed around high-ranking necks. Pageantry especially loves royalty, and royal blood was present in abundance. France's Louis XV, then thirty-five years old, had come, along with his sixteen-year-old son and heir, the Dauphin. Maurice of Saxony, the French commander, was the illegitimate son of a Saxon king of Poland; the Duke of Cumberland, head of Britain's forces, had King George II for a father.

To the ordinary soldier, though, things looked and felt quite a bit less splendid. The troops at Fontenoy, on both sides, staggered under sixty pounds of equipment and supplies, including all their valuable personal possessions (certain to be lost or stolen if left behind in the luggage train). Following days of marching in the wet weather with little food, they were quite possibly suffering from dysentery, rheumatism, pleurisy, infections of the throat or eye, or others of the many maladies enumerated by the British physician John Pringle in his classic *Observations on the Diseases of the Army*, based in part on the experiences of the Fontenoy campaign. Maurice of Saxony himself, suffering from dropsy, conducted the battle from a stretcher. The soldiers were also, quite possibly, drunk. Eighteenth-century armies may have provided bad food, abysmal pay, savage discipline, and unspeakable medical care, but they were liberal with beer, wine, and spirits, and many recruits signed up for no other reason.

Once the battle began, the pageantry quickly disappeared into an all too literal cloud of smoke. Cannon and musket fire produced great billows of dark, foul-smelling gunpowder smoke, which covered everything in its path with a black, greasy film. The soldiers had the taste in their mouths as well, for in order to load their muskets, they had to bite powder-coated musket balls out of their cartridges. The mud generated by tens of thousands of men, horses, and wheels grinding through the wet fields added to the filth, while cannonballs threw up huge gouts of dirt (and blood and flesh) as they splashed and bounced through the armies. King Louis and the Dauphin burst out laughing when one ball, landing nearby, soaked a particularly resplendent officer with mud from head to toe.

But guns and cannon were no laughing matter. Iron cannonballs, traveling at up to 750 feet per second, could whip through files of men like bowling balls through porcelain pins: human beings disintegrated on impact. Even after expending most of their energy, the balls could still crush or rip off feet as they rolled to a stop. Musket balls two-thirds of an inch across could do horrific damage as well. Moving far more slowly than modern rifle bullets, they did not pass cleanly through the body but bounced off bones and organs, dragging bits of dirt and clothing with them in a sure-fire recipe for dangerous infection. Worst of all was canister, with its bullets and scrap metal. We know the damage such ammunition can do when stuffed into a backpack with plastic explosive and detonated, along with the owner, in a restaurant or a nightclub. In eighteenth-century battles, the effects were just as horrible but multiplied many times over.

At Fontenoy, canister made the difference. Maurice had established fortified redoubts along a line parallel to the river, and for much of the morning, Cumberland's troops battered against them with little result. But Maurice had left one spot unprotected, between Fontenoy and the woods of Barry, and there Cumberland broke through. Pushing into the gap, his redcoats squeezed into a single massive column that battered the French backward more than a quarter of a mile. Salvos of musket fire failed to stop it (under battlefield conditions, French soldiers would have been lucky to get two shots a minute out of their cumbersome, heavy muskets, and even at two hundred feet, only a quarter of the shots were likely to strike home). For a moment, the battle seemed lost, and King Louis's aides urged him to withdraw from the field. But at that moment, Maurice and the other French commanders realized that the British column was out of control and vulnerable. Desperately dispatching orders, they managed to line up cannon loaded with canister directly in front of it. Unable to attack or retreat, Cumberland's men died where they stood, and by 1:30, the battle was over. Thousands of bodies lay on the ground, some turning yellow and beginning to swell with putrefaction, others screaming, moaning, and twitching, very likely not to be rescued for hours or days — very likely to die from their wounds. Overall, total casualties — dead and wounded — amounted to at least 15,000 of the 95,000 participants.

These were the horrors of Fontenoy, and the participants were in no sense blind to them. "Sire," Maurice allegedly told Louis XV, "now you see what war really means." One senior French officer clearly suffered from posttraumatic shock: "This terrible spectacle scarcely had any effect in its first moments. I walked about and informed myself about my friends, and I saw a great number dying, with a calm that astonished me." As for another eyewitness, the brilliant, eccentric Marquis d'Argenson, then serving a short and unhappy term as France's foreign minister, he wrote an extraordinarily explicit and moving letter about the battlefield: "The corpses stripped naked, the enemies dying in agony, the awful scenes, the wounds steaming in the air." At one point, he confessed, he turned aside and vomited. "Triumph," he continued, "is the most beautiful thing in the world . . . but its foundation is human blood, and shreds of human flesh."

It would be easy to stop here, with the implicit conclusion that the aristocratic culture of war amounted to little more, in the end, than a pretty façade pasted over trauma, agony, and death. Such a conclusion would certainly appeal to our modern sensibilities. At least since World War I, serious literature, drama, and film in the West have mostly presented the horrors as the essence of war, justified going to war only as a grim necessity, and dismissed talk of honor and glory as shoddy hypocrisy. In fact, we take for granted that "war literature" really means "antiwar literature," with World War I as the great example: think of Remarque's *All Quiet on the Western Front,* Siegfried Sassoon's "How to Die," or Wilfred Owen's savage "Dulce et Decorum Est" ("If you could hear, at every jolt, the blood / Come gargling from the froth-corrupted lungs"). A similar trend has developed in military history, in which many of the most successful and innovative works, such as John Keegan's *The Face of Battle,* promise readers a glimpse of the hideous, unvarnished reality of war, stripped of all evasion and glamorization.

This approach, however, has the effect of making the way eighteenth-century men and women understood war almost impossible to grasp, let alone take seriously. We make much of exceptional letters like d'Argenson's, because they resonate so well with our own expectations. But we quietly put aside the much larger mass of material that fails to do so: that strikes us as oddly dry, abstract, and uninformative. In the eighteenth century, however, d'Argenson was the exception. Lauzun again provides a more typical example. On the war in Corsica: "It was the sort of life that suited me best: musket shots all day long, and supper with my mistress in the evening!" Or on a battle in the American

Revolutionary War: "I marched on the English; I charged their cavalry, and my infantry exchanged fire with theirs . . . There were two or three hundred men killed and captured, and many wounded." End of story. This style is absolutely typical of most European military memoirs from the Renaissance through the late eighteenth century, and it expresses an important aspect of aristocratic culture.

To see how, consider the most popular contemporary description of the battle of Fontenoy. It was written by Voltaire, and he most certainly knew of the horrors, because he was the recipient of d'Argenson's letter (they were school friends). Later in his career, as we will see, Voltaire showed himself eminently capable of conveying war's horrors in gripping detail. But in the days after the battle, working feverishly, he composed a 348-line celebratory poem, entitled *Fontenoy,* which proceeded in an entirely different manner. It avoided the gruesome details almost entirely. Instead, it used a style that reduced the battle to sonorous and decorative abstractions:

> A hundred bronze thunderclaps gave the signal:
> At a firm and quick pace, with implacable brows,
> The deep column advanced towards our ranks,
> Preceded by Terror and surrounded by flames,
> Like a thick cloud, which, on the wing of the winds,
> Bears thunderbolts, lightning, and death in its flanks.

Voltaire could not entirely avoid scenes of carnage, but he preferred to present them through the lens of classical metaphor, casting the dead and wounded as bloodied leopards or as birds fallen from the sky. He made sure to devote a line or two to the exploits of each prominent French officer, and when it came to King Louis, he lost his sense of proportion entirely:

> The French are great when their Master guides them! . . .
> He strides forward, he is like the Master of the Gods . . .
> He strides forward, and his steps echo in distant lands,
> The Escaut flees, the Sea complains, and the Sky darkens.

Voltaire also loyally singled out his friend Richelieu, "who bears his courage wherever he goes / Ardent but enlightened, lively and wise." And he was as clearly thinking of the duke elsewhere in the poem, when

he wondered at the mysterious alchemy of eighteenth-century aristocrats at war:

> How is it that these gentle, jocular, affable Courtiers
> Become indomitable Lions in battle?
> What a happy union of graces and valor!

Voltaire at least made a distinction between what now appear to be the
two halves of Richelieu's persona. Richelieu himself would probably
not have done so. In his mind, he was a noble, pure and simple. Nonetheless, the lines perfectly capture the aristocratic ideal of warfare.

A cynic might well ascribe Voltaire's efforts to nothing more than
sordid self-interest. We know that he wanted to curry favor with the
king and the king's mistress, Madame de Pompadour, for at this point
in his career, he had not yet given up hope that the people who counted
in France would pardon him his extensive record of insolence, sedi-
tion, and religious heterodoxy. He particularly wanted to join the elite
French Academy, and after his poem featured in France's official victory
celebrations, he was in fact duly admitted. He also, incidentally, made a
fortune investing with military contractors. Still, in the eighteenth century, such ulterior motives did not automatically discredit the final
product. (Imagine, by contrast, how contemporary American poets
would judge one of their number who celebrated President Bush and
the Iraq War in return for an appointment as Poet Laureate, while also
investing in Halliburton!)

More to the point, Voltaire's *Fontenoy* was entirely typical of the period. He was only one of several poets to rush into print with celebrations of the battle, and verse of the sort oozed off European printing presses after every major military engagement of the century. There
were ballads on the battle of Blenheim, odes on the battle of Oude-
naarde, couplets on the battle of Culloden. As the British man of letters
Joseph Addison explained in a typical piece of work: "Thus would I
fain Britannia's wars rehearse / In the smooth records of a faithful
verse." Eleven years after Fontenoy, French poets greeted a single engagement, Richelieu's seizure of Minorca from the British, with nothing less than a 330-page anthology of (mostly dreadful) ballads and
odes. French readers expected a literary giant like Voltaire to celebrate a
major French victory, and they gave his poem a rapturous reception
when he did. The first printing sold out in days, and within a week, the

work had gone through five more; within two months, forty. Audiences *wanted* sonorously abstract invocations of splendor and glory, not vivid descriptions of pain and death.

The reason the style appealed is that in the aristocratic culture of war, the texture of individual experience and individual feelings — including feelings of pain and horror — mattered very little. What mattered was how well the leading participants, and the army as a whole, lived up to an impersonal aristocratic ideal of splendor, courage, and honor. Voltaire, in fact, had almost precisely the opposite goal from present-day creative authors: not to bring out what made an event original and unique but to emphasize what made it exactly like other events of the same type — other great battles, other epic victories. Hence the abstract language and the liberal imitation of classical models. Aristocratic officers like Lauzun imagined their performances on the battlefield, and wrote about them, in very much the same manner. Paradoxically, to our eyes, they made a spectacle of their individual selves by trying to conform as closely as possible to a standard model of what an aristocratic officer should be.

It is still tempting to separate the representation from the reality — to say, in effect, that regardless of how Voltaire chose to write about Fontenoy, eighteenth-century war remained what d'Argenson saw: an indescribably bloody horror. And, of course, it was. But insisting on seeing it only as a Wilfred Owen or Erich Remarque would later see it, as opposed to the way Voltaire saw it in his poem on Fontenoy, doesn't simply render a great deal of eighteenth-century culture mysteriously alien. It also blinds us to a paradoxical fact: that eighteenth-century aristocratic culture helped place surprising limits on war. These limits existed *despite* the gruesome tolls of the major battles and *despite* the fact that European elites had war as their principal purpose. Indeed, in some ways, they existed *because* the elites had war as their principal purpose.

To see these limits, we need to place the eighteenth century against the bloody background of earlier periods. During the struggles between Catholics and Protestants of the sixteenth and early seventeenth centuries, when, in Froude's words, "religion made humanity a crime," the technology of war was still less deadly than in the age of Enlightenment (many soldiers still used pikes rather than muskets and bayonets; artillery was less mobile and destructive). Armies were smaller as well. Yet the effects of war spilled over into the civilian world in a torrent of gore and suffering. Soldiers routinely massacred the inhabitants of towns they had captured, and the overall population statistics tell a story unmatched in their grimness until the days of Stalin and Hitler. From 1600 to 1648, the population of Germany fell from around 21 million to as little as 13 million. The Thirty Years' War of 1618–48 was not total war in the modern sense: it did not involve the same systematic mobilization of resources, the same systematic destruction of enemy societies, and the same political dynamic driving the adversaries toward ever more extreme measures, with no outcome possible but one side's complete collapse. But the scale of horror was similar.

By the early eighteenth century, this scale of horror had diminished. The battle of Fontenoy was ghastly, but it is worth noting that Maurice of Saxony did not follow up his victory by pursuing and destroying the remnants of Cumberland's force, as earlier generals might have done (and as Napoleon would have done sixty years later). Peter the Great behaved with similar restraint after Poltava, although, admittedly, he had few enough survivors to pursue. Most important, although battles were murderous, most generals did their best to avoid them. "I am not at all for battles," wrote Maurice of Saxony, "especially at the start of a war, and I am convinced that a skillful general can go all his life without being forced to fight one." Few soldiers saw more than three or four major battles during their careers — enough to have ample chance to demonstrate their bravery without making the military into a necessarily suicidal career choice. Only after 1792 did the frequency of battle increase. One simple reason for the generals' reluctance to fight was their preference for relatively small, well-trained armies of career soldiers. Maurice once again expressed the era's conventional wisdom: "It is not large armies that win battles, but good ones." His preference was born of necessity, since even the partial-conscription systems used in many European states could not produce the sort of mass armies that would trample the Continent during the French Revolution. Sometimes, European states indeed needed to recruit soldiers out of prisons and poorhouses and even to force prisoners of war to fight against their homelands, as Frederick the Great did with 18,000 Saxons he captured in 1756. Soldiers were expensive to find and train, and so generals did their best to keep them alive. As one of them remarked during the Seven

Years' War: "It's a great shame to lose a grenadier; it takes time to make men like that."

What is more surprising is that eighteenth-century armies did their best to keep civilians alive as well. As late as the 1680s and 1690s, French armies invading present-day Belgium left an appalling reputation behind them. French bombardments destroyed much of Brussels, and French troops, left to their own devices, raped and pillaged, causing widespread panic. But when the French returned in the first decades of the eighteenth century, they largely spared civilian populations, sometimes in return for large, up-front payments by the local authorities. By 1745, when it was the turn of Maurice of Saxony's troops, Belgian civilians largely went about their business unmolested. Adam Smith dubiously claimed that Dutch peasants actually looked forward to military occupation because they could stop paying rent and sell provisions to the invading armies at inflated prices.

Farther east, the situation was not always much different. When Russian soldiers occupied the East Prussian capital of Königsberg in 1757, one German eyewitness described their behavior as follows: "It became fashionable to drink punch. The Russian authorities held balls — invariably at their own cost — and the ladies were not conscripted, but invited by gallant, nimble and handsome aides-de-camp . . ." Compare this scene to what happened when a different Russian army came to Königsberg, in the spring of 1945. In Anthony Beevor's words:

> The destruction was terrible. Thousands of soldiers and civilians were buried under the bombardments . . . Any civilians left alive hung sheets from windows in a signal of surrender . . . On the morning of 10 April [1945] . . . the surviving garrison of just 30,000 troops marched out to imprisonment. Their watches and any useful items were promptly grabbed by Red Army soldiers, who had managed to find stores of alcohol. The rape of women and girls went unchecked in the ruined city.

One could make similar comparisons between Maurice of Saxony and the Germans who occupied Belgium in 1914 and 1940.

Eighteenth-century Europeans also made increasingly important attempts to establish legal limits on war making — and thus formally to outlaw atrocities. The Hague and Geneva conventions still lay in the future. But as early as 1625, the Dutchman Hugo Grotius had provided the first great modern model for them, after observing "a lack of restraint in relation to war, such as even barbarous races would be ashamed of." Grotius did not believe it possible to banish war altogether, but he proposed rules for limiting and humanizing it. His thick tomes amounted to a code for monarchs, generals, and soldiers: when they could legitimately go to war in the first place; when they could confiscate enemy property, enslave, and kill; and the rules to be followed vis-à-vis neutrals, enemy noncombatants, prisoners of war, and so forth. By the eighteenth century, Grotius had acquired a host of imitators and correctors, including Jean-Jacques Rousseau, who brilliantly distilled into a few lines of his *Social Contract* the basic distinction that underlay the new approach to military conflict. "War," he wrote, "is not a relationship between individual men, but between states," and therefore, "states can only have other states, not men, as enemies." Force was justified only against men wearing the uniform of their state. Against noncombatants, it was purely and simply illegitimate.

Admittedly, the limits took time to develop in practice and did so very irregularly. The armies of France's Louis XIV, who reigned from 1643 to 1715 and fought many aggressive wars, not only wrought terrific damage on Belgium but also, in 1688–89, deliberately undertook the physical destruction of the German region called the Palatinate (Pfalz). By the standards of the earlier seventeenth century, they behaved rather mildly. They razed property on a vast scale (as Heidelberg tour guides still point out, with somewhat inappropriate indignation). But for the most part, they followed a cruel but rational strategic plan for protecting French territorial gains, maintained a reasonable degree of military discipline, and engaged in relatively little arbitrary slaughter. Still, they caused great human suffering.

Even in the middle of the eighteenth century, several campaigns stand out for their ferocity, especially in the Seven Years' War. Frederick the Great gambled the existence of his kingdom in this war, and central Europe suffered terribly for it, with Prussia alone losing as much as 500,000 dead. If at least some Russians behaved themselves in Königsberg in 1757, in nearby Memel, other Russians were accused of horrors "not seen since the invasion of the Huns — they hung the inhabitants after having cut off their noses and ears, they ripped off legs and tore out hearts and entrails." It is also difficult to downplay the well-documented atrocities committed by the Russians thirty years later at Otchakoff and Izmail, in the Balkans, where they killed as many as 26,000 Turkish prisoners out of hand and as many as 6,000 civilians. Nonetheless — and distasteful as it may be to weigh atrocities against each other — it is still the case that such horrors took place less frequently, less systematically, and on a smaller scale than during the age of religious wars — especially in Western Europe. Neither does the eighteenth century compare to the period of total war that began after 1792, to say nothing of the first half of the twentieth century.

Some historians persist in thinking of the eighteenth century as a time of uncontrolled conflict that fed directly into the excesses of 1792–1815. In doing so, however, they disregard the astonishing increase in the scope and intensity of warfare in the French Revolution and also misunderstand the aristocratic context of eighteenth-century warfare. If we assume that the political elites of the time abhorred war and wanted to end it forever, then the record indeed looks like a dismal failure. But if we accept that they saw war as a natural, unavoidable part of human existence and simply wanted to limit its scope and damage, then they did not do so badly, compared with other periods of European history. Indeed, the eighteenth century represents in some ways a remarkable historical moment: a time of relative restraint between the age of the religious wars and the total war of 1792–1815.

Eighteenth-century observers themselves saw the transformations at work very keenly. "There are fewer cannibals in Christianity than there once were," wrote Voltaire with characteristic sharpness in 1751. The officer and essayist Vauvenargues agreed: "Today war is waged . . . so humanely, so deftly, and with so little profit that it could be compared, without paradox, to civil trials." The Swiss Emeric de Vattel, one of Grotius's most important successors, commented that "the Nations of Europe almost always carry on war with great forbearance and generosity." And the French revolutionary Jean-Paul Rabaut Saint-Etienne claimed, with more than a little hyperbole, before the outbreak of the Revolutionary wars:

> Armies slaughter each other politely; heroes salute before killing each other . . . No longer is it nations which fight each other, but just armies and professionals; wars are like games of chance in which no one risks his all; what was once a wild rage is now just a folly.

According to Joseph Cornish, the clergyman from Devon: "wars have in general of late been carried on with less cruelty than formerly."

True, these "limits on warfare" did themselves have one crucial limit: they applied above all to war between uniformed European armies. When it came to civil war involving irregular insurgents and also sometimes to wars against non-European "savages" and "barbarians," then that familiar historical specter, European elite hypocrisy, quickly reared its head. The French practiced brutal counterinsurgency tactics against Protestant Camisard rebels on their own soil in the first decades of the century and against Paoli's supporters in Corsica in 1768–69. Less than a year after his defeat at Fontenoy, the Duke of Cumberland crushed Bonnie Prince Charlie, Stuart pretender to his father's throne, at the battle of Culloden and proceeded to savage the Highlands with a fury that Scotland has neither forgotten nor forgiven. The distinction between "civilized" and "noncivilized" opponents constituted one of the century's most dangerously double-edged legacies, for if the first had to be treated with every courtesy, the second, sometimes defined as "enemies of the human race," were left open to every horror. During the French Revolutionary wars, the ability to define an opponent — even a uniformed European one — as "savage" would do much to bring the era of limited warfare to an end.

So why did this shift to limited war take place? The decline of religion as a cause of hostilities certainly mattered. As Cornish remarked: "Religion used to be made a pretence for stirring up men to cut another's throats, but this mad frenzy has lost much of its power." Significantly, the worst slaughter of the eighteenth century tended to occur where religion still divided the adversaries: in the Camisard civil war in France, for instance, or in the Russo-Turkish conflicts. The war that saw the destruction of the Palatinate still had a strong religious component, with Catholic France, then in the midst of trying to eradicate Protestantism from its own soil, arrayed against Protestant Britain and Holland. There is the classic argument that European powers practiced restraint because of the emergence of a rough balance of power, which obliged them to fight for limited goals and to banish all thoughts of knockout blows and Continent-wide hegemony. And historians have also cited the growth of state power, which allowed larger and more disciplined armies to take the field, thereby making it more difficult for bands of uncontrolled "soldateska" to rampage through Europe. The growth of the state had the crucial effect of subordinating European nobilities to central authorities, both politically and militarily.

All these explanations have something to be said for them. Indeed, the seventeenth-century developments they point to formed a necessary prelude to the eighteenth-century age of military restraint. Still, the explanations are incomplete. Culture matters too, enormously. On the battlefield, European monarchs and generals did not practice the new style of warfare because of conscious calculations about the balance of power or conscious reflections about the waning of religious passions. They did so because it came naturally to them as aristocrats: to fight, to fight bravely and gloriously but also with restraint, with self-control, with honor; to live up to the ideals praised in Voltaire's *Fontenoy*. What governed the experience of warfare for Europe's ruling classes and kept it functioning as a system was aristocratic culture.

Tellingly, the atrocity cited most often in eighteenth-century writings on war was not an incident from the Thirty Years' War, involving ravenous military brigands or wide-eyed priests. It was France's campaign in the Palatinate, which, for all the impressive destruction of property, had a much smaller death toll. Nonetheless, it shocked cultured eighteenth-century Europeans in a way that the earlier rampages did not. To quote the French *philosophe* Denis Diderot, "I should hate to have been the ferocious beast who ordered the devastation of the Palatinate." The beast in question, he knew perfectly well, was France's own Louis XIV. Yet the event was shocking precisely because it had been the work of that most polished and aristocratic of kings and therefore seemed utterly aberrant. By contrast, one of the greatest cultural heroes of eighteenth-century France was Nicolas Catinat de la Fauconnerie, a marshal of Louis XIV who worked conspicuously to spare civilian populations.

Although it had its own, independent roots, the jurisprudence of war in the eighteenth century also fell into line with aristocratic cultural ideals. Unlike medieval commentators on the subject — and unlike Grotius — jurists such as Vattel devoted relatively little attention to questions of justice and responsibility in war. That is to say, they focused less on establishing criteria to judge which, if any, side had the morally superior cause — what today goes by the name of "just war theory" — than about how the sides actually fought. In other words, as Carl Schmitt has observed, they treated war as something like the formal duel, whose rules likewise made no reference to the cause of the conflict but pertained only to the forms observed by the combatants. If the forms were honorably observed, it did not matter which side was in the right. Nothing could be closer to the aristocratic code. (On the other hand, Vattel judged those who did *not* adhere to the forms as "monsters" in need of extermination.)

Finally, remember that most eighteenth-century officers who reflected on the subject did not see anything massively unstable about the prevailing system of international relations and warfare. Whether they saw it as a lark, in the manner of Lauzun ("the chance of musket shots was too precious to pass up"), or as a fundamental law of nature, in the manner of Vauvenargues, they treated it as an utterly ordinary part of the order of things. And when they saw it under threat, they did not hesitate to defend it. "I cannot, as certain philosophers do, resolve to see war as a detestable scourge," wrote the French officer the Chevalier de Ray, in his memoirs. "I prefer to see it as a time of salutary ordeals." Such remarks, incidentally, should caution us against attributing the growing moderation of war to the influence of Enlightenment thought, which tended to portray war more as a scourge to be ended than as a salutary activity in need of correction and restraint. The process of moderation also began well before the heyday of Enlightenment thought in the mid-eighteenth century.

Soldiers like Ray believed that their form of aristocratic warfare could continue indefinitely. But soon after he wrote his memoirs in 1787 or 1788, his aristocratic world would dissolve forever. It would do so as a result of a tremendous political and cultural upheaval: the French Revolution, which began in 1789 and led to the total war of 1792–1815. But as his remark indicates, the change had roots in a very different quarter: those "certain philosophers" who attacked the ideas that lived in aristocratic heads well before the heads themselves came to decorate the ends of revolutionary pikes. In response to an aristocratic code that placed honor and loyalty above moral judgment, these philosophers had raised the claims of conscience. Rather than glorifying war, they reviled it. If it had to be fought, they demanded armies of citizens, not aristocrats. Just as important, they convinced an ever-expanding body of readers to accept their judgments. And so, it is to them that we now must turn.

2

Conscience, Commerce, and History

War is a great and profound subject which concerns the philosopher as much as the general.

— JOSEPH DE MAISTRE

IN ONE SENSE, the claims of conscience against war have always been with us — or at least since a Hebrew prophet carved the words "thou shalt not kill" onto a stone tablet. The scriptures that lie at the foundation of Western culture abound with promising visions of a world free from violent conflict. By the time the French National Assembly issued its 1790 declaration of peace, a hundred generations had already had their hopes (fleetingly, elusively) raised by the words of Isaiah: "and they shall beat their swords into plowshares, and their spears into pruninghooks: nation shall not lift up sword against nation, neither shall they learn war any more" (Isaiah 2:4). For seventeen centuries, the West had hearkened to the man who told his followers, "blessed be the peacemakers" and "love your enemies" (Matthew 5:9, 5:44). True, Jesus also told his listeners, "Think not that I am come to send peace on earth: I came not to send peace, but a sword" (Matthew 10:34). And, in a parable: "These mine enemies . . . bring hither, and slay them before me" (Luke 19:27). Yet his message was still, overwhelmingly, interpreted as a peaceful one, particularly when blended with the classical tradition of natural law, which held out the prospect of harmony among mankind. And although the subsequent history of Christianity reeks of blood as strongly as any other major religion's, it has also been dotted, throughout its length, by the presence of groups that have taken the apparent scriptural message of peace literally, refused to bear arms, and preached the virtues of absolute nonaggression.

In the eighteenth century, the most visible of these groups were the Quakers. Arising out of the millenarian chaos of the British civil wars of the 1640s and spreading across the Atlantic under the leadership of William Penn, much about them utterly shocked their contemporaries: their rejection of baptism, their disdain for etiquette and polite forms of speech, the mournful sobriety of their dress and behavior — and especially their absolute refusal to fight for their country. In January 1661, they issued a solemn declaration promising never "to fight and war against any man with outward weapons." They stood, it could be said, at the precise opposite end of the European cultural spectrum from such extravagant, lordly, and aggressive warriors as Lauzun or Richelieu. Not surprisingly, when Voltaire visited Britain in the 1720s, he found the Quakers to be the strangest thing about that strange island and wrote wonderingly about their unwillingness to slaughter their fellow men. Even in the twentieth century, as many as 45 percent of British Quakers would still become conscientious objectors.

Individual Quakers could and did preach the merits of perpetual peace to others. "When it pleases God to chastise us severely for our Sins, it is with the *Rod of War,* that, for the most Part, he whips us . . . [the] Saviour . . . *came to save, and not to destroy the Lives of Men.*" Thus William Penn in 1693. "Let the Holy Jesus . . . be the Example for all Christian Princes to Imitate" — and not "those Heathen Heroes, such as *Alexander, Caesar,* or *Hannibal* . . . who Sacrificed the Lives of Thousands, to their restless Ambition, and Honour." Thus Penn's fellow Quaker John Bellers in 1710. Both men proposed the establishment of a European superstate to suppress warfare. But their works went largely unread at the time, and by the middle of the century, the Quakers, who numbered no more than 50,000 in Britain, had largely given up trying to convert others to their doctrines. They argued mostly by example alone, and this example elicited mockery rather than admiration: they were sectarian curiosities more than an embryonic peace movement. By the time of the American Revolution, the British government had long ceased to see Quakers as any sort of threat to its military efforts and did not even prosecute those who resisted militia service.

The eighteenth century did, however, see one enormously influential example of Christian pacifism. In time, it would help inspire new, secular varieties of pacifist thought, and they, in turn, would provoke new and troubling glorifications of war, as we will see in this chapter. But this pacifism arose out of a very different and unlikely quarter of Christianity.

This quarter was a ramshackle, towered castle in the Périgord valley of western France. There, in August 1651, a man had been born whom the eighteenth century would know simply as Fénelon — but let us give his name its full, luxuriously aristocratic dimensions: François de Salignac de la Mothe Fénelon. There was nothing remotely pacific about the castle's atmosphere. The walls were hung with portraits of family members who had bled and killed for France since the tenth century, including at least one Crusader. Fénelon's uncle and surrogate father, Antoine, had a reputation as one of France's finest fencers and duelists — and this in the golden age of French swordsmanship, immortalized by Dumas in *The Three Musketeers*. It is not impossible to imagine that Fénelon himself, despite a sickly youth and his family's impoverishment, might have entered the army.

In fact, his inclinations took him into the priesthood, but the humility of the cassock did little to disguise the bearing of the aristocrat. He was not only polished, charming, and learned but also knew it and combined grace with ambition in equal measure. Joseph Vivien's portrait accords well with the tart description given by the great memoirist of the age, the duke of Saint-Simon: "A tall, thin, handsome man with a large nose, from whose eyes flowed ardor and spirit in a torrent, and whose countenance was unlike any other I have known, and impossible to forget . . . It had both gravity and gallantry, seriousness and gaiety, and was at once that of a theologian, a bishop and a great lord."

For years, according to Saint-Simon, Fénelon "knocked at all the doors, without any opening for him." He cultivated the right clerical patrons, engaged in the right theological controversies, and supported King Louis XIV's attempt to exterminate Protestantism on French soil. He tried desperately hard to please everyone he came across, whatever their rank. But only in 1689, at age thirty-eight, did the great position he dreamed of finally materialize, when he was named tutor to the seven-year-old Louis, duke of Burgundy, the king's oldest grandson and eventual heir. Taking up residence at the court of Versailles, Fénelon

Joseph Vivien: *Archbishop Fénelon*

quickly established a deep psychological hold over the willful prince (some called it breaking the boy's spirit). He also took on the role of spiritual adviser to the king's former mistress and secret wife, the sober and devout Madame de Maintenon. He was now a power at court and could quite plausibly hope that when his young charge ascended the throne, he himself would become the second-most-powerful man in the kingdom. He could hardly have failed to think of an earlier clergyman, the original duke of Richelieu, who had used his hold over Louis XIV's father to accumulate vast power and wealth, becoming France's effective prime minister and a prince of the Roman Catholic Church.

Yet at this very moment of triumph, Fénelon's life took a strange and unexpected turn, setting up what must have been an agonizing struggle between his ambitions and his beliefs. In 1688, he had met a Catholic mystic and supposed "prophetess" named Jeanne Guyon, who advocated a set of beliefs known as Quietism. A wealthy forty-year-old widow, Guyon taught that Christians should abandon themselves abso-

lutely and entirely to the love of God, in a spirit of total disinterested-
ness — unconcerned even with the fate of their own souls. Those who
succeeded in this renunciation of the self, through an intense regimen
of prayer and devotion, would eventually find God actively taking possession of them, bringing about an ecstatic state of "pure love." Quiet-
ists made the Catholic authorities distinctly nervous — some of them,
although not Guyon herself, had taught that if true love possessed the
soul, the body could give in to carnal temptation without sin. Nonetheless, Fénelon was enraptured by her, and the two slowly fell into an intense, entirely platonic friendship.

From the point of view of someone coming to believe in the utter renunciation of the self, the court of Versailles must have looked like a
very strange and sinful place. Louis XIV built it as a temple to his own
royal self, with the greatest art and architecture of the age sumptuously
and strategically deployed to emphasize his utter superiority to ordinary
humans. Everything at the huge and lavish palace and its enormous
grounds — from the arrangement of the central building around the
royal apartments to the famous motifs of the sun to the allegorical and
historical paintings hanging in the magnificent galleries — glorified this
single individual. It compared him to Phoebus and Hercules, celebrated his strength and wisdom, praised his taste and physical beauty,
and, above all, saluted his achievements in war. Since taking personal
control over the French government at age eighteen, Louis had devoted
his reign largely to conquests, fighting a virtually uninterrupted series
of campaigns against nearly every major European power. In the process, he had greatly extended France's borders. He had shown little
compassion to rulers who dared oppose him and had allowed his troops
to devastate the Palatinate with very little regret. But even with these excesses, his reign marked the apotheosis of warfare as a form of aristocratic self-expression.

This obsession with the royal self would have been terrible enough
by itself, from a Quietist point of view, but within a few years of
Fénelon's arrival at court, it seemed to have dragged France to the brink
of the abyss. The most recent of Louis's aggressive wars, the War of the
League of Augsburg (1688–97), had brought into being a grand coalition opposed to France. The king's armies had met with repeated defeats, including the 1690 Battle of the Boyne, which secured British
Protestant supremacy in Ireland. Then, in 1693–94, the worst harvest

failure of the century struck in France itself. The price of bread, the principal foodstuff for most of the population, reached record heights, until the cost of the ordinary two-pound loaf far outstripped most families' daily income. The mortality rate climbed in grim lockstep with bread prices, as hundreds of thousands succumbed to starvation and disease. The birth rate fell precipitously as well — the sign of a population too sick and starved to reproduce (with grim understatement, demographers call such moments a "mortality crisis"). Yet Louis XIV fought obstinately on. Was the king devouring his own people for the sake of military glory?

Sometime in 1694, Fénelon made precisely this charge in one of the most extraordinary letters ever written to a French monarch. It was not a letter he actually sent — for all his belief in self-renunciation, he still had enough sense of self-preservation to realize that doing so would land him in prison or worse. At most, Fénelon showed it to a few confidants and then hid it away so carefully that it came to light only a century later (its authenticity remained in doubt until a manuscript copy in Fénelon's hand turned up in the 1820s). It is nonetheless a remarkable document. It shows Fénelon not only harshly condemning his king in the name of Christian morality but also moving toward the view that the root of the king's offenses lay not merely in excessive pride but more particularly in the form of pride that goes by the name of military glory. The trouble went back at least twenty years, to Louis's first unabashed war of conquest, against the Netherlands:

> It is useless to say, Sire, that these conquests were necessary for your State. The property of others is never necessary for us. What is truly necessary for us is to observe an unerring justice . . . This is reason enough, Sire, to admit that you have lived your entire life apart from the paths of truth and justice, and therefore apart from the paths of the Gospel. All the hideous troubles that have devastated Europe for more than twenty years — all the blood spilt, all the outrages committed, all the provinces sacked, all the cities and towns reduced to ashes — are the deadly consequences of this war . . . And your people, whom you should have loved like your own children, and who once so adored you, are now starving to death. The tilling of the soil is almost abandoned, the cities and the countryside are emptying out . . . All of France is nothing but a great, starving sick ward, and it is you yourself, Sire, who have brought all these troubles to pass.

At a court addicted to the sickly sweet perfume of flattery, words of this sort were almost literally unthinkable — a monstrously shocking act of secular blasphemy, even in private.

Although Fénelon never sent the letter, he began, in the early 1690s, to do something potentially just as seditious. At the court of Versailles, under the gaze of a thousand images of its warrior king, he decided to use his position as tutor to mold a very different sort of heir to the throne, committed to the happiness of the people and to peace. For the king's grandson, he would design an educational program that combined classical and humanist political teachings with a powerful Christian morality, all infused by the spirit of "pure love." When Louis XIV and his doltish son and heir finally passed away, the duke of Burgundy would take the throne, bring the days of aristocratic warfare to an end, and usher in an age of perpetual peace and prosperity.

It was a hopelessly naive project, unlikely to succeed even with the most pliant of the princes of the house of Bourbon (a species notoriously resistant to education of any kind and inordinately fond of firearms) — and in any case, Fénelon never got the chance to put it into practice. For a brief while, he remained influential at Versailles and was even rewarded with an archbishopric and the title of duke. But clerical attacks against Madame Guyon were intensifying, and Fénelon stubbornly insisted on defending his spiritual friend, in words and in print. Finally, the king turned against him and, in 1697, permanently exiled him to his see of Cambrai in northern France, "to age under the useless weight of his hopes," as Saint-Simon put it. These hopes revived momentarily in 1711, when the king's son died, leaving Burgundy first in line to the throne. The former pupil still remembered his tutor affectionately, and with Louis XIV himself aged and ailing, Fénelon eagerly sketched out ideas for a new regime with the duke's advisers. But just a year later, without warning, Burgundy himself succumbed to an infectious disease, along with his wife and young son. It was the final blow. "I cannot resist the will of God, which crushes us," Fénelon wrote in black resignation to a confidant after hearing the news. "He knows what I am suffering, but it is His hand which strikes, and we deserve it. There is nothing to do but to detach ourselves from the world and from ourselves, to abandon ourselves, unreservedly, to God's designs." Less than three years later, Fénelon too was dead.

Yet his program of pacifist royal education, naive and short-lived as it may have been, bore unexpected fruit. For the priest not only tried to influence the young prince through personal lessons but also put his program into writing. From his arrival at Versailles, he started to compose a series of moralistic fables and fairy tales, in the style of Aesop and La Fontaine. He supplemented them with *Dialogues of the Dead,* a series of readings intended for the adolescent prince, composed of encounters in the underworld between pairs of famous figures from world history: Romulus and Remus, Confucius and Socrates, Hannibal and Scipio, and so forth. Stilted and humorless but possessed of a certain orotund elegance, the dialogues served up a relentless moral menu of humility, patriotism, self-sacrifice, and pacifism. Into the mouth of Socrates, Fénelon put these words: "War is an evil which dishonors the human race . . . All wars are civil wars, because it is always man who sheds the blood of man, who tears open the entrails of man." Only in the last extremity, with a kingdom under vicious attack, could a king ever legitimately resort to force.

Most important, Fénelon wrote a novel for his pupil. Called *Telemachus,* it was a sequel to Homer's *Odyssey* but focused on the son of the wandering Ulysses rather than on the man himself. Published (supposedly without Fénelon's consent) in 1699, it is this book, more than anything else, that has saved him from the thickets of scholars' footnotes and made him a sizable figure in European history and literature. It drew both from the Christian tradition and from humanist teachings of the Renaissance, and in these respects, it was not enormously original. But the spirit of "pure love" breathed through it, insisting that true virtue demanded the utter renunciation of the self. And in each of its eighteen long sections, Fénelon insistently put forth the claims of conscience, denounced war, and urged Christian pacifism on Christian rulers. The book caused an immediate sensation, going through fifteen French editions in 1699 alone and at least sixty more over the course of the eighteenth century. Translated into every major language, it had particular success in English, where it appeared in at least fifty separate editions before 1800. It was one of the great bestsellers of eighteenth-century Europe.

Today, it is exasperatingly difficult to see why. Telemachus roams the

Mentor Bringing Peace

Mediterranean, searching for his lost father, but his adventures — unlike the *Odyssey* — involve little suspense and boast few compellingly
monstrous characters to match Homer's Polyphemus the Cyclops or
Circe the Enchantress. Instead, Telemachus has by his side the drearily
wise counselor Mentor, who ensures that his pupil's slightest surrender to temptation meets with quick and loquacious correction. Many
chapters — even Telemachus's despairing search for his father amid the
ghosts of Hades — consist of little but large helpings of unadulterated,
virtually indigestible virtue, accompanied by verbose sermonizing and
much shedding of pious tears. Alfred Tennyson would later capture

something of the book's well-meaning, earnest tedium in his poem "Ulysses":

> This is my son, mine own Telemachus . . .
> Well-loved of me, discerning to fulfill
> This labour, by slow prudence to make mild
> A rugged people, and thro' soft degrees
> Subdue them to the useful and the good.
> Most blameless is he . . .

Unlike Homer's dazzlingly individualistic and amoral warrior-princes, Fénelon's heroes conform to a single, Christian model of humility and restraint, despite the classical setting. It hardly comes as a surprise when, at odyssey's end, Mentor reveals himself as Minerva, goddess of wisdom, in disguise.

Certainly, some readers saw *Telemachus* as a simple *roman à clef*. The eponymous hero seemed an obvious stand-in for the duke of Burgundy, and if so, then who could the divine Mentor possibly represent, if not Fénelon himself? (So much for priestly humility!) Less probably, readers saw the shadow of Louis XIV stretching out from other characters: the cruel Phoenecian tyrant Pygmalion or the tragic Idomeneus, King of Crete, who suffers exile for sacrificing his own son to the gods and then reforms his new kingdom of Salentum under Mentor's exacting and long-winded supervision. But this uncertain guessing game alone could hardly have kept many readers going through endless variations on lines like "shipwreck and death are less hideous than the pleasures which attack virtue."

Our own inability to understand what eighteenth-century readers saw in Fénelon's orgy of high-mindedness is frustrating but also offers us a starting point for understanding something that was beginning to change in European culture. As Robert Darnton has written: "When you realize that you are not getting something — a joke, a proverb, a ceremony — that is particularly meaningful to the natives, you can see where to grasp a foreign system of meaning in order to unravel it." To our own sensibilities, Telemachus and his tutor may seem unbearably sentimental. But contemporary readers found in them characters who seemed to speak directly from their own hearts and from nature, who followed the precepts of simple reason, and who were rewarded with genuine happiness. Fénelon's story therefore stood as a powerful rebuke to the aristocratic court culture that dominated European societies, with its perceived artificiality, hypocrisy, and monumental selfishness. The book did not simply express these feelings; it helped shape and popularize them. From its wellspring of sentimentality, a river of tenderly shed tears would flow straight through the eighteenth century, fed by Richardson, Greuze, and Rousseau, among others, finally to pour out into the broad sea of Romanticism.

And of course, *Telemachus's* sentimental ethos had powerful implications for contemporary warfare. Remaining true to nature demanded the renunciation not only of luxury and self-promotion but also, above all, of war and military glory. In his efforts to construct a utopian kingdom in Salentum, Mentor drives home the lesson relentlessly. "All peoples are brothers," he insists. "And all men must love each other as such. Woe to those profane souls who seek a cruel glory in their brothers' blood . . . ! War may sometimes be necessary, but it is the shame of the human race." These words posed a profound challenge to the aristocratic military code and the notion that war was a large-scale duel, with moral issues subordinated to the thirst for honor and glory. Just as important — if ironically, given the author's deep faith — the novel posed the challenge in resolutely secular terms that could not be dismissed as mere pious sermonizing.

Unfortunately, historians of pacifist thought have tended to slight Fénelon's importance or even to ignore him altogether. Fixated on questions of pure intellectual originality or on finding authors who anticipated their own exacting doctrines and definitions, they tend to skirt quickly over his writings, despite his popularity. Most often, they lump him in with other literary figures of the period who condemned war in language drawn from the Christian and humanist traditions. Notable among these was the moralist Jean de la Bruyère (1645–96), who more than once suggested, with mordant skepticism, that glory amounted to nothing more than a fiction veiling the reality of senseless slaughter. Also invoked is the famous mathematician and religious writer Blaise Pascal (1623–62), who observed sardonically that the only thing distinguishing murder from heroism is whether it occurs on your side of an arbitrary borderline or the other. But war hardly figured centrally in their thought as it did in Fénelon's.

Of all the protopacifist writers of the period, historians have devoted the most attention to the curious figure known as the *abbé* de Saint-Pierre (1658–1743). He does have some importance to our story. Like Fénelon, he came from an ancient family of the military nobility, and he too fell victim to a precocious religious vocation. But unlike Fénelon, he soon lost his faith and decided instead to make a career as a man of letters. Armed with a small private income and rather more enthusiasm than talent, he arrived in Paris in the 1680s and tried to gain entrée to literary circles — initially, with embarrassing eagerness. Eventually, though, he succeeded and spent the rest of his life haunting the more intellectual of the Parisian *salons,* ingratiating himself with their hostesses through his good manners, and gaining a carefully cultivated reputation for unworldly goodness. From his pen flew an endless number of supremely well-intentioned reform projects: for repairing roads, suppressing duels, improving the theater, stopping Barbary piracy, creating newspapers, adjusting the tax code, curing mendicity, revising the judicial system, and even ending clerical celibacy (a cause particularly close to his heart). If his projects had anything in common, it was that nothing ever came of any of them, and, indeed, many were printed up at his own expense. Yet Saint-Pierre was neither a saintly simpleton nor a crank and in some ways stands as an early, if somewhat comic, example of that great eighteenth-century social type, the *philosophe.*

In 1713, he published his most important book, *A Project for Making Peace Perpetual in Europe.* It was not exactly pacifist, for it wasted little space condemning war per se and suggested that one reason for peace in Europe was to bring about a grand crusade against the Turks. It consisted mostly of detailed plans for the construction of a federation named, in a moment of lucky prophecy, "the European Union." In this, it resembled the earlier plans of Sully, Penn, and Bellers. It differed mostly in Saint-Pierre's claim that states would have no incentive to abandon war unless they sacrificed most of their sovereign rights to a superior authority. At the time, the plan attracted more ridicule than applause, with French prime minister Fleury calling its author "the apothecary of all Europe," and Voltaire dubbing him "Saint Pierre of Utopia." But it later attracted close attention from the philosophers Rousseau and Kant and occupies a small but serious place in the history of political thought. It has the dubious honor of counting among the intellectual antecedents of the United Nations. Still, this self-published text, which circulated mainly among denizens of the Parisian *salons,* had only a tiny fraction of *Telemachus's* readership. And when it comes to widespread attitudes toward war and peace, what matters most is what men and women read, discussed, and took to heart — not the most advanced philosophical treatments of the subject.

As attitudes began to change in early eighteenth-century Europe, it was Fénelon who marked them more than any other single author. Indeed, his influence is difficult to overstate. "*Telemachus* appeared," swooned the novelist Jacques-Henri Bernardin de Saint-Pierre in 1784, "and it summoned Europe back to the harmonies of nature. It produced a great revolution in politics. It brought peoples and kings back to useful arts, to commerce, to agriculture, and above all to affection for the divinity." Another critic burbled that "if any poem could engender the happiness of the human race, it would be [*Telemachus*]." Even as entirely un-Fénelonian a character as Lauzun read the book and referred to it familiarly in his memoirs. The word "mentor," which we owe to Fénelon, remains a telling sign of its appeal.

Telemachus even, eventually, reached the royal audience it was intended for. After King Louis XIV's death in 1715, the regent to his successor quoted directly from the book in a speech before being confirmed in office, as did the court preacher Massillon, who warned the young heir to the throne that even the most legitimate of wars brought more sorrow than glory in their train. In his funeral elegy for Louis XIV, Massillon had daringly asked what the old king's victories signified and answered, as Fénelon might have done: "nothing but an entire century of horror and carnage." Royal panegyrists repeatedly hailed the young king as a new Telemachus and flattered his tutors as new Mentors. Later in the century, royal tutors gave the book itself to their charges, and King Louis XVI (1754–93) was strongly marked by it.

Fénelon's influence shows through most dramatically in the way the French saw their own history. In the seventeenth century, efforts to commemorate the national past had highlighted the achievements of French kings in war and of great aristocratic commanders. The eighteenth century, however, saw a very conscious reevaluation of this tradition. As the literary historian Jean-Claude Bonnet has shown, inner moral qualities, as opposed to heroic actions, became the chief criteria of historical "greatness." Legislators, scholars, literary and artistic figures, and even merchants became candidates for commemoration. Even kings now qualified only if they had governed as true "fathers of their peoples." The indefatigable *abbé* de Saint-Pierre helped define the trend, in an essay on the difference between mere "fame" and authentic greatness. But Fénelon — "the true key to the museum of the eighteenth-century imagination," in Bonnet's words — provided the great and decisive example in his portrayal of Telemachus and Mentor. Not surprisingly, Fénelon himself soon became the archetype of this new type of national icon. Stories of his own life multiplied: in biographies, poems, paintings, and essay contests. In the 1770s, when the French crown decided to commission official sculptures of France's greatest men, Fénelon numbered among the first four subjects chosen.

Yet Fénelon and *Telemachus* were by no means the whole story. For one thing, although kings and nobles might have read the book, they continued, at regular intervals, to turn peaceful fields, such as Fontenoy, into reasonable approximations of hell. Their conduct remained shaped by the logic of aristocratic warfare. And in the great intellectual revolution called the Enlightenment, which in France took a strongly anticlerical direction, Christian love did not exactly offer a convincing basis for pacifism, even when it came dressed in *Telemachus's* decorous classical robes. Still, by the later eighteenth century, a large swath of Europe's intellectual elites was in fact beginning to condemn war and to prophesy its quick disappearance. In the words of Condorcet, the greatest and most optimistic of the late eighteenth-century *philosophes:* "War, like murder, will one day number among those extraordinary atrocities which revolt and shame nature, and drape opprobrium over the countries and centuries whose annals they sully." But this intellectual transformation required an intellectual base different from the one Fénelon had provided.

It required, in the first place, the redefinition of war as something fundamentally irrational — a phenomenon akin to the superstition, prejudice, and intolerance against which the Enlightenment had arisen in the first place. Here, surprisingly, the most famous example was provided by an author who had earlier done as much as anyone to glorify aristocratic warfare: Voltaire. In 1745, he had celebrated the victory of Fontenoy, and from 1750 to 1753, he had served Frederick the Great as a sort of *philosophe*-in-residence. But by 1759, Frederick had finished with him ("one squeezes the orange and one throws away the peel," the king remarked contemptuously), and Voltaire had withdrawn into an embittered, if luxurious, Swiss exile. There he wrote his best-known work, *Candide,* the tale of human suffering that, while satirically thrashing everything from the Inquisition to slavery to philosophical optimism, exposed precisely those aspects of war that the poem *Fontenoy* had occluded. The title character, forced to flee his native town in Germany, is tricked into joining the Bulgarian army. When he accidentally deserts, he is caught and forced to run a gauntlet of 2,000 men, who rip every last inch of skin from his back. There follows an utterly pointless battle in which 30,000 men lose their lives. Meanwhile, soldiers have gang-raped and disemboweled the object of his affections. A wise man later explains war to him as follows: "A million assassins in uniform, roaming from one end of Europe to the other, murder and pillage with discipline in order to earn their daily bread." *Candide* ends on a famously ambiguous note, with Voltaire seeming to despair of ever demolishing the world's thick ramparts of folly and telling his readers to look inward — to cultivate their own gardens. Nonetheless, the book proved enormously popular and inspired numerous imitations.

The most important and influential Enlightenment arguments for peace, however, used more than satire. They drew, instead, on a new sort of science just then coming into being: the science of society. To illustrate this change, however, it is best to leave Fénelon and Voltaire behind and to introduce a very different sort of figure: Paul-Henry Thiry, known as the Baron d'Holbach (1723–89). The son of bourgeois German landowners, he inherited fabulous wealth at an early age and used it to buy both a noble title and a sumptuous Parisian townhouse, where he entertained lavishly. His largesse helped him gather one of the century's most significant circles of thinkers around him: "Holbach's coterie," which included the *philosophe* Denis Diderot and the soldier-poet Saint-Lambert. D'Holbach was also a zealous and uncompromising atheist, who might well have died for his beliefs in earlier, less tolerant ages (or later, less tolerant ages, for that matter). Human beings, he taught, were physical matter and nothing more. There was no God, no heaven, no such thing as the soul. Nothing could be further from Fénelon's Christian zeal. But d'Holbach was an equally dedicated critic of warfare.

If d'Holbach offers a particularly clear example of French Enlightenment thinking on war and peace, it is not because he was a "typical" *philosophe* (if such a thing can even be said to have existed): his atheism was stomach-turning stuff even for liberal eighteenth-century digestions, and he published his books abroad, anonymously, so as not to endanger his position in society. Nor is it because of his intellectual importance, for in comparison with the sublimities of a Montesquieu or a Diderot, his thought was rigid and derivative. But where Montesquieu and Diderot were gloriously disorganized, d'Holbach was firmly, indeed often pedantically, systematic, laying out his points in long, carefully organized treatises. And, like Fénelon and Voltaire, he was popular — enormously so. Although his books were banned in France, the French public had grown addicted to illicit literature by the 1770s, and a vast black market had grown up to supply its habit. According to Robert Darnton, d'Holbach's "materialist" tract *The System of Nature* ranked third among the bestsellers of pre-Revolutionary France; his reform program, *The Social System,* came in at a respectable twenty-nine. His black-market works, in fact, outsold those of any other major *philosophe,* although they could not quite match the pornography, scandalmongering, and utopian fantasies that dominated the list.

Unlike in the case of Fénelon, d'Holbach's views on war and peace do not seem to have arisen out of any profound personal experiences. Indeed, he is open to charges of hypocrisy on this score, for even while condemning aristocratic warfare in the strongest terms, he managed to procure a place for his son in a prominent regiment of French dragoons and married his daughter to another dragoon officer. But this was behavior entirely typical of France in the twilight of the Old Regime. Social elites, confident in the power of the human mind and admirably tolerant of intellectual experiment, openly cultivated the philosophy that was corroding the foundations of their own status and power. They gamely pursued intellectual exercises to their logical conclusions, even while living by a set of codes that these exercises condemned. "We were walking on a carpet of flowers," one aristocratic memoirist would remark much later, "and did not notice the abyss beneath."

D'Holbach's thinking on military matters was grounded in a simple but deeply seditious idea: namely, that peace was the natural condition of humankind; war, an unnatural aberration. "Is there anything more contrary to equity, humanity and reason than to maintain between Peoples these hereditary, absurd and unreasonable hatreds?" Thus a typical passage from *The Social System.* It was a point of view that had developed against a great deal of opposition. It not only jibed uneasily with much evidence of actual human behavior but also ran contrary to Christian teachings. Most forms of Christianity offered a compelling promise of future peace, but they held too bleak and pessimistic a vision of Fallen humanity to expect much from it in the present. Even Fénelon, who anticipated so much Enlightenment thought in other respects, remained apart from it in this one, giving the young Telemachus a "wicked natural state" in need of correction, not natural goodness. Peace, for Fénelon, was not a gift of nature but something painfully and laboriously learned.

Nor was it only devout Christians who held to this idea, for the most powerful of early modern secular philosophers, Thomas Hobbes, had restated and reinforced it. Writing in the bloody middle of the seventeenth century, Hobbes had famously asserted that mankind's natural state was in fact nothing but "the war of all against all," which could be overcome only if everyone surrendered their rights to an all-powerful sovereign. Lest his readers think that he was writing only about individuals, Hobbes explicitly and repeatedly compared individuals to nations, which likewise existed in a state of nature in regard to each other — and so, most often, in a state of war. Hobbes had vast influence in early modern Europe, including on the *abbé* de Saint-Pierre, whose plan for states to surrender their rights to a European Union followed closely from the logic of the Englishman's masterpiece, *Leviathan.*

Nonetheless, even in the seventeenth century, some theoreticians had begun to challenge this view and to dispute Hobbes's conclusions about the international order. By the time d'Holbach came on the scene, the notion that "the state of peace is the natural state of nations," to quote the French economist Pierre-Paul Mercier de la Rivière, had become common among Europe's educated classes. Denis Diderot and Jean le Rond d'Alembert put the case authoritatively in their great compendium of Enlightenment thought, the *Encyclopédie:*

> Hobbes claimed that men always exist in a state of war of all against all; this bilious philosopher's sentiment would have been just as unconvincing had he said that the state of pain and sickness were natural to man . . . War is a convulsive and violent sickness of the body politic; this body is only healthy — that is to say, in its natural state — when it is at peace.

D'Holbach's thinking expressed this new consensus. Men were not naturally bellicose, he insisted. Bad rulers made them so. In his own unsubtle attack on Hobbes in *The System of Nature,* he concluded that the English philosopher had gotten things exactly backward: "The state of society is a state of war of the sovereign against all, and of each of its members against the others."

What d'Holbach added to the consensus, and what gave his pacifism its particular bite, was his close association of warfare with the prevailing aristocratic order and his venomous criticism of aristocratic notions of honor. Of course, others had come before him in this regard. "What is honor? A word. What is that honor? Air . . . Who hath it? He that died o' Wednesday." Thus Shakespeare's Falstaff. "War, he sung, is toil and trouble; / Honor, but an empty bubble." Thus John Dryden's Timotheus. Fénelon had criticized aristocratic concepts of honor as well, not to mention Voltaire in *Candide.*

But d'Holbach developed the critique with unprecedented thoroughness and psychological insight. "What does this [present-day] *honor* consist of?" he asked in *The Social System.* "Of ridiculous vanity, of imaginary advantages, of titles and sounds, of futile symbols." True nobility and honor, he added in his book *Universal Morality,* belonged only to those who had earned it by their own achievements, whether on the battlefield or off. Europe's modern nobles, with no real achievements of their own, shined only by the reflected glory of their ancestors — an especially ridiculous pose, given that those ancestors had gained preferment mostly through "murder, theft, rape and infamy." In order to maintain their position, modern nobles abjectly enslaved themselves to powerful monarchs and squandered their time and energy in bouts of competitive conspicuous consumption and dueling. Clearly referring to such figures as the dukes of Richelieu and Cumberland, with their servants and china services and endless baggage trains, d'Holbach dripped scorn on "the commanders, who, by their luxury, liberality, and sumptuous meals, starve the camp, drenching a mob of do-nothing servants in abundance while the exhausted foot soldier goes wanting." What did such monstrous extravagance signify if not a pathetic attempt to compensate for the aristocrat's personal inadequacy? Honor, in short, had degenerated into a pathology: "the fear of being despised, because one knows that one is, in truth, despicable."

Having presented this evidence of human selfishness and stupidity, d'Holbach might well have thrown up his hands, like Voltaire in *Candide.* Instead, he offered hope that humanity's natural tendency toward peace might yet prevail over prejudice and greed. And, crucially, he offered this hope with a theory to back it up: a theory of history. It was this step — exemplified by d'Holbach, although in no way invented by him — that gave Fénelon's sentimental opposition to war real intellectual grounding and persuasiveness.

"The glory associated with conquest, war and valor in almost all countries," d'Holbach wrote in *Universal Morality*, "is visibly a remnant of the savage customs that prevailed in all nations before they were civilized ... Thanks to a series of opinions mistakenly handed down by our barbarian ancestors, the deadly profession of war has been reputed the most noble profession." These lines summed up an idea that, in the heyday of the Enlightenment, entranced Europe's educated classes: the idea of scientifically measurable historical progress. In its classic form, developed above all in the "conjectural histories" of the French and Scottish Enlightenments, it was believed that all societies naturally followed roughly the same path from a primitive state, in which small tribes subsisted on hunting and gathering, through pastoral and agricultural phases, to a modern stage characterized by the rise of large-scale commerce. In the course of this evolution, manners grew gentler and more refined, passions were restrained, and brute force gave way to peaceful negotiation. The persistence of warfare among the great commercial powers of Europe therefore testified to nothing more than their incomplete embrace of modernity — to "remnants" of barbarism. Warfare itself, in other words, amounted to a social pathology, just as the cult of honor amounted to an individual psychological one. Even Voltaire, in an ambitious world history written before Fontenoy (*Essai sur les moeurs*), saw progress introducing "a new humanity into the scourge of war." For him and d'Holbach, and for many others, the solution lay in properly educating Europe's rulers so that they no longer believed they were living in the Middle Ages.

Today, this vision of history has utterly lost its power in most Western cultures. The twentieth century offered altogether too much proof that the most sophisticated of cultures stands only a breath away from relapse into the most terrifying barbarism. Yet in d'Holbach's day, the case for humanity's steady progress struck many as overwhelming. D'Holbach himself had too abstract a turn of mind to compile much empirical evidence for it, but a member of his "coterie," François-Jean de Chastellux, did so in an engaging book that owed a great deal to d'Holbach's influence. Chastellux, yet another member of France's ancient military nobility, had served as an army officer since age thirteen and won laurels in the Seven Years' War and in the American Revolution. But in between these tours of duty, he proved a graceful writer, whose 1772 *Essay on Public Happiness,* wildly overpraised by Voltaire, became the most popular statement of Enlightenment historical optimism until Condorcet arrived on the scene. Chastellux was a model of the soldier-authors we met in the previous chapter, and yet his literary efforts happily prophesied the coming extinction of his own profession and class.

Like the English clergyman Cornish, Chastellux believed that religious hatreds no longer had sufficient power to provoke large-scale warfare. They too, he wrote, properly belonged to a more primitive age. Furthermore, alliances among the European powers had become so strong, and modern weaponry had made warfare so difficult and expensive, that the age of conquests had definitively passed — most states were too deeply sunk in debt even to attempt it. The only thing left to provoke Europeans to aggressive warfare was "national hatred," which existed "only amongst the mob" and was being "daily more and more deadened by commerce, and that frequent intercourse which a taste for travelling hath of late established." Even the powerful tensions developing in the early 1770s between Britain and its American colonies, Chastellux stated confidently, could not possibly lead to open war, still less American independence.

As this last point suggests, Chastellux made a very bad prophet. Yet the facts that he adduced in his support were quite real. Religious hatreds *were* on the wane. And as we have already seen, warfare *had* grown less cruel and violent, at least relative to the wild carnage of the seventeenth century. A style of warfare that today seems a consequence of the aristocratic code and of the relative absence of religious and ideological conflict impressed eighteenth-century observers as part of the inevitable advance of civilization. "Barbarians," explained the Scottish writer William Robertson, "rush into war with impetuosity, and prosecute it with violence . . . nor does their rage subside until it be satiated with inflicting . . . every possible calamity." By contrast, "civilized nations, which take arms upon cool reflection . . . carry on their hostilities with so little rancor or animosity, that war among them is disarmed of half its terrors." Eighteenth-century thinkers, in other words, not only noticed the change in warfare that had taken hold by the early eighteenth century but also drew much of their inspiration from it. But they attributed a very different meaning to it from the one aristocratic officers had done, seeing it not as the achievement of a proper state of affairs that could now continue indefinitely but as an indication of war's imminent disappearance.

European elites, furthermore, *were* drawing steadily closer to one another. As the great *philosophe* Jean-Jacques Rousseau, the most important critic of the phenomenon, lamented: "there are no longer any Frenchmen, Germans, Spaniards, or even Englishmen: there are only Europeans. They all have the same tastes, the same passions, and the same customs." Across the Continent, the upper classes increasingly followed the same fashions, read the same books, and even, to a certain extent, spoke the same language: French was heard more than Russian at the court of the tsar, and Frederick the Great of Prussia dismissed his native German as fit only for commanding servants and dogs. A well-developed postal system allowed easy communication between the principal European cities, and a rapidly multiplying number of periodicals spread news from Cádiz to Saint Petersburg within weeks. Travel had grown easier and safer than ever before. And, of course, no class of person participated more eagerly in these changes — traveling more readily, perusing the newspapers more greedily, or writing letters more earnestly — than the *philosophe*. D'Holbach, a German living in Paris, who counted the radical English politician John Wilkes and the Neapolitan polymath Ferdinando Galliani among his closest friends, offered a perfect example: he was a true cosmopolitan. And naturally, he extrapolated from his own experience to humanity as a whole:

> The entire human race forms one vast society, of which the various nations are members, spread out over the face of the earth, but heated and lit by the same sun, washed by the waters of the same ocean, shaped in the same fashion, feeling the same needs, conceiving the same desires, occupied by the same cares of self-preservation . . . It must necessarily be concluded . . . that each people is bound to other peoples by the same ties, and the same interests, that binds each man to his fellow citizens in a particular nation or society.

In such passages, the Enlightenment formulated its secular equivalent of Fénelon's Christian universalism: all men are brothers.

Finally, commerce *was* binding the states of Europe more closely to one another. Commodities imported from the Americas and Asia — sugar, coffee, tea, tobacco, textiles, spices, precious metals — clogged every port in Europe with heavily laden ships and drove the European economy into unprecedented expansion. Bordeaux alone saw its maritime trade increase sixfold between 1724 and 1789 (most of the cargo moved straight out again to other European destinations). Much of this vast wealth came directly out of slave labor in the killing fields of the Caribbean sugar colonies, but this inconvenient fact did not as yet bother more than a small minority of Europeans. The development of commerce was further aided by the slow rise of "cottage industry" — textile piecework, which had transformed half the farmsteads in some areas of France, Britain, and the Netherlands into scattered elements of what amounted to a giant, primitive factory. Commodities flowed across borders. They were hindered by the dams and sluices of archaic tariffs, obstructionist guild statutes, and protectionist mercantile legislation but they flowed nonetheless and left glittering wealth behind.

To eighteenth-century thinkers, this was the single most important point. The decline of religious hatreds and the rise of cosmopolitanism might remove causes for war, but commerce acted as a positive force for peace, since it created mutually beneficial international relationships that war would disrupt or destroy. Commerce could even act to soften a nation's warlike spirit. The *abbé* de Saint-Pierre had made these points as early as 1713, in his plan for perpetual peace. Thinkers throughout the century agreed: "The spirit of conquest and the spirit of commerce are mutually exclusive in a nation" (Jean-François Melon, 1734); "the natural effect of commerce is to lead to peace" (Montesquieu, 1748); "Commerce tends to wear off those prejudices which maintain distinction and animosity between nations" (Robertson, 1769); "It is the *spirit of commerce* which cannot coexist with war" (Immanuel Kant, 1795).

In short, there was every reason for such writers as d'Holbach and Chastellux to believe their own rhetoric. If peace was not the natural state of mankind, at least it was fast becoming the ordinary state of modern commercial society. No active intervention was required to bring it about. True, in the eighteenth century, well-meaning projects for leagues of nations, international federations, and European superstates proliferated, many of them claiming to improve on the early efforts of Penn, Bellers, and "Saint Pierre of Utopia." Some of the most eminent philosophers of the age — Rousseau, Bentham, Kant — tried their hand at the exercise. But they worried that the public would greet their proposals as "hopeless . . . visionary and ridiculous" (Bentham's words), and they were right. Few readers believed that such well-meaning utopian projects, however original and sophisticated, had any chance of success in the real world. They *were* ready to believe, though, that the world itself was changing. History, wrote Condorcet in a more typical formulation, drove itself forward. It did not need the help of impractical projects devised by idle philosophers.

So widespread did the belief in historical progress become, it even percolated into the ranks of the military itself — helped by soldier-philosophers, such as Chastellux. Consider one rather prominent example. The young George Washington, scion of a patrician Virginia family who had brothers in British military service, initially seemed bound for a typical career as a genteel army officer. After first coming under fire as a twenty-two-year-old militia officer in 1754, he boasted in good courtly fashion that he found something "charming in the sound" of whistling bullets. But thirty-four years later, despite his own triumphant military career, he had also come in contact with the European philosophy of the day and could speak a very different language. In a remarkable letter to Chastellux himself from 1788, Washington echoed the *Essay on Public Happiness* and summed up virtually all the points just discussed:

> It is time for the age of Knight-Errantry and mad-heroism to be at an end. Your young military men, who want to reap the harvest of laurels, don't care (I suppose) how many seeds of war are sown; but for the sake of humanity it is devoutly to be wished, that the manly employment of agriculture and the humanizing benefits of commerce, would supersede the waste of war and the rage of conquest; that the swords might be turned into plough-shares, the spears into pruning hooks, and, as the Scripture expresses it, "the nations learn war no more."

The words "mad heroism" recall d'Holbach's mocking of the aristocratic code of honor, and the passage as a whole recapitulates the idea of war as a fundamentally selfish activity that needed, in an age of reason, to give way to the pursuit of the common good.

By providing serious intellectual grounding and apparent empirical evidence for the idea that historical progress would make perpetual peace possible, the Enlightenment therefore marked a fundamental new stage in human thinking on the problem. It built on the Christian pacifism exemplified by Fénelon and, in many ways, grew directly out of the cultural climate he had helped create, in which the pursuit of peace and the common good had come to seem more natural and more worthy than the pursuit of military glory. But the story is more complicated, because this same Enlightenment thought departed from Fénelon's writings not only in its secularism but also in another, more ominous way. Nothing makes this point more clear than considering the work of the man generally credited with bringing Enlightenment thinking on war and peace to its logical conclusion but who, in fact, broke with it in some very significant respects.

This man was Immanuel Kant (1724–1804), whose life had none of the drama of Fénelon's and none of the glitter of d'Holbach's. Almost all of it passed within the chill gray walls, streets, and skies of the Baltic Prussian city of Königsberg, where he taught philosophy uneventfully at the university (and where he experienced the Russian occupation during the Seven Years' War). But, like Hamlet, he could "be bounded in a nut shell and count [himself] a king of infinite space." By reworking much of the philosophy of the Enlightenment in a breathtakingly new manner, Kant founded his own kingdom in the infinite space of the intellect and, in the process, recast Enlightenment reflections on war and peace into the form in which they are best known.

In a short, abstract 1784 essay entitled "Idea of a Universal Cosmopolitical History," Kant restated the Enlightenment creed of progress. Yes, humankind was undergoing historical evolution. Indeed, in doing so, it was fulfilling the hidden purposes of nature itself. But nature was not benign, and human progress did not consist of a simple move out of shadowy barbarism into the sunlit uplands of civilization. The "means of nature" consisted of "mutual antagonism" among humans — competition and conflict up to, and including, war. So war had its purposes and could not be expected to disappear until historical evolution had reached its end point. Kant also introduced a critical distinction that the French authors — especially "materialists," such as d'Holbach — had largely missed: "We are civilised, even to excess . . . But there is still much to be done before we can be regarded as moralized." As Kant stressed throughout his philosophy, the laws of nature and the moral law were both present in the human mind, but they were not identical. And without morality, "all apparent good . . . is nothing but mere illusion and glittering misery."

Already in this work, Kant prophesied that the antagonistic experience of war would eventually push mankind to form a great International Confederation. In his landmark 1795 essay "Perpetual Peace," he pursued the theme further and devised a series of constitutional provisions for this organization. Unlike the *abbé* de Saint-Pierre, from whom he took his title and model, Kant had no illusions that peace required only that enlightened princes recognize the genius of his plan. He sardonically noted that the inscription "to perpetual peace" had once appeared on a signboard painting of a graveyard, and he accepted Hobbes's bleak postulate that the state of nature was a state of war. For states even to recognize that their real self-interest lay in peace, they could not have despotic forms of government, driven by passion. Only representative governments, in which the separation of powers prevailed, could qualify. This argument, incidentally, made Kant the intellectual ancestor of the idea that the spread of democracy brings peace, since democracies do not fight each another. Kant also warned that even if representative government became ubiquitous, it was too much to expect that separate nations might ever fuse into a single world state. All that could be hoped for was "the negative substitute of a *union* of nations." Still, he insisted that the movement of history would inevitably bring something like his confederation about.

Throughout the text, he also insisted, however, as before, on the primacy of the moral law. *Fiat justitia, pereat mundus,* he quoted: Let justice be done, though the world perish. He also asserted his "categorical imperative" — the version of the golden rule that he developed in his major works of moral philosophy and that has become the modern world's definitive statement of the claims of conscience: "act in such a way that you could want your maxim to become a general law." This principle, he argued, drawn from the moral sense that is within all humans, must take precedence over any claim based on empirical observation of the material world — including theories of history.

In this way, Kant set himself apart from such French philosophers as d'Holbach and Condorcet, for whom history offered not simply a promise of better times and a theory of human events but, crucially, a blanket justification for political action. In Condorcet's *Sketch for a Historical Tableau of the Progress of the Human Mind,* composed during the

French Revolution, the lessons of history had amounted to a series of "truths" obvious to every "enlightened" person — and more, to a "judgment" passed on "enemies of reason" and "oppressors of freedom." From this perspective, the goal of perpetual peace had value not because it conformed to a fundamental moral law but because it conformed to the historical progress of civilization. It was a point of view that Kant found fundamentally flawed.

But it is a point of view that has had an enduring and deadly success. *Die Weltgeschichte ist das Weltgericht:* The history of the world is the world's court of judgment. This line, composed by a great Enlightenment poet and later adopted by Hegel as a fundamental maxim, has passed into many modern ideologies. And in the process, the "judgment" of history has been invoked to justify many unspeakable things, whereas its "dustbin," to which Lenin scornfully consigned his opponents, has often turned into a mass grave. Already in the French Revolution, as we will see, the architects of the Terror justified mass murder with a language of historical progress not dissimilar from that used by d'Holbach and Chastellux. The French Revolution, Maximilien Robespierre declared in 1794, had not only fulfilled the historical predictions of the *philosophes* but also accelerated them. It had placed the French two thousand years ahead of the rest of the human race, so that "one is tempted to see them . . . as a different species." As Kant might have asked: can a general law prevail for members of different species? Does human conscience have any claim over a human's behavior toward wild beasts?

In short, the Enlightenment theories of history, which promised the imminent arrival of perpetual peace, concealed unsuspected dangers. Building on the general cultural climate that Fénelon helped bring into being, the *philosophes* gave intellectual rigor to his irenic Christian sentimentality. But in the process, they transformed peace from a moral imperative into a historical one. And so they opened the door to the idea that in the name of future peace, any and all means might be justified — including even exterminatory war. It is an idea that Fénelon would have utterly rejected and that Kant *did* utterly reject. In "Perpetual Peace," he insisted that no state should ever treat another as an "unjust enemy" against which it might wage a "war of extermination." Such a war "would allow perpetual peace only upon the graveyard of the whole human race." It should be "wholly forbidden."

Yet despite these differences, Fénelon, the French *philosophes,* and Kant did stand together: not only in their desire for peace but also in their rejection of war as an ordinary part of an aristocratic social order. In opposition to the dramatization and glorification of the aristocratic self that was so visible in the officer corps of most eighteenth-century armies and on the battlefields of Poltava and Fontenoy, these eighteenth-century philosophers urged the renunciation of the self and the relinquishing of glory — whether in the name of the common good, of conscience, or of historical progress. Even before Kant published "Perpetual Peace," antiwar teachings in these different forms had become something close to the conventional wisdom of Europe's intellectual elites.

But was peace, in fact, such a good thing? Even as the conventional wisdom spread, certain writers were asking the question — and not only traditional aristocrats, such as the Chevalier Ray, who had rejected the idea of war "as a detestable scourge." And so this story has one last twist. From within the Enlightenment itself, critiques of the new theories of peace were taking shape, grounded in the belief that the progress of commercial civilization represented anything but an unalloyed benefit. "Primitive" societies, in this view, might lack refinement and restraint, but they had something else: a vital fire and a passion that the civilizing process was steadily leeching away, leaving humanity lethargic, soft, and decadent, incapable of great deeds or great beauty. Civilization resembled a degenerative disease, but war could provide a vaccine.

Almost without exception, these new advocates of war had no admiration for the aristocratic warfare of their own day. They dismissed its armies as collections of slaves, mercenaries, and well-drilled "automata." Instead, they sought models in the Greeks and Romans, whose languages and cultures still dominated the education of European elites (indeed, well-educated Europeans often knew Roman history and literature far better than that of their own countries). In the Greek city-states and republican Rome, they argued, the obligation of all male citizens to serve in the military had reinforced both physical vigor and civic virtue. Man for man, they contended, these citizen-soldiers could fight better than any other soldiers in history. And they celebrated the great examples of classical heroism and glory: Spartan warriors sacrificing themselves at Thermopylae to hold off the invading Persians, Roman armies reducing Carthage to rubble and sowing its fields with salt, Caesar subjugating the peoples of Gaul. Needless to say, none of these examples fit in particularly well with the prevailing aristocratic culture of limited war.

Jean-Jacques Rousseau provided the first great blast of the critique in his 1750 *Discourse on the Sciences and the Arts*. Later in his career, Rousseau would write with sympathy about the *abbé* Saint-Pierre's peace plans, but in this early, relatively crude work (the one that first brought him notoriety), he came close to judging a people's worth by its military prowess. In particular, he favorably contrasted the masculine, warlike Spartans ("who made Asia tremble") to the soft, decadent, enervated Europeans of his own day. The progress of the sciences and the arts, he asserted repeatedly, led to the decline of something much more valuable: "military virtue." Rousseau lavished extravagant praise on the states that had preserved this virtue by obliging all male citizens to serve: Sparta, republican Rome, his native Geneva. "Every citizen should be a soldier by duty, no citizen should be a soldier by trade. This was the military system of the Romans . . . and this should be the military system of every free state."

Over the next decades, this classical republican fantasy proved increasingly beguiling. In France, the *philosophe* Mably argued that citizens of republics should take part in military training on a daily basis and bring the "habits of discipline of an army camp" to ordinary civilian life. The *comte* de Guibert, France's most influential pre-Revolutionary military reformer (and an habitué of "philosophical" salons) gained renown with a massive *Essay on Tactics,* whose preface urged France to emulate the Romans. An aggressive people, he wrote, who combined austere manners with universal military service, could carve out an empire for itself "as easily as the north wind blows over frail reeds." Guibert also insisted that if a truly free state *were* forced into war:

> Its style of war will not be the one practiced by states today . . . Terrible in its wrath, it will bring fire and steel to its enemy's hearth. In its vengeance, it will shock all the peoples who might have been tempted to disturb its peace. And let no one call barbarism, or a violation of the sup-

posed laws of war, these reprisals grounded in the laws of nature. If this happy and peaceful people is insulted, it will rise up, leave home, and perish, to the last man if need be.

This vision of total war, the most striking of the pre-Revolutionary period, earned Guibert harsh reproofs from many of his aristocratic colleagues, even though his more specific proposals for reform involved the creation of small, mobile, highly trained armies of professional soldiers, not mass armies of peasants.

A vision of exterminatory war, on the model of the Punic Wars between Rome and Carthage, even crept into French and British war propaganda. In both countries, the idea of the "nation" was becoming a staple of political rhetoric, and both governments made use of it to mobilize their populations during the exhausting Seven Years' War of 1756–63. Both countries celebrated the heroic acts of ordinary soldiers, who supposedly exhibited typically "national" qualities of bravery and determination. In both, scholars drew up exhausting lists of historical parallels to cast their own country as the modern Rome and their enemies' as the modern Carthage. The propagandists also highlighted atrocities committed by enemy soldiers, in order to demonstrate the perfidious qualities of the enemy nation. Most spectacularly, French authors seized on an incident in which British colonial militia had surprised a detachment of French marine troops in the Ohio Valley, killing ten. They labeled the British troops — and, by extension, all Britons — horrific "barbarians" who deserved no mercy in war. The militia commander — none other than the young George Washington, still enamored of whistling bullets — came in for particularly vicious treatment (a fact the French had to quickly forget twenty-four years later, when they became his ally). As part of the barrage, French poets called their nation to battle with such phrases as "to arms, citizens!" and insisted that the "impure blood" of the British would water their own furrows. Pirated and put to music during the Revolution by the military engineer Rouget de Lisle, these lines became part of his song the *Marseillaise*, which remains France's national anthem.

In France and Britain, the advocates of revived Greek and Roman military values still generally drew the line at praising war for its own sake. Military training might promote civic virtue and so might help a society survive. But there is little evidence that Rousseau, Mably, or even Guibert saw the experience of war itself as beneficial. In Germany, however, the line was crossed. The German literary movement known as the *Sturm und Drang* (Storm and Stress), which flourished in the last decades of the eighteenth century, eloquently denied that all human societies followed the same, roughly linear path of evolution. Johann Gottfried Herder, in particular, proposed that each nation had its own particular, organic "genius," linked to its own particular language. He found the most authentic expressions of a national culture among the people of the countryside, closest to its "primitive" past, not among the supposedly decadent elites of the cities.

But how did a nation develop and grow? Through careful, peaceful education? Or, perhaps, through violent struggle? Herder famously commented that "men desire harmony, but nature knows better what is good for the species: it desires strife." Kant himself, as we have seen, characterized war as nature's way of bringing the species to the highest stage of humanity — although in that highest stage, it would finally disappear. He even remarked briefly, in his *Critique of Judgment,* that "war . . . has something sublime about it" and associated "prolonged peace" with "debasing self-interest, cowardice, and effeminacy" — a position somewhat at odds with his later work *Perpetual Peace*! The more obscure scholar Johann Valentin Embser went even further, in 1779, praising war as a necessary phenomenon without which virtue, courage, friendship, and generosity would all wither and die. "War . . . rejuvenates the people," he wrote. God had put conflict and evil in the world for a purpose, and to deny them amounted to idolatry. Therefore: "The project of perpetual peace cannot be realized, and even if it could, should not be. A terrible proposition, I admit, but a true proposition!"

The strongest of these defenses of war was composed in 1792 by a prominent philologist and liberal statesman linked to Herder: Wilhelm von Humboldt. In a tract written in reaction to the French Revolution (although only partially published at the time) and devoted to exploring the purpose and limits of state action, Humboldt joined Rousseau and Mably in deploring the way contemporary societies had deprived most citizens of military experience. Professional soldiers, he lamented, led a "machine-like existence." Only in antiquity, he continued, had the "noble character of the warrior" achieved "its highest beauty." He also went a step further, as we saw in the Introduction, calling war "one of the healthiest phenomena for the cultivation of the human race." And he continued: "It is unwillingly that I see it disappearing more and more from the scene. It is the admittedly fearful extreme, through which active courage in the face of danger, labor and fortitude are tested and steeled." Although Humboldt did hope for the eventual coming of perpetual peace, he insisted that it should not come about through "artificial paralysis."

Ironically, these new enthusiasts of war had a far less realistic vision of eighteenth-century combat than did the advocates of peace. With hindsight, their words might perhaps seem to foreshadow the mass levies and conscriptions of the Revolution. But to contemporaries, they conjured up Romans with spears and shields, not infantrymen firing disciplined musket salvos or artillery tearing into helpless ranks of close-packed bodies. What would it mean to have citizen armies in the age of gunpowder and in kingdoms of millions or tens of millions of people? The enthusiasts did not say. By contrast, such writers as the Voltaire of *Candide* had described the unpleasant realities of the eighteenth-century battlefield quite clearly indeed.

The enthusiasts' glorifications of war might also seem a rejection of Enlightenment arguments for perpetual peace, whether of the d'Holbachian or Kantian variety. In one vital sense, however, they shared the same fundamental perspective as the more pacifist *philosophes*. That is to say, they too entirely rejected the aristocratic conception of war as an ordinary, unexceptional element of the social order. For them too, war was something entirely *extraordinary* — but dynamically, and perhaps even sublimely so, not destructively so. In this sense, they too belong to what could be called a new culture of war in embryo, one grounded precisely in the assumption of war's exceptionality.

Before 1789, however, all these various currents of thought remained abstractions, with little relationship to the actual conduct of European politics and war. The new glorifications of war, in particular, still amounted to a very narrow current indeed. The arguments for peace had become conventional wisdom for a large section of Europe's intellectual elites, but they had yet to gain much purchase on Europe's *ruling* elites, to say nothing of its military elites. In *these* circles, the aristocratic code still flourished, despite such exceptions as Chastellux or Guibert (and even they found it all too easy to keep their social ambitions and their advanced philosophy in separate compartments). For the separations to be overcome — for the glass walls dividing philosophy from war to shatter — would require nothing less than the collapse of the aristocratic system that maintained them. It would require cool, abstract questions of state building to turn hot and palpable with urgency. Which is to say, it would require a revolution.

3

Declaring Peace; Declaring War

The French nation renounces the undertaking of any wars aimed at conquest, and will never employ its forces against the liberty of any people.

— FRENCH NATIONAL ASSEMBLY, MAY 22, 1790

It is a cruel thing to think, but it is becoming more clear every day: peace is taking us backwards. We will only be regenerated by blood.

— JEANNE-MARIE ROLAND, JUNE 25, 1791

October 6, 1789. Dawn. As the sun rises in a clear sky over the palace of Versailles, it illuminates the gilt images of itself placed there by Louis XIV to boast of his glory. It shines on the polished floors that generations of aristocratic red heels have crossed in light, measured, well-practiced steps. Its light even creeps into the west-facing Hall of Mirrors, where, for a century, the grandest of the grand have stolen silent, adoring glances at their gaudy selves.

But in the hall this morning, the light uncovers an unusual scene. Men and women are moving through, not at a delicate walk, but at a heavy, purposeful run. Their feet are not shod in red-heeled shoes but in thudding workboots, clacking clogs, and all manner of cheap, decaying leather — the footwear of the working poor. They trail mud and dirt behind them, for yesterday they walked here from Paris, twelve miles or more, in bad weather, and have mostly spent the night outdoors. They are tired, hungry, and enormously angry.

For months, they have been waiting for their king, Louis XVI, great-

great-great-grandson of Versailles's builder, to relieve their hunger and misery, the product of the worst economic slump France has known in decades. In May, they waited expectantly as the Estates General, the country's long-dormant parliament, met to consider long-needed reforms. In June, they listened excitedly to the news that the commoner deputies to the Estates had broken an impasse by declaring themselves a National Assembly and had won the king's reluctant authorization to begin writing a new constitution. In July, they trembled at rumors that the king was massing troops around Paris in preparation for a *coup d'état*; in response, some of them took up arms to storm a royal fortress and prison called the Bastille. And they danced with wild joy when they realized that the Bastille's fall had effectively ended what they could now call the Old Regime. In August, they applauded as the National Assembly swept away centuries' worth of social privileges and proclaimed the Rights of Man and Citizen. A revolution was under way. But little happened to relieve their hardships.

And then, a few days ago, they heard indignantly that while the royal family looked on approvingly, symbols of the Revolution had been trampled underfoot at a banquet thrown by the royal bodyguards for aristocratic officers of the Flanders Regiment. Their anger crested yesterday: a huge crowd, dominated by market women, crammed into the square in front of the Paris city hall, demanding action and bread. The cry went up, "to Versailles," and so thousands of women and men set out for the palace in a great, bedraggled, singing mass, protesting their love for their sovereign but taking pikes, muskets, and even cannon along with them. The Revolutionary authorities in the city, unable to stop the march, sent National Guards after the crowd as an escort. Hours later, the Parisians arrived in Versailles, and the king himself met with a small delegation, promising immediate shipments of grain to the capital. Tensions seemed to ease.

But crowds can be strange, chimerical things. At dawn, a group of the marchers finds the palace's main gate unguarded and charges inside. A soldier fires at them and is killed on the spot. Simmering resentment now swells up into incandescent rage and comes to focus on the haughty, spendthrift, Austrian-born queen, Marie-Antoinette, for a decade the target of ugly rumors and libels. The Parisians rush toward her apartments, through the Hall of Mirrors, screaming threats of murder, and the queen barely escapes. Barefoot and hysterical, she runs shrieking toward her husband's quarters with her children and pounds on the doors for more than ten minutes. The royal bodyguards, outnumbered and confused, cannot help her. Finally, someone hears her cries and opens the door, and she makes it — barely — inside to safety.

But neither she nor her husband is really safe. As the sun rises higher, it is only the immediate danger that dissipates. The National Guard moves in to protect the royal family, more royal appearances take place before the crowd, and more promises of bread are made. Again a modicum of calm returns. But the Parisians, by now as many as 60,000 strong, have won a new victory, and they are not about to leave their prizes behind. As they begin the long, weary walk home, they force the royal family to accompany them in a hastily packed carriage, listening to their raucous songs and watching the pikes bob up and down outside the window (by some accounts, the heads of royal bodyguards adorn the tips of several). The king and queen have become prisoners of the Revolution. On October 6, as the sun sets, the people of Paris are gone from the Hall of Mirrors, but they have nonetheless, effectively, taken possession, in one of history's most tangible and dramatic displays of popular sovereignty. No monarch will ever live in this place again.

A year later, a horrified observer across the English Channel, Edmund Burke, will remember this moment as a decisive one in history — the one in which the French Revolution moved irredeemably beyond the pale of civilization. In a book-length letter to a French correspondent that he will publish as *Reflections on the Revolution in France* and that will become the founding text of modern conservatism, he will first recount the events of the morning in horrifying, gory detail. And then he will drift into a haunting, elegiac reverie:

> It is now sixteen or seventeen years since I saw the queen of France . . . at Versailles, and surely never lighted on this orb, which she hardly seemed to touch, a more delightful vision . . . I thought ten thousand swords must have leaped from their scabbards to avenge even a look that threatened her with insult. But the age of chivalry is gone. That of sophisters, economists, and calculators has succeeded; and the glory of Europe is extinguished forever . . . All the decent drapery of life is to be rudely torn off. All the super-added ideas, furnished from the wardrobe of a moral imagination, which the heart owns and the understanding ratifies as necessary to cover the defects of our naked, shivering nature, and to raise it

to dignity in our own estimation, are to be exploded as a ridiculous, absurd, and antiquated fashion.

Today, it may be difficult to share Burke's enthusiasm for a "decent drapery" whose delicacies veiled vast inequalities, unfathomable miseries, and very real oppression. But there is no denying his insight. October 6, 1789, better than any other date, marks the end of the age of aristocracy. Versailles has been the capital of this age. With its abandonment, the class that flourished there will not be able to survive.

With the end of the aristocracy, the practices of aristocratic warfare stand in imminent danger of extinction as well. Over the next three years, a series of remarkable debates will take place in France's legislative bodies, in which the abstract ideas debated by the eighteenth-century philosophers will bubble over the rims of treatises and newspapers and salons, to drench the nation's new, Revolutionary politics. Initially, in May 1790, in a dramatic debate pitting Revolutionary radicals directly against eloquent aristocratic conservatives, these ideas will lead France to embrace the pacifist creed of Fénelon, d'Holbach, and Chastellux and to renounce aggressive warfare altogether. But then, with the sort of vertiginous speed that delights the cynical at heart, the claims of war will reassert themselves in a new and ominous manner. In 1792, less than twenty-three months after declaring peace, France will go to war, in a different sort of conflict from anything it has previously known.

Unbeknownst to anyone in Europe, the events that would trigger these legislative showdowns had begun even before the new legislatures were born. In the first days of May 1789, the Spanish warship *Princesa* had sailed into the waters of the Nootka Sound, on the Pacific shore of what is now Vancouver Island, and asserted Spanish sovereignty over the region. The sound was remote indeed from Europe. Five thousand miles from Paris as the crow flies, European ships had to slog nearly three times that distance to reach it, making the howling, treacherous passage around the tip of South America. The sound's thickly wooded shores were one of the last coastal areas in the Americas free from European settlement, and its indigenous population had so far met only a handful of white explorers and traders. An unlikely place, it would seem, to emit tremors capable of reaching into the deliberations of French Revolutionaries.

But the late eighteenth century was already an age of globalization, and at least three European empires had extended covetous gazes toward the Pacific Northwest, drawn by its untapped reservoirs of wood and fur. So it was not surprising that Captain Estéban José Martínez of the *Princesa,* claiming the territory for Spain, would accuse several British and American ships he encountered in the sound of trespassing. And it was not surprising that when Martínez seized two British ships and sent them down the coast under prize crews, the British would consider it a cause for war.

The dispute might still seem remote from French concerns. But in the late eighteenth century, just as at the start of World War I, a web of treaties bound the principal European powers into alliances like chains of firecrackers. Spain's King Carlos IV was a cousin of France's Louis XVI, and since 1761 a so-called Family Pact had pledged the various branches of the House of Bourbon to defend each other in case of hostilities. In the 1770s, when France had intervened in the American struggle for independence, Spain loyally came into the fight and, as a reward, snatched back its former colony of Florida from Britain at the peace table. A war might also conceivably envelop France's other major ally, the Austrian Empire, and Russia and Prussia as well. France felt under particular pressure to intervene because in 1787, its pre-Revolutionary troubles had kept it, humiliatingly, from supporting Dutch allies during a Prussian invasion of the Netherlands. So Nootka, despite its remoteness, could easily have come to signify for the late eighteenth century what Sarajevo did for the early twentieth.

As news of the clash finally trickled back to Europe in the spring of 1790, this outcome seemed likely. Britain wanted revenge for its defeat in the American war and hoped to lop off a few Spanish American colonies in compensation for its recent losses. Patriotic opinion in Britain raged over the "outrage" to the British flag. The British government demanded apologies and restitution from Madrid, which gave no sign of wishing to comply. The cumbersome baroque machinery of several European states started to creak into action, to raise money for ships that might soon be blasting each other to splinters on the high seas.

It was precisely with this financial goal in mind that on Friday, May 14, 1790, France's foreign minister, the count of Montmorin, sent a letter to the representative Assembly created the previous year. The king, he informed the deputies, was watching events unfold with concern and had ordered fourteen ships of the line equipped for possible wartime service. He also mentioned, almost as an afterthought, that the government did not have enough money for the ships and was counting on the deputies to act patriotically and vote the necessary funds.

Despite his confident tone, the foreign minister knew that he was sailing into the political equivalent of poorly charted waters. Since the previous summer, and particularly since the October Days, the French state had existed in uneasy limbo. The National Assembly was carrying out its promise to write a new constitution for a limited monarchy but had not yet come close to completing the task. According to the *Declaration of Rights of Man and Citizen,* which it had issued the past August, all sovereignty resided in the nation. But in practice, it was unclear which powers had now passed to the nation's elected representatives and which still belonged to the once-absolute king, Louis XVI. In its daily business, the Assembly lurched back and forth between practical matters of governance and abstract constitutional principle, one minute haggling over small-town municipal loans and tax exemptions and the next, floating up into the most ethereal reaches of political theory. As of May 14, it had not yet confronted a pressing issue of foreign policy, and Montmorin's request was likely to trigger a charged discussion. Did the king still have the right to send his country to war?

In order to avoid an unwelcome discussion on this subject, Montmorin tried to load the deck, arranging in advance for twenty friendly deputies to speak for his motion. With luck, the Assembly would quickly and quietly approve the request and move on to other business. But the ploy backfired. No sooner was the list of speakers announced than several other deputies protested that such a weighty matter as war demanded an open and extended exchange of views. The Assembly as a whole clearly favored delay, and so further argument was postponed until the next morning.

Take a moment and imagine this body, the French National Assembly, in the spring of 1790. It consisted of nearly 1,200 men, originally elected the previous year to the Estates General. Around 300 came from the clergy (the former First Estate) and 278 from the nobility (the former Second), each of which had possessed its own, separate legislative chambers at the time of the elections. As we have seen, most of the nobles had held military commissions at some point in their lives. The other 600-odd deputies hailed from the "Third Estate," which constituted the vast majority of the French population. Since the previous summer, all three estates had come together to sit in the same chamber, and their numbers made the body massive and unwieldy: more than twice the size of Britain's House of Commons and fully eighteen times larger than the U.S. House of Representatives at the time. Luckily, fewer than fifty men spoke with any regularity, but this was still a considerable number. In May 1790, no fewer than thirty-five deputies would deliver major speeches on the war issue, making the debate less of a duel and more of a relay race.

To accommodate its numbers, the Assembly had taken over the "Manège" — an indoor riding arena built in 1721 for King Louis XV in Paris's Tuileries Gardens, conveniently close to the Tuileries palace, which now housed the royal family. Long, narrow, and high-ceilinged, the building had poor lighting, abominable acoustics, and worse air quality, especially in cold weather when the windows were closed and two large stoves smoked away to provide heat. On hot spring days, the deputies — most of whom saw regular bathing as dangerous to their health — provided their own fragrances. Félix Faulcon, from western France, blamed the poor air for his continual headaches, bloody noses, and episodes of spitting blood.

The ideological atmosphere was often no less poisonous. As in most countries new to democracy, the concept of a "loyal opposition" barely existed in Revolutionary France. If two groups disagreed over policy, each was likely to accuse the other of ignorance and stupidity at best, corruption and treason at worst. In the National Assembly, a hard core of conservatives, drawn mostly from the privileged orders, vehemently tried to preserve what they could of the old social and political order, whereas Revolutionaries of various stripes strove to reduce the king's powers and enact far-reaching reforms. As the conservatives gathered largely on the right side of the hall and their opponents on the left, the very geography of the Manège contributed to the polarization, while also engendering the "left-right" terminology that the world has known ever since. The Left was further divided between radicals, who belonged mostly to the so-called Jacobin Club, and moderates, who gathered in the Society of 1789.

Although a degree of decorum generally prevailed during debates,

The Manège

the specter of disorder frequently hovered nearby. Spectators in the galleries continually interrupted and intimidated the deputies with loud catcalls, applause, or threats. Outside the hall, the crowd's conduct often verged on violence. On one occasion, supporters of the Left surrounded *abbé* Jean-Siffrein Maury, a prominent conservative, as he left the hall, promising to hang him from a lamppost. "Well, *Messieurs,*" he wittily retorted, "if you hung me there, would it add to your enlightenment?" On the afternoon of May 14, Antoine Barnave, twenty-eight-year-old star orator of the moderate Left, complained about Montmorin's ploy to a liberal aristocrat, the viscount de Noailles. But Noailles, who had figured on Montmorin's list of speakers, took the complaint as a personal insult and furiously challenged Barnave to a duel. That evening, the two men faced each other with pistols in the Bois de Boulogne. Barnave shot first and missed. Noailles, whose temper had cooled, then fired into the air, and the opponents embraced. Barnave and other members of the Assembly fought several other duels, some of which ended in bloodshed.

Historians often call 1790 the "peaceful" year of the French Revolution, but in fact, the divisions in the Assembly mirrored even deeper ones in the country, and the danger of social unrest swirled around nearly everything the deputies discussed. Scarcely a day went by in which they could not read in the newspapers or hear a parliamentary report about riots, acts of rough "popular justice," or the murder of pro-Revolutionary "patriots." Journalists competed to uncover the most terrible conspiracies, report the largest massacres, and demand the bloodiest vengeance. In the Assembly, during the first debate on war, a report on strife in southern France led one histrionic conservative to shout out: "I see civil war approaching!"

With hindsight, we can see the deeds of later Revolutionary bloodshed prefigured in this hugely combustible atmosphere. We can see the predictions of civil war fulfilled. We can see, in the case of deputy after deputy, the thread of life snipped unnaturally short. Yet this is by no means the whole story. For despite all the violence and instability and all the haggling and windy philosophizing, the Constituent Assembly was embarked on an astonishing project. The deputies were attempting to dismantle a massively complex, inefficient, and discriminatory system of government and to rebuild it according to principles of reason and justice. If they collectively brought most human flaws to the task, they also brought determination, passion, and, impressively often, breathtaking eloquence. And despite their many failures, a great deal of what they built would in fact survive down to the present day — notably, France's principal administrative and judicial structures. Nothing of the sort had ever been seen in Europe. To describe it, observers had to redefine the word "revolution" itself, from the older meaning of a sudden, unpredictable shift in a nation's fortunes to the more capacious modern one of an explosive, open-ended expression of a nation's collective will.

For all the rhetorical frenzy, few people in France in the spring of 1790 doubted the momentous nature of the Assembly's work. As the debate on war and peace began, Félix Faulcon forgot his headaches and marveled, in a letter to a friend, at the role that he, a humble provincial magistrate, was now playing: "Who would have said, when I was walking in my woods in philosophical reverie, that the day would come when I would be the judge of such great questions!" Men and women lined up every day in the early morning to get one of the numbered seats in the high galleries at each end of the Manège. Helen Maria Williams, a young British poet who attended one day in the spring of 1790, wrote fizzily of having seen history in the making:

> And this, repeated I with exultation to myself, this is the National Assembly of France! Those men now before my eyes are the men who engross the attention, the astonishment of Europe; for the issue of whose decrees surrounding nations wait in suspense, and whose fame has already extended through every civilized region of the globe.

During important debates, crowds massed outside in the Tuileries Gardens; inside, spectators would jot down bulletins, attach them to clips, and send them sliding out the windows down strings to friends below. The Revolution, by ending press censorship, had given birth to hundreds of newspapers, and they devoted long columns to the Assembly's doings, reprinting the most important speeches in full.

As the deputies took their seats on the morning of Saturday, May 15, an arrogantly handsome liberal noble rose to deliver the first speech on the war issue. It was none other than Lauzun, the rake, seducer, and war hero we met in Chapter 1. Now forty-three, he had long since squandered his fortune, but he remained irresistible to women and popular with his fellow aristocrats. He had also become a boon companion of Philippe d'Orléans, the king's cousin and a natural intriguer who had embraced the cause of the Revolution, possibly because he hoped it might bring him to the throne. Lauzun had joined a leading reform society in 1788, won election to the Estates General, and sat with the moderate left: a good example of the liberal aristocracy that did so much to bring the Revolution about. He now went by the name Biron (after his *second* dukedom), but to avoid confusion, I will continue to call him Lauzun.

The issue of war and peace left him torn and troubled — so much so that after his initial speech, he contributed nothing further to the debate. He knew that his allies on the Left saw the looming conflict with Britain as nothing but a ploy to rally the country around the king — or possibly even to raise military force against the Revolution. Yet as an exemplary aristocratic soldier, he could not imagine disobeying the king on a military matter and squirmed at the thought of France betraying an ally. Three years before, as a senior soldier and diplomat, he had pressed the crown to support France's Dutch allies against Prussia and privately concluded the French failure to intervene had made the period "one of the most humiliating in the history of the French monarchy." In his speech, he tried to justify his support of the royal position to the Left. The king, he explained, wanted only to mediate between Britain and Spain. But if France were to be listened to, it had to be strong and respected. Nor should the Assembly fear putting more armed force in the king's hands. Even if Louis XVI *were* plotting against the Revolution, what could he do against the millions of citizens who had taken up arms in defense of liberty? Besides — and here Lauzun fell back instinctively into the language of the aristocratic code — France had obligations of loyalty to fulfill. "Peace can be bought at a great price, but not that of honor and our national character," he declared. "One of our kings said: 'All is lost, save honor,' and all was saved . . . Honor will always be our strength, as it has always been our law."

Stirring words, designed to squelch debate, and deputies from the Right rose to press for an immediate vote on the requested funds. Was there really anything at stake beyond money? asked the *abbé* Maury. But more was indeed at stake, and everyone knew it. Alexandre de Lameth, a noble from the northern town of Arras, explained: "This incidental question has given rise to a question of principle. We must decide . . . whether the sovereign nation need delegate to the King the right to make peace or war." A squall of protests interrupted him, and for a moment, he could not continue.

Lameth made for an unlikely radical on this issue, for he had a background similar to Lauzun's: son of a marquis, presented at court, an officer since the age of seventeen. But at twenty-nine, he had taken a leading role in the Assembly and had come into continual conflict with the court and the conservatives, leaving him hardened, intently suspicious, and anxious about a military *coup d'état*. He had a classic Enlightenment faith in history and war's eventual disappearance and nothing but scorn for the way monarchs "sacrificed entire peoples to their personal resentments and despicable whims," as he had put it in a recent speech. Now, on May 15, Lameth argued that the talk of war was in fact no more than a plot to restore Louis XVI to his former powers. "This," he explained, "is the cause of the kings against the peoples." The Assembly needed to examine the evidence carefully, and, more important, it needed to decide whether the king should have "the terrible right" to declare war in the first place: "the right to shed blood, to drag thousands of citizens far from their homes, to put the national territory in jeopardy."

In this way, a debate on war and peace began and immediately threatened key elements of the aristocratic code. Lameth was no pacifist. But at the heart of the code was the ideal of personal service to the king. If the right of making war passed from Louis XVI to an elected assembly, that bond of service would be broken. Indeed, could an aristocratic army, bound to the king by personal loyalty, remain in place in a constitutional regime? Many on the Left thought the very idea ridiculous and believed that the royal army would remain the greatest threat to the Revolution until brought under control. Lameth himself was now heading a military committee charged with examining precisely how such a reform might be brought about.

Lameth's challenge was radical enough, but a few minutes later, another deputy rose and moved into entirely new territory. Like Lameth, he came from Arras and was almost the same age, but he otherwise made a severe contrast to the polished, elegant, and confident army officer. Maximilien Robespierre was a fussily dressed, round-faced man with a stiff, charmless manner. Before 1789, as a lawyer with literary inclinations, he had shown a preference for cases that showcased Enlightenment ideals. In the Assembly, he had gotten off to a bad start, speaking poorly and once being laughed off the speaker's platform for his preachy manner. But he persisted, improved, and slowly built up a reputation for sincere, unwavering, and utterly humorless radicalism. Lameth and his allies thought little of him, but one prescient British observer, accurately perceiving his monstrous determination, called him "a character to be contemplated" who would shortly "be the man of sway . . . and govern the million."

Speaking on the morning of May 15, Robespierre supported Lameth but was not willing to stop there. Instead of voting for the mobilization, he argued, the Assembly should take a "great step" forward. "For example," he asserted:

> you could show the nations of the earth that, following principles very different from those that have cast the peoples of the world into misery,

the French nation, content to be free, has no desire to engage in any war, and wishes to live with all nations in the fraternity commanded by nature.

There it was, stiffly phrased but unmistakable: a renunciation of warfare altogether. Robespierre would say little more during the following days, but his intervention had been critical. From now on, the debate would concern not only who had the right to declare war but also the legitimacy of war itself. Whether the Assembly as a whole would adopt this radical position was another matter.

For the moment, however, the deputies forgot Robespierre's proposal, because the next deputy to speak was the *comte* de Mirabeau, the Assembly's most striking personality. At age forty-one, his resumé included several terms in prison: twice at the request of his temperamental father and once for seducing and abducting a married woman. His voluminous published writings included pornography, pamphlets designed to manipulate the stock market, and thunderous denunciations of the judicial system under which he had suffered. Notoriously spendthrift and dissolute, he had won election to the Third Estate despite his noble title and quickly emerged as one of its leaders. He had a commanding, well-trained voice and a daunting appearance, his face covered with smallpox scars and topped with a wild mass of hair. "It is hard to know the full power of my ugliness," he liked to boast. Rather than engaging with Robespierre's ideas, Mirabeau ignored them and again tried to squelch the debate. He had recently entered into a secret agreement to advise and support the king, in return for a payment of no less than 1 million French pounds, a vast sum for the period. He now argued that only the immediate problem of mobilization was at issue.

Mirabeau did not win this argument, however. Another liberal aristocrat and army officer, the thirty-nine-year-old baron Jacques-François Menou, replied that if war came, it should be "a national, not a ministerial war," waged with the full "courage and power of a truly free nation." It therefore belonged to the representatives of the nation to decide the question. Loud applause greeted him, and Mirabeau, sensing a shift in the Assembly's fast-running currents of opinion, quickly and cunningly suggested a compromise: the deputies would formally thank the king for his vigilance but proceed, the very next morning, to discuss whether "the nation should delegate to the King the right of peace and war." Put to a vote, this measure passed almost unanimously. Yet even as it did, the twenty-six-year-old duke of Lévis (yet another liberal officer) proposed an amendment: "The National Assembly furthermore declares, in the most solemn manner, that the French nation will never undertake anything against the rights of any people, although it will repel, with all the courage of a free people and all the power of a great nation, any attacks on its rights." Robespierre's idea, the renunciation of war, was back on the agenda.

By the next morning, May 16, everyone who had followed the debate felt that the National Assembly had reached a decisive moment in its history. While Félix Faulcon expressed his wonder at judging the affairs of kings, the duke of Lévis wrote tenderly to his twenty-year-old wife, apologizing for not joining her in the countryside: "The great question keeps me here. Never will we deal with a greater one." With comic self-satisfaction, he also praised his own ideas: "I think they are new and fine . . . you can call them gigantic, but not boring!" In the Manège, the public galleries filled early, foreign ambassadors wangled for seats, and crowds waited outside for news. Scores of journalists descended on the hall, armed with pencils to scribble down notes. In London, the *Times* reported the exchanges at length. "This question," it commented, "the most important that ever was agitated in a Monarchy, will probably be determined NEGATIVELY, and thus the glory of the throne of France will set, to rise no more."

One of the French journalists, Jacques-Pierre Brissot, would have a particularly strong impact on this and future war debates. Brilliant, quarrelsome, unscrupulous, and desperately ambitious, he was one of the most fascinating and repellent figures of the Revolution. Born the son of an innkeeper in 1754, he received a good education and dreamed of climbing the social ladder as a lawyer, only to run afoul of the powerful Paris bar association. Throughout the 1780s, he then tried to establish himself as a *philosophe,* publishing voluminously on many subjects. But his writings offended the monarchy's censors, and he spent four months imprisoned in the Bastille, after which he probably agreed to spy on other pamphleteers for the police in order to survive. The Revolution, however, repaired his fortunes: he started editing a newspaper, *Le patriote françois,* and it quickly emerged as a leading voice of the radical left. In its pages, on May 15 and 16, Brissot repeated the claim that the war talk was a plot, blasted Lauzun for reviving "the dreams of the old politics," and slopped scorn over the duke's contention that French honor was at stake. "French honor! This honor no longer consists of getting mixed up in every foreign quarrel, in fighting on all sides. It consists of being free, of settling our affairs, of paying our debts, of being fair to all."

This day, May 16, marked the full arrival of Enlightenment thinking on war and peace into the National Assembly. The duke of Lévis defended his proposed antiwar amendment and then went further and posed questions that challenged the entire structure of European diplomacy: "Are alliances more useful than harmful to France? Does a great people of 25 million men . . . need allies and alliances? Shouldn't it rather provide an example for that grand universal alliance that should unite all nations and all men?" As with George Washington in his 1796 farewell address, with its similar warning against foreign entanglements, Lévis insisted that in a democracy, foreign interests should never trump the will of the people. Jacques Jallet, a poor village priest from western France, chimed in with the sentiment that any use of force other than self-defense violated natural law. In what the *Times* called "a speech replete with the purest sentiments of enlightened philosophy," he told the deputies: "May all nations be as free as we wish to be, and there will be no more war."

The conservatives had so far remained largely silent in the face of such arguments, but now they counterattacked. The count of Sérent, twenty-seven-year-old colonel of the prestigious Angoulême Infantry regiment, belonged to the same narrow stratum of the military aristocracy as Lameth, Lévis, and Lauzun but had not embraced the Revolution. Now, defending the king's right to make war, he presented a largely pragmatic case. Giving control over the issue to an Assembly rather than to a single individual would make military affairs slower, more cumbersome, and less reliable, he argued. It might even — "though it pains me to say it" — open the way for foreign powers to influence French policy by bribing deputies. But Sérent also fell back, tellingly, into a fundamentally antidemocratic attachment to a different system of values: "It is the people's interest, and not its desires, which we must consult," he declared.

It can hardly have escaped notice that members of the old military aristocracy had so far dominated both sides of the discussion. They would continue to do so, and it made for an extraordinary spectacle:

colonels and generals, counts and dukes, and members of France's oldest noble families exchanging arguments and accusations across the floor of the Manège (Lameth could trace his family's nobility to the fifteenth century; Sérent, to the fourteenth; Lauzun, even further). Those nobles on the Left must have felt the clash between their convictions and their vocation with painful intensity. In the case of Lauzun and several others, the weight of more than three decades in uniform trumped left-wing political sympathies. Lameth and Lévis, each under thirty years old, found it far easier to renounce their vocation in the name of their liberal politics.

But it is hardly surprising that the old military aristocracy played such a key role here, for their very existence was at stake, and they knew it. Even before 1789, as we have seen, France's aristocratic military ethos had come in for concerted criticism, both from *philosophes,* such as d'Holbach, and from the French state, in its halting efforts to produce a more professional, full-time officer corps, committed to the army itself rather than to an aristocratic way of life. Furthermore, as we have also seen, some thinkers had begun to call for a society in which all citizens were soldiers, thereby destroying the aristocracy's traditional monopoly on military vocations. Already, a plan for universal conscription had come before the Assembly, although the deputies had rejected it.

The Revolution had greatly intensified the threats to the officer class. The 1789 Declaration of Rights stated baldly that social distinctions could be founded only on the general good, and by this standard, the nobility's control of the officer ranks looked plainly illegitimate. The Assembly's military committee was working on a new system of officer recruitment, and it seemed only a matter of time before a crowd of newly minted middle-class officers pushed aside their noble competitors. Although Alexandre de Lameth, who headed the military committee, welcomed this development, other officers, especially the older ones, looked aghast.

There was also a more immediate and alarming danger. From the start of the Revolution, French officers feared that common soldiers under their command might turn against them, and the events of 1789 had amply justified these fears. In July, the rank and file had fraternized with the Parisian crowds, and some even participated in the storming of the Bastille. Inflammatory pamphlets, distributed among the regiments, contrasted the luxury and comfort of noble officers' lives to the misery of the common soldiers' and excoriated the savage code of discipline that still ruled life in the ranks. "We are citizens first and soldiers second," proclaimed a *Notice to the Grenadiers and Soldiers of the Third Estate.* "We belong to the Fatherland and not to the Nobles, we are Frenchmen and not slaves." In some cases, whole battalions defected. The Counter-Revolutionary writer Rivarol would speak truth when he quipped: "The army's defection was not one of the causes of the Revolution. It *was* the Revolution."

In 1790, far from subsiding, this insubordination had metastasized. In this single year, more than one-third of the units in the Royal Army experienced large-scale disobedience, often encouraged by local Revolutionary clubs or National Guard units. In April, infantrymen in Corsica handed their colonel over to a lynch mob, and men of the Royal Champagne Cavalry Regiment rioted to free one of their comrades from prison. During the debate on war and peace, more regiments mutinied against their officers. In short, the pillars of the traditional military hierarchies were visibly turning to sand.

Given the emotions that these developments could stir, it is not surprising that the May 16 session of the Assembly, which had begun on a lofty plane of seriousness, finished in a muddy shouting match. Charles de Lameth, Alexandre's brother and fellow deputy (and also a former officer), rose to insist that democratic assemblies could indeed act efficiently in the nation's interest, whereas even the best kings could start wars on a whim. When right-wing deputies shrieked protests at this blasphemy, Lameth grew hysterical in turn, adducing conspiracy theories and predicting that if the Right won the debate, "the Constitution will be attacked and perhaps destroyed, the kingdom will be covered in blood." The rich and privileged would stop at nothing to destroy the Revolution, Lameth bellowed to ecstatic applause from the public galleries, but they would not prevail, "for if they have gold, we have steel and know how to use it!" So much for pacifism!

"The speaker's platform had become a battlefield where it seemed that the fate of the Revolution would be decided." Thus Alexandre de Lameth, nearly forty years later, recalling the debate over war and peace. The military analogy is apt, if a bit obvious, but the "battle" had distinct phases. The exchanges over the weekend were skirmishes: quick, sharp, scattered, and sometimes confused, as each side deployed its forces and determined the position of the adversary. Monday, May 17, by contrast, saw the heavy battalions lumber into action. The speeches were better prepared, more closely argued, and heavily fortified with reams of erudition, and as a result, they took much longer: some certainly lasted well over an hour. The most prolonged and intense combat took place over the king's right to declare war, but throughout the day, the voices of Enlightenment thinking made themselves heard over the din.

The first and most important speech came from the moderate Pierre-Victor Malouet, whose thirty-year career as a diplomat, colonial administrator, and military bureaucrat had given him a deeper and more varied experience of war and foreign affairs than that of any other deputy (it included being captured by a British corsair on the high seas during the American Revolutionary War). Transferring control of war to the Assembly would do little to ensure peace, Malouet argued. "Free peoples have fought as many wars of ambition as despots." Indeed, the only European sovereign of late *not* to launch aggressive wars in recent times was the Ottoman sultan, the most despotic among them. Yes, Malouet continued, the French could solemnly renounce aggressive wars, but "Europe is used to such declarations; they can be found in every manifesto." The best way to avoid conflict lay rather in a compromise: allowing the Assembly to evaluate royal actions after the fact. Louis XIV himself would not have laid waste to the Palatinate if he had faced an Assembly's censure for doing so, Malouet argued. Cunningly, he then deployed the Enlightenment vision of historical progress against the Left, which had so far laid uncontested claim to it. "Commerce has changed the face of the globe," he declared. "Customs, laws, needs, wealth, freedom, slavery, war and peace: everything has felt its influence." Everything had become interdependent. But for this very reason, France could not renounce alliances and pretend to stand alone. It needed colonies and alliances, it needed a balance of power, and therefore it needed armed force.

Malouet's analysis was, in fact, exceptionally keen. The history of the Greek city-states and the Roman Republic, which the classically educated French elite knew better than that of their own country, certainly supported his point about the aggressive potential of democracies. (And might not the subsequent history of democratic France and, dare we say, democratic America support it as well?) His point about the impossibility of autarky and the necessity of diplomacy in a modern, commercial, interdependent world was incontestable. But in the French Revolution, such moderate reason usually stood little chance against ideological passion, whether of the Left or the Right.

That passion burst forth from the next speaker, Jérôme Pétion de Villeneuve, a lawyer from Chartres — and also, unbeknownst to his fellow deputies, quite possibly a paid agent of the Prussian ambassador, who hoped that a victory for the Left would destroy the Franco-Spanish alliance. In a speech whose Brezhnevian length would have reduced even Helen Williams's fizzy enthusiasm to flat ennui, Pétion gave the Assembly a lesson in history, drawn straight from the *philosophes*. In ages past, he lectured (inaccurately and in interminable detail), the Estates General, not France's kings, had possessed the right over war and peace. But the kings had usurped this right, putting the nation at the mercy of their unbridled ambitions. Pétion flayed Louis XIV with a savagery that would have made even Fénelon blanch: "This vain, superstitious and despotic king, [who] breathed nothing but war and waged it with barbarity, [who . . .] wounded the state so deeply that even today, it still bleeds." "Open the history books," Pétion thundered,

> and contemplate these many political crimes, these crimes against humanity [*crimes de lèse-humanité*], committed by these masters of the world. You will see that every page is stained with the blood they have shed; you will see that the earth has been a perpetual theater of war and carnage.

He might have been quoting from d'Holbach. And he concluded, to loud applause, by reiterating Robespierre's call for a "noble and generous declaration" of peace. Eventually, the peoples of the world would see that "battles are only good for slaughtering men, and ruining their countries," and the French could set them on this path. Again, it was the pure language of Enlightenment pacifism, and Pétion even invoked the shade of the *abbé* de Saint-Pierre in his final peroration. Lost amid the swells of rhetoric was his brief description of the Barbary pirates, who still preyed on Mediterranean commerce and sold captured Europeans into slavery: they were "hateful monsters" who deserved "extermination." Here lay a dark hint that "universal" peace and harmony, as the French Revolutionaries understood them, might not, in fact, extend to all of humanity.

The hour was growing late and the deputies tired, but in the Manège of 1790, zealotry on such a scale could not help but call forth equal and opposite zealotry from the other side of the hall. It came from François-Dominique de Montlosier, one of the Assembly's smartest, most eloquent, and extreme reactionaries (and, of course, a former officer). After repeating that only the king could properly conduct military affairs, Montlosier ridiculed Pétion's proposed declaration of peace: "It is a shelf of metaphysics, a book of philosophy. And this is what the honorable member claims will check the interests, ambitions, and passions of the peoples who surround us." In his conclusion, all Montlosier's anguish about the fate of his class poured out of him in an angry, chilling lament, while the deputies of the Left tried to howl him down:

> It is a grand, sublime spectacle to see the French nobility . . . deprived of its ancient and legitimate property by the National Assembly, and then insulted in this Assembly . . . And here are these all too patient men, these men who have been plundered, offended, and outlawed . . . here are these men who you claim are calmly plotting death and destruction, surrounded by heaps of gold. *They have gold,* you said, *but we have steel* . . . Oh, yes, you have steel, the steel with which the King's most loyal servants were slaughtered under his eyes, and which threatened his wife's life. Oh, yes, you have steel. You have forged your laws out of it.

Brilliantly, Montlosier had flung Charles Lameth's words back at him, evoking the primal moment of October 1789, when the Parisian crowds spilled blood in the palace of Versailles. Even Brissot, in his account of the debate, could not resist quoting the "delirious" passage in full.

The debate wore on for several more days and rapidly grew repetitive. In a rhetorical carpet bombing that exceeded even Pétion's in length, the *abbé* Maury forthrightly defended the absolute monarchs, including Louis XIV, while denouncing the Revolution for making France "a sad object of pity for all nations . . . covered with ruins and debris." Constantin-François Volney, a writer of some note, replied with the debate's last, and most lyrically idealistic, expression of Enlightenment pacifism and cosmopolitanism:

> Until this day . . . empires were owned as pieces of private property, and whole peoples given in dowries like herds of sheep . . . Gentlemen, you will change such a deplorable state of affairs . . . Until this moment you have deliberated in France and for France, but today you will deliberate

for the universe and in the universe. You will, if I dare say so, convoke
the assembly of nations . . . Resolved: that the National Assembly con-
siders the entire human race as forming but a single and same society,
whose object is the peace and happiness of each and all of its members.

The speech brilliantly distilled the opinions of the cosmopolitan *philosophes,* while unconsciously expressing a formidable French nationalism. (What right did French deputies have to "deliberate for the universe"?) But even Brissot found it a little much: "This pacific Congress
lies too far above our sublunary world," he wrote in the next issue of his
newspaper. "We should limit ourselves to what is possible."

The climax came on Thursday, May 20. The morning brought several speeches, most notable for right-wing attacks on the supposed
naiveté of Robespierre, Pétion, and Volney, who were predictably linked
with the naive and dreamy *abbé* Saint-Pierre. The Left answered with
arguments that had become tediously familiar. But the deputies and the
public galleries were no longer listening so carefully. They were waiting.
For they knew that after five days' silence, Mirabeau, the Assembly's
most imposing and charismatic figure, was finally preparing to weigh in
again.

Rumors had already spread that Mirabeau would side with the king.
The evening before, Alexandre de Lameth had challenged him on the
issue, whereupon Mirabeau asked for a private discussion. It took place
late at night, at the home of another deputy, with Barnave and Adrien
Duport, the other two "triumvirs" of the nonradical Left, also present.
But the group reached no agreement. "I am not entirely the master
here," Lameth later remembered Mirabeau saying; "I am *spoken for.*" In
fact, just days before, Mirabeau had signed his secret agreement to advise the king.

Nonetheless, the proposal that Mirabeau made on May 20 and defended at great and vigorous length was a genuine compromise. "Must
we make an exclusive choice?" he asked the deputies. Rather, the Assembly and the king should exercise the power over war and peace
"concurrently." But while the king should have the right to conduct
foreign policy and to take the military initiative in case of emergency,
the Assembly should have complete oversight. It should even have the
right to prosecute "agents of the executive power" if France committed acts of unjustified aggression. And here, to justify his position,

Mirabeau borrowed the ideas initially proposed by Robespierre and Lévis: "The French nation renounces the undertaking of any wars aimed at conquest, and will never employ its forces against the liberty of any people."

Since, in practice, it would be difficult to deny the executive power control over the armed forces during an emergency, Mirabeau was in fact giving the Left much of what it wanted — including the declaration of peace. But his own rhetoric disguised the concession, while seeming to confirm the swirling rumors of his dealings with the royal family. He repeated, at great length, the Right's pragmatic arguments about the need for secrecy and speed in foreign policy, and he blithely dismissed fears that the king might use the army against the Revolution. Republics, he claimed, launched many more aggressive wars than monarchies and had far more to fear from ambitious generals. The events of the next decade would amply demonstrate his sagacity on this point, but for the moment his words did little but infuriate the Left.

On Friday, May 21, the heavy guns of the Left and Right opened up for the last time, with Mirabeau now in the middle of the field. The speakers, again, did little but repeat the earlier arguments. Still, one remarkable exchange revealed just how much things had changed. It came when the right-wing deputy Jacques-Antoine de Cazalès, a noted duelist, denounced the proposed declaration of peace:

> Many orators . . . have set out here the principles disseminated by modern philosophy. But legislators cannot base what they do on vague principles of humanity, for these principles extend to all the peoples of the world. Put aside this sentiment, which is no more than ostentation. The only proper object of our exclusive affection is the fatherland . . . It is not Russians, Germans or English whom I love, it is the French whom I cherish. The blood of a single one of my fellow citizens is more precious to me than that of all the peoples of the world.

A banal piece of chauvinism of the sort that would not have raised eyebrows in the France of 1788 or the France of 1914 (or, for that matter, the America of 2007). But in the France of 1790, it was greeted by loud and prolonged boos from all sides of the hall, which eventually forced Cazalès into silence. And this reaction proved that whatever the Assembly's final decision on the war-making powers, in a crucial sense, the radical Left had already won. If a simple statement of preference for

French over foreigners could provoke such horror, then "modern phi-losophy," as relayed by Robespierre, Pétion, and Volney, had indeed taken possession of the Manège. Even for some of the officers in atten-dance, if not for veterans, such as Lauzun, the aristocratic code of honor and unquestioning loyalty had become something alien. The deputies had not assembled a year before with the intention of destroy-ing that code. But the experience of the twelve months that followed — the hitherto unimaginable experience of Revolution — had given them a new and extraordinary sense of the possible. On this, as on so many other issues, it had transformed attitudes into intentions, abstract ideas into political will.

The question of the war-making powers still remained. Indeed, for many observers, dazzled by the rhetoric, the fate of the entire Revolu-tion seemed to hinge on it. On Saturday, May 22, crowds of up to 50,000 gathered outside the Manège, waiting for a final resolution. Brissot could not help marveling that in the gardens where once he had seen only brilliantly dressed idlers given over to frivolity and gossip, there now appeared something very different: "the spectacle of a people returned to liberty, taking an interest in its own affairs, and most heat-edly debating rights whose very names they had not known before."

But as at so many moments in the history of the Revolution, heated discussion quickly condensed into vengeful anger. In this case, it was directed against Mirabeau, whose speech of May 20 had made his break with the Left unmistakable, despite his concessions to the radicals. By the afternoon of the next day, no less than six thousand copies of a crude pamphlet entitled *The Treason of the Count of Mirabeau Revealed* were already circulating in Paris. "You have now brought your crimes and lies to new heights," it rebuked him. "Take care that the people do not end up parading your head" (i.e., on the end of a pike). Barnave, the only orator on the Left to match Mirabeau, angrily refuted his pro-posals point by point. On May 22, as Mirabeau entered the Manège, it was to cries of "Treason!" and "Hang him from the lamppost!" from the crowds.

But it was not for nothing that Mirabeau had become the dominant figure in this raucous and often unmanageable collection of men. His political skills were exceptional. In an inspired address, delivered en-tirely off the cuff, he denounced the slanders against him, defended each article of his proposal, and answered Barnave's critique with scalpel-edged humor and condescension. "He has talent as a speaker," Mirabeau conceded of his opponent, "but he knows nothing of being a statesman, or of human affairs." Hours of parliamentary haggling followed, but eventually, Mirabeau's amended proposal passed, giving the king the right to conduct foreign policy and run the armed forces, but entrusting the Assembly with extensive oversight powers. The final decree also codified Mirabeau's version of the declaration of peace, which would find its way unchanged into the French Constitution of 1791. The debate, arguably one of the greatest in the history of representative institutions, was finally over.

Immediate reactions were mixed. In Paris, some confusion prevailed over the meaning of Mirabeau's compromise. The journalist Camille Desmoulins reported wryly that "the question was decided 1) in favor of the nation 2) in favor of the king 3) in favor of both." Some on the Left hailed Barnave and Lameth for supposedly forcing Mirabeau over to their side, but the radical press interpreted the result mostly as a victory for the Right and its alleged criminal machinations. Since the king kept the initiative in declaring war, the weekly *Révolutions de Paris* declared: "Frenchmen, you are still slaves." The ultraradical journalist Jean-Paul Marat agreed, telling his readers that attempts to deprive a people of its liberty always began with war.

Further afield, however, it was not the mechanics of declaring war but the renunciation of aggression that attracted the most attention. In London, the *Times* praised the deputies as "an assembly of Statesmen and Philosophers" and claimed to see in their decision nothing less than "that renovation of the golden age of society, when human victims will no longer be sacrificed to the resentment and ambition of Princes." The Scottish writer Sir James Mackintosh called the decree a "Manifesto of Humanity" and held that it refuted Edmund Burke's indictment of the Revolution. Across the North Sea in Germany, the poet Klopstock rejoiced that now, "even the most ghastly of monsters, war, will be enchained." A French diplomat, on the other hand, expressed his misgivings, complaining that "universal peace, a principle which no one will adopt . . . is as foreign to men as men are to ideas of perfection." Most foreign courts remained silent, no doubt sharing Malouet's cynical observation that it was really nothing new for a country to protest its peaceful intentions.

Most historians of the French Revolution have either agreed with this point of view or joined the diplomat in scolding the Assembly for dangerous naiveté. "Platonic proclamation of a congress of metaphysicians speculating in a vacuum on the mysteries of perpetual peace" is how Albert Sorel scathingly described the decree in his classic history of Revolutionary diplomacy, after a swift and error-ridden account of the debates. It is almost irresistibly tempting to do what the conservatives did during that week in May: identify the Assembly with the well-meaning but risible figure of the *abbé* Saint-Pierre and equate their declaration of peace with his impractical and never-enacted plans for an eighteenth-century league of nations.

But in truth, the Assembly's decision was neither empty rhetoric nor simple naiveté, and the spirit presiding over the deliberations was not Saint-Pierre's but rather — though his name was never mentioned — Fénelon's. For the Assembly never came close to proposing an international federation, as Saint-Pierre had done, and it was in no sense renouncing all military force, as if 1,200 French Catholics and Deists had suddenly, simultaneously discovered the inward light and turned Quaker. What the Assembly was doing, rather, was breaking decisively with aristocratic practice and precedent in the realms of both war and diplomacy. The Assembly was rejecting war waged for the honor and glory of kings, and it was rejecting all manner of entangling alliances that might drag the French into fighting for the honor and glory of someone else. It was, as Malouet had quite accurately seen, adopting a credo of openness and self-sufficiency in dealings with other nations and renouncing secrecy and deception. "The reign of the charlatans is over," as a left-wing deputy said, in reference to professional diplomats. It was exactly the foreign policy prescribed by Mentor to Idomeneus, King of Salentum, in *Telemachus*.

Most important, the Assembly was emphatically not saying that France would never fight another war. It was saying that France did not *want* war but that if war came, it would be waged in a new and different way. France would fight in self-defense and with the full "courage and power of a truly free nation," as baron Menou had put it. Furthermore, as was hinted in Pétion's threats to "exterminate" the Barbary pirates, France might not fight according to all the aristocratic niceties of eighteenth-century dynastic conflict but rather so as to eliminate "monsters" once and for all. The "declaration of peace" certainly expressed the view that if all nations followed France down the path of liberty, then war would vanish from the world. But until that happy moment arrived, France would defend itself with newly righteous fury.

We will see, in the next chapter, just what this righteous fury entailed, but some of the implications of the May debates emerged very quickly. On June 19, with scarcely any debate, the Assembly abruptly abolished all titles of nobility. The reasons for its decision remain obscure. But it is undeniable that the nobility, after having lost its legal privileges and much of its wealth in 1789, had now lost its great traditional *raison d'être:* war. Following the declaration of peace, the continued existence of a noble order seemed utterly superfluous. Then, a few months later, Spain yielded extensive rights in the Pacific Northwest to Great Britain, bringing the Nootka Sound controversy to an end. Spain accepted this humiliation in large part because its prime minister felt that he could no longer count on his French ally. For all practical purposes, the Family Pact was dead: France had effectively withdrawn from the existing European system of alliances. An era in the history of international relations had come to an end as well.

The sponsors of the declaration of peace might well have hoped that international tensions would now ease, but if so, they were badly mistaken. The opposite occurred, thanks above all to the steadily increasing political temperature within France itself. During the fifteen months that followed the May debate, the Assembly did finish drafting a constitution for a moderate, constitutional monarchy. But at the same time, the Assembly deeply antagonized the king, the pope, and many Catholics, inside and outside France, by voting to subordinate the Catholic Church radically to the French state. It spurred angry protests from German princes by eliminating their traditional privileges in the eastern French province of Alsace. Meanwhile, the other major powers, although distracted by such matters as Nootka Sound, gazed on French events not only with increasing apprehension but also — since they might profit from French troubles — with increasing greed.

Matters grew much worse in June 1791, when the French royal family absconded from the Tuileries Palace in the middle of the night and fled toward the eastern border. Louis XVI, goaded by Marie-Antoinette, had finally taken a stand against the Revolution and planned to return to Paris at the head of loyal troops, backed by the forces of the queen's brother, Emperor Leopold of Austria. But the daring plot crumpled into a comedy of errors as the royal family's heavy, overloaded carriage fell disastrously behind schedule. They were spotted and, finally, arrested in the village of Varennes before they could reach their goal. Moderates scrambled to save the situation, claiming that the royal family had been rescued from kidnappers, but few believed the transparent fiction. In September, Louis duly took up his new role as a limited monarch under the new constitution, but millions of his subjects now saw him as an enemy, not a legitimate king. On the other side, thousands of nobles, priests, and wealthy commoners were leaving the country, with many gravitating to Koblenz, in Germany, to join a Counter-Revolutionary army taking shape under the command of the prince of Condé and sponsored by Louis XVI's two younger brothers.

Meanwhile, related events not only completed the destruction of the old officer corps but also raised the serious possibility that in a new war, more French officers would fight *against* France than for it. In September 1790, the National Assembly approved a new military constitution drawn up by Alexandre de Lameth's military committee, which formally abolished any preference for the now-abolished nobility and set aside a quarter of new commissions for promotions from the ranks — something unprecedented in the aristocratic armed forces of the day. Radical attacks on the royal army intensified. "Any nation which sees in its midst a large and disciplined army under the orders of a monarch, and which thinks itself free, is insane," Robespierre told the Assembly in a typical speech in December 1790. In the provinces, political clubs continued to push soldiers to mutiny, leading, in more than one case, to bloody confrontations and scores of executions. Noble-born officers reacted predictably to this dissolution of everything that they held dear. "Every day," one later remembered, "we asked each other privately, *when are you leaving and where will you go?*" By the end of 1791, over 60 percent of them had not only resigned but also emigrated — many to join the Counter-Revolutionary army in Germany.

Even so, war with the powers that backed these émigrés was not inevitable. The armed émigrés at Koblenz numbered only 20,000 and did not pose a serious threat to France. The apparent weakness and chaos within the country certainly tempted Austria and Prussia to behave more aggressively — they threatened to intervene militarily if the Revolution continued to radicalize — but this factor by itself was not sufficient. What proved decisive was that an influential group of French radicals began to push for aggressive international action, in apparent contradiction of the declaration of peace. They included the philosopher Condorcet (the exponent of enlightened theories of history) and also a number of powerful speakers who went by the collective name of the "Girondins" (many came from the department of the Gironde, in southwestern France). The single most important figure, though, was the left-wing journalist Brissot, who by 1791 had moved the short but significant distance from the Manège's spectators' galleries to the deputies' benches and become one of France's most important politicians.

The Manège in late 1791 continued to host France's legislature, under much the same unpleasant physical conditions as before, but a new body of 745 legislators, chosen by new elections, according to the new constitution, now sat there. With the vote limited to a wealthy minority of the population, these men did not come into office with particularly radical inclinations. Nonetheless, their Legislative Assembly differed hugely from its predecessor. As nobles and priests no longer enjoyed special electoral privileges, nearly all the deputies came from the former Third Estate. And thanks to one of those moments of ostentatious self-denial so beloved by men who fancied themselves reborn Romans, the old National Assembly had prohibited its members from serving in the new body (it was Robespierre who proposed the measure). At a stroke, all the men who had become such grand political presences during the debates of 1789 and 1790 found themselves banished from France's main political stage. Among the deputies from the old aristocracy, many emigrated, but a few on the Left — including Lauzun — went back into the army. The new denizens of the Manège were mostly young and mostly unknown, so those few among them with any degree of celebrity enjoyed outsize influence. Brissot, thanks to the reputation he had made with his newspaper, quickly took on a decisive role.

From the start, Brissot's great cause was war against Austria and Prussia, the principal supporters of the émigré Counter-Revolutionaries. It was a position that gave off more than a faint stink of hypocrisy, given his earlier support of the 1790 declaration, but some degree of principle did enter into it. Even during the 1790 debates, Brissot had never indulged in full-fledged pacifism. Like so many at the time, he saw international relations in idealistic terms straight out of *Telemachus:* Diplomacy was a corrupt game, states should practice nonaggression, but peoples had the right to defend themselves vigorously if attacked. Brissot also sincerely believed that the king's flight in 1791 had made war inevitable — so why let Emperor Leopold and the émigré armies choose the moment for it? Finally — and this was perhaps Brissot's most attractive feature — he was a true, convinced internationalist. Even before 1789, he had founded the Society of the Friends of the Blacks to push for an end to slavery in France's Caribbean colonies. Few other Revolutionaries took the idea of universal human brotherhood as seriously as he did. If it would take a war to bring this brotherhood about, then France might just have to fight it.

Still, there is no denying that Brissot was playing a cynical game. On October 20, soon after taking office, he made an incendiary speech denouncing the plotting of the émigrés and the "hostile plans" of the other European powers. But he clearly didn't believe his own words, for only two days later, he calmly wrote to his brother-in-law that since France was looking forward to a period of "tranquillity," he was ready to take part in some new real estate speculations. In order to rally support for war, Brissot also brazenly contradicted his own long-standing internationalist principles by developing a suspiciously sudden concern about France's slipping status as a great power since its ill-fated alliance with Austria in 1756. The man who had ridiculed traditional notions of honor just a year earlier now told his colleagues: "avenge your glory or condemn yourselves to eternal dishonor." The most charitable explanation for Brissot's conduct is that, having by now become a convinced republican, he wanted to isolate the king politically: if the king opposed a patriotic war, he would look like an enemy of the Revolution. But the evidence makes clear that Brissot also thought that stirring up war fervor would help him steal support away from more moderate left-wing rivals.

In any case, the first ploy failed, for in December, to everyone's surprise, the king and queen came out in favor of war as well. Their motives were even more cynical than Brissot's and tinged with desperation. Only defeat and foreign occupation, they now believed, would save the French monarchy (they assumed that France would lose, although if it unexpectedly won, the king could take credit). "The best way to help us," Marie-Antoinette wrote to her Swedish former lover and confidant, Axel Fersen, "is to fall on us." As for Brissot and the Girondins, the queen had only dark scorn: "These imbeciles don't see that they are helping us, because in the end all the powers will have to join in." The unholy alliance between the royal couple and the radicals would soon make war all but inevitable. Still, before it came, there took place a debate nearly as profound as the one of May 1790. Thanks to the 1790 compromise, the king retained the decisive role in declaring war, but the Assembly had its oversight powers, and so their deliberations mattered.

The new debate is not worth chronicling as closely as its predecessor, for it lacked the concentrated intensity and drama and was also much more one-sided. It took place over many months rather than a single week and did not center as firmly on the Manège, where few of the new deputies had the brilliance or oratorical flair of a Mirabeau, Barnave, or Malouet. Instead, the debate spilled out into the newspaper press and also into political clubs, which had now gained immensely in importance, in part because they provided a forum for the members of the old Assembly to speak in public. The debate also took place largely between radicals — a sign of the Revolution's rapid move to the left. The right-wing firebrands of 1790 had largely emigrated or otherwise fled the scene. Barnave and the Lameths, once heroes of the moderate Left, now found themselves on the right of the shifting political terrain and increasingly marginalized. Mirabeau, the one man who might possibly have slowed the process of radicalization, had died in April 1791. The principal exchanges took place between Brissot and his followers on the one side and, on the other, the lonely figure of Maximilien Robespierre, who had first proposed the declaration of peace the year before. Now, banished from the Manège (by his own "self-denying" ordinance!), he led the resistance to war from his perch in the radical Jacobin Club — but less out of pacifist principle than out of mistrust of the warmongers. He had few allies.

The new debate also had a very different character in another respect, for unlike the allegedly "naive" legislators of 1790, the dominant Girondins really did see the looming conflict almost entirely through the prism of classical fantasy — very much in the manner of Rousseau, Mably, and the other Enlightenment-era enthusiasts discussed in the previous chapter. As early as July 1791, in a speech in the Jacobin Club, Brissot made the absurd boast that France had nothing to fear from foreign powers, because freedom made men into supermen, capable of "prodigious, supernatural efforts." His allies repeated these optimistic claims throughout the fall, none more fantastically than an irrepressible German baron named Anacharsis Cloots, who had emerged as a leading advocate of war and French expansionism. Cloots had come to Paris in 1789 to join the Revolution, dubbed himself the "Orator of the Human Race," and in 1790 staged a gimcrack tableau of cosmopolitan brotherhood before the National Assembly (in part using actors quickly scrounged up from nearby theaters to play exotic foreigners). Invited to address the Legislative Assembly in December 1791, he told the members that within a month of declaring war, the French flag would be flying over twenty liberated enemy capitals. French bayonets, he added nonsensically but to loud applause, would prove ten times as deadly as the enemy's musket fire. Even the philosopher and former pacifist Condorcet, who had also won election to the new Assembly, got into the act. In March 1792, the newspaper he edited published an extract from a "history" of the as yet undeclared war. No sooner would French troops cross the borders, it predicted, than foreign soldiers, impressed by both French discipline and French Revolutionary principles, would throw down their arms, surrender, and embrace the invaders.

With two centuries of hindsight, it is difficult not to share Marie-Antoinette's contempt toward men who could indulge in such dangerous delusions. Out of a toxic mixture of ignorance, wishful thinking, and pure, naked ambition, the Girondins were pushing France toward wars that would last for twenty-three years and take millions of lives. It is difficult not to reflect on the differences between the 1791 Assembly in which Brissot sat and its predecessor, which had debated the declaration of peace. The new body was chosen in a far more democratic fashion, but for this reason, it had almost no members with military experience. Unlike the seasoned officers who had deliberated in May 1790, the new legislators were largely lawyers and officeholders who knew war only from books (and mostly ancient books, at that).

Still, it is worth looking a little more closely at their arguments. Rather like those made by certain modern democratic war leaders, these arguments may have held only a tenuous relation to military reality. But they foreshadowed, and arguably helped invent, several critical elements of the new culture of war that would soon dominate Europe and out of which a true total war would soon begin.

First, throughout the debate, the Girondins made the classic, modern, oxymoronic argument that they wanted war only for the sake of peace. In no sense, they insisted, had they renounced the 1790 declaration of nonaggression. War was being forced on them by the plotting of the émigré nobles and the conniving of foreign regimes. But the war they wanted would be more than a war of self-defense. It would be a war to end all wars. This slogan may not have been coined until World War I, but its essence was already present in Revolutionary rhetoric. Even before the flight to Varennes, for instance, the radical Charles-Philippe Ronsin called for war in a highly successful stage play and predicted that victory would bring "from the bosom of natural law . . . that deep, universal peace which has been mocked as a dream." In a climactic speech in December, the Girondin orator Pierre-Victurnien Vergniaud told the Assembly to "hate war, it is the greatest human crime and humanity's most terrible scourge" — and proceeded to argue for the opening of hostilities against Austria. A few days later, with brazenly dismal logic, Anacharsis Cloots added: "It is because I want peace that I am asking for war." And once the war started, as we have seen, the Girondin general Charles-François Dumouriez declared starkly: "This war will be the last war."

Second, the Girondins believed that the war would turn into a worldwide war of liberation. "There has been in this Revolution a character that belongs to no other: to generalize its principles, to make them applicable to all peoples, all countries, all governments. It is a true spirit of conquest, or rather of proselytism." Thus Pierre-Victor Malouet, the eloquent moderate of 1790, well before the second debate on war even started. The radicals would prove him right. "War is declared upon all the oppressors of the world," proclaimed Ronsin hopefully in his 1791 play. "This expiatory war . . . will renew the face of the world, and plant the standard of liberty in the palaces of kings, the seraglios of Sultans, and the castles of petty feudal tyrants alike; on the temples of popes and of muftis." Thus Brissot, in his newspaper, on December 13, 1791. "Remember those crusades in which Europe, [took] up arms for a few superstitions . . . The moment has come for a new crusade, and it has a far nobler, and holier object. It is a crusade for universal liberty." Thus Brissot again, on December 30.

And, of course, a war for such stakes could only be apocalyptic — something entirely different from the limited, restrained wars of the Old Regime. The French had to be prepared to conquer and live free or to perish to the last man. This theme had already sounded in the 1790 debate. In early 1791, as the temperature of international relations rose, the liberal aristocrat Menou stated it more forcefully, as we have seen: "All the nations of Europe must learn that if ever we are forced to make war . . . it will be a war to the death . . . We will fight to destroy or annihilate those who have attacked us, or to be destroyed ourselves." The Girondins echoed the same theme again and again, none more vividly than the reliably unbalanced Cloots. If war were to come, he said:

> The French, like lions, will defend themselves in such a way as to leave not a single man alive, not a single tree standing. They will bury themselves under the ruins of their doorposts and their huts . . . The land of France may be enslaved, but we will perish as free men, with our wives, our children and our cattle. So! princes of Germany, monarchs of the north and south, there you will be, bathing in the blood of an exterminated nation.

The Assembly itself literally took an oath to die. On January 14, a close ally of Brissot's named Marguerite-Elie Guadet was making yet another appeal for war: "Let us then, Messieurs, tell the princes of Europe that the French nation is determined to maintain its constitution unaltered. We will die here." At these words, according to the semiofficial transcript published in the newspaper *Le moniteur*, the Assembly interrupted him with wild cries of "yes, yes, we swear it!" and then raised their arms in unison, in imitation of ancient Roman salutes, and solemnly swore to live free or die.

Scenes like this one — and there were many in the excitable winter of 1791–92 — suggest that something else, rather strange, was taking place in the Manège. The delirious deputies swearing fervent oaths were not behaving like men of peace who reluctantly take up arms as a last resort, in self-defense. They were not behaving like men who truly believed war to be "humanity's greatest scourge." Even Vergniaud, who used these words, belied them in the very same speech. "Hate war," he thundered, but he added: "if you are forced to it . . . follow the course of your great destiny . . . glory awaits you." In the frenzied atmosphere of the 1791 Manège, the Girondins were not remaining true to the pacific principles of 1790. They were not even arguing for war as a spur to civic virtue, in the manner of Rousseau or Mably. They were arguing for war as a holy cause. Brissot and his allies had no love for the Catholic Church, but they obsessively invoked religious language — "crusade," "holy war," "expiatory war" — to describe the conflagration they longed for. The great orator Georges Danton even spoke, chillingly, of "the exterminating angel of liberty."

In fact, the Girondins were falling in love with war — or at least, with the idea of war. They were romanticizing it and exulting in its creative force. An astonishingly frank letter composed by one of the group's guiding spirits, Jeanne-Marie Roland, just a few days after the king's flight in 1791, demonstrates this point very clearly. "It is a cruel thing to think," she wrote, "but it is becoming more clear every day: peace is taking us backwards. We will only be regenerated by blood. Our shallow national character, and our frivolous or corrupt morals, are incompatible with liberty, and can only be reformed by the rasp of adversity." The key word in the letter — "regenerate," a favorite of the radical Revolutionaries — had not only religious connotations of redemption but also organic ones of regrowth, and this organic vision would permeate Brissot's prowar speeches in particular. Incessantly, he spoke of France as a nation turned "dessicated" and "listless" by centuries of royal despotism, in need of "consolidation" and a violent purgative. "I have only one fear," he told the Jacobin Club on December 30: "it is that we will not be betrayed . . . We need great treasons, they will be our salvation; for there is still strong poison in the body of France, and we need strong explosions to expel it." In this sense, Girondin language came eerily close to that of the German enthusiasts for war discussed in the previous chapter — for instance, Johann Embser, who had characterized war as "rejuvenating," or Humboldt, who claimed that it could help "cultivate" the human race. The Girondins almost certainly had no awareness of their German counterparts, but their words expressed a similar reaction against the Enlightenment dream of universal peace and a similar vision of war as something exceptional — but sublimely, and redemptively, so, at least when fought for the right cause.

The Girondin rhetoric had an inebriating effect on the Assembly, but it did not carry the day for several months. While the king's stance undercut right-wing opposition to the war, a small band of politicians on the left struggled against the Girondins throughout the winter. In the Jacobin Club, Robespierre made a series of biting, brilliant speeches against Brissot, laying out three reasons why France should not go to war — at least, not yet. First, the principal danger to the Revolution did not come from the pitiful handful of émigrés in Koblenz but from within France itself, from shadowy Counter-Revolutionaries — including some who disguised themselves as patriots. Second, premature hostilities would only play into the hands of the king and the Counter-Revolutionaries and open the way to ambitious generals establishing a dictatorship. War, he stressed, would accustom the soldiers to "passive obedience, separate them from the people," and bring about "idolatry for the supreme head of the army."

Finally, attempting to impose Revolutionary democracy on neighboring peoples would backfire, for they were not ready to receive it. On this point, incidentally, Robespierre showed a better grasp of some basic principles of political sociology than have some more recent democratic leaders, and his words are worth quoting:

> The most extravagant idea that can arise in a politician's head is to believe that it is enough for a people to invade a foreign country to make it adopt their laws and their constitution. No one loves armed missionaries . . . The Declaration of the Rights of Man is not a beam of sunlight which shines on all men, and it is not a lightning bolt which strikes every throne at the same time . . . I am far from claiming that our Revolution will not eventually influence the fate of the world . . . But I say that it will not be today.

Robespierre also ridiculed Brissot's defense of "French honor" — which Brissot himself had ridiculed so recently — as a childish enthusiasm at best and at worst, a cunning ploy to plunge the French back into slavery.

Robespierre lost the debate, but it is difficult to deny that he had the better arguments. His denunciation of ubiquitous Counter-Revolutionary plots may have anticipated his later paranoia, but on the substantive issues, history would confirm his judgment. France did *not* in fact have much to fear from the émigrés or the Austrian emperor. The attempts to impose Revolutionary democracy on neighboring states *would* backfire. And war *would,* soon enough, bring a military dictator to power, although not the sort Robespierre imagined. But the members of the Legislative Assembly could not see into the future. They looked instead into the distant past and saw columns of brave Roman legionaries cleaving the ranks of their enemies. On April 20, 1792, despite Robespierre's words, the Girondins and the king got their wish, and war was declared on Austria. Within days, French troops would cross the border into the Austrian Netherlands (modern Belgium). But what were they supposed to achieve there? On this question — how to translate the lofty goals of ending war and universal liberation into practical military strategy — the Assembly gave fatefully little guidance. It was sending its army into the void.

4

The Last Crusade

Revolutionary war is an antitoxin which not only eliminates the
enemy's poison but also purges us of our own filth.

— MAO ZEDONG

THE STORY OF REVOLUTIONARY FRANCE at war is a remarkable one, but despite the countless books devoted to the
subject, it remains surprisingly ill-understood. For generations, an impressive line of French scholars insisted, patriotically but
unconvincingly, on the simple truth of the Revolutionaries' own incandescent myths: the People rose up as one, their ideological *élan* making
up for their lack of training, and heroically overwhelmed their adversaries. Meanwhile, a line of self-proclaimed commonsense realists have
gleefully debunked the myths but in the process badly underestimated
the role of myth as a historical force in its own right. A full account is
impossible without a sensitivity to the ways in which myth and practice
influenced each other, often in unexpected ways. Yet untangling these
influences is far from easy. The texts that are our principal sources do
not offer anything like a clear window onto the past. The voices of the
dead are sometimes faint, sometimes deceptively clear. We must listen
carefully.

The best place to start listening is with ordinary soldiers. Take,
for instance, Gabriel-Nicolas Noël. A well-educated young man from
Lorraine, he volunteered for the French army in December 1791 and
over the next months wrote a series of evocative, startlingly intimate let-

ters back to his adoptive mother and sister. Although he had his moments of patriotic exaltation, the letters mostly expressed his longing
for his family (he called himself a dog who ached to lick their hands!)
and described his ordinary routine. One day, his subject was his comrades' off-putting penchant for "filling the mouth and throat with
stinking smoke." The next, he joked about the difficulty of communi-
cating with the German-speaking peasants on whom he was billeted.
To get milk from them, he had to hold his hand down to resemble an
udder and then pretend to milk it. The peasants did not have enough
beds to go around, which led to other problems. On February 27,
1792, Noël devoted most of a letter to rhapsodizing over his new bed-
mate, a chandler's son named Gilbaut. Unlike his predecessor, Gilbaut
was clean, a good conversationalist, and didn't complain when Noël
thrashed around in the middle of the night. "We sleep together as
peacefully as if we each had our own bed."

After the war started in April, of course, hardly any soldiers had such
luck in their sleeping arrangements. Gilbert Favier was the son of a lawyer from the mountainous Auvergne region. On August 2, 1792, he
wrote home from eastern France that, for an entire week, "a rain that
hardly ever stopped made our camp impassable; despite the ditches we
dug, the water flowed into our tents and made the little bit of straw we
had to sleep on as putrid and foul as manure." Waking up after a night
on the cold, wet ground, Favier's limbs trembled violently for a full
hour. Another volunteer had similar complaints: "We're always sleeping
on the ground, camping close to the enemy, always drenched in mud
up to our knees. I don't know how I have managed to stay alive." As for
Claude Simon, a grenadier from Paris, he wrote to a friend in March
1793: "It has now been fourteen days and fourteen nights, my friend,
since I've set foot in a house or slept for more than two hours in a row
. . . for fourteen times twenty-four hours I've had nothing hot to eat.
I've lived with army bread, not always any water, and sometimes a little
bad *pecquet* (a horrible eau-de-vie)."

The letters and memoirs of Revolutionary soldiers are filled with
such complaints: bad food or no food, rotting shoes, filth, boredom,
sickness, fatigue, poor mail service. And then there were the battles.
Louis-Joseph Bricard, an artilleryman from Paris, had the bad luck to
take part, along with his brother Honoré, in France's 1793 disastrous defeat at Neerwinden, in Belgium. In a harrowing journal, he recalled

that during the preliminaries, an inexperienced officer ordered their battery to fire too early on approaching Austrian cavalry. Taking advantage of the mistake, the unscathed Austrians rode in, chopping down with their well-honed sabers and causing a "horrid butchery." Nearby French artillery made things worse by targeting the Austrians and hitting friend and foe alike. Bricard survived only by desperately parrying a saber thrust with a long-handled brush and startling his attacker's horse. Finally, new French columns advanced and drove the Austrians (who, Bricard reported, were mostly drunk) from the position. But in the mêlée, Bricard had lost sight of his brother. As evening fell, temporarily suspending the hostilities, he searched in anguish, "running from corpse to corpse." He visited the barns and stables where the wounded had been taken and spent much of the night tormentedly wandering the battlefield. But finally he learned that Honoré was dead, literally blown apart by a friendly shell. Bricard fainted at the news. In shock, hungry, and sleepless, he barely noticed the rest of the battle or the ensuing French retreat. Several days later, he wrote to his parents that Honoré had been taken to the hospital to be treated for exhaustion. He feared that the truth would kill them.

The soldiers rightly considered the lot of the wounded particularly dreadful. Ten days after Neerwinden, the grenadier Simon had his leg crushed and received a severe concussion when a cannonball knocked a heavy tree limb onto him. He woke up fifteen hours later to find himself being carried south in a jolting cart, "suffering unspeakable pains in my head and legs, my hat and breeches all torn. I asked where I was and what had happened: they replied that since I was speaking, I wasn't dead, as they had thought." Arriving at Mons, in Belgium near the French border, Simon was brought to a hospital that lacked doctors, bandages, or proper beds. He finally received a rotting mattress on the floor and a cup of hot water, only to be dragged outside soon afterward when the French decided to evacuate the town. It took a further, agonizing twelve-hour ride in an ammunition cart to reach Valenciennes, where, as Simon put it sardonically, "compassion and my money won the heart of the attendants," who put him in a proper bed. At least Simon survived. Most of the badly wounded did not.

These accounts give us a vivid and immediate sense of the soldiers' experiences, yet in one way, they are deceptive, for in their utterance of timeless soldiers' complaints, they give the impression that relatively little had really changed since the start of the Revolution. It is quite true that if a combatant from the 1745 battle of Fontenoy had fallen asleep and then awoken, Rip Van Winkle–like, in a French army camp of the early 1790s, he would have found himself far more at home than a veteran of the World War I trenches similarly plucked out of time and dropped into the mechanized armies of Rommel or Eisenhower. Uniforms looked and felt much the same, and so did the equipment: the same heavy, awkward, inaccurate musket; the same cumbersome swords and packs and ammunition pouches; marching under this load entailed the same pains. The sleeper might notice some important modifications in artillery and military engineering, soon to be joined by major reforms in battlefield tactics. Army organization, however, remained largely the same in most European countries. At the decisive French victory of Fleurus, in 1794, one vivid novelty did appear: a one-hundred-foot-wide balloon, christened the *Enterprising,* from which French observers viewed the battle and reported down to their commanders. But this first attempt at a French air force had more of a symbolic than a practical effect. Generals still relied more heavily on spyglasses to survey the smoke-clogged fields.

In a crucial sense, though, the soldiers' accounts reveal something truly new: the fact that they exist at all. Before 1789, French common soldiers wrote very few witty, colorful letters like those of Noël or Simon, for the simple reason that the army of the Old Regime had relatively few soldiers who could write at all, let alone who had received good educations. This is why, to recreate the experience of warfare under the Old Regime, we must rely overwhelmingly on the testimony of officers, who tended to follow the flat conventions associated with the aristocratic code. Common soldiers remained, for the most part, frustratingly mute. The Revolution, however, radically transformed the armed forces. As we have already seen, it decimated the old officer corps, opened up new avenues of promotion and recruitment, and saw many units mutiny. It also led to the emergence of a new type of European soldier (prefigured, in many respects, by the soldiers of the American Revolution): the articulate citizen-soldier, of whom Noël, Simon, and Favier were perfect examples.

It took time and some false starts, though, for anything approximating a real citizen army to emerge. Before the Revolution, various prominent readers of Rousseau and Mably had composed plans for one, with the idea that it would supplement (though not replace) France's regular army of professionals and mercenaries. In December 1789, Edmond Dubois-Crancé, a deputy and former officer, formally proposed to the National Assembly the creation of a conscripted, 1,200,000-strong reserve force. "In France every citizen must be a soldier, and every soldier must be a citizen, or we will never have a constitution," he argued. In keeping with the optimistic tenor of military thought in 1789–91, he and the other reformers assumed that since the new force would make France too strong for any sane enemy to attack, and since the French were now "cured of the sickness of conquest" (as the future war minister Joseph Servan blithely put it in another argument for national service), the country would never fight foreign wars again.

Yet armies, of course, do not exist simply to fight foreign wars. In 1789, the National Assembly grandiosely proclaimed the end of the old "feudal" social system, with its complex and suffocating system of titles, tithes, taxes, and seigneurial obligations. With the foundations of a new social order barely even scratched in the ground, fear and confusion spread, especially among the long-suffering peasantry, leading to social unrest that swelled in great waves through the countryside. Armed force would be needed to keep the peace. But the sort of suspicions Robespierre had voiced in regard to the royal line army kept the deputies from taking steps to increase its size (they voted down Dubois-Crancé's plan). In fact, they let it shrink radically as mutinies spread and the officer corps crumbled.

Instead, the Revolution began to raise and train a new, separate force to maintain order and promote civic participation: the so-called National Guard, commanded by George Washington's former aide-de-camp the Marquis de Lafayette, now a leading Revolutionary moderate. Hundreds of thousands of men, mostly from relatively prosperous and literate segments of French society, volunteered for it. They initially had to scrabble together their own makeshift flags, uniforms, and weapons, but the Guard quickly grew in efficiency and took over such crucial tasks as ensuring the food supply for the city of Paris. Then in 1791, as war loomed, the Assembly authorized the incorporation of a portion of the Guard into new "volunteer" military units that would supplement the line army. Noël and Favier both came into active service as volunteers of this sort. Meanwhile, the opening up of avenues of promotion was making careers in the regular army more attractive to men such as Claude Simon (who expressed admiration for the volunteers in his letters).

In one sense, this transformation of the armed forces was breaking down the barriers between "military" and "civilian" life, giving a taste of the former to men who, before 1789, might well have scoffed at the very idea of enlisting. The phenomenon would presumably have pleased Rousseau and Mably, those devotees of citizen armies. But the creation of the National Guard and its volunteer units also served to *create* new distinctions between things military and civilian. As Noël and Favier's letters illustrate, the new soldiers tended to see military service as something strange and extraordinary. They continually marveled at the differences from the civilian life they had known (and, soon enough, were longing to return to it). If they generally accepted service as a patriotic necessity, they also saw it as a distinct and extraordinary phase of their lives that they would eventually leave behind.

The Revolution also emphasized the contrast between military and civilian spheres by putting military force on display before the civilian population more conspicuously than at any time in recent history, and not only because of the need for order. In much of France, the armed, uniformed National Guard was becoming the most visible symbol of political change. On July 14, 1790, the anniversary of the fall of the Bastille, the National Assembly decreed a gigantic festival of commemoration — the *fête de la fédération* — celebrated in Paris and throughout France. Ordinary citizens marked the occasion in their own raucous manner, but guardsmen and soldiers dominated the official proceedings: they drilled, paraded, listened to sermons and patriotic homilies, watched priests bless their flags, solemnly pledged to "federate" with each other, and took oaths of loyalty to the nation and the king. It may be going too far to say that the militarization of France was beginning. But many observers saw something of the sort at work and criticized it. The left-wing newspaper *Révolutions de Paris,* for instance, denounced the Guard early on for adopting military-style dress, arguing that "the military spirit is always a spirit of oppression." The ultraradical journalist Jean-Paul Marat, who preferred his bloodshed anarchic and "popular" rather than disciplined and military, wrote in late 1790 that "never was there a more ridiculous project than that of forcing the entire nation to become a people of soldiers." Other Revolutionaries, however, simply saw the National Guard as a necessary counterweight to the line army.

The new shape of the French armies was one crucial early novelty of the Revolutionary wars, but there were many others as well. The political stakes attached to campaigns increased enormously. The line between combatants and noncombatants, which pre-Revolutionary armed forces had done so much to sharpen, turned blurry, both in regard to enemy populations and to what we would today call the "home front." The absolute destruction of the enemy became a moral imperative, raising the prospect of the conflict stretching out indefinitely into the future. These changes too can be glimpsed, imperfectly, in the soldiers' accounts. But to grasp the overall contours of what was becoming total war, we need, like the balloonist at Fleurus, to rise up over the battlefield and survey broader trends.

At the start of the war, the most obvious change involved France's strategic goals — or lack thereof. To listen to Brissot and the other prowar orators in the Convention, France was now embarking on a crusade for universal liberty. But how did such a grandiose vision translate into practical war plans? To a surprisingly great extent, the Girondin government had no clear idea. Despite the obsession with the French émigrés in Germany, France had issued the declaration of war against Austria, not the German princes hosting those émigrés. Prussia, as Austria's ally, immediately entered the war as well. But neither the Austrians nor the Prussians posed an imminent threat to France. So where should France attack? In the absence of a clear strategy, the government essentially obeyed the force of deeply rooted habit and sent its forces north, into what is now Belgium. The country had belonged to Austria since 1714, its border lay dangerously close to Paris, it had been a perennial target of French territorial ambitions, and it had seen major political disturbances of its own since 1789. Perhaps, some officials thought, the Belgians would "embrace the cause of liberty," making Girondin dreams come true.

Nothing of the sort happened. "I can't conceive how we could declare war without being ready for anything," wrote Lafayette, now commanding France's Army of the Center, a few weeks after the declaration of war, and his bafflement was eminently reasonable. Thanks to the departure of mercenaries and other professional soldiers, the wave of mutinies, and administrative chaos, the strength of the French armed forces had fallen to a dangerous low, even with the new "volunteer" units. The volunteers themselves were poorly trained — particularly those who had come into service in the spring of 1792. The shortage of experienced officers was desperate, and the volunteer units made matters worse by electing their officers: popularity often trumped merit. At the highest ranks, meanwhile, the Girondins had no choice but to put their trust in men they profoundly mistrusted: aristocrats who had resisted the lure of emigration, such as Lafayette, Lauzun, or Nicholas Luckner, a crotchety seventy-year-old Bavarian who did not even speak good French. There were simply no other generals available. The army, in other words, was in anything but an ideal state for launching a full-scale war, let alone a crusade for liberty. The initial result was an all too predictable fiasco.

Witnessing it on the front lines was Lauzun, who had returned to the army after the end of the National Assembly in 1791. He remained loyal to the Revolution but had nothing but scorn for many of the volunteers under his command: "They do not know how to use their weapons, they have no idea of discipline," he wrote. "All the officers to whom I want to give them, fear them more than they want them." Soon after the declaration of war, he led a column of the Army of the North across the frontier toward the Belgian town of Mons. But on reaching the heights of Bertaumont and Jemappes, he found his route solidly blocked, while the country, as Robespierre had predicted, gave absolutely no sign of rising up to greet its "liberators." Meanwhile, rumors of a massive Austrian counterattack swirled insistently through his ranks. In early May 1792, Lauzun managed to drive the Austrians out of Quiévrain, but when he directed two battalions forward to occupy the town, they refused, and before he could restore order, a blind panic seized his entire force, which dropped all unnecessary weight and ran back south. "In the blink of an eye," one of Lauzun's deputies remembered, "the roads and the plain were covered with muskets, swords, sacks, broken equipment, carts run into ditches, dying men." Lauzun at least avoided the fate of another French general, Théobald Dillon, whose troops likewise panicked after coming under strong Austrian ar-

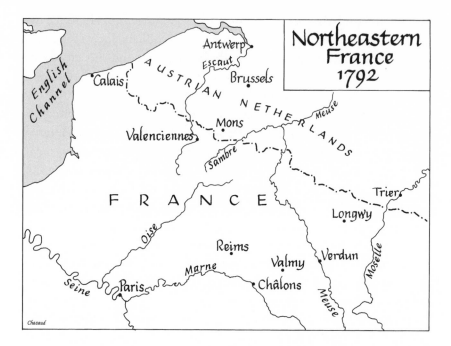

tillery fire. Soldiers accused him of betrayal, dragged him from his carriage in the French city of Lille, lynched him, and hung his mutilated body from a lamppost.

Luckily for the French, the Austrians did not follow up on their initial successes, and so, for the first few months of the war, the most important violence did not take place on the northern frontier at all. As a radical French newspaper announced, quite correctly: "The first battle we will fight will be inside the walls of Paris, not outside." Opponents of the monarchy, backed by the popular groups known as the "*sans-culottes*" (i.e., those who did "without the breeches" of the male upper classes), were now openly accusing the king of treason and demanding the establishment of a republic. On August 10, 1792, after months of tension, armed *sans-culottes* and National Guardsmen stormed the royal palace of the Tuileries, in a grimmer and much bloodier replay of the October Days of 1789. Through the smoke and blood that turned parts of central Paris into a combat zone, the terrified royal family took refuge in the Manège and saved their own lives, but the French monarchy had come to an end. Among the Girondins, rejoicing was muted, for they had staked too much on their unholy alliance with the king on the war issue. But they now had no choice but to clutch desperately to the Revolution that they had so deliberately sent careening into the unknown. Lafayette, in shock, desperately tried to rally his troops to march on Paris, but when the effort failed, he defected to the Austrians, who promptly threw him into prison.

This political radicalization soon affected the war and sent it hurtling in unprecedented directions as well. Even before August 10, Prussia had been preparing to strike into France from the German Rhineland. The Prussian commander, the Duke of Brunswick, issued a manifesto threatening to destroy Paris if any harm came to Louis XVI. But for the moment, the Prussians still behaved as if they were fighting a familiar, limited conflict against opponents similar to themselves. After the fall of the monarchy, this idea was no longer credible, and a key shift in Prussian strategy soon reflected the change. The Prussian army, accompanied in its march by King Frederick William in person, had initially met with easy success capturing several key fortified towns. But what next? Should it march straight west, toward Paris? Or should it wheel north and establish positions from which it might drive toward Paris the next spring?

Brunswick, a cautious fifty-seven-year-old campaigner made very much in the aristocratic eighteenth-century mold, favored the latter course. The autumn end of the traditional campaigning season was coming on. Worse, a foe as powerful as the French — dysentery — was affecting some two-thirds of his troops. Many Prussians suffered so greatly that they could not even drag themselves to the latrines, turning their bivouacs into mephitic "shit camps." Of the 42,000 who crossed the French border, fully a fifth did not even make it to the site of the first major battle, and many of those who did could barely stand. But in a council of war held in the first week of September, French émigré officers accompanying the Prussians insisted that too much was at stake to wait. Peddling optimistic fantasies to match those of the Girondins, they depicted a French population just waiting to rise up against the Revolution and greet the invaders with flowers. After the fall of the fortified town of Verdun, despite a conspicuous lack of flowers, the Prussian king gave the order to march west.

When the news of the enemy advance arrived in Paris, the discrepancy between radical fantasy and military reality proved a frighteningly efficient generator of terror. If the French were as invincible as the

Girondins had claimed, then Verdun could not have fallen through any fault of the army but only through acts of treason, such as the one La- fayette had just committed. Rumors of conspiracies abounded, and in the first week of September, crowds of *sans-culottes* stormed the Paris prisons, dragging out all manner of suspected traitors. In the streets, a brutal, rapid popular justice was administered, with death sen- tences immediately following impromptu "trials." At least 1,100 prison- ers died, and the stories of bloodied, horrifically mutilated corpses piled high in fashionable streets immediately turned much of European opinion against the Revolution. The *Times* of London, once so favor- able to the changes in France, inflated the death toll to 12,000, de- scribed how "two legged Parisian animals" had dragged the mutilated corpse of Marie-Antoinette's former lady-in-waiting around Paris for two days, and compared the French to Goths and Vandals.

Yet it is in this same moment of Parisian hysteria that historians tra- ditionally detect the origins of a heroic Revolutionary "élan" that sup- posedly turned the tide of the war. It remains the official version of the story in France, as anyone can testify who has walked down the Boule- vard Saint-Germain in Paris and seen, near the rue de l'Odéon, the statue of the Revolutionary orator Georges Danton. A physically im- posing, rough-hewn figure, Danton made his reputation in the streets and political clubs of Paris, not the Assemblies, speaking off the cuff rather than from carefully crafted texts. So we have few records of his speeches. But carved on the base of his statue are the climactic words of his most famous one, delivered to the Assembly on September 2, 1792: "The bells that will ring are not a signal of alarm, but an order to charge against the enemies of the *patrie*. To defeat them, *Messieurs,* we need boldness, again boldness, forever boldness, and France is saved." (It is better in French: *"Il nous faut de l'audace, encore de l'audace, toujours de l'audace et la France est sauvée."*) Danton also demanded the death penalty for anyone who did not cooperate, although this part of the speech is quoted less often.

The Parisians certainly did respond with boldness, clamoring by the thousands to "rush at the enemies en masse." Even before Danton's speech, the Assembly had authorized another large-scale levy of volun- teers, this time drawn heavily from the *sans-culotte* lower classes. In Paris, the National Guard paraded in the streets, to the sound of can- non and drums, and raised 15,000 recruits in a single week. More volunteers flooded into the ranks after the speech. But this zeal had some-what mixed military effects. The *Times* did not altogether exaggerate in its tabloid description of the new recruits: "The army marching from Paris exhibits a very motley group. There are almost as many women as men, many without arms, and very little provision." Nor were other re-cruits much better. General François-Christophe Kellermann, com-manding the Army of the Center, wrote on August 23: "Most of these soldiers, without guns, ammunition packs, and dressed in the most pitiable rags, cannot be of the least use." In the wake of August 10, the government was barely functioning, to say nothing of being able to train, equip, and feed thousands of new soldiers who for the most part lacked any military experience. And they were out of time.

On September 20, 1792, this ragged French army met the Prussians at the battle of Valmy, twenty-five miles west of Verdun. It was a relatively small affair, and for sheer number of men killed, it would hardly deserve inclusion in books like Sir Edward Creasy's canonical *Fifteen Decisive Battles of the World,* alongside Marathon and Hastings and Waterloo. It did have the good fortune to be witnessed by a famous poet, Goethe, who accompanied the Prussians and claimed to have told his companions in its aftermath: "From this place, and from this day forth begins a new era in the history of the world, and you can all say that you were present at its birth." Historians rarely fail to quote these words. But Goethe wrote his account decades later, after the legend had already taken shape, and borrowed heavily from the descriptions of others while doing so.

Yet Valmy deserves its symbolic importance. In the campaign, both sides deliberately raised the political and military stakes alike in a way that directly foreshadowed the total war to come. The Prussians, as we have seen, threw everything into a march on Paris, hoping for a quick and decisive victory. They ran the risk, however, of giving the Revolu-tion a propaganda triumph and the opportunity to recover from its po-litical and administrative chaos. And the French too gambled at Valmy, in a manner that would have dismayed the generals of the Old Regime.

The key French gambler was the new general commanding the Army of the North after Lafayette's treason: Charles-François Dumouriez. An astonishing character, he had far more in common with Napoleon than with earlier French generals. Born in 1739, he came from a noble family

— but, like Napoleon, from the minor nobility that could never have hoped for high rank before 1789. Small, olive-skinned, and vivacious, he spent much of his twenties and thirties as an adventurer, offering his services as soldier or secret agent to any power that would employ him. He was friends with the military reformers Guibert and Servan and with Lauzun as well. He had grandiose ambitions.

The Revolution finally brought him the opportunities he thought he deserved, and he pursued them recklessly. In 1791, having gained a certain prominence, he entered into a dangerous political double game, promising his loyalty to both the Girondins and the king. It worked for a time, and in early 1792, Louis XVI named him minister of foreign affairs in the new Girondin government. In this capacity, he played a key role in designing France's initial offensive in Belgium. However, as tensions developed between the Girondins and Louis XVI, he ended up losing the confidence of both sides and was dismissed. It was abundantly clear by this time that Dumouriez cared about no political principle other than Dumouriez. But experienced military talent was scarce in France and became more so after August 10. When Lafayette crossed the lines to the Austrians, Dumouriez replaced him as general in chief of the Army of the North.

In this new position, he essentially invented a new and important type of French figure: the political general. Far more than their predecessors under the Old Regime, these generals actively maneuvered and schemed within the treacherous world of Parisian politics. In the field, they routinely took decisions about matters well removed from their military expertise, including the negotiation of treaties. They wrestled with civilian superiors for control of the strategic direction of the war and frequently exceeded their instructions. Dumouriez and Lafayette were the first examples, and many would follow; Bonaparte perfected the type. They typified, and helped advance, the dissolving of boundaries between politics and the military that characterized the age of total war.

Dumouriez's first weeks in command in August did not inspire confidence. First, he pushed the new transitional government in Paris to support his pet project, a renewed invasion of Belgium to distract the Prussians. With difficulty, the new minister of war, Servan, impressed on him the urgency of stopping the Prussians. Dumouriez finally agreed and took his army on a forced march toward the Argonne forest, which stretches out in a north-south line ten miles west of Verdun. Five narrow passageways led through the thick woods, and if the French could hold them all, they could hope to block the enemy advance, despite the fall of Verdun. But an Austrian general under Brunswick's command seized one passageway, and a French detachment fled from another. In the second week of September, the Prussians crossed through the Argonne, then regrouped on the main road leading west toward Paris.

Desperately, Dumouriez rushed to meet them. He also ordered the Army of the Center, commanded by the stolid, reliable General Kellermann, to rendezvous with his own Army of the North. On September 19, the two French forces met and spread out on both sides of the main road, near the little village of Valmy. Brunswick's army had already passed and stood to the west, closer to Paris. However, with the Prussian troops sick and loaded down with baggage (including the officers' typically mammoth aristocratic carriage-loads), Brunswick could not risk having his retreat cut off. He turned to fight, and Dumouriez turned to face him. In an ironic nod of history, no fewer than five present and future kings were present at this first great battle of the Revolutionary wars: Prussia's Frederick William; his son; the two younger brothers of Louis XVI, both of whom would reign after the fall of Napoleon; and their cousin Louis-Philippe, who would follow them between 1830 and 1848. Only the last, whose father had renounced his ducal title and embraced the Revolution, stood on the side of France.

By accepting battle at Valmy, Dumouriez was running an awesome risk. True, he had 52,000 soldiers, facing only 34,000 of the dysentery-racked enemy. But while the French artillery and cavalry were largely professional soldiers, half the infantry were new volunteers, and half of the others had enlisted since the start of the Revolution. A panic, of the sort that had hobbled Lauzun, doomed Théobald Dillon, and led to the desertion of the Argonne passageway, was a distinct possibility. With France's principal armies concentrated in a single spot, and with the road open to the west, such a panic might well have spelled the end of the Revolution.

The night of September 19–20, rain poured down, quickly soaking through the canvas tents and particularly affecting the miserable Prussians. At dawn, the weather finally began to clear, but the fields around Valmy had turned into plains of mud, into which soldiers sank up to their ankles. As the Prussians struggled to place their cannon, the mud covered their wheels in great, glutinous clumps. The battle itself started soon after dawn and quickly saw a decisive move by the French. On Kellermann's orders, Louis-Philippe seized the windmill that lay at the village's highest, most strategic point and placed an artillery battery in front of it.

The battle lasted all day, but for most of it, the fighting belonged almost entirely to the artillery. The seasoned French artillerymen had ample opportunity to demonstrate recent technological improvements in their art — especially the development of light, maneuverable, easily reloadable guns. As at Fontenoy, forty-seven years earlier, the wet ground minimized deadly cannonball ricochets. Instead, great gouts of mud sprayed up into the air wherever the balls hit. Goethe, behind the Prussian lines, later claimed that the balls passing through the air sounded like the humming of tops, the gurgling of water, and the whistling of birds. Such fanciful analogies did not occur to the soldiers themselves, but experienced French troops later reported that they had never heard so many cannon used so intensely. Overall, the day saw more than 20,000 cannon shots.

Finally, at noon, King Frederick William himself ordered the Prussian infantry into action, over the hesitations of the cautious Brunswick. With the precision brought by years of merciless drilling, the troops formed three columns, marched to within 1,200 yards of the height, and then reformed into lines to attack it. Behind them, fifty-four guns fired cannonballs and explosive shells at the French. It was the decisive moment. Kellermann, at the windmill, barely escaped death when a cannonball struck his horse. At two in the afternoon, a Prussian shell hit a group of French ammunition carts, setting off a huge explosion, and several ranks of French troops came close to fleeing in terror. Nearly all artistic representations of Valmy, including Horace Vernet's famous nineteenth-century tableau, depict this moment.

But the French held. The troops cheered every French shot and every Prussian miss with the cry "*Vive la Nation!*" They sang Revolutionary songs, particularly the bloodthirsty "*Ça ira*" ("it'll be all right"), which promised that the aristocrats would hang from lampposts, and the new favorite called the *Marseillaise*. The French could not compare with the Prussians for discipline, but their very indiscipline could give them a degree of bravura. In one anecdote from the battle, a general told a can-

Horace Vernet: *Battle of Valmy*

noneer that he was aiming too high, to which the man replied, "You'll see I'm not, General," and fired. The shot hit its target, and the general and soldier embraced, to shouts of "*Vive la Nation!*" Better substantiated is the story that, at the moment of the Prussian infantry attack, Kellermann stood up in his stirrups, held up his hat with its Revolutionary cockade on the end of his sword, and led his troops in shouts of "*Vive la Nation!*" Meanwhile, the French fired round after round at the Prussians. Even without ricochets, the balls wrought their usual, hideous carnage, tearing off heads and limbs. Finally, with his suffering troops still six hundred yards from the height, Brunswick called the attack off and ordered a retreat. "*Hier schlagen wir nicht,*" he remarked laconically. "Here we do not fight."

On the evening of September 20, the Prussian leaders retreated to a tiny four-room inn near the battlefield. Most of their troops remained outside, as a new, glacial rain began falling. Desperate to stay warm, they made bonfires of the poplar trees that lined the road. The next morning, they began to retreat toward Germany. On the French side, the soldiers were just as uncomfortable but in better spirits. One wrote home the next day: "Try to decipher my letter as best you can. I am sitting on the ground and writing with a piece of straw. We are sleeping on the ground like rats, and it's neither warm nor pleasant. But despite that, *ça ira, ça ira, ça ira.*"

The Duke of Brunswick had behaved in good, aristocratic, Old Regime style and did not think that he had been defeated. Rather than risking the lives of thousands of expensively trained soldiers, he had chosen the path of cautious withdrawal, the war of maneuver, and kept his weakened force intact. As a result, the "battle" remained more of a simple artillery duel with a few hundred casualties on each side and almost no real action by the infantry, apart from the aborted Prussian attack. The volunteer Gabriel-Nicolas Noël, now part of the Army of the North, quite accurately wrote home the next day that "the soldiers were, so to speak, simple spectators" at Valmy. But what Brunswick could treat practically as a nonevent, the French rapidly elevated to the level of myth. "Valmy, you do not explain it," the French statesman Georges Clémenceau would later remark. "You do not relate to other things, far or near . . . It is an aurora, an aurora of hope . . . a moral phenomenon."

Kellermann, with his decision to fortify the windmill and his patriotic theatrics, was the hero of the moment. When offered a peerage by Napoleon many years later, he chose the title Duke of Valmy. But the overall campaign belonged to Dumouriez. Napoleon himself later criticized Dumouriez for taking too bold a position at Valmy, adding caustically: "that ought to count for a great deal, too, for I consider myself, in war, the boldest man who ever existed." But the gamble had paid off. A regime and a Revolution had been at stake, and Dumouriez had committed all his forces to a single encounter. First the Prussians and then the French had therefore decisively abandoned the traditional cautious chess game of military maneuver. In its place, they had begun to develop a style of rapid movement and decisive clashes, linked to an acceptance of massive political risks. "They continually risked all to gain all," an admiring Russian officer wrote a few years later. In this respect, from Valmy to Waterloo, the road runs straight.

In Paris, even as the cannons were firing at Valmy, yet another assembly was meeting in the Manège: a National Convention, elected, for the first time ever in Europe, by universal adult male suffrage and including both Brissot and Robespierre among its 749 members. Although in theory only a temporary body, it would rule France for three years, during which there occurred what can only be called a tremendous compression of history: decades' worth of events crammed into an intense spiral of radicalization. I will mention only the highlights.

The day after Valmy, the Convention dissolved the monarchy and proclaimed France a republic. In the winter of 1792–93, the Convention put Louis XVI on trial, found him guilty, and condemned him to death by decapitation, courtesy of the new, supposedly humane execution device called the guillotine. The next spring, factional fighting almost tore the Convention apart, leading to the fall and eventual execution of Brissot and the Girondins. Throughout the country, rebellions broke out against the Revolutionary government. In the fall of 1793, the Convention's dictatorial, twelve-man Committee of Public Safety, increasingly dominated by Robespierre, began to direct what became known as the Terror, which claimed the lives of tens of thousands of people in Paris and far more in the provinces. The Convention also attacked Christianity, abolished the Christian calendar, and devised impossibly ambitious plans for a new social order. "And today, after eighty years have flowed by, every time that the Convention appears before the thought of a man, whatever he may be, historian or philosopher, that man stops and ponders. Impossible not to be attentive to this great passing of shadows." Thus Victor Hugo in his great novel of the Revolution, *Ninety-Three*.

The war intensified at an equally vertiginous pace. In the wake of Valmy, Dumouriez won a decisive victory over the Austrians at Jemappes. The French went on to occupy Belgium and much of the German Rhineland. But in 1793, the Netherlands, Spain, and Britain came into the fight alongside Austria and Prussia, pitting France against a broad European alliance. In March, Dumouriez met with a disastrous defeat at Neerwinden, again opening the possibility of the enemy armies' marching on Paris. Dumouriez himself tried to stage a coup d'état but failed and defected to the enemy, as Lafayette had done before him — yet another figure washed away by the Revolutionary tsunami. A desperate struggle for military survival had begun, and over the next year, the Convention worked convulsively to overcome its rapidly multiplying enemies. Under these conditions, even former advocates of peace, such as Robespierre, turned into remorseless advocates of military victory.

The French had distinctly modern military needs: muskets, cannon, well-trained officers, and willing recruits. Nonetheless, the classical dreams first cultivated by the Girondins continued to shape the conduct of the war in surprisingly important ways and remain one of the period's most significant elements. These dreams amounted to much more than simply a romanticization of the war effort — something that has occurred in most wars, ancient and modern. A significant section of the political leadership believed fervently in this fundamental truth: that the Revolution had transformed war as much as politics, making all the old military science designed for aristocratic commanders of mercenary armies largely or even totally irrelevant. The Revolution had, they believed, brought war back to its supposedly natural condition of an extraordinary break in human history, one that would forever transform the societies that fought it. And so they struggled to bring battlefield realities into line with their vision of an apocalyptic fight to the finish between heroic free citizens and miserable slaves.

There is a great irony here. Dreams inspired by a reading of the classics and grounded in a rejection of modern, scientific warfare were driving the French toward a sort of warfare we now see as quintessentially modern, characterized by unprecedented mobilization of the population and an abandonment of the regime of restraints that had prevailed before 1789: total war. In time, a group of leaders more sober and ruthless than Brissot and the Girondins would find practical, successful ways of "revolutionizing" war and of translating the classical dreams into reality. But along the way, other elements of the radical leadership implemented policies that were distractions at best and dangerously counterproductive pieces of fantasy at worst.

Take, for example, the durable belief that freedom gave "citizen-soldiers" something close to supernatural abilities, despite their lack of training and experience. In keeping with it, the Revolutionary armies refused to subject their soldiers to traditional disciplinary codes. Offenses were judged by panels of fellow soldiers, and instances of insubordination that would have put a World War I *poilu* up in front of a firing squad sometimes earned only mild reprimands or symbolic punishments, such as the shaving of eyebrows and hair. This leniency arguably had a powerful motivational effect, giving ordinary soldiers a sense of being truly equal citizens. But it could be taken to a reckless extreme. "Those who command and those who obey are equal," wrote the radical journalist Jacques Hébert.

Then there was the curious matter of the pike. As a weapon, it had not featured seriously on western European battlefields for a century. When used to impale the horses of oncoming cavalry, it still had some utility, but for soldiers to rely on it when facing companies of well-trained musketeers was little more than suicide. Nonetheless, the Girondins had blithely promoted it as the true weapon of free citizens before the war, and its cult continued to flourish even as the Prussians began their march. In September 1792, the department of the Marne, on the Prussians' route to Paris, ordered smiths and locksmiths to abandon all other work in favor of pike making. The sober military engineer Lazare Carnot, a future member of the Committee of Public Safety, argued for the distribution of pikes to the entire adult population. In a revealing exchange in the Legislative Assembly, a deputy criticized Carnot for holding up the pike-bearing Macedonians and Romans as models. France's enemies, the man sensibly observed, "do not carry out their assaults with slings and pikes, the weapons of savages, but with firepower directed by scientific calculations. The terrible art of war is far from its infancy." But another deputy immediately shot back, to huge applause: "If we have not been either Spartans, or Athenians, we should become them." In 1793, a Revolutionary general would complain that the government had burdened him with no less than "sixty thousand [pikes] that are good for nothing."

It could, perhaps, be said that pikes also had a psychological effect, since they were key symbols of the *sans-culotte* movement, which had adorned them with the severed heads of aristocrats on more than one occasion. And among an intellectual elite addicted to the study of "national character," the use of the pike was held to accord with the supposedly "impetuous" nature of Frenchmen, who would never tolerate laborious, Prussian-style drill. But other ideas advanced by Revolutionary leaders were simply delusional. Jean Bon Saint-André, a member of the Committee of Public Safety, argued enthusiastically for ignoring a century's worth of change in naval technology and relying on boarding parties, rather than cannon, to overcome enemy ships — as if the British would not blast into flotsam any French ship that failed to make utmost use of its artillery. Meanwhile, war minister Bouchotte argued that it made sense to promote officers solely on the basis of political orthodoxy. When Robespierre's younger brother protested the promotion of a young second lieutenant to the rank of adjutant general, he replied tartly: "The *sans-culottes* regard patriotism and republicanism as the most important talents." Bouchotte and several more of his deputies belonged to the radical faction led by the journalist Hébert, who wrote his newspaper, *Le père Duchesne,* in the voice of a foul-mouthed, blood-thirsty, and fanatical *sans-culotte* and fancied himself the spokesman of the popular movement. After the fall of the Girondins, this faction, the "Hébertists," did most to promote the classical dreams.

Although easy to ridicule, these dreams proceeded directly from the conviction that war was more a matter of morality than science or aristocratic art. From the Hébertists' viewpoint, as from that of the Girondins before them, there was in fact something distinctly *immoral* about fighting from a distance, with guns and cannon — about putting more faith in science and technology than in the strength and courage of individual warriors. Here, ironically, these men echoed quite precisely the lamentations of noble knights at the start of the gunpowder age while spurning the very technology that had saved the Revolution at Valmy. But they were anything but throwbacks to the age of chivalry. True, like the aristocratic officers of the Old Regime, they saw war as a test of the self. But unlike those officers, they did not see this test as involving primarily skill, precision, and elegance — they did not see it as a performance grounded in rigid mastery of the body and emotions. To the contrary, they saw it as a test of a person's very essence, his moral qualities and intentions. It was not a question of self-control but of self-expression. In the hallucinatory images of fighting at close quarters — weapons ripping into the flesh of enemies — can be seen the same exaltation of death, the same hope for "regeneration through blood," that ran through the Girondin war rhetoric of 1791–92. An allegorical *sans-culotte* print, entitled *500,000 Republicans Defending the Constitution,* illustrates precisely this fascination with elemental, physical combat. At the back, farthest from the action, are cannon, and below it stand soldiers with muskets, although mostly raised up, with their bayonets in the air, like pikes. But in the foreground, the weapons are pikes, swords, axes, and in the center, a *sans-culotte* swinging a huge, exquisitely primitive, wooden club.

Coupled with these images of sweaty masculine aggression were ones of sacrificial death and martyrdom. In September 1793, the Convention began to publish *Collection of Heroic and Civic Actions of French Republicans,* a periodical whose readers may well have numbered in the millions (it was distributed free to schools, political clubs, and the armies). Its editors liked nothing more than gruesome accounts of heroes doing their best to die bloodily for France. For instance:

500,000 Republicans Defending the Constitution

Félix Cabanes, grenadier in the Third Battalion of Gers, hit with a bullet in the thigh, at the camp in Sarre, fires twenty cartridges, and sustains the shock of the enemy cavalry. Taken to the hospital, he pulls out the bullet with his corkscrew . . . On 23 July, he receives a bullet wound on the back of the head . . . but fires two hundred cartridges, and kills six Catalans with a knife. On 23 August, a cannonball falls at his knees and buries him with earth, while another . . . makes a deep gash in his right side; at the same instant a poisoned bullet penetrates his hat, gouges out an eye, and remains lodged in the right eyesocket. Carried to the hospital, he falls into a state of asphyxia that makes him seem dead. They are ready to bury him when suddenly he cries out: "Wretch, you want to bury me alive! I still have some blood left to shed for my country!"

The Convention itself played host to a steady parade of the atrociously mutilated (over a hundred altogether): soldiers without arms, without legs, with terrible chest wounds, even one who had lost the upper jaw, nose bones, eyes, and eye sockets ("none of us would refuse glory at the price it cost you," Carnot declared to him, unconvincingly).

Most spectacularly, a virtual cult of martyrdom developed around two very young volunteers — Joseph Bara and Agricol Viala — who had been killed by Counter-Revolutionary rebels. The report of the thirteen-year-old Bara's death reached the Convention in December 1793, and Robespierre praised it as a perfect example for French youth. On cue, writers rushed to produce speeches, stage plays, and poems commemorating the boy. The painter Jacques-Louis David left an astonishing, unfinished painting of the dying Bara. It bears little relationship to the actual circumstances of the boy's death, and the general who first reported the case later protested: "I think he should be shown as he was when he received the final blows, on foot, holding two horses by the reins, surrounded by brigands and replying to [them]: 'You [fucking] brigand, give you the horses . . . ? Certainly not!" David's figure, naked, androgynous, unmarked, and serene neither conveys the story of the real Bara's pluck nor tries to evoke the horror of the real wounds paraded by soldiers on the floor of the Convention. Rather, it associates sacrificial death with a deeply sensual, disturbing image of beauty and purity, turning it into nothing less than an object of desire. As the poet Augustin Ximenez wrote at the time: "It is beautiful to perish." *Il est beau de périr.*

The fantasies had one final, disturbing aspect. Just as martyrs were to

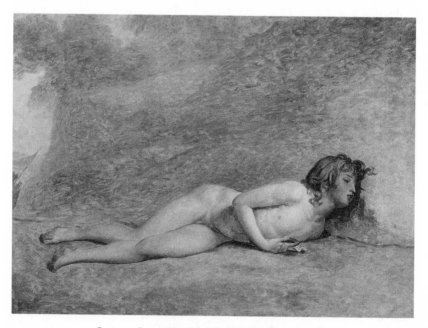

Jacques-Louis David: *The Death of Joseph Bara*

be exalted and envied, enemies — moral monsters — were to be utterly abhorred and eradicated. Once the war began, not only did the rhetoric of a "war to the death" intensify, it also was joined by a ferocious outpouring of hatred against anyone who dared take up arms against France. They were damned as "sanguinary hordes," "barbarians," "vipers," "monsters." The English, who posed the greatest longterm threat to France and whose own revolutionary heritage made their enmity look like betrayal, came in for the worst of this abuse. "National hatred must sound forth," thundered Bertrand Barère, a member of the Committee of Public Safety, in 1794. "Young French republicans must suck hatred of the name of Englishman with their mother's milk . . . [The English] are a people foreign to Europe, foreign to humanity. They must disappear." Orators throughout France called for the "extermination" of the English, and the Convention formally endorsed the idea when it issued a decree forbidding French commanders from giving quarter to English soldiers. "Only the dead do not come back to fight again," Barère and Carnot both remarked. True, when another deputy earlier proposed sending assassins to kill British prime minister Pitt, the members shouted him down in horror. In this instance, at least, the warfare of the late eighteenth century seems more restrained than that of the early twenty-first. Still, the Convention seemed ready to approve mass murder.

Historians often dismiss the significance of this exterminationist rhetoric, noting that unlike in the cases of military discipline or the pike, it had very little real impact on the armies. In practice, they observe, French forces largely ignored the "take no prisoners" decree. The story even circulated of soldiers who received orders from visiting deputies to kill prisoners, only to retort that the deputies would have to do the deed themselves. The deputies might denounce the fraternity of men at arms as an aristocratic sham, but commanders in the field knew perfectly well that their men would be the ones to pay the price, in the form of enemy revenge, for shooting prisoners.

The rhetoric does matter, however, for it shows just how completely the French state had now rejected the older regime of limited war. "War is a violent state of affairs," Lazare Carnot commented laconically. "It must be waged to the utmost." Robespierre went even further, invoking the high court of history beloved of the *philosophes*. In a draft for a new declaration of rights, he wrote: "Those who make war on a people to

halt the progress of liberty and destroy the rights of man must be attacked by all, not as ordinary enemies, but as assassins and rebel brigands." In defending the "take no prisoners" decree, he frostily insisted
to the Committee of Public Safety that between free men and the
henchmen of despotism, there could be no common ground: any notion of treating the enemy as an honorable adversary was simply absurd. Robespierre was now, strikingly, casting the war in religious terms
as "a clash of proselytisms." But after all, he and his radical allies believed that any means were justified, for this was to be the last war. "Prepare for universal peace," insisted Carnot, even as he was working frantically to strengthen France's military capacities.

The clearest sign that the Old Regime norms no longer held did not
involve the treatment of foreign prisoners but foreign territory. Under
the Old Regime, it had been understood that any formal transfer of territories, and any modification of the political and social systems in
them, would wait until a formal peace settlement and then proceed, at
least in theory, by mutual agreement. But soon after Dumouriez's victory at Jemappes in 1792, the Convention signaled that it would no
longer respect the rights of enemy powers, declaring that it would
"grant fraternity and aid to all peoples who wish to recover their liberty"
— that is, encourage revolution throughout Europe. True, it soon
backed off from this breathtakingly ambitious program and then, less
than a year later, explicitly renounced "philanthropic ideas" in war altogether. From now on, it stated, French armies would "behave towards
the enemies of France in the same way that the allied powers are behaving towards us, and will apply the ordinary rights of war." But this
change of direction did not imply that France would return entirely to
traditional practices. In fact, France soon began to annex conquered
Belgian and German territories, without waiting for a treaty. The full
gamut of Revolutionary reforms followed there, including attacks on
religion, the elimination of "feudal" privileges, the abolition of nobility
— and, most important, the introduction of a state apparatus capable of
squeezing the territories for the war effort.

The rejection of Old Regime norms, it should be emphasized, was
not entirely limited to the French, even if they articulated the point
most forcefully. Across the Channel, English public opinion exploded
in outrage at the "take no prisoners" decree, yet prominent English pol-

iticians had themselves demanded much the same policies even before the outbreak of hostilities. "The mode of civilized war will not be practiced," wrote Edmund Burke as early as 1791, "nor are the French . . . entitled to expect it . . . The hell-hounds of war, on all sides, will be uncoupled and unmuzzled." With France and Britain still at peace in 1792, the British diplomat Lord Auckland had called for executing French prisoners and dispensing with "the courtesies of the age." Thankfully, British commanders greeted such advice with even less enthusiasm than did their French counterparts.

Still, it was in France that the rhetoric was fiercest. It was also in France that the government made the greatest effort to spread the apocalyptic vision of war to the general population. It subsidized the writing of stage plays, which were performed in major cities and army camps. Six thousand copies of a stage fantasy about the worldwide triumph of the *sans-culottes* were sent to the Army of the North, along with 400,000 copies of the new constitution and well over 1,000,000 copies of Hébert's newspaper *Le père Duchesne.* These numbers dwarf anything previously seen in French history (and furthermore, each copy had multiple readers). And the efforts were not limited to the literate. "The people still sing much more than they read," the composer Thomas Rousseau reminded the war minister; in response he received a commission to send the army 100,000 songbooks. Eyewitnesses agree that French soldiers sang continually: on marches, in camp, in battle:

> *Courons en masse mes amis*
> *Pour écraser nos ennemis*
> *Que ces lâches guerriers,*
> *Sortent de nos foyers,*
> *En mordant la poussière,*
>   *Au joli son,*
>   *Au joli son,*
> *En mordant la poussière,*
>   *Au joli son,*
>   *Du canon.*
>
> *La patrie attend de nos bras*
> *La mort de tous ces scélérats . . .*

[Qui] mordront tous la poussière,
  Au joli son, etc.

Let us run en masse my friends
To crush our enemies
May those cowardly warriors
Leave our land
Biting the dust
  To the lovely sound,
  To the lovely sound
Biting the dust
  To the lovely sound
  Of the cannon

The fatherland expects from our arms
The death of all those wicked men . . .
[Who] will all bite the dust
  To the lovely sound, etc.

This song, just one of hundreds from the period, appeared in 1794 in the newspaper *The Evening in Camp.* The song was not very good, to say the least. But it was simple, easily understood, and sung to a popular tune, and the editors could reasonably expect that within days, it would be warbled, off-key but enthusiastically, from the Channel to the Pyrenees.

It is frustratingly difficult to say how soldiers and the general population reacted to this propaganda barrage. Revolutionary newspapers reported that they greeted it with wild enthusiasm, but then, such descriptions were propaganda themselves. It is easy enough to find the songs and newspaper articles echoed in soldiers' letters, but the soldiers knew that their letters could be opened and read. Still, it is missing the point to think that such propaganda "succeeded" only if it turned its readers and listeners into obedient zealots. Simply through its amplitude, through the incessant repetition of its images of death, martyrdom, and extermination, the propaganda drove home a set of simple but potentially transformative ideas. This war, it was emphasized, was indeed different from anything that had preceded it. It was extreme, all-encompassing. It would not end with a compromise treaty but with utter victory or defeat. The fact that twice, in the summers of 1792 and 1793, there seemed nothing to prevent allied armies from taking Paris, gave credence to the message. And in this way, the propaganda prepared the population for the drastic, unprecedented demands of the real war effort.

In 1793–94, the French state finally began to take more effective steps to translate the classical dream of total mobilization into reality. Two men in particular embodied the shift. First was Carnot, "the organizer of victory," a skilled mathematician and engineer who had once advocated the traditional tactics of maneuver and siege against innovators, such as Guibert. Carnot knew the business of war better than did any member of the Convention, but he too had drunk of the classics and was not immune from the temptations of fantasy. As a young officer in Arras at the end of the Old Regime, he had participated, along with Robespierre, in a literary society that gathered the sort of young professionals who devoured Rousseau and Voltaire (it provided a setting, bizarre in hindsight, for these two future leaders of the Terror to exchange comic verse and read love poetry aloud). At the start of the war, it was not entirely surprising to find Carnot one of the officers advocating the return of the pike to European warfare.

Much more of a fantasist was Louis Saint-Just, who once famously declared that "the world has been empty since the Romans." Born the son of a nonnoble army officer in 1767, he spent his adolescence and early twenties feverishly seeking a literary and political reputation. Among his more regrettable achievements was a long erotic poem called *Organt*, which included scenes of rape and bestiality. Elected to the Convention at only twenty-five, he made his reputation in passionate speeches calling for the death of Louis XVI and quickly attached himself to Robespierre, who became his idol and brought him into the Committee of Public Safety. Saint-Just's cold insistence on purging and executing those Revolutionaries who diverged from his rigid standards of classical virtue earned him a reputation as the archangel of the Terror.

But it was Carnot and Saint-Just, backed up by the other members of the Committee, who directed the war effort in the crucial years 1793–94. Using savage methods to overcome daunting obstacles, they managed in an incredibly short time to mobilize and redirect the resources of the French nation to the overriding goal of military victory. The three key elements to their success were manpower, political control, and the reconstruction of the army. With these in place, the total mobilization promised since the debates of 1791–92 would start to take palpable form.

Manpower was obvious. As the reformer Dubois-Crancé had observed back in 1789, with the French population of 28 million dwarfing that of other western European states, France had the theoretical ability to overwhelm enemies with ease. The trick was actually getting men into the army. The levies of volunteers in 1791 and 1792 did little but make up for the shortfalls caused by the disintegration of the old royal force. And so, in early 1793, the Convention tried again, this time ordering France's departments to supply an additional 300,000 men. It was a move toward conscription, and it met with widespread disobedience, even revolt. It did probably succeed in raising 150,000 men, but this number was not sufficient. At the start of August 1793, a moment of maximum peril for the infant Republic, deputies from the Convention in the northern departments called for total mobilization. In Paris, Hébert picked up the cry, and spokesmen from across the country demanded that the Convention formally order a general rising, a *levée en masse.* On August 23, the Convention complied: "From this moment until our enemies will have been driven from the territory of the Republic, all Frenchmen are permanently requisitioned for service in the armies."

The *levée* had its own strong elements of fantasy. Although generally seen as a prelude to the age of conscripted mass armies, the measure in fact looks back to the ancient past as much as to the future. In calling for it, Hébert tellingly exhorted men to arm themselves with pikes, swords, scythes, and cooking spits and for women to heat oil and sulfur to pour on the enemy. The text of the decree, drafted by Carnot and rewritten by Barère, owed more than a little to classical reverie:

> The young men will fight; married men will forge weapons and transport supplies; women will make tents and uniforms and serve in hospitals; children will turn old linen into lint; old men will have themselves carried into the public squares to rouse the courage of those who fight, to preach hatred of kings and the unity of the Republic.

In practice, admittedly, the Convention did not bother much with lint-spinning children and managed to avoid scythes and cooking spits entirely. Instead, it quickly transformed the high-flown language into a deadly serious summons to every adult male between the ages of eighteen and twenty-five to report for military service. By doing so, it succeeded in raising another 300,000 men, which brought the size of France's armed forces up to well over 750,000, far larger than those of any of its adversaries.

The Convention still faced huge obstacles in equipping, training, and deploying these masses. In September 1793, for instance, the principal French armory was producing muskets at a rate of only 9,000 per year. But the Committee of Public Safety acted decisively to address the problem, setting up a workshop to improve the precision of machine tools, which increasingly allowed for interchangeable parts — a crucial innovation given the tendency of musket parts to fail under battlefield conditions. By October 1794, five thousand munitions workers were making guns at the rate of 145,000 per year, and a single Parisian factory was producing 30,000 pounds of gunpowder per day.

Meanwhile, it was becoming clear that levels of education and physical fitness among the new recruits did not come close to matching those of the volunteers of 1791, while their sheer numbers overwhelmed the army's capacity to make use of them. But again, with surprising speed, the government adapted to the new conditions. As early as January 1793, one of the best military thinkers of the period, Philippe-Henri Grimoard, had written that a democratic France, "supplementing art by numbers," would need to abandon "aristocratic" notions of sophisticated maneuvering and simply direct overwhelming strength against particular points. The idea initially met with little favor among the generals. But it was taken up by Carnot, who applied it in person at the battle of Wattignies, on October 15–16, 1793, after the British and Austrians had frittered away their chance to take Paris during the summer, and it had immediate success.

Wattignies was a crucial moment. At first, the French forces under General Jean-Baptiste Jourdan made little progress against the better-trained Austrians despite two-to-one superiority in men. However, the French detected a weak spot, and the next day, over Jourdan's objections, Carnot insisted on concentrating the French overwhelmingly against it. Three marching columns advanced, with most of the troops initially kept out of range of direct enemy fire, to prevent them from panicking. Instead, in a tactic that would become characteristic of the Revolutionary armies, a smaller number were first deployed as skirmishers, to snipe at and weaken the enemy. Then the bulk of the army was brought forward all at once, in a rapid, disorganized, but successful charge, to the sound of Revolutionary songs. "Fifty thousand savage beasts, foaming at the mouth like cannibals, hurl themselves at top speed," wrote a French *émigré* officer about such tactics.

The battle was not as richly symbolic as Valmy, but it mattered nearly as much to the survival of the Revolution. Within months, Carnot and the Committee on Public Safety were issuing decree after decree urging the new tactics on all French forces: "The general rules are always to act *en masse* and offensively"; "Be attacking, constantly attacking"; "Stun like lightning and strike like thunder." The use of skirmishers greatly increased. Staff officers started to divide the armies into divisions of 5,000 or more soldiers — great mobile masses of men. Victories followed. They did so, however, at a terrible cost, for the wild infantry charges entailed huge French casualties. In the two years 1794 and 1795, according to the best available research, 200,000 French soldiers died. But thanks to the "requisition," the Convention easily replaced them, and the generals adjusted with cold pragmatism to the change. As the historian Gunther Rothenberg writes laconically: "soldiers had been expensive, now they had become cheap." The painters and poets might dream of heroic self-sacrifice, but in practice, victory demanded the more grisly and prosaic tactic of feeding young men into the pulverizing hell of enemy artillery and musket fire.

Carnot's presence on the battlefield illustrates the second element of the Convention's winning formula: tight central control of the war effort. Again, this was not something the idealists had envisioned. The persistent radical dream had been that virtuous patriotic intentions would automatically generate desirable outcomes, without any need for rigid discipline and order. "No battle plans, no order in the army, no officers, no generals, no superiority of rank: everyone is a soldier, and they all fight as heroes." This was how the Girondin playwright Olympe de Gouges imagined the victorious French armies at Jemappes, and it was, of course, absurd. Not only did the soldiers need battle plans and generals, but also the generals themselves needed coordination, direction, and all the support they could get from Paris. This work of organization was not going to come from a general staff, which did not exist, and it was not going to come from the war ministry. The apparatchiks who prevailed there were more than willing to compile thick dossiers on the political reliability of the officer corps (on Ney and Hoche, future Marshals of Napoleon: "worthless"). But they did not provide much real assistance to the military.

Instead, the real work was done by the Committee of Public Safety and by members of the Convention sent into the field as all-powerful "representatives on mission." Here is where Saint-Just stood out. In late October 1793, after Wattignies but with the military situation still perilous, he came with another representative to the Army of the Rhine in the Alsatian city of Strasbourg. He delivered inspirational rhetoric, but he also delivered the Terror. Between his arrival and early March, a military tribunal in the city handed down twenty-seven death sentences to soldiers and officers, mostly for the unforgivable crime of failure. Saint-Just imposed a huge forced loan on the city, and when he realized how many troops lacked proper shoes, demanded that the citizens bring in their own. With the rasp of the guillotine in his words, he quickly collected 17,000 pairs, along with 21,000 shirts. The methods were brutal but effective and helped the French to chase enemy forces out of Alsace by the end of the year. "Saint-Just appeared not as a representative, but as a king, as a God," Jules Michelet would later write. Throughout France, the years 1793–94 saw the execution of no fewer than 84 generals and the dismissal of 352 others — a performance incentive if ever there was one.

The following spring, Saint-Just accompanied the Army of the North in a decisive campaign that removed the allied threat to French territory. When the commander of the Austrian garrison at Charleroi asked to negotiate, Saint-Just haughtily insisted on unconditional surrender. That would dishonor the garrison, the officer protested. Saint-Just's chill reply echoed Robespierre's warning against battlefield fraternization: "We can neither honor you nor dishonor you, just as you have not the power to honor or dishonor the French Nation. There is nothing in common between you and us." In late June, as the observation balloon hovered above the battlefield of Fleurus, Saint-Just galloped among the troops, urging them on. In the fusion of military and dictatorial political authority that he represented, there can be glimpsed a hint of the Napoleonic future.

The political control exerted by the Convention was decisive to the war effort. But its efforts would have been useless without a final reconstruction of the army. In 1793, political purges completed the decimation of the officer corps, leaving nobles accounting for barely 3 percent of it. A motley group was taking their place: predominantly former soldiers and noncommissioned officers of the old royal army, as well as former civilians elected in the new volunteer battalions. Among both groups, representatives on mission detected a frightening abundance of inexperience, ignorance, and incompetence, often compounded, in the case of the old soldiers, by illiteracy. In Marseilles, officers of a volunteer battalion included a mason, a locksmith, a miller, a carpenter, a cooper, a tailor, a stocking maker, a machinist, and an apothecary. And among such officers, some of the most competent actively shunned promotion, seeing the deadly price that failure in a higher rank might entail. In early 1793, battalions of the old royal army remained separate from — and often in dangerous rivalry with — battalions of new recruits.

The Convention, however, worked frantically to address these problems. In February 1793, the old line army and the new volunteer battalions began, slowly, to "amalgamate" into a single force. And as this occurred, the Convention began to show a distinct preference for placing literate, experienced former soldiers from the line army in leadership positions. In other words, Robespierre, Saint-Just, and Carnot were opting decisively for competence over ideological purity. Heroic martyrs were all well and good, but above all, France needed men who knew how to fight. The Committee also began to restore harsher military discipline. The Parisian artilleryman Bricard noted the results of the shift in August 1794, when six drummer boys from his battalion were found pilfering. The two oldest were shot, one crying out piteously for his mother, while the younger four were made to watch.

The great beneficiaries of these newly practical attitudes were the newly promoted officers. In the years 1791–94, thousands of men from relatively modest backgrounds, who never could have dreamed of high rank under the Old Regime, achieved it, at astonishingly young ages. Lazare Hoche went from sergeant in 1792 to general in chief of the Army of the Moselle a year later, at age twenty-four; François Marceau, a common soldier turned attorney's clerk, rose through the National Guard and became general in charge of a division in 1793, also at twenty-four. Guillaume Brune, a proofreader and failed poet turned revolutionary journalist, entered the army through the National Guard and made general in 1793, at age thirty. The average age of new generals in the 1790s was just thirty-three. Among them was the intense, literarily inclined young Corsican officer named Napoleon Buonaparte.

These new soldiers were, needless to say, of a very different stamp from the aristocrats who had commanded the French armed forces before 1789. They did not have courtly manners, and many, like Napoleon, spoke French with a heavy provincial accent. They preferred uniforms to fancy civilian dress. They did not have elaborate estates or sumptuous Parisian mansions (yet!). Once they entered the army, it usually became their entire life. They saw themselves as professionals devoted to the task of war, not as members of a privileged order of the state who could move seamlessly from court to campaign and back again. They did not spend hours a day practicing dance steps. In a little-noticed but significant development, in early 1792, the dancing master at the military school at Brienne was dismissed and left destitute.

Much of the rest of this book is concerned with these new officers and the bloody trails they blazed across the European continent and beyond in the years after 1794. Before turning to this later period, however, one final episode of the French Revolution deserves attention. For during the Terror of 1793–94 and the events I have just described, the idea of total, physical extermination of France's enemies did not remain comfortably theoretical, as in the case of the "take no prisoners" decree. In one theater of operations, it turned all too piercingly real. The enemies in question, however, were not English or Austrian or Prussian, and the fields of battles were not in Belgium or the Rhineland. Instead, the torch of total war was first applied to a region of France itself: the Vendée.

5

The Exterminating Angels

The hirelings of despotism will be vanquished by the exterminating angel of liberty.

— GEORGES DANTON, 1791

You must decide in advance about the fate of the women and children I will encounter in this rebellious country. If they must all be put to the sword, I cannot carry out such a measure without a decree which relieves me of responsibility.

— LOUIS-MARIE TURREAU, 1794

January 28, 1794, Châteaumur (department of the Vendée).
   Vincent Chapelain is nervous. The thirty-six-year-old mayor of this tiny hamlet in western France, he has been trying for months to restore order in the wake of horrendous civil war between the forces of the Revolutionary government and rebels fighting for the French monarchy and the Catholic Church. It has not been an easy task, for a rebel army remains active nearby, and the memories of savage killings on both sides are still unbearably raw. Nonetheless, Chapelain has managed, in his own words, to "patriotize" the local district, where he is the chief remaining representative of the Republic. He has successfully confiscated hundreds of guns, recruited a National Guard unit to maintain order, and put local government back to work. He has also removed church bells from more than twenty churches, to be melted down and recast into armaments for the national war effort. Now, he believes, it is time for forgiveness and an end to the violence.

But more violence is coming, in the form of columns of Republican soldiers — "blues" — who are crisscrossing the Vendée, with orders to kill all remaining "brigands" and make the region uninhabitable for them. A few days before, Chapelain himself played host to one detachment of two hundred soldiers, giving out food and wine and providing beds for those who got too drunk to stumble back to their bivouacs. Another detachment passed through a village five miles away and shot twenty-five young men who belonged to the National Guard, as well as two local officials wearing the official sash of the Republic. The blues claimed that the men were really rebels. And now, yet another detachment has arrived in Châteaumur itself.

Chapelain, as mayor, goes out to meet their commander, General Louis Grignon, a forty-five-year-old career soldier whom the Revolution has vaulted to the rank of brigadier general. Still recovering from a leg wound inflicted by the rebels the previous fall, Grignon has given his troops orders to burn every building they come across and to kill every human being. "I know there may be a few patriots left in this area," he has allegedly told them, "it doesn't matter. They must all be sacrificed." Now he screams, "Who are you?" at the trembling Chapelain. The mayor lists the various offices he holds and cites the authority of the former commander in the region, General Antoine-Marie Bard. Grignon fiercely replies that he doesn't recognize any local offices and doesn't recognize General Bard, either. From somewhere, a voice cries out, "The mayor is a suspect!" and that is enough: Grignon gives orders for Chapelain to be shot. At the last minute, however, a soldier recognizes the mayor as someone who stayed loyal to the Republic all through the war. Chapelain himself frantically insists that far from helping the "brigands," he has helped hunt them down. Finally, Grignon relents. By this point, however, his blues have already killed eight of Chapelain's guardsmen and ransacked his house.

Grignon then makes Chapelain guide the blues down the road to a neighboring village, La Flocelière. Chapelain offers to provide a list of the leading rebels there, in the hope of limiting the violence, but the general waves him off. When the column arrives, the soldiers run amok, killing six men and pillaging the houses. "They raped the women," Chapelain will later recount, "thirty of them taking turns on just one; another didn't escape despite being sixty years old, with a disfigured eye." Over the course of the afternoon, thirty more people are killed, including six men who had valid passes but the bad luck to be passing through on the road. Grignon then moves on to the town of Pouzauges, where he has dinner in the local château. Several young women are being held prisoner there, and Grignon and his staff invite them to coffee. Later, Chapelain hears soldiers boasting that the women have been raped and shot — all except "the pretty one," to whom the officers had taken a fancy. Finally, on January 31, Grignon and his column move out of the district. "We burned and broke heads like usual," he reported to his superiors in a laconic report. But Chapelain would remember that "for two and a half miles, you could follow the column as much by the trail of bodies that they left as by the light of the fires they had lit."

Civil wars are the cruelest wars. By definition, neither side recognizes the legitimacy of the other (at least at the start): there are no honorable adversaries, only traitors. By definition, the fighting takes place on home territory, and by definition, friend and foe are difficult, if not impossible, to tell apart. As we have seen, even during the century of relatively restrained warfare that preceded the French Revolution, civil war took a terrible toll on several areas of western Europe: notably, the Cévennes mountains of southern France after the Protestant Camisard revolt of 1702–4, and the Highlands of Scotland after the Jacobite rebellion of 1745, with thousands dead in each case.

The Vendée, however, occupies a different dimension of horror. According to the most reliable estimates, from 220,000 to 250,000 men, women, and children — over a quarter of the population of the insurgent region — lost their lives there in 1793–94. The principal campaign against the Vendée's "Catholic and Royal" peasant armies, which lasted from March to December of 1793, set a new European standard in atrocities. Then, at the start of 1794, the Republican general Louis-Marie Turreau sent twelve detachments of two to three thousand soldiers each marching across the territory in grid fashion, with orders to make it uninhabitable. These "hell columns" burned houses and woods, confiscated or destroyed stores of food, killed livestock, and engaged in large-scale rape, pillage, and slaughter. In some cases, they killed only suspected rebels. In others, as at La Flocelière, they liquidated men, women, and children indiscriminately, including "patriots" who had remained loyal to the Republic, on the grounds that no one still living in the Vendée could truly be loyal. In the port city of Nantes, the Republican authorities devised appalling new methods of mass murder to eliminate the "brigands" more efficiently and to reduce stress on the killers. Most hideously, they lashed thousands of prisoners into barges and lighters, which they then towed out into the Loire estuary and sank. The Vendée was "the most horrible civil war that ever took place," remarked Turreau — the man who did more than anyone else to make it so.

Ever since the Revolution, the Vendée has divided the people of France like nothing else except Vichy. From the very start, Counter-Revolutionaries transformed it into a virtual religious icon: a symbol of pure, simple faith; of resistance to Revolutionary evil; of martyrdom. In 1939, the Catholic Church even began a process of beatification for several hundred children allegedly slaughtered in the twin villages of Les Lucs at the end of February 1794. Today, monuments to the Vendéan generals, to crucial battles, and to Revolutionary atrocities dot the region, in a manner that recalls Southern U.S. commemoration of the Confederate "lost cause." Writers favorable to the Revolution, meanwhile, while deploring "excesses," have insisted that horrors were committed on both sides and that the insurgents did, after all, side with France's enemies during wartime. Historians remain so bitterly opposed that one of the best short books on the subject, by Claude Petitfrère, has a bibliography with separate sections for pro- and Counter-Revolutionary works.

In the past twenty years, the Vendée has achieved new, worldwide prominence thanks to a distinctly contemporary and disturbing twist in the arguments. In 1985, a native of the region, Reynald Secher, published an incendiary book on the war entitled *A French Genocide*. He presented little original research, wrote sloppily, and claimed a conservative total death toll of 117,257 with absurdly exaggerated precision. But the book appeared at a moment when the French were confronting the legacy of their collaboration with Nazi genocide, and far-right politicians seized with delight on Secher's implicit message that the First Republic, not Vichy, had been France's worst, most criminal regime. The 1980s were also a time, however, when historians across the political spectrum were taking a more critical view of revolutions in general, and Secher's allegations struck a deep and resonant chord with many readers beyond France. Simon Schama and Norman Davies repeated

them uncritically in best-selling books, and the idea of a Vendéan genocide became widely accepted. In 1993, no less a figure than Alexander
Solzhenitsyn traveled to Les Lucs to inaugurate an elaborate new monument to the Vendée and its victims. He and its builders ignored careful new research demonstrating that the supposed massacre in the villages had not, in fact, taken place — at least not on the scale and with
the degree of premeditation that had been claimed.

Was the Vendée a genocide — a deliberate and systematic attempt to
exterminate a distinct ethnic population? Secher was not, in fact, the
first to say so. As early as 1795, the proto-Communist agitator Gracchus
Babeuf accused the Revolutionary government of "turning the scythe of
death against the totality of the Vendéan race" and called its representative in Nantes, Jean-Baptiste Carrier, "populicidal." But Babeuf made
the charge as part of a demented conspiracy theory, and his book was
rightly ignored at the time. Secher has used "genocide" as a rhetorical
trump card, designed to expose detractors to the charge of minimizing,
or even justifying, the original crime. But it is no insult to the memory
of the victims to recognize that in this case, the word is misplaced.

To begin with, the Revolutionaries did not consider the Vendéans a
distinct ethnic group. The word "race," which appeared frequently in
Revolutionary rhetoric, did not yet have its modern biological connotations and meant little more than "group." Today, we shiver on reading
the Revolutionary radical Bertrand Barère's call for "measures to exterminate this rebel race" (August 1, 1793), but the context makes clear
that he was discussing only armed rebels, and two sentences later, he
insisted that their families be treated with compassion. Several of
Turreau's columns *did* deliberately slaughter avowed "patriots," as at La
Flocelière, but not because they believed that a person was indelibly
stained by Vendéan birth. To the extent that they carried out these killings systematically, it was either because they believed no true patriots
were left in the Vendée after nearly a year of war or because they
thought the murders a military necessity. Significantly, Vendéan "patriots" *outside* the rebel province were never persecuted on account of
their birth, as one would expect had a true racial theory been operating.

Furthermore, as the historian Jean-Clément Martin has demonstrated, the massacres committed by Turreau, Carrier, and others did
not belong to any sort of master plan of extermination. True, Revolutionary leaders rarely missed an opportunity to call for the "destruc-

tion," "extermination," "pulverization," or even "depopulation" of the Vendée. But they made such threats against *most* of their enemies, including aristocrats, royalists, "refractory" priests, and the entire populations of Austria and England. Jules Michelet once quipped that Barère "exterminated the royalists twice a week from the speaker's platform." If the Jacobins turned particularly apoplectic on the subject of the "inexplicable Vendée," it was because they saw it as the keystone of a much larger structure of Counter-Revolution, *all* of which deserved destruction. The sanguinary language is not at all without significance, but there is still a world of difference between Barère's overheated speechifying and, for instance, the 1942 Wannsee conference at which Nazi officials methodically planned the extermination of European Jewry. On three or four occasions, a handful of Revolutionaries speculated about killing on a large scale with poisoned brandy or even poison gas, but there is no evidence that anyone ever tried to implement these ideas.

The Convention *did* call for the physical devastation of the Vendée: woods and thickets burned or cut down, crops destroyed, livestock seized, women and children deported from the rebel region. It also declared all rebels captured in arms or wearing the white cockade of the Vendéan armies to be outlaws, subject to summary execution. Some of its agents ordered such executions on an industrial scale (two thousand people in the town of Angers alone), whereas the Committee on Public Safety told others "to take whatever measures they deem necessary." But when Turreau requested a decree explicitly authorizing him to kill women and children, the Committee hesitated for weeks and then issued only an ambivalent endorsement of his "intentions." Arguably, they were giving tacit approval. Still, the politicians in Paris, distracted by their own ferocious political battles, were reacting to facts as they developed on the ground, not systematically planning mass murder. Many deaths were the result of the independent action of local "revolutionary tribunals." Turreau himself later wrote that his columns acted "without any authorization." In the Vendée, conflicting orders from the Committee, the radical war ministry, and numerous "representatives on mission" produced administrative chaos, in which military officers often acted on their own initiative and with virtually no coordination.

Although Martin and his colleagues have refuted the theory of "genocide," they have been less successful in advancing their own explanation for the Vendée's gushing tide of blood. There remains no cogent, reli-

able overview that accounts for the war's extraordinarily gruesome nature. Babeuf, in his delirium, strikingly compared the Revolutionary
forces to the Spanish conquistadors in Mexico and Peru: "There . . . it
was said to people who had never heard of Jesus the Galilean, *acknowledge your God or die.* Here . . . those who never developed ideas of liberty are admonished, *believe in the Tricolor, or feel my dagger.*" The element of religious or ideological fanaticism was indeed crucial. But then,
it was present in the Camisard Revolt of the early eighteenth century as
well. What made the Vendée so much worse?

The difference was total war. It was not simply that the Vendée took
place in wartime (so did the Camisard revolt, so did the 1745 Scottish
rising). It was that it took place in the context of a kind of warfare
whose scale had little or no precedent, whether in the mobilization of
population and resources, the ambitious and ill-defined war aims, the
demonization of entire enemy populations, or the threats to the French
leadership in case of defeat. It was a perceived war to the death, in
which, as we have seen, parts of the Revolutionary leadership were beginning to romanticize combat in a new and sinister way. In this sort of
war, the threats of "extermination" dealt out on all sides were in fact
meant in deadly earnest. Enemies of the Revolution, whether Vendéan,
aristocratic, Austrian, or English, were perceived as an existential evil.
They were inhuman monsters. They were barbarians condemned by
the high court of history for a failure to accept the blessings of Revolutionary civilization. They were obstacles to the triumph of liberty and
therefore to the coming of a final, universal peace. They did indeed deserve death. In its very theory, warfare was turning exterminatory.

On most of France's battlefields during 1792–94, the practice did not
live up to this theory. But in the Vendée, three exceptional conditions
combined to produce a convergence between them. First, after December 1793, the Revolutionary forces in the region did not face serious
military opposition and therefore could act without the possibility of
reprisals that elsewhere helped limit atrocities — for instance, staying
the hands of French generals ordered to execute British prisoners. Second, the experience of civil and guerrilla war, with massacres on both
sides and the constant threat of ambush, generated powerful states of
hatred and fear that allowed soldiers to overcome their natural human
repugnance for slaughtering helpless prisoners and civilians.

Third, for a brief but decisive period in late 1793 and early 1794, control of military operations in the Vendée, to the extent that it existed, passed partly into the hands of the Revolutionary faction known as the Hébertists, after Jacques Hébert, editor of *Le père Duchesne*. As we saw in the previous chapter, the Hébertists were the Revolutionaries who combined the most fervent dedication to classical fantasies of total war with the least actual military experience. They were also those most likely to demand that insufficiently victorious or sanguinary generals be sent to the guillotine. Turreau followed what was to a great extent their plan and acted under their influence, while fearful, as he later put it in a self-justifying memoir, that "the least refusal — what am I saying, the least negligence — would have led to the scaffold." It was thanks to these factors that in the Vendée, the rhetoric of total war was fully translated into blood-streaked, exterminatory fact.

The Vendée did not even exist as a distinct region before 1789. It was born out of the war, in the western coastal regions south of the Loire River, in parts of the old royal provinces of Poitou, Anjou, and Brittany. In 1790, the National Assembly abolished the provinces and created eighty-three new "departments," one of which bore the name "Vendée" after a hitherto insignificant river. The insurgent region centered on it, but spilled over its borders and included a variety of terrains, economies, and patterns of political activity.

Like much of western France, this region vibrated to a basso continuo of rural tension throughout the early years of the Revolution. In 1789, the wretchedly poor peasants had demanded better roads and lower taxes. The Revolution gave them mostly higher taxes and largely excluded them from the land boom brought about by the confiscation and sale of Church property. In many of the more isolated areas, the Revolution's subjection of the Catholic Church to secular state authority cut deep into the tissue of communal life, with villages enraged at the dismissal of long-serving priests. In reaction, bubbles of anxiety and rage burst angrily on the surface of rural life. The most serious rioting took place after the fall of the monarchy in the fall of 1792, when crowds of peasants armed mainly with pikes and scythes occupied several towns in the region, leading to fighting that left up to a hundred dead.

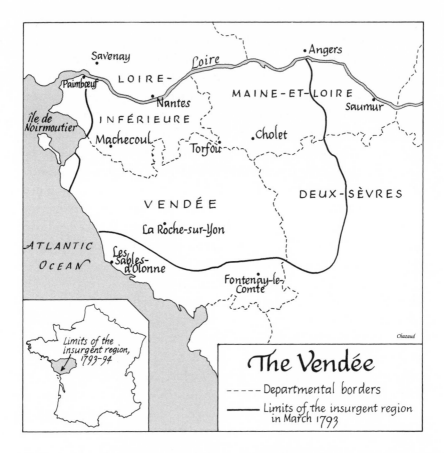

Savenay

Loire

•Angers

Paimbœuf

LOIRE-

Nantes

MAINE-ET-LOIRE

Saumur

île de
Noirmoutier

INFÉRIEURE

•Cholet

Machecoul

Torfou

VENDÉE

DEUX-SÈVRES

La Roche-sur-Yon

ATLANTIC

OCEAN

Les
Sables-
d'Olonne

Fontenay-le-
Comte

Chazaud

Limits of the
insurgent region,
1793-94

The Vendée

----- Departmental borders

——— Limits of the insurgent region
in March 1793

Then came the draft. In February 1793, as we have seen, the Convention called for a levy of an additional 300,000 troops. With supplies of
willing volunteers largely exhausted, local officials across the country
prepared to draw lots for conscripts. But in several regions, already
shuddering with discontent over taxes, the religious struggles, and the
execution of the king, the idea of sending more young men off to die
for the Republic touched off explosions. In hundreds of *communes,*
crowds of peasants, often numbering in the thousands, descended on
villages and towns, armed with whatever sharp implements and firearms they had to hand. They made a frightening spectacle. In Machecoul, in the Vendée, the sound they produced reminded seven-year-old
Germain Bethuis of a tempest on the sea; looking onto the road that led

to town, he mistook the rioters for a "loud, black cloud." Local officials saw them as irrational, murderous brutes and fled, if they could. The revolt had begun, with the demands of total war abroad sparking what would soon turn into total war at home.

What were the peasants hoping to accomplish? We have few accounts of the revolt that have not passed through a thick filter of hindsight and mythology, but it seems that to a large extent, the rebels were following a familiar, and not at all irrational, script. For centuries, the "jacquerie" — insurrection against nobles, town dwellers, and especially tax collectors — had been the last resort of France's perennially impoverished rural classes. Fear, rage, and exaltation could make them murderous and susceptible to the millenarian messages of charismatic leaders and "prophets." They expected savage repression by the government, and their leaders could hope for little other than a minimum of torture before execution. But the revolts also served a purpose, for once the initial wave of exemplary retribution had passed, the government often quietly granted some of the peasant demands. The 1793 rioters in western France initially remained true to this pattern and, at least at first, hoped principally for the end of conscription and the return of long-serving priests, not the overthrow of the Revolution.

They sought out leaders among local nobles, who mostly, at the start, showed little initial enthusiasm for the cause. True, several belonged to a secret Counter-Revolutionary organization, the Breton Association. But almost by definition, the most virulently Counter-Revolutionary nobles had left France by this time, to fight for the émigré armies. The Marquis de Bonchamps insisted correctly to the peasants of his district that a revolt would bring them nothing but pillage, slaughter, and misery; Louis-Célestin Sapinaud de la Verrie tried his hand at homely metaphor: "You want to dash an earthen pot against an iron pot. We'll be shattered." In several cases, the frustrated peasants replied by offering their nominees a choice between the roles of leader and victim. Initially, they did not even trust Sapinaud with a horse, and as for the former naval officer François-Athanase Charette, soon to be one of the most famous of the Vendéan commanders, the peasants literally dragged him out from underneath his bed.

Poorly armed, untrained, and reluctantly led, the peasants nonetheless had sheer numbers on their side, and in hundreds of towns and villages, they easily overcame the National Guard — which consisted mostly of poorly trained, inexperienced countrymen like themselves. The army, which had helped maintain rural order earlier in the Revolution, was now mostly off fighting on the frontiers. In some towns, the rebels murdered Republican officials and sympathizers, and in Machecoul, a district official turned rebel named René-François Souchu condemned hundreds of them — including Germain Bethuis's father — to death. The prisoners were tied together at the arms to make "rosaries," marched to the edge of the moat of the local château, and shot or stabbed. When the blues recaptured Machecoul a few weeks later, Souchu rushed out to greet them, wearing a red liberty cap, claiming he had been held in the town against his will — but to no avail, for he was quickly denounced and killed.

In Paris, news of the revolt caused consternation and was treated as proof of yet another gigantic conspiracy against the Revolution. Charged with informing the Convention of the situation, André Mercier du Rocher, an administrator from the Vendée, witnessed a hallucinatory scene in which the ultra-Revolutionary Marat waved in his colleagues' faces a model of a dagger he proposed distributing to the population: "Look carefully at this blade!" he repeated, as if uttering an incantation. "How sharp it is! How cutting!" Barère told him that the deputies had more urgent business to take care of, Marat accused Barère of treason, and the two almost came to blows. The Convention soon passed its draconian measure allowing for summary execution of rebels.

As soon as it could muster regular military units, the Republic did start, in most regions, to bring the revolts in the west under control. In Brittany, Republican troops routed peasants at the bridge of Kerguidu and retook the city of Châteaubriant, executing ninety-six rebels in the process. In other areas as well, experienced soldiers slowly and painfully began to douse the brushfires provoked by the conscription decree, which continued principally in the form of low-level but dangerous guerrilla campaigns known as the Chouannerie. But the Republic was stretched too thin. Even as the insurrection smoldered, the disaster of Neerwinden exposed northern France to Austrian attack, and the widening of the war to include Britain and Spain placed further demands on an overburdened, undermanned, and inexperienced army. In the Vendée, the result was disaster.

The heart of the Vendée, known as the Bocage, was nightmarish terrain for an army. The modern visitor, seeing its well-paved roads, broad fields, and lush meadows, will get little sense of what the land looked like at the time of the revolt. Moderate temperatures and plentiful rains made it inordinately fertile, but a multitude of small hills, ravines, and streams left much of it unsuitable for farming, and fields lay fallow for years on end. In place of crops, there sprouted an infinity of brightly flowering gorse, heather, thistles, and small trees, while fields were lined with ditches topped by large, strong, prickly hedges. Thanks to the saturation of the soil, streams and roads flooded at every heavy rain. The perpetually muddy, deeply rutted roads were rarely wider than six feet or so, making it almost impossible for carts and wagons to turn around. Military convoys rarely traveled more than seven miles a day. Mercier du Rocher remembered the Bocage as "enchanted . . . teeming with fruit trees . . . and birds of every sort," but the Republican general Jean-Baptiste Kléber damned it as "a deep, dark labyrinth," and Turreau bitterly remembered hedges that resembled "palisades around a fort." He called the land "an asylum of brigandage and crime."

On March 19, 1793, General Louis-Henri-François Marcé, a veteran officer and hero of the Seven Years' War, marched north from the town of Chantonnay, deep into the Bocage. He was accompanied by 2,400 mostly raw recruits, 9 cannon, and 2 members of the Convention. In the afternoon, as he stopped to repair a small bridge, a large crowd of armed men came into view on a nearby height. Marcé opened fire with his cannon, only for one of the deputies to countermand the order, claiming that he had heard the men singing the *Marseillaise.* Were they friendly? By the time a scout confirmed they were not, it was dusk. Marcé decided to pitch camp and fight in the morning. But the Vendéans, led by the once-reluctant Sapinaud and armed with guns seized from government arsenals, had taken advantage of the confusion to sneak into the thick hedges that lined the narrow route. At nightfall, as Marcé's men started to set up tents and light campfires, a blaze of musket shots erupted at the front of his column, followed by screams from the attackers. Marcé frantically tried to move up additional battalions, but the confusion was overpowering. His young soldiers, crushed together on the road, could see little except the flash of gunfire and hear little except the detonations and screams. The Vendéans shot at will into the struggling mass; not surprisingly, the blues panicked and fled, trampling each other and yelling *"sauve qui peut!"* ("every man for himself!"). The next day, Marcé had no choice but to gather up the remnants and retreat all the way to La Rochelle, on the coast, outside the Vendée, having lost at least five hundred men.

Marcé's defeat, a classic example of guerrilla warfare that the Vendéans would successfully copy many times (and that Marcé himself would expiate at the guillotine), marked the first great turning point of the rebellion. As Jean-Clément Martin has argued, despite later mythologizing, there was nothing uniquely reactionary about the Vendée, compared to many other areas of France. But in the Vendée, because of Marcé's defeat, the Republic lost control. On March 21, with the blues in retreat, the various irregular peasant forces began to coalesce into a Catholic and Royal Army, some 20,000 strong, known as the "whites." It was led mostly by former noble officers, including Charette, Sapinaud, Bonchamps, and the dashing twenty-one-year-old Henri de La Rochejaquelein. But there were also commoners, including a tall, brooding, deeply pious carter named Jacques Cathelineau, who became the Vendéans' first commander in chief. The whites later formed a High Council, which claimed authority over the insurgent region in the name of the dead king's young son (whom the Convention was holding as a prisoner in Paris). It declared all Revolutionary laws invalid, started to issue its own paper money, and reinstituted obligatory tithing to the Catholic Church.

Even after their early victories, the Vendéans never adopted real military discipline. They remained essentially a force of untrained peasants who obeyed orders when they wished and left when necessary to take care of families and farms. They had no uniforms other than squares of white cloth adorned with a red heart and cross. Even after capturing several cannon, they rarely managed to stand in formal, pitched battles against the Republican forces. They preferred ambushes in the broken-up and overgrown terrain and sudden, frenzied charges to the sound of their own rebel yell: "Rembarre!" Victor Hugo later wrote: "Invisible battalions watched and waited. These unseen armies snaked under and around the republican armies, leapt out of the earth in an instant only to disappear, bounded up numberlessly and vanished, everywhere and nowhere, an avalanche one moment, dust the next."

What sustained them, above all, was religion. Witnesses described them marching in solemn silence, telling rosary beads, stopping for prayers, and crossing themselves before charging into combat. Priests accompanied them and before battles gave out remissions of punishments for sin. In battle sermons, the priests cited biblical passages that supposedly predicted the triumph of their cause. "Let us march. The God of battles is fighting with us. What can the blasphemers do against Him?" General Cathelineau, quite possibly in conscious imitation of Joan of Arc, spent hours prostrated before church altars and became known as the "saint of Anjou." At times, the wave of faith turned frankly superstitious. In the town of Cholet, the whites seized an ancient, intricately engraved, but still-functioning cannon cast for Cardinal Richelieu more than 150 years before. The peasants covered it with ribbons, dubbed it "Marie-Jeanne," and declared that it would always lead them to victory. Perhaps the strangest episode of all concerned a former priest named Guyot de Folleville, whom the Republic had conscripted into the army. Taken prisoner by the whites in the town of Thouars, he showed them a sacred heart emblem and claimed to be a secret envoy from the pope, who had ordained him Bishop of Agra. His captors not only believed him but also made him president of the High Council and did not take action even after real envoys from the pope refuted his story. He became a fixture of the army, riding among the peasants in a semblance of episcopal robes, followed by a priest carrying his miter and crosier.

In the spring of 1793, this amazingly unlikely army won several victories, capturing guns and ammunition each time, and held off the Republican forces. Then, in early June, it received an unexpected windfall. In Paris, the Girondins were purged from the Convention (after armed *sans-culottes* had insisted on the point by surrounding the Manège with cannon), and in the resulting uproar, several major cities across France revolted in their turn against the government. These new rebels considered themselves loyal Revolutionaries and had little love lost for the Vendée. The turmoil, however, left the blues distracted and obliged again to divide their forces at precisely the moment when Austrian and British armies seemed poised to descend on northern France. On June 9, the Vendéans captured Saumur, a major town in the Loire valley, some eighty miles inland, killing at least 1,500 Republican soldiers and taking 8,000 prisoners. It was the Republic's moment of greatest peril.

But the general unrest in the country does not explain why the blues performed so badly against untrained peasants. Many other factors contributed to the debacle. The Convention, trying to douse several fires at once, starved the Vendée of troops, and those they did provide were all too often ill-trained volunteers who tended to desert and to panic under fire. And the blues suffered from the same problems as their counterparts in Belgium and Germany: chronic shortages of food, clothes, shoes, and tents; newly promoted officers incapable of restraining their unruly, hungry men. The various commanders quarreled incessantly with one another and with the deputies from the Convention who hovered around them.

All these problems were shockingly obvious to the general who arrived to take command of the Army of the Coasts of La Rochelle at the end of May. It was none other than Lauzun, who once again, though not a pivotal figure himself, had gravitated to the epicenter of the changes in warfare, as if drawn by an irresistible magnetic force. "I have found unimaginable confusion," he wrote from the Vendée to Bouchotte, the minister of war, "a heap of men it is impossible to call an army." The success of the whites, he continued, was due entirely to "the incoherent and insufficient measures which have been partially taken against them . . . The cause of these misfortunes is the neglect and abandonment of all organization, of all military principles." He complained bitterly about the lack of food: "We cannot secure a day's rations in advance, and if we attempted a march we should inevitably have no bread."

I have already discussed one other factor at work. Just a few years before, the French army could have drawn on considerable experience fighting with or against irregular troops, such as the Vendéans. Many of its officers and men had taken part in such operations in Corsica in the late 1760s or in India in the early 1780s or alongside American revolutionary forces. But the decimation of the officer corps and the overhaul of the ranks effectively left the army to rebuild itself from scratch. Lauzun, with his extensive colonial experience, was now the exception, not the rule, and the Vendée itself became the matrix against which *future* colonial wars were set. When French forces found themselves bogged down in Haiti in 1797, Lazare Carnot quickly labeled the Caribbean territory "the colonial Vendée."

The whites, then, had important initial advantages. But they also suffered from a limitation experienced by nearly all guerrilla armies: an inability to operate far from their base. From Saumur, in June, they could have followed the Loire east without opposition toward Orléans, just seventy miles south of Paris. Napoleon later commented: "Nothing would have stopped the triumphant march of the royal armies. The white flag would have been flying from the steeples of Notre Dame before the Armies of the Rhine could have rushed home to save their government." But Charette and Cathelineau hesitated to lead their men into hostile territory so far from home. Instead, they turned west. On June 18 they took the Loire valley town of Angers and a week later laid siege to the major port city of Nantes. A victory there might itself have proved decisive in the long run, for it would have opened up western France to British arms. But in Nantes, the whites faced a more competent enemy than before: five thousand experienced soldiers, backed up by five thousand National Guards, under the command of the tough and seasoned general Jean-Baptiste Canclaux. A badly coordinated white assault on June 29 failed, and Cathelineau, the "saint of Anjou," was mortally wounded. Discouraged, the peasant armies withdrew south, back into the hedgerows of the Vendée.

The battle of Nantes marked the last time the Vendéans posed a serious threat to the Revolution. During the summer, the Catholic and Royal Army, now under the command of aristocratic generals, won several more victories and held off the blues but did not venture outside the insurgent region. Meanwhile, the heavy, grinding machinery of national mobilization was finally being swung around, slowly but remorselessly, to crush them. On August 1, the Convention formally adopted its literal scorched-earth policy against the Vendée. It also voted to send a new force to the region: the French garrison of Mainz, in the Rhineland, which had surrendered to the Prussians during the general military crisis of the spring of 1793 but had been allowed to return home. Desertion was steadily draining the whites, who had scarcely 40,000 fighting men left by the end of the summer (the blues would soon have close to 75,000 in the region). The whites did deliver a significant drubbing to the former Mainz garrison on September 19, but they could not put off the inevitable. On October 17, a large blue force confronted the Vendéans in the town of Cholet, twenty miles south of the Loire, and decisively routed them. If "war" is defined as a conflict between armies, then the war of the Vendée was over. The slaughter, however, had only just begun.

By the battle of Cholet, the Catholic and Royal Army was already less a military force than a frightened city on the march. Wives, children, and parents of the remaining combatants had flocked to its ranks for safety, as had thousands of priests, swelling its numbers to well over 60,000. And they were right to do so, for by the fall of 1793, the massacre of noncombatants was becoming a common currency that the blues and whites traded back and forth in a gruesome inflationary spiral. It had started with the "rosaries" of Machecoul but continued incessantly thereafter. In the spring, after taking the town of Montaigu, the whites allegedly filled a 240-foot well with bodies of slain "patriots." In September, the blues retaliated, allegedly throwing no fewer than four hundred victims, many of them still alive, into the mammoth well of the Château de Clisson, which belonged to one of the Vendéan generals. Throughout the insurgent region, both ordinary courts and special "revolutionary tribunals" handed down so many death sentences that a shortage of guillotines developed, and towns drew up schedules to share the limited supply. Both sides routinely put captured enemy soldiers to death. Each side justified its conduct by reference to the other. The Republican general François-Nicolas Salomon put the matter brutally on June 17: "Since this is a war of brigands, we must become brigands ourselves. We must, for a time, forget all military rules."

None of this behavior represented much of a novelty in the history of European civil wars. But it quickly generated the sort of ferocious, unforgiving hatreds that can turn ordinary soldiers into mass murderers. On the side of the blues, the Revolutionary authorities did everything possible to maintain and intensify these emotions by relentlessly publicizing white atrocities in newspapers, pamphlets, songs, plays, and popular prints. In early October, even as the blues were gaining the upper hand, Parisians strolling down the Boulevard du Temple could stop to take in a "vaudeville opera" entitled *The Brigands of the Vendée,* which featured predictably bloodthirsty rebels who pillaged, burned, and slaughtered innocent patriots. Lest the audiences fail to draw the proper conclusions, one of the heroes spelled it out: "Fall on them without pity. Don't spare a single one." In the Vendée, the blues, who lived in constant fear of ambush or sabotage, hardly needed to be persuaded.

But it was after Cholet, and the end of the serious military threat, that atrocities and war crimes started to coalesce into something even worse. It began with the extraordinary flight of the defeated Vendéans. Fearful of returning to their homes, which had now fallen largely under blue control, the vagabond bulk of the Catholic and Royal Army took the desperate decision to flee north, across the broad Loire, toward the English Channel. In skiffs and makeshift rafts, some 80,000 men, women, and children crossed in less than two days. Regrouping on the other side, they began what has been dubbed the "Virée de Galerne," or the Northwind Turn: a forlorn attempt to raise Normandy and Brittany, and to open a French port to the British navy, which had been seeking one since France and Britain had gone to war in the spring. Lacking even basic supplies, the huge shapeless column spread out for miles on either side of its route, scavenging for food. Marie-Louise-Victoire Donissan, the widow of a Vendéan general, remembered that on some days, she and her family survived on onions dug out of the ground. On other days, they ate unripe cider apples that caused violent diarrhea and even dysentery. This twenty-one-year-old *grande dame,* a marquise who had spent her childhood at the palace of Versailles, now found herself clothed in old blankets tied together with string and covered with lice. It was an irony not lost on the blues, one of whom later remembered that "it was a curious spectacle to see these great ladies, who once had barely managed to shuffle along without the help of two tall lackeys, now trudging through the mud." Among the Vendéan leaders, one wrapped himself in a lawyer's robe; another, with a Turkish costume and turban taken from a theater on the route.

The provinces north of the Loire did not rise en masse, and the increasingly hungry, frantic hordes had no choice other than a desperate lunge for the coast. In the middle of November, they arrived at the small Norman port of Granville, just north of Mont-Saint-Michel. But on the dismal gray waters, there were no British sails — not surprising, since contact between the Vendéans and the British had been sporadic, and the fleet had not been told of the rendezvous. Worse, Granville was tenaciously defended, and the exhausted whites could not capture it. Reluctantly, they turned around and headed back toward the Loire. Scarcely thirty miles offshore, just beyond the chill gray horizon, lay the British island of Jersey, utterly unreachable.

The sick, snuffling army now stumbled back in agony through country it had already stripped clean. Frigid autumn rains poured down incessantly, soaking the Vendéans' tattered clothes and slathering them with mud until the brown-gray mass of humanity seemed to dissolve into the brown-gray fields of western France. But increasingly, the palette was enlivened by scarlet showers of blood. The blues had initially pursued the Vendéans with the same incompetence they had shown throughout the campaign, but slowly, their attacks started to take a toll. And, as the Parisian playwright had instructed, they showed no mercy. One commander in particular distinguished himself in ferocity. François-Joseph Westermann was a forty-two-year-old minor noble who had once served in the entourage of the king's brother. Turned Revolutionary, he fought at Valmy and became an aide to Dumouriez, a connection that almost cost him his life after the general's defection. Thereupon, he acted as if he could prove his loyalty only through extreme rashness and brutality. During the summer of 1793, he took a major Vendéan stronghold but lost it again in a surprise attack, with the whites killing or taking prisoner nearly all of his six thousand men. Put on trial for negligence, he told his judges that "we can only defeat the Vendée by destroying it" and won acquittal. Pursuing the Vendéans north of the Loire, he would make a show of stripping off his jacket, rolling up his shirtsleeves, drawing his saber, and leading his men in bloody charges, after which he would dash off a letter to Paris, boasting of the death toll.

After a month of agonized flight, the decomposing Vendéan forces marched into the city of Le Mans on December 10, meeting with minimal resistance. Witnesses claimed they had left so many bodies behind on their route that the air had turned unbreathable for miles around. In the city, they greedily took whatever food, clothing, and shoes they could find. Two days later, the blues approached from the southeast. Westermann, eager to take credit for a victory, attacked prematurely, made little headway, and started frantically beating his own troops with the flat of his sword to keep them from retreating. But the next day, General Kléber arrived with 15,000 more soldiers. In the central marketplace, the remaining Vendéan cannon blasted them with canister, but the blues brought up artillery of their own and set about reducing the area to rubble. The outnumbered, exhausted whites broke and fled.

Now, the killing reached a new level. The brilliant young general François-Séverin Marceau stopped a "hideous slaughter" only by beating the call to arms, but not all the authorities on the scene approved. Three deputies from the Convention wrote back to their colleagues with satisfaction: "Heaps of bodies are the only obstacle the enemy can put in the way of our troops. The massacre has been going on for fifteen hours." A Republican official pursuing the Vendéan survivors on the road to Laval reported that the road was littered with corpses. "Women, priests, monks, men and children, all were put to death. I took no prisoners. I did my duty, but there is pleasure in avenging one's country." Westermann gloried in the bloodshed as well:

> Without stopping for a moment, I followed the enemy on the road to Laval . . . the brigands fled into the woods, abandoning the army, but the citizens of the area tracked them down and brought them back by the dozens. All of them were hacked to pieces. I harried them so closely that the princesses and marquises had to abandon their wagons and splash through the mud.

One Republican reported seeing a hundred naked bodies stacked neatly on the side of the road, reminding him of dead pigs waiting to be salted at the butcher's shop. Where rebels fell into the hands of local Revolutionary tribunals, death sentences followed with implacable speed.

Over the next eleven days, the survivors of the Vendée covered another 150 miles, with Marceau and Westermann hounding them. Approaching the Loire, thousands attempted to cross back to the Vendée on boats, rafts, even barrels. Thousands more were chased into nearby marshes, to be shot or to drown. The remnants of the Catholic and Royal Army made a futile last stand near the village of Savenay, on December 23, and were annihilated. Westermann again made sure that the Parisian authorities knew the full extent of his merciless zeal, in a letter that has become justly notorious:

> There is no more Vendée, citizens. It has died under our free sword, with its women and children. I have just buried it in the marshes and woods of Savenay. Following the orders you gave me, I have crushed children under the hooves of horses, and massacred women who, these at least, will give birth to no more brigands. I do not have a single prisoner with which to reproach myself. I have exterminated everyone.

In the two months since Cholet, more Vendéans had been killed than would be put to death in Paris throughout the entire period of the Terror. And the slaughter was still not close to ending. Turreau's columns had not yet marched.

What explains the ferocity with which the blues hunted the pitiful remnants of the insurrection? The desire for revenge against Vendéans they considered guilty of massacres, ambushes, and the torture of prisoners certainly counted for a great deal. Equally important was the conviction, born out of the experience of guerrilla war, that *all* Vendéans were potentially soldiers. The Vendéans themselves had not hesitated to boast that their entire population had gone to war. Several women who fought openly for the whites became folk heroes. But in early October, Antoine-François Momoro, a delegate from the radical Paris municipal government, turned this fact against the whites:

> This war does not at all resemble the one the allied powers are waging against us . . . It is against an entire population that we must fight . . . We can therefore consider as enemies the entire population of the area, including the women who serve as spies, and even as soldiers where necessary — even as cannoneers, for several have been killed in their ranks, and blown to pieces, from which their disguised sex was later recognized.

Three deputies from the Convention employed the same deadly logic: "*All* the present inhabitants of the Vendée are dedicated rebels; it is the women, and the girls and boys older than twelve who are the cruelest. They practice unspeakable cruelties on our volunteers. Some of them have been cut to pieces, and others burned, and it is women who are committing these atrocities."

If the blues had motive, they also had opportunity. After mid-October 1793, the remnants of the Vendéans could still overwhelm lightly defended towns and cities, but they could no longer hold their ground against a serious Republican force. The blues could therefore act without fear of major reprisals. And as military historians have long observed, armies never pose a greater threat to prisoners and noncombatants than when they have won a major engagement, are shuddering with pent-up tension and fear, and have their enemy at their mercy. One Republican official took possible reprisals so lightly that he invited more of them: he ordered white prisoners shot at the approach of the enemy, because the whites "would then do the same," and Republican soldiers would not dare surrender.

Still, if these conditions help explain the bloodshed, they are not sufficient. For one thing, they have characterized portions of almost all modern guerrilla insurrections. What ultimately distinguished the Vendée was the politics — and not simply the general background of the Revolution. What also mattered was the influence of a particular radical faction during the Revolution's most astonishing, exalted, and perilous stage, under conditions of total war. True, we cannot talk of Revolutionary factions the way we might talk of modern political parties. French Revolutionaries loathed the very idea of party — of anything that implied division within the fraternal body politic — and groupings in practice were often slippery and elusive. Nor can we talk of any particular constellation of figures absolutely dominating the Vendée, for as Turreau himself remarked, a principal characteristic of the Revolutionary army was "incoherence." Nonetheless, during the crucial period between the battle of Nantes (June 1793) and the end of Turreau's "hell columns" (March 1794), a rough pattern is visible.

A key figure in the Vendée in the summer of 1793 was a man we met briefly in a previous chapter: Charles-Philippe Ronsin. Born in 1751, he served briefly in the army in his youth, rising to the rank of corporal, but gave it up to write a series of mediocre stage plays, all of which went unperformed. Physically imposing and given to tremendous rages, he became one of the "poor devils" mocked by Voltaire, flitting resentfully around the margins of a literary world that had shut its glittering doors to him. As with many figures out of what Robert Darnton has called the "literary underground of the Old Regime," his anger found hot expression in the Revolution. In August 1789, he published a demented pamphlet claiming that a debauched, nymphomaniacal Marie-Antoinette had tried to assassinate her husband. He also joined the radical Cordelier Club, political home of Danton and Marat. As he became politically prominent, Paris theaters finally started to stage his plays; in 1791, he had particular success with the play that called precociously for war on all Europe in the name of universal peace. After the fall of the monarchy, he became part of the circle around Hébert and went to work for the war ministry, which the Hébertists controlled.

Sent to the Vendée as a civilian agent in May 1793, Ronsin devoted as much time to political purges as to the war effort. He conceived a particularly savage hatred for Lauzun, and for several weeks, the two fell into a complex, intense bureaucratic duel. It expressed far more than simply personal rivalry. On the one side was the angry, foul-mouthed former private soldier and playwright, a creature of the political clubs, who fluently spoke the language of mass murder. Later in his career, Ronsin would insist that in the city of Lyon, which had also rebelled against the Convention, only 1,500 of the 140,000 inhabitants deserved to live. On the other side stood the infinitely suave, courtly duke and peer of the realm, habitué of Versailles, equally at home on campaign and in aristocratic boudoirs. Lauzun was capable, even in the white heat of the Vendéan war, of writing to the Committee of Public Safety a letter in which there breathed something of the old spirit of aristocratic restraint: "Here, Frenchmen fall under the blows of other Frenchmen; the villages which we are despoiling are our own, and the blood which is flowing is ours as well; these deluded men will cease to be our enemies as soon as they recognize their errors." Needless to say, it had no effect.

In the battle between Ronsin and Lauzun, in short, two opposing cultures of warfare came face to face. But there could be little doubt as to the outcome. The playwright accused the duke of losing Angers through incompetence: "[his] conduct is really appalling . . . His tardiness . . . his persecution of the best patriots, and above all, his position as a *ci-devant* [former noble] give cause to fear that he will allow our army to perish." The Hébertists in the war ministry supported the charge, and soon, Lauzun was recalled to Paris and placed under arrest. A few months later, the public prosecutor issued a predictable indictment: "Born in the caste of the formerly privileged, having passed his life at the heart of a corrupt court . . . he only put on a mask of patriotism . . . to deceive the nation." On December 31, Lauzun went to the guillotine. Meanwhile, Ronsin's allies rewarded him with a transfer into the army and the most rapid promotion in French military history. A captain on June 30, he rose successively over the next four days to the ranks of major, lieutenant colonel, colonel, and brigadier general. Napoleon himself had a slower time of it.

Lauzun's fall formed part of a campaign in which Ronsin and his allies, during the summer and fall of 1793, fought to take control over the war effort in the Vendée. In September, they managed to replace Canclaux, the defender of Nantes, with a *sans-culotte* nonentity named Jean Léchelle, who soon received a new, unified command over all the Republican forces. Léchelle in turn gave way to an unstable former goldsmith who encouraged soldiers to disobey the orders of insufficiently radical officers. Ronsin also made generals of two actor cronies who had seen only stage battlefields, not real ones. But for the Hébertists, as we have already seen, political orthodoxy had an absolute primacy over military experience. When appointing Turreau supreme commander in November, war minister Bouchotte instructed him to dismiss any officer "who is not recognized as Republican or totally devoted to the popular system." Professional soldiers, such as Canclaux and Kléber, could not conceal their disgust for the Hébertists. After one particularly humiliating defeat, Léchelle openly exclaimed: "What did I do to deserve to command such cowards?" One of Kléber's wounded men replied: "What did we do to deserve being commanded by such a *Jean-Foutre?*" (roughly, "fucking bastard").

The soldier had a point. Ronsin had little discernible military talent, and his protégés proved complete disasters in the field (of course, so did some of the professional soldiers). They favored abstract, unworkable plans of battle and the reduction of the Vendéan forces through sheer bloody attrition. During the Virée de Galerne, one of these protégés, over Kléber's protests, lined up his entire force of 20,000 men in a single column to attack the whites, with predictably disastrous results. In an attempt to cover up the mistake, he then accused Kléber of being in the pay of the British and tried to send him to the guillotine. Historians have long recognized that such bumbling contributed as much as rebel doggedness to the long survival of the "inexplicable Vendée."

But the very lack of military experience and the utter devotion to orthodoxy had another, considerably more sinister effect, which historians have largely ignored. Failing to meet the Convention's demand for a complete end to military resistance, the Hébertist generals had no way of demonstrating their progress other than a high body count. Meanwhile, their military inexperience left them relying on little other than the rhetoric of total war. As we saw in the previous chapter, it was the Hébertists who made the most frequent and extreme use of this rhetoric in 1793–94, demanding the total mobilization of the French population and the total extermination of France's enemies, both foreign and domestic, as part of what they presented as an apocalyptic confrontation between good and evil. It is no coincidence that the most extreme ideas for cleansing the Vendée came from Hébertist generals. It was one of Ronsin's protégés who asked the Convention to have chemists develop a means of poisoning the entire region. It was another who similarly requested mines laden with poison gas.

Nothing came of either of these requests, but during the Virée de Galerne, the Hébertists did anything but restrain the army in its conduct toward the fleeing Vendéans. Even those high-ranking officers *not* aligned with the faction felt pressure to go along with the general tendency, lest they be accused of the grave sin of "moderation" and sent to join Lauzun on the guillotine. Westermann, already under suspicion, is the prime example of this deadly dynamic. In his case, however, it did not work. Just days after the victory at Savenay, the Convention recalled him and eventually put him on trial with his patron, Danton. They went to the guillotine together in April 1794.

But the deadliest attempt to translate the abstract rhetoric of total war into military reality was yet to come. After Savenay, only a few thousand men under Charette, who had refused to cross the Loire, still put up any serious military resistance in the west. The Revolutionary government therefore had the luxury of deciding how to "pacify" the Vendée once and for all. Kléber proposed a sober plan involving a series of fortified outposts throughout the territory, with flying columns that would pursue and destroy the remaining bands of "brigands." He stressed the exhaustion of the Vendéan population and their readiness to abandon the struggle as long as the blues could gain their confidence "through painstaking discipline." He also warned: "It is impossible to cover the entire extent of this vast territory with our troops." The only result of trying to do so would be to set the ashes of the rebellion in flame again.

Against this plan, Turreau proposed his own: the hell columns, or what he called a "military promenade" across the Vendée, from one end to the other. As we have seen, the Committee of Public Safety, although not explicitly approving the plan, did confirm Turreau's authority as supreme commander in the west and allowed him to proceed. On January 20, the columns marched.

Neither a *sans-culotte* nor a creature of the political clubs, Turreau was not himself a Hébertist. Born in 1756 into a family of modest legal functionaries in Normandy, he had barely begun a career as a professional soldier when the Revolution broke out. Like many other new officers of the period, he rose rapidly through the ranks of the National Guard and served in Belgium and the south before taking command in the Vendée. But the Hébertists counted Turreau as a friend, and he knew Ronsin well (he would later, in fact, marry Ronsin's widow). He, in turn, feared the Hébertists and followed their advice. His plan for the "promenade" came in part from Ronsin's crony Joseph Robert, who served as his chief of staff. The plan fit exactly into the Hébertists' vision of the Vendée: it was gratifyingly apocalyptic, fearsomely abstract, and hugely impractical.

The results of the "promenade" were so gruesome that historians have never really stopped to consider just how fantastical it was in the first place. It is worth quoting the orders Turreau gave to the commanders of the columns on January 17: "All means will be used to uncover the rebels; all will be put to the sword; villages, farmsteads, woods, heaths, thickets and generally everything that can be burned will be set on fire." The heartland of the insurrection, it should be noted, covers around five thousand square miles — over 3 million acres — and has one of the wettest climates in western Europe. How, exactly, did Turreau — in the dead of winter — expect to burn the woods and heaths? And how did he expect slow-moving columns of men on foot, carrying heavy packs, to catch rebels who could easily escape into their native woods? There is little indication that he gave any of these matters serious consideration. He was simply attempting a literal application of Barère's rhetoric from August, which the Convention had approved but not taken steps to implement: "to exterminate this rebel race, to destroy their hiding-places, to burn their forests, to cut down their crops."

In the short term, the columns were all too predictably inefficient in their principal mission. Antoinette-Charlotte de La Bouëre, the wife of a Vendéan leader, later wrote a vivid description of how the most committed rebels, knowing they could expect no mercy from the blues, ran off each day to the woods, hiding in thickets, curling up for hours under blankets on the wet ground. They easily spotted the columns, which marched to the sound of drumbeats and whose attempts at arson sent greasy clouds of smoke into the air wherever they passed: "a cruel signal," she called it, "but it saved three quarters of the inhabitants, one would guess." As a result, in a cruelly ironic twist, the Vendéans most vulnerable to the columns were those like Vincent Chapelain, who assumed that they had nothing to fear. Predictably, the "promenade" did little to hinder Charette, who recruited more soldiers from among its targets and who delivered a drubbing to two of the columns in early

February. Turreau himself wrote to the Committee of Public Safety on January 25 to confess: "I am in despair about being able to burn down the forests." Deliriously, he suggested they should be cut down instead. To him, the steady flow of volunteers to Charette only made his plan of extermination more urgent.

Faced with the impossibility of carrying out their plan in a systematic manner, Turreau's 30,000 men could deal out little but random rampage and murder. Not all of them carried out their orders. Officers under General Nicolas Haxo later claimed that he refused to obey "immoral" commands, whereas General Bard was suspended for a similar refusal. "Patriotic" towns and villages in the areas tried to prevent the columns from carrying out massacres, and one, Luçon, succeeded in having a particularly sadistic deputy of Grignon tried and executed for theft, rape, and murder. Nor did all the columns gain the barbaric reputation that those commanded by Grignon and Cordellier did. Nonetheless, after long months of unremitting bloodshed, plenty of Republican soldiers were ready to wreak vengeance on a largely helpless population.

The letters written by the blues speak for themselves. Here is the volunteer François-Xavier Joliclerc, writing home on January 25 from Cholet as his column prepared to march: "We are going to be bearing iron and fire, a gun in one hand and a torch in the other. Men and women, all will be put to the sword. All must die, except the small children." Or a certain Captain Dupuy, writing to his sister in January:

> Wherever we go, we are bearing fire and death. Age, sex, nothing is being respected. Yesterday, one of our detachments burned a village. One volunteer killed three women with his own hands. It is atrocious, but the safety of the Republic demands it imperatively. What a war! We haven't seen a single individual that we haven't shot. Everywhere the ground is strewn with corpses.

Or a local Republican official, describing the blue tactics to a friend on February 24:

> Destroy the watermills, burn the windmills, smash the ovens. Depend on the humanity of the cavalry each day to gather up those children who can be given a republican education; send them out to follow the grain convoys, the livestock . . . put everyone else to the sword, both sexes,

young and old. I have become cruel. The pains that this cursed war has
made me suffer force me to be so.

Or the provisioning agent Beaudesson, recalling the scene on the road
from Cholet to Vihiers: "Everywhere the eye fell on bloody scenes; . . .
inside the half-burned houses, what did I find? Fathers, mothers, children . . . swimming in their own blood, naked, and in postures that the
most ferocious soul could not envisage without shuddering."

The blood-drenched stories of what the columns wrought could be
continued almost endlessly. Charles-Louis Chassin, a historian favorable to the Revolution, who published the definitive documentary
collection on the Vendée in the late nineteenth century, has hundreds
of pages of them. Historians loyal to the memory of the Vendée have
even more. Even today, their histories read like Catholic martyrologies.
They indiscriminately mingle well-attested accounts from contemporary letters and depositions with tales recounted decades later in half-
fictionalized memoirs. They give credence to wild stories of sadism
that evoke the cruelties of the SS. Some of these may be true, but as
with the alleged massacre at Les Lucs, many are probably exaggerated,
misremembered, or simply invented out of whole cloth.

The atrocities committed in the city of Nantes under the rule of
Jean-Baptiste Carrier are better attested, in part because Carrier was
later tried for them and executed. Carrier also had ties to the Hébertists, but in his case, mass murder did not follow from a fantastically
abstract plan of campaign. As representative on mission in Nantes in
the fall of 1793, he was faced with the problem of how to deal with
thousands of Vendéan prisoners crammed into insecure, unsanitary
jails, posing the twin dangers of breakout and epidemic, with more arriving each day. Horrifically, he and his fellow representatives decided
to solve the problem by killing as many as possible.

The guillotine, however, proved too slow and also quite literally too
nauseating for the patriots of the city: no method of execution spills a
greater quantity of blood. The authorities then turned to mass firing
squads, but as one Nantais recounted to a deputy: "shooting them takes
too long and uses up too much gunpowder and too many bullets." So
there then was devised the ghastly expedient of lashing the prisoners
into barges and lighters and sinking them in the Loire. The Revolutionaries devised many euphemisms for this mass murder: "sending to the

water tower"; "sending to Nantes by water"; most horribly, in post-1945 retrospect, "deportation." Carrier sadistically reported to the Convention that prisoners had "accidentally" drowned (similarly, General Robert reported that two thousand Vendéans had "unfortunately" drowned farther upstream while trying to escape, because they "unfortunately" had their hands and legs tied). "What a revolutionary torrent the Loire has become," Carrier declared. It is reliably estimated that between 2,800 and 4,600 people died in these mass drownings at Nantes, and that another 1,896 were executed by guillotine or firing squad. Corpses washed up on the banks of the river for months. "It is out of a principle of humanity that I am purging the land of liberty of these monsters," said Carrier on December 20, 1793.

As spring came to western France in 1794, the pace of the killings finally slowed. In Paris, one of the titanic political battles of the Terror ended with Hébert, Ronsin, and several other "ultra-Revolutionaries" going to the guillotine. The victors, led by Robespierre and Saint-Just, were hardly moderates, but they liked their bloodshed well ordered and efficient, not wild and anarchic. Their success was very bad news indeed for political suspects in Paris, who went before kangaroo courts and thence to the guillotine at a steeply rising pace: between April and July, the Terror turned in a totalitarian direction. But the victory was better news for the Vendée, where the episode of the hell columns was not repeated.

In July, the Terror itself came to an end. A number of deputies to the Convention, fearful for their lives, persuaded their colleagues to arrest Robespierre, Saint-Just, and a number of allies. The next day, the man who had proposed peace to the world in 1790 and argued fiercely against war in 1791–92, only to find himself at the head of the most intense war effort Europe had ever known, died, hideously, by the guillotine to which he had condemned so many others (a failed suicide attempt had left him with a mangled jaw; to fit his neck under the blade, the executioner ripped the bandages off). The new rulers of the Convention, though themselves stained by the Terror, now sought rapidly to distance themselves from its excesses. In the fall, in the Vendée, the government started to issue amnesties. The region remained unsettled, and smaller-scale risings would continue for many years, as would the low-level Chouannerie, throughout the west, but the "war of the

Vendée" was over. As for Turreau, he was recalled and put on trial. During his imprisonment, he wrote his long, self-pitying memoir, which insisted, in retrospectively chilling language, that he had done nothing but follow orders:

> What is the cause for this inconceivable obstinacy with which you are now prosecuting those under orders, the *very passive* executors of the Government's wishes? You have now substituted softer measures for the terrible ones you thought you needed to end the war; none too soon, but admit at least that you intended the complete destruction of the Vendée, and do not persecute your agents!

Carrier had gone to the guillotine six months before.

Turreau, however, did not join him. He was acquitted, then reinstated in his rank. Between 1797 and 1801, he fought for France in Belgium, Germany, Italy, and Austria. In 1803, Napoleon named him ambassador to the United States, where he stayed for eight years, helping oversee the transfer of the Louisiana Purchase and gaining notoriety for having his secretary play music to cover the screams when he beat his wife (Ronsin's widow). Back in the French army as Napoleon's empire was collapsing in 1814, he chose the right moment to surrender the citadel he commanded and to declare his loyalty to the brother of the executed Louis XVI, who awarded him France's highest military decoration. Turreau died peacefully at home in 1816. Twenty years later, his name was carved on the Arc de Triomphe in Paris, alongside that of Napoleon's other generals, where it is still visible today. Seeing it makes one realize that Reynald Secher, despite his flagrant exploitation of the term "genocide," has a point when he complains that France's Fifth Republic has yet fully to come to terms with the crimes of the First.

The war in the Vendée was not a genocide. That, however, is probably the only positive thing that can be said about it. It was a tragedy of unspeakable dimensions, and its suppression was a ghastly crime, as well as an indelible stain on the Revolution, which allowed men like Westermann, Ronsin, and Turreau to rise and flourish. Responsibility for this crime cannot be laid entirely at the feet of the Revolutionary leadership, which did not run as efficient a dictatorship as some historians imagine. But to the extent that there existed a dynamic of radicalization within the Revolution, a competition for power that consistently favored exponents of the most extreme stances and policies, the Vendée condemns it, and condemns those who helped to drive it forward.

The Vendée was the face of total war, which followed its own dynamic of radicalization. It was the place where the modern version of the phenomenon was first revealed to its full, gruesome extent. As in most modern cases, its "totality" did not derive primarily from the battlefield clashes between organized armies (World War I is a distracting exception in this case). What made it total was rather its erasure of any line between combatants and noncombatants and the wanton slaughter of both — and at the behest of politics more than military necessity. In fact, from a strictly military point of view, Turreau's "hell columns" had no serious purpose at all. His plan was a witches' brew of hatred, fear, fantasy, and pure folly; its execution an unmitigated horror, and counterproductive to the extent that it spurred further resistance. But then, extermination of the enemy, as opposed to disarming it, has hardly ever served a serious military purpose. "We destroyed the village in order to save it." And to say that the barbarism of one side impelled the barbarism of the other is not much of an excuse. It is General Salomon's excuse: to defeat the enemy, we must become him.

Thankfully, nothing in the next twenty-one years of Revolutionary and Napoleonic warfare quite matched the Vendée's level of bloodshed. But the Vendée nonetheless served as a precedent, a matrix of French experience. During those twenty-one years, the French Republic and Empire would face many cases of insurrection and irregular warfare, most often from traditional rural Catholics fairly similar to the Vendéans. The Vendée gave an apparent warning of just how dangerous such insurrections could turn and just what methods might be necessary to suppress them. And it was not just a general national memory that taught this lesson but a living skein of military memory. Even beyond 1815, many veterans of the Vendée held prominent positions in the French army and continually referred back to it as the crucible of their military experience. "A point worth noting, and which gives the war of the invasion of Spain a special character, is that, just like the war of the Vendée, it was entirely a people's war." Thus General Joseph Hugo, who served in both campaigns.

The Vendée was not a genocide, but it nonetheless stirs memories of recent genocidal horrors — enough to make one think that it must have scoured every last trace of romance out of European warfare. Except that it did not. Even as the hell columns were marching, the Vendéans were weaving their own romantic myths about the conflict, while Robespierre, as we have already seen, was constructing the romantic cult of the boy hero Joseph Bara, killed by Vendéan rebels. Then, and for a century to come, the Vendée would exert a deeply romantic hold on the European imagination, so much so that some of the Continent's greatest writers — Balzac, Dumas, even Anthony Trollope — tried their hands at portraying the war. Not to mention General Hugo's son, Victor, who made the Vendée the subject of one of his greatest novels, *Ninety-Three*. "This War of the Ignorant," he wrote in it, "so stupid and so splendid, abominable and magnificent, devastated France and gave it pride. The Vendée is a scourge which is also a glory." But the Vendée was not what struck Victor Hugo and his readers as the *most* seductively romantic aspect of the wars. For *that* they looked elsewhere, to what they saw as the incarnation of military glory in the life of a single man.

6

The Lure of the Eagle

Ambition, like all disordered passions, is a violent and unthinking
delirium . . . Like a fire fed by a pitiless wind, it only burns out after
having consumed everything in its path.

— NAPOLEON BONAPARTE, 1791

DURING HIS FIFTY-ONE YEARS, Napoleon Bonaparte exposed himself to enemy fire in scores of battles and survived at
least four serious assassination plots. So it is not unreasonable
to ask how history might have remembered him had he died earlier
than he did. Of course, counterfactual speculation of this sort always
has a parlor-game feel to it, but in this case, it reveals a great deal about
both Napoleon and the beginnings of total warfare described in the
previous chapters.

Imagine, for instance, that the man who still signed his name "Napoleone Buonaparte" had died in his first military engagement, a bungled
assault by Corsican French forces against the island of La Maddalena,
off the coast of Sardinia, in early 1793. He might well have done so, for
Corsican leader Pasquale Paoli probably sent the annoyingly ambitious
young officer on this dangerous expedition precisely to get rid of him.
Napoleon was then an unknown twenty-three-year-old artillery officer
who would have left few traces in the history books. But if historians
later came across him in the archives, would they have found hints of
possible greatness? Despite the tales that acquaintances later retailed of

his precocious strategic genius — for instance, in schoolyard snowball fights — the answer is likely no. The sources from this time mostly present Napoleon as a typical junior officer of the Old Regime. Born into the minor nobility of Corsica in 1769, a year after the island's annexation by France, he benefited from the eighteenth-century attempts to professionalize the French officer class and won admission to the new military school at Brienne. Yet after receiving his commission in 1785, he did not undertake anything like a dedicated professional career. As we have seen, like many of his peers, he spent more time on leave than with his regiment. Even when supposedly on duty, he favored solitary study over military business, whenever possible.

Although ravenously ambitious from the start, the young Napoleon knew quite well that minor Corsican nobles had little hope of rising high in the French army. A glittering military career could be found only in foreign service — as late as 1794, he toyed with enrolling in the Turkish army. To shine in France would mean following another path, and before 1789, Napoleon thought most seriously of becoming a writer. He did dream, passionately, of Corsican independence, but this seemed a lost cause before 1789. He therefore devoted much of his energy to sketching out philosophical dialogues, historical essays, even love stories. In this juvenalia, incidentally, he expressed an utterly banal late-Enlightenment contempt for the sort of military ambition "that feeds on blood and crimes" and that led such figures as Alexander, Cromwell, or Louis XIV "to conquer and devastate the world."

Now leap ahead a few months, and imagine that Napoleon's death came during France's late-1793 attempt to retake the port city of Toulon from the British. In the battle, he did in fact have a horse shot out from under him and received a bayonet wound to the thigh, leading an English newspaper to report him killed in action (the historian Trevelyan, who discovered the article, quipped that "everything I have learned since has increased my regret that the news proved inaccurate"). Napoleon still would not have merited more than a few lines in specialized history books, but now he would seem less a typical noble officer than a quintessential young soldier of the Revolution. True, between 1789 and mid-1793, his attention had remained fixed on Corsica and on ingratiating himself with Paoli, the aging hero of the island's earlier campaigns for independence. "General, I was born as the fatherland was dying," he wrote cloyingly to the old man by way of introducing himself. But after several snubs and rebuffs, Napoleon grew disillusioned and began scheming against Paoli — who schemed back, rather more effectively, forcing the entire Bonaparte family to flee to the mainland.

Even before this flight, Napoleon had also shown genuine enthusiasm for the Revolution. He rhapsodized in print over the leading figures of the National Assembly ("O Lameth! O Robespierre! O Mirabeau! O Barnave!") and, after reading of a political murder, told his older brother: "that's one fat aristocrat less." He set up a Revolutionary club in the Corsican town of Ajaccio and maneuvered unscrupulously to win election to a high rank in the local National Guard contingent. After arriving on the mainland in 1793, he composed a pamphlet in favor of the Jacobins, which brought him the patronage of Augustin Robespierre, Maximilien's brother, who found for him a coveted artillery post in the army besieging Toulon. After Napoleon's ideas for how to end the siege proved successful, he won promotion to brigadier general. He was just twenty-four. "I would add to the list of patriots," wrote Augustin Robespierre afterward, "the name of citizen Buonaparte . . . an officer of transcendent merit." Thanks to the Revolution, Napoleon no longer contemplated a career as a writer but had thrown himself wholly into the cause of a revolutionary nation engaged in total war.

Finally, skip ahead four more years, and imagine that Napoleon had died in November 1796 at the battle of Arcola, in northern Italy. Again, he almost did, for at a crucial moment, his horse slipped down an embankment, hurling him into a marshy canal. Several of his soldiers dragged him out again under heavy fire, and one was killed. By now, Napoleon had established a formidable reputation and would deserve a major place in any history of the Revolutionary wars. Taking command of the Army of Italy in the spring of 1796, he had carried out a brilliant campaign, separating his Austrian enemies from their Sardinian allies, knocking the latter out of the war entirely, and then defeating the Austrians in one battle after another, until most of northern Italy had fallen into his grasp — a goal that had eluded French generals for centuries.

This Napoleon, however, had a very different social and political profile from his earlier self. His days as a radical Revolutionary ended when the Thermidor coup of 1794 toppled Robespierre and Saint-Just and brought the Terror to an end. Napoleon himself, thanks to his radical ties, spent a nervous eleven days in prison after the coup. Thereafter, he rapidly altered his profile and behaved less as a convinced Revolutionary than as a classic "political general" of the type pioneered by Dumouriez in 1792–93 — that is to say, one who unapologetically placed his own interests ahead of ideology and campaigned for political influence in Paris as vigorously as he did for enemy territory. When the government tried to send him to the Vendée to chase the remnants of the white army through the ruined province, he balked at this classic Jacobin assignment, malingering, delaying, ignoring orders, and almost leaving the army in protest. He also attached himself to a new patron he had met at Toulon — an unscrupulous deputy named Paul Barras, who had helped plot the Thermidor coup. When royalist crowds marched on the Convention in the late summer of 1795, Barras called on Bonaparte, who turned artillery on them in central Paris — the famous slaughter by "whiff of grapeshot," whose scars still mark the walls of the church of Saint-Roch. But his ruthlessness served the same purpose as his earlier Jacobin pamphlet writing: it brought him attention and vaulted him up the ladder of promotions. Within a year, thanks to Barras, he had taken command of the Army of Italy. At least one fellow general (Suchet, whom Napoleon would name a marshal in 1811) dismissed him as a "general known only by the Parisians . . . an intriguer supported by nothing." Only with the Italian campaign of 1796–97 would the Napoleon known to our own history books begin to come into focus.

This little counterfactual exercise therefore shows us a Napoleon very different from the popular image of the man as always and everywhere the same uncontainable force of nature. His early career reflected the changing contours of war so precisely that it does a fair job of recapitulating the first chapters of this book. At each stage, Napoleon's strategies for advancement grew out of his uncanny sense of the existing possibilities for someone in his position. His own younger brother, Lucien, sensed as much and dilated on the implications for Napoleon's character in a revealing letter to their older brother Joseph, written in 1792:

> There are no men more hated in history than those who bend with the wind. I will say to you in full confidence that I have always detected in Napoleon an ambition that is not altogether selfish, but which over-

comes his love for the common good; I truly think that in a free state, he would be a dangerous man . . . He seems inclined to be a tyrant, and I think that he would be one if he were king.

Prophetic, to say the least. Napoleon's "bending to the wind," however, amounted to more than mere cynical opportunism. As we shall see, he was more psychologically complex than this and could come to believe fervently in the roles he played, the mask becoming the man. Even his Jacobinism, which he seemed to peel off like a tattered paper disguise after Thermidor, kept enough of a grip on him that twenty-five years later, after having claimed an imperial title and married the great-niece of Marie-Antoinette, he could still express admiration for Robespierre and regret at his fall.

An emphasis on Napoleon's adaptability is particularly useful for understanding the years of his rise to power: 1794–99. In these years, Napoleon sensed ongoing changes in the nature of European war and politics with preternatural precision, exploited them with incomparable skill, and rode them to a concentration of power heretofore undreamed of in European history. He is necessarily the central figure of these years, to the extent that the vivid, brilliant colors of his story leave everything else looking pale and wan.

The changes of 1794–99 were some of the most far-reaching of the entire eighteenth century. In these years, the French gave up all but the slimmest pretense of fighting for a just and perpetual peace among the nations. They now pursued expansion and conquest with relatively little apology, and if they granted the conquered peoples a role in their new European order, it remained emphatically *their* order. At best, French leaders proceeded out of the belief that only a French-led Europe could continue along the path of historical progress sketched out by the writers of the late Enlightenment. At the same time, these years saw military officers again occupy leading positions in French politics and society, after the civilian ascendancy of 1789–94. And the period saw a sustained reglorification of war: a growing conviction in the culture that it was an activity worth pursuing not only for a greater good but also for its own sake.

But these years emphatically did not mark a return to the old regime of war that had prevailed before 1789. War remained total, in the Revolutionary manner. At key moments, the French leadership continued to see the ongoing conflict in garishly apocalyptic terms, and this vision prompted them to attempt to use every political means at their disposal to mobilize the nation's resources. It led them to fight not simply to defeat France's enemies but also to destroy them and to absorb the broken pieces of their regimes into new configurations of power. It led them to treat these enemies as monsters rather than as honorable adversaries. When enemy populations resisted French occupations, they were to be fed the acid medicine of the Vendée.

In France itself, the nation and the military, after having supposedly melted into each other in the white heat of the *levée en masse,* did not solidify back into the earlier, complex social latticework dominated by a hereditary military class. Instead, a far more radical process took place, which saw "the military" separate out into a society and culture far more distinct than before from a sphere that could now be fully characterized, in opposition to it, as "civilian." Finally, the reglorification of war in no way entailed a return to the traditional aristocratic code of splendor, self-control, and dedication to the service of the hereditary prince. The new model of military glory was less a model of aristocratic perfection than of Romantic transcendence. It had a relationship to the Revolution's febrile celebration of patriotic self-sacrifice, but it now came to focus less on the Revolution's cold and high ideals than on the prowess of individual warriors. In short, war was becoming evermore something that societies might desire, and this desire took physical form in the person of Napoleon.

The France in which these changes took place has a poor historical reputation. The standard account long held that after the pitiless, austere virtue of the Terror came a time of luxuriant debauch. In this view, the fall of Robespierre and his allies opened the door to a corrupt whirl of pleasures. Under the unscrupulous leaders who governed between 1794 and 1799, the poor suffered malign neglect, whereas the bourgeoisie engaged in a riot of conspicuous consumption. Preening dandies dressed their mistresses in diaphanous gowns. At the so-called *bals des victimes,* relatives of those guillotined under the Terror tied red ribbons around their necks in macabre memory of the dead.

Recent scholarship has done its best to dissolve this collage of clichés. Revolutionary ideals, it emphasizes, did not evaporate between 1794 and 1799. Throughout the country, some democratic practices spread and solidified. New state institutions to promote education, welfare, and justice took root. A cadre of influential intellectuals sought to stabilize the Revolution by grounding it in scientific principles. The *bals des victimes,* it has been revealed, never took place — they were an invention of early nineteenth-century Romantic authors.

There is no denying, however, that between 1794 and 1799, a stable constitutional regime utterly failed to materialize. In the year after the Thermidor coup, the survivors in the Convention bloodily put down challenges from the Left and the Right. They also eventually managed to devise yet another new constitution. In a self-conscious retreat from their earlier radicalism, they again restricted the electorate to the well-to-do and divided power among a bicameral legislature and a five-man executive Directory. Through this profession of moderation, they sought to unite the warring political factions that had emerged from the Terror. But they sacrificed their own democratic credibility almost immediately by decreeing that two-thirds of the new legislature would come from their own ranks, so as to ensure their political survival. The collapse of the fragile Revolutionary paper currency did little to soothe popular discontent.

For a couple of years, it nonetheless seemed as if this newest new regime might yet consolidate itself. A relatively moderate, "neo-Jacobin" political grouping emerged as a prominent force, committed to revolutionary reform without accompanying terror. But by the summer of 1797, the Right was rapidly increasing in strength and seemed close to replacing the Republic with a restored monarchy (Louis XVI's younger brother was now claiming the throne). Rather than allow this to happen, three Republican "directors," backed by the army, carried out a coup, dismissing two hundred deputies and their own two more conservative colleagues. Two further minor coups took place in 1798–99, stripping the regime of virtually all legitimacy. Worst of all, as aftershocks of the Terror continued to rip apart local communities, criminality and political violence rose to unprecedented levels. To contain them, the regime felt that it had no choice but to call out the army and try civilians before military courts. By the fall of 1799, 40 percent of France had fallen under effective military rule. It was predictable that by this point, the dominant figure in the Directory — Emmanuel Sieyès, a hero of the early Revolution — should want to take these various trends to their logical conclusion. "I need a sword," he declared.

Material conditions were just as bad in the armies. The government had done little large-scale recruiting or conscription since the *levée en masse,* so the burden of the fighting fell heavily on the same soldiers who had entered the ranks in 1791–94. The economic collapse, moreover, left these soldiers with worthless pay and a miserable supply situation. "We are not living, only suffering," wrote a lieutenant in the summer of 1795, who laconically described his daily rations: "no bread, just two pounds of sprouted potatoes, and three ounces of dry, worm-eaten peas . . . on August 10, having caught a cat, we had no choice but to introduce it to our stew-pot." The low point came in early 1796, when the Army of Italy saw a staggering four-fifths of its men spend time in the hospital. A soldier wrote home bitterly of having to march without proper shoes or coats in the snow-covered mountains, while at home, citizens enjoyed warm beds. "Why did we fight?" he asked in a badly spelled letter. "They led us to believe it was for our liberty, but it was the reverse, we are slaves more than we ever were before."

Yet despite these handicaps, the armies enjoyed a remarkable string of successes that contrasted dramatically with French domestic strife. The devastation of the Vendée had already reduced the western insurrections from a mortal threat to a lingering, if serious nuisance, and the victories of 1794 had driven the allies back from the French borders. Then, in a winter offensive, when ice prevented the Dutch from opening the dikes to bog down the invaders, French forces surged north to occupy the Netherlands and transform it into a puppet state. In the spring of 1795, France signed a peace treaty with Prussia, which wanted to concentrate its energies in the east; another French army penetrated deep into northern Spain, forcing the Spanish to switch sides and ally with their former enemy. With these flanks secure, the Directory then planned a triple thrust at France's chief remaining enemy on the Continent: Austria. In the spring of 1796, three armies would attack eastward: one from the Rhineland, one from Alsace, one from the Mediterranean coast. The last and smallest of these, Napoleon's Army of Italy, would attack mostly as a diversion, allowing the other two to strike for the Austrian heartland.

The first two armies, however, saw their offensives rapidly bog down. Napoleon, meanwhile, sliced into northern Italy, dazzling his opponents with his precise maneuvers and his ability to bring superior forces into action at the right time and place. On May 16, he entered Milan and then turned south. The small states into which the Italian peninsula was still divided could not resist him, and within a month, everything north of Rome had passed under his control. Austria continued to resist, holding on to the great fortress town of Mantua. But Napoleon continued his series of victories: Castiglione, Arcola, and finally, in January 1797, the decisive battle of Rivoli.

The negotiations that followed eventually led to the treaty of Campo-Formio, signed in October 1797, which left Great Britain the only power still at war with France. Austria acknowledged French rule over Belgium and also Napoleon's creation of a new puppet state in Italy: the Cisalpine Republic, whose constitution followed the French model. In five years of war, France had decisively broken the old balance of power. In its territorial gains and its Italian victories, it had fulfilled the long-frustrated dreams of the monarchy and reached what its apologists liked to call its "natural boundaries": the Rhine, the Alps, the Pyrenees, and the sea. Such a far-reaching and decisive shift could never have occurred so quickly under the old regime of warfare, with its careful campaigns of maneuvers and its code of aristocratic restraint. Even Frederick the Great, the most daring of eighteenth-century leaders, did not come close to redrawing the map and reweighting the powers in such a dramatic way so quickly.

Would the new era continue? Napoleon sent some clear signals that it would not. The huge prestige he had garnered with his victory allowed him to behave like a little king in the territory he had conquered, and he did. He established a virtual court for himself, at Montebello, and insisted that it follow strict rules of social etiquette. He dined before spectators, like the Bourbons at Versailles, and when he arrived in Rastatt, Germany, for negotiations, did so in an elaborate *berline* pulled by eight horses — a privilege traditionally reserved for monarchs. Most significantly, in the negotiations themselves, which he tried to present to the Directory as a fait accompli, he no longer even gave lip service to the right of peoples to self-determination. To compensate Austria for its loss of Belgium, he blithely agreed to let it annex the republic of Venice, which had existed as an independent republic — if no model of democracy — for centuries. The decision, worthy of an aristocratic diplomat of the Old Regime, shocked the French neo-Jacobins, who had heretofore counted the young general as one of their own. But in the end, Napoleon's taste for royal splendor and Realpolitik was deceptive. If he was embracing traditional forms of legitimation, he would do so without rejecting the new regime of war. This desire to have things both ways would be an enduring characteristic of Napoleon's career. And in fact, war in the late 1790s was taking yet another radical turn.

To understand this turn more closely, there is no better place to start than with Napoleon himself at the moment he took command of the Army of Italy: March 27, 1796. He was still just twenty-six, and by all accounts, he did not yet cut a very impressive figure. Numerous descriptions of him from the period call attention to his poor clothes and untidy appearance, especially his hair: badly cut, badly combed, and badly powdered, falling down to his shoulders in a lank mess. Subordinates in the Army of Italy initially had trouble believing that he was the General-in-Chief. The wife of General Junot later wrote: "I can still see him crossing the courtyard of the Hôtel de la Tranquilité with an awkward and uncertain gait, with a horrible little round hat thrust down over his eyes . . . long, thin, dark hands . . . wearing badly made, badly polished boots, and that overall sickly appearance which came from his scrawniness and yellowish complexion." He spoke incorrect, heavily accented French.

Yet Napoleon had several qualities that augured well for his success. First, he had genuinely extraordinary mental capacities that included, by some accounts, a near-photographic memory. Second, he had a phenomenal energy and capacity for work. As proof, one need only consult the nearly two thousand letters he wrote or dictated in the years 1796 and 1797 alone, which take up over a thousand tightly packed pages of his *General Correspondence.* In it, we see him taking charge of matters ranging from the number of carts needed to carry a regiment's paperwork to the amount of munitions carried by soldiers to the position of drummer boys in a marching column. In his campaigns, his success came in large part from his ability to keep the positions of thousands of men in scores of separate units in his head, along with information about munitions and supplies, and to calculate how to maneuver them all for maximum effect.

Napoleon could also draw on a military training perfectly suited to the way warfare was developing. Well before 1789, the French army had developed a new system of mobile heavy guns, equipment, and service personnel to facilitate the movement and rapid concentration of separate units. As a young artillery officer, Napoleon received intensive training in it, which gave him a natural inclination for the tactics that the French army embraced during the Revolution, involving rapid deployment of large, mobile masses of soldiers and the concentration of overwhelming force against a single enemy position. Whereas the commanders of 1793–94 had to deal with crudely organized masses of poorly trained troops, Napoleon could count on smaller units of seasoned and disciplined soldiers — the same men as before but now with the experience of several campaigns behind them. He could and did push them very hard, marching men with sixty-pound loads on their backs as much as fifty miles over a thirty-six-hour period. As one of his soldiers proudly complained years later: "The Emperor has discovered a new way of waging war; he makes use of our legs instead of our bayonets."

These are the factors that Napoleon's biographers have called the most attention to in explaining his rise to prominence. They certainly help explain the stunning military successes he had in Italy. But just as important was the way Napoleon crafted his own image as an extraordinary figure — as the god of the new age of war. In Italy and throughout his early campaigns, he demanded more of his soldiers than any general of the period and could not have done so without their active enthusiasm — indeed, without what sometimes amounted to fanatical devotion. He also quickly established a popularity in the French population unmatched by any other figure, civilian or military. He could not have accomplished this all without a very keen sense of how to speak to his fellow countrymen — and more, how to touch them, emotionally.

The first, key element was simply to show his soldiers he cared for them. On taking command of the Army of Italy in 1796, he immediately devoted himself to improving its living conditions. He raised pay and tried to frighten crooked contractors into supplying his forces at an honest rate. Much of his correspondence from the end of March deals with the banal but fundamental subject of meat, which one of his divisions had not seen for months. He ordered that it receive fresh meat every second day and salt meat on the others. Within three days he was boasting: "I have given out meat, bread, forage . . . my soldiers are showing me inexpressible confidence." Once in Italy, he did not hesitate to pick the country bare to keep his men well fed and comfortable.

Wherever his armies arrived, there followed demands for hefty "contributions": oxen by the hundred, bread rations by the hundreds of thousands, bottles of wine and brandy by the tens of thousands, as many coats and pairs of shoes as possible. In battle, he often led his soldiers in person, ostentatiously sharing their dangers.

Napoleon also understood the importance of less tangible rewards — of honor and distinction — and never thought to limit these things to the officer class. In November 1797, for instance, he drew up a list of a hundred soldiers, including simple privates and drummer boys, who would receive specially engraved sabers for such feats as carrying letters through enemy lines or refusing to surrender even after receiving seven sword wounds. He then had the awards splashed across the front page of the French-language newspaper published under his supervision in Milan. His code of honor could dole out disgrace just as easily. When two French units broke and ran in Italy, he excoriated them in astonishing terms: "Soldiers, I am not happy with you . . . you gave in at the first setback. Soldiers of the 85th and 39th, you are no longer French soldiers." The men in question begged for a chance to redeem themselves and at the next battle suffered horrific casualties but covered themselves with glory.

Just as important, Napoleon treated his soldiers as equals. As a second lieutenant, his training had included a stint as a simple gunner, learning how to load, fire, and swab cannon. It was an experience that taught him a crucial lesson: not to condescend. As he told his brother Lucien as early as 1792, chiding him for composing an overly abstract, verbose public proclamation: "This is not the way to speak to the people; they have more tact and more sense than you think." In his own first proclamation to the Army of Italy, he chose to call himself the soldiers' "brother in arms," and six weeks later, at the battle of Lodi, he supposedly stepped in to help aim the artillery pieces. It was a piece of bravado that won Napoleon an enduring nickname, which no general of the Old Regime would have tolerated: "the little corporal." He even allowed some common soldiers to address him with the informal "*tu*." In proclamations and speeches, which he made more frequently than any other general, he addressed the soldiers in loose, familiar, emotional language. "I can't express the feelings I have for you any better than by saying that I bear along in my heart the love that you show me every day."

Yet, like a talented composer, Napoleon could speak to his men in different registers and frequently modulated the intimate warble of the second-person singular with the basso profundo of the epic proclamation. April 26, 1796:

> Soldiers, the fatherland has the right to expect great things of you . . . Are there any of you whose courage falters? . . . No, there are none . . . All of you burn to carry onwards the glory of the French people . . . All of you wish to be able to say with pride, upon returning to your villages, "I was part of the conquering Army of Italy!"

May 20, 1796:

> Soldiers, you have rushed like a torrent from the heights of the Appenines, you have overthrown, dispersed and scattered everything that hindered your advance . . . Yes, soldiers, you have done much, but does not much remain to be done? . . . So then, let us depart! We still have forced marches to make, enemies to subdue, laurels to gather, and insults to avenge.

May 10, 1798:

> Soldiers, Europe has its eyes on you. You have a great destiny to fulfill . . . You will do more than you have yet done, for the prosperity of the fatherland, the happiness of mankind, and your own glory.

To modern sensibilities, the bombast is almost unbearable. But it worked. The soldiers responded.

Although Napoleon's rapport with the troops had many precedents, in one sense he was entirely original. He was the world's first "media general," exploiting every possible means of communication to diffuse and popularize the image he crafted of himself. Most important, he founded newspapers: in the Italian campaign, the *Courier of the Army of Italy* and *France Seen from the Army of Italy.* The first, printed every other day, reported army news and French news to the soldiers and probably had a considerable free circulation in France as well. Its closely printed four-page issues borrowed copiously from left-wing Paris papers, but Napoleon himself contributed a number of articles. The second, filled with longer, more thoughtful, and more politically moderate articles, aimed at a French civilian audience.

The *Courier* in particular faithfully reflected the various aspects of

Napoleon's carefully constructed image. It breathed concern for ordinary soldiers, echoing their complaints and reporting lovingly on them. It faithfully reported on the doings of the "little corporal" as well, stressing how he shared his men's dangers and discomforts. But it could adopt the epic tone of his proclamations with relish, particularly in a long report on the campaign, which appeared in October 1797:

> Today, glory has written a new name on its immortal tablets, with no fear of it ever being erased. The divinations which predicted a brilliant destiny for the young islander have come true. The time is past in which he locked himself up in his tent, a voluntary prisoner, a new Archimedes always at work . . . He knows that he is of those men who have no limit to their power but that conferred by their own will, and whose sublime virtues complement their overwhelming genius . . . He promised victory, and brought it. He flies like lightning, and strikes like thunder. The speed of his movements is matched only by their accuracy and prudence. He is everywhere. He sees everything. Like a comet cleaving the clouds, he appears at the same moment on the astonished banks of two separate rivers.

Such shameless self-promotion, so far removed from the cold abstractions of the radical Revolution, does not deserve simply the label *propaganda*. It marks the beginning of a cult of personality. If war was now to be seen as an extraordinary phenomenon, utterly at odds with the ordinary life of society, Napoleon was the extraordinary man, of almost supernatural accomplishments, who embodied it.

The cult quickly spread. In Paris, another newspaper began publication under the modest title *Journal of Bonaparte and Virtuous Men*. Popular engravings proliferated, including one that showed Napoleon being crowned with laurel leaves, like a classical conqueror. Theaters in 1796–97 put on no fewer than twelve separate plays and at least one opera devoted to his exploits. Several popular biographies appeared as well, which invented all manner of boyhood exploits for him — including the famous victory in the schoolyard snowball fights and a dramatic balloon flight over Paris at the age of fifteen. Poets who had hailed kings now turned their flattery on Napoleon: "Hero, dear to peace, the arts and victory / In two years he conquered a thousand years of glory."

The leading French poets of the late 1790s are a forgettable bunch, but the leading French painters are not, and they too made Napoleon a

Antoine-Jean Gros: *Napoleon on the Bridge at Arcola*

favorite subject. Antoine-Jean Gros, in particular, immortalized the moment when Napoleon supposedly led his men to glory at Arcola, seizing a flag and advancing over the bridge under Austrian fire. In fact, the attack did not succeed, and Napoleon's subordinate, General Augereau, who first led men onto the bridge, had the more truly heroic role. Yet little of this mattered to Gros, who painted a stunning, complex work. Unlike popular engravings of the battle, which show Napoleon (or Augereau) holding tricolor Republican flags and supported by their men, in Gros's rendition, Napoleon is alone, and his (non-tricolor) flag dissolves into the somber background, the better to highlight his shining face and brilliant costume. He strides confidently forward but looks back toward his men, perfectly conveying the image of a superior leader. It has been argued that Gros consciously modeled Napoleon's pose after a famous Renaissance engraving of the winged figure of History, making the bridge of Arcola a symbolic bridge between past and future.

It is difficult to say just how much of this tremendous media production was orchestrated by Napoleon himself. He certainly sponsored the newspapers. He also commissioned Gros's portrait, although legend has it that in his impatience, he had trouble standing still for the painter and that his wife had to sit and grasp his knees to keep him from striding off. But his popularity was genuine, not manufactured. How could it be otherwise for someone who could already claim, in 1797, to be the most successful general in French history and who had just negotiated a triumphant peace settlement with Austria after five years of weary combat? Memoirs of the period all testify to the widespread adulation for Napoleon. And while the 1790s were blissfully free of opinion polling, there was a rough equivalent: police spies who lurked in cafés and squares in order to assess the state of public opinion. In their reports, they repeatedly attested to the "flood of praise" the young general received.

How did Napoleon craft an image for himself so much more successfully than any of his Revolutionary predecessors did? Was it simply a matter of his successes or of his freakish genius? In fact, although Napoleon nurtured the cult of his heroism with unparalleled skill, the shape that the cult took, and its impact on European war and politics, also grew directly out of new understandings of the human self that were emerging in the late Enlightenment and Revolutionary period, particularly in the world of literature.

To understand this point, we first have to recognize just how thoroughly the cult of Napoleon broke with earlier forms of celebrating "great men." The elites of eighteenth-century France had a gluttonous appetite for such celebrations, for they fervently believed that virtue was best stimulated by placing great examples of it continually before the people. The Académie Française began annual essay contests honoring designated "great Frenchmen" in 1758, and the French crown commissioned expensive series of paintings and sculptures of "great men": statesmen and soldiers, of course, but also, increasingly, artists and writers (including Bishop Fénelon). The Revolution crowned the trend by transforming the vast, gloomy new Paris church of Sainte-Geneviève into a Pantheon of national heroes, a function it still holds today.

Yet the eighteenth-century eulogies and monuments were curiously one-dimensional. They adopted as their principal measure of "greatness" a person's selfless dedication to the common good and tended to push everything else out of the focus. As a result, a long line of tediously self-sacrificing patriots blended colorlessly into one another. The cult of Napoleon was different. It had a palpable, vivid quality. Although focusing on his great deeds, it delighted in his unique, even idiosyncratic qualities. It did not try to occlude the Corsican upbringing or the early struggles for attention. The portrait by Gros, while conforming to a model of classical heroism, nonetheless depicted a distinctive, original personality. In general, the cult owed less to the earlier celebration of great men than to the way literature was beginning to shape new perceptions of the individual human character.

Napoleon's own literary tastes help reveal the nature of these perceptions. As we have seen, he had a genuine love for literature, which did not desert him even after he gave up hope of a literary career. He adored history, philosophy, and the tragedies of Corneille and Voltaire. Poetry mostly bored him, although like many other Europeans of the day, he fell for the bombastic verse of the ancient Celtic bard Ossian, recently "discovered" and "translated" by James MacPherson (in fact, forged by him). On board ship to Egypt in 1798, Napoleon read out loud from Ossian and declared him superior to that "rambler," Homer.

But the most important creative literary form for Napoleon was the novel. He did not himself say as much. Yet although he never tried his hand at poetry or drama, he wrote — or at least started — several short stories and even a novel, *Clisson and Eugénie,* the sentimental story of a young officer in love. He read many of the most popular novels of the day, including Goethe's *Young Werther* and Rousseau's *The New Héloïse.* Later in his career, he put together a traveling library that included, amid a flood of history books, forty volumes of epic, forty of theater, and one hundred novels, including Goethe, Rousseau, and, surprisingly, Fénelon's pacifist *Telemachus.*

As literary critics have explained, the rise of the novel in the eighteenth century brought readers a fundamentally new way of relating to literary characters — which Napoleon clearly shared. Although these creations might take part in extraordinary adventures and come across as extraordinary human types, the genre also seemed to provide unprecedented access to their innermost, unique selves, allowing for a new degree of psychological intimacy between character and reader. It is a commonplace of cultural history that eighteenth-century readers could take characters for real people in a disturbingly literal manner. Fanatical readers of Rousseau sent letters to the characters, care of the author, drawing attention to the stains of their tears on the paper.

Steven Englund has written, elegantly, that Napoleon "chose to 'write' his novel on the world, not on paper." I would go further and suggest that Napoleon saw himself, throughout his life, as something of a character in a novel. Novels gave him a way of understanding his own unique and extraordinary life story. In exile on Saint Helena, he famously declared: "What a novel my life has been!" He also claimed that with a few more years in power, he would have made "Paris the capital of the universe, and all of France a true novel." His companion added: "The emperor often repeated these last words." But there is more serious evidence from the period of the Italian campaign itself. And nowhere more than in his relationship with women.

Napoleon's love affairs certainly seem worthy of a novel. In 1794, in Marseille, he met and briefly fell in love with Désirée Clary, the pretty, charming daughter of a local merchant. She, like Napoleon himself, later became the subject of a good many real novels, because after marrying a different French general, the era's tornado of possibilities landed her, improbably, in Stockholm as queen of Sweden (her descendants sit on the Swedish throne to this day). Her relationship with Napoleon did not last long, but while it did, he gave her a new name — Eugénie, like the heroine of his novel.

A few months later, Napoleon met a woman whose life seemed even more worthy of novelization. Rose Tascher de la Pagerie came from a family of wealthy, noble plantation owners in the sugar islands of the French Caribbean. She married Alexandre de Beauharnais, a liberal noble who remained in the French army even after 1792, but during the Terror, they were both imprisoned as aristocrats, and Alexandre died under the guillotine. After Thermidor, Rose became the mistress of Napoleon's patron Paul Barras and through him, met Napoleon himself. He was instantly besotted with the beautiful, worldly Rose, caring nothing for the fact that Barras had effectively handed her down to him. In 1796, in the midst of his preparations to depart for Italy, they married.

His letters to her are extraordinary documents. Once again, he gave his love a new name: Joséphine (did he name her after his older brother Joseph, the man "to whom my heart entirely belongs"? A question best left to a psychoanalytical biographer). And once again, he strained desperately for romantic eloquence. December 1795:

> Sweet and incomparable Joséphine, what a strange effect you have on my heart! . . . I draw from your lips, from your heart, a flame that burns me . . . I will see you in three hours. In the meantime, *mio dolce amor,* here are a thousand kisses; but give me none, for they burn my blood.

Or March 31, 1796: "Joséphine! Joséphine! Remember what I have sometimes told you: nature gave me a strong and determined soul; it built you out of lace and gauze." At times, his thoughts turned positively purple. "A kiss lower, lower <u>than the heart!</u>" Even: "your little white breast, springy, so firm . . . and the little black forest, I send it a thousand kisses."

Joséphine herself, however, could not respond with anything like this ardor and clearly felt rather oppressed by it. Indeed, once Napoleon left for Italy, she took a young officer, Hippolyte Charles, as a lover. Pressed by her husband to come to Italy, she pleaded illness and (false) pregnancy and stopped writing. He responded with letters worthy of the most overblown romantic melodramas. June 8, 1796:

> Cruel one! How could you make me hope for a feeling that you didn't have! . . . Farewell, Joséphine, stay in Paris. Do not write me again . . . A thousand daggers tear at my heart, do not stick them in any farther.

October 17, 1796:

> Your letters are cold like middle age; they resemble fifteen years of marriage . . . Fie, Joséphine! It is so mean, so bad, so treasonous of you.

November 23, 1796:

> I no longer love you at all. To the contrary, I hate you. You are fiendish, awkward, stupid and decrepit . . . What do you do with yourself all day, Madame? What is so important that you have no time to write? . . . Who could this marvellous new lover be who takes up all your time . . . ? Be-

ware, Joséphine! One fine night the doors will be smashed in and there I
will be in your bed. Remember! Othello's little dagger!

But are these writings pure effusions of emotion? A window into the
depths of Napoleon's heart? If we read them closely, it becomes clear
that Napoleon didn't mean for Joséphine to take them entirely seriously. "In truth, I'm worried, my dear friend," he continued, immediately after his outlandish threat of murder. "I haven't had any news
from you. Write me quickly . . . I hope I'll be holding you in my arms
soon." In other words, the outburst was at least in part an act. Napoleon was consciously taking on a role and expressing his emotions in the
way that he had learned, at least in part, from novels. It is not so
strange. We all follow models, literary or otherwise, consciously or unconsciously, when we release our feelings. But Napoleon seems to have
taken this banal cultural habit to something of an extreme.

In this move from the battlefield of Arcola to the intimacy of Joséphine's boudoir, we may seem to have strayed rather far from the theme
of total war. But in fact, love and war are hardly so far removed from
each other (if you doubt it, read Stendhal). And Napoleon's sense of
himself as a character in a novel, which comes out so forcefully in his
letters to Joséphine, was in no sense incidental to his military and political careers. His novelistic sensibility, his ability to make a spectacle of
his inmost original self, goes a long way toward explaining how he
could forge the sort of bond that he did with his soldiers and, later, with
much of the French people. It explains their sense that they knew him
— the "little corporal" — personally, that they could care for him.

This sort of public self-presentation, it is worth stressing, was something quite new in French history. France's kings never allowed this degree of intimacy and familiarity with their subjects. As for the leaders of
the Revolution, *their* literary references were, for the most part, to the
great moralizing works of classical antiquity. Robespierre and Saint-Just
never let themselves be seen as figures with whom the ordinary French
person might feel comfortable, let alone intimate. They were men of
grand, windy abstraction. Mirabeau, perhaps, came closer to Napoleon
but died too soon. Marat also had something of Napoleon's inclinations, except that the intimate persona he chose to offer to his readers —
that of a raving, fanatical psychopath — attracted only a limited set of ad-

mirers. Danton had great popular skill but rarely committed his words to writing, and the sort of relationship that Napoleon enjoyed with his public was one that could be forged only through the medium of print. Indeed, without the explosion of the periodical press during the French Revolution, Napoleon's success would have been unimaginable.

Napoleon, in short, was the first true, great populist of the Revolutionary era: the first who could speak to his audiences in familiar, personal terms and be accepted as a man of the people even while presenting himself as an extraordinary genius. It is this quality, grounded in his literary sensibility, that explains the richness and depth of the cult that he helped develop around himself from the start of the Italian campaign. And, when coupled with his extraordinary successes, it is this quality that explains how he forged such an intense bond with his soldiers and indeed with the French as a whole.

In forging this bond, Napoleon could on occasion pose as a character surprisingly close to the Enlightenment tradition of hostility to warfare: Napoleon "the peacemaker of this vast universe," as one pamphlet called him. In Italy, he put up a monument whose inscription called for the breaking of swords and the "slaying of death" itself. During the campaign, he displayed an ostentatious concern for Italian arts and letters, declaring that all distinguished artists and scholars should have French citizenship, whatever their birth (his troops, meanwhile, were making Italian artworks French in a rather more literal manner, stripping the country of them wholesale and shipping them off to the Louvre). After his return from Italy in 1797, he ostentatiously joined the new scholarly National Institute and showed up regularly for its sessions, wearing civilian dress.

But Napoleon was never going to adopt Telemachus as a role model. To the extent that he saw himself as a literary character, his story was first and foremost one of military glory. As he himself recounted it, its key moment was the battle of Lodi, on May 10, 1796, when he personally directed operations, forcing his way across the Adda River and spectacularly defeating an Austrian army that was already in retreat. Years later, in exile, he told the members of his little entourage that "it was only on the evening of Lodi that I believed myself to be a superior man, and that the ambition came to me of executing the great things which so far had been occupying my thoughts only as a fantastic dream." In his own reckoning, then, his innermost self was defined by war — war was its ultimate test, what marked him as a unique personality.

And indeed, as the cult of Napoleon grew, a reglorification of war took place in France, centered on the notion that war might prove a regenerative, redemptive experience for individuals, as well as societies. The Enlightenment creed of peace now came in for more direct criticism than at any time in the Revolutionary period. Fittingly, it was in Napoleon's newspaper, the *Courier of the Army of Italy,* that a journalist wrote what amounted to its obituary, and an explicit renunciation of the National Assembly's 1790 declaration of peace:

> If we only consulted our feelings, we would wish ardently for fate to put an end to this deluge of blood . . . But if we . . . turn our glance to the future, we will see the sad necessity of new battles. The [National] Assembly . . . declared that France renounced all conquests. This idea might seem sublime at first, but it was driven by false philanthropy rather than by an enlightened love of humanity . . . A conquering republic is the benefactor of the nations that it conquers . . . And you, young hero, who have already shown yourself the equal of the greatest men of all time, and who may yet surpass them all . . . You can yet bring together the double glory of conqueror, and of benefactor of the nations.

Note the last sentence. Despite the author's care to defend war in the name of a higher, Revolutionary good, he nonetheless makes the title of "conqueror" a source of glory in its own right. And as Napoleon's career progressed, the glory of conquest would shine forth ever more powerfully from behind the thin gauze of ideological justification, until the latter was barely visible at all. Consider, for instance, the hero's next great adventure.

On July 1, 1798, a French armada appeared off the sun-bleached, palm-studded coast of Egypt, bearing an army of 25,000 men under Napoleon's command. That night, in a difficult operation, some 4,300 of them disembarked and drew up at dawn in front of the gates of the ancient city of Alexandria. Its governors refused the French demand to surrender, and so at midday, the invaders brought up ladders, scaled the walls, and attacked. Soon, Alexandria was in French hands.

A week later, the army began a 120-mile advance on Cairo. Napoleon made the usual, grueling demands on his men, forcing them to march every day, even in the midafternoon, in the savage midsummer heat of North Africa. A staff officer wrote to his parents that many soldiers, dressed in heavy cloth and bent double under their heavy packs, could not take the strain: "We saw them die of thirst, of starvation, of heat; others, seeing how their comrades were suffering, blew their brains out; others threw themselves into the Nile with their guns and their packs, and drowned." The army had no bread and made the march on a menu of pumpkins, melons, scrawny chickens, and the occasional withered vegetable. But Napoleon himself shared these discomforts and sometimes himself went a whole day without food. The army remained intact.

On July 21, in sight of the pyramids, the French confronted the forces of the Mamelukes, the warrior caste that ruled Egypt under the distant aegis of the Turkish sultan. Napoleon later claimed to have told his men, "Soldiers, forty centuries look down upon you." Six thousand Mameluke horsemen, supported by 12,000 foot soldiers, gallantly charged the French positions, but they had no hope of prevailing against Napoleon's well-drilled army, which fired salvos from impregnable infantry squares and wrought havoc with its powerful, mobile artillery. The battle was more of a massacre, and on July 24, the French made a triumphal entrance into the capital.

Over the next several months, Napoleon made efforts to transform Egypt into a model French colony — a supposed example of enlightened civilization at the heart of the Middle East. He set up a new government, grounded in a system of native councils, although he routinely overruled them. He ordered up a new system of courts, a postal service, a mint, hospitals, and a National Guard. He began a process of land reform. He set up printing presses and published a weekly newspaper. Whatever his lingering admiration for Robespierre, he had obviously forgotten the man's warning that "no one likes armed missionaries." Just as significantly, Napoleon established an Institute of Egypt staffed with 160 eminent French scholars, artists, and engineers. It met twice a week and discussed everything from the wings of Egyptian ostriches to the composition of the slime of the Nile to the discovery of Egyptian antiquities. In this last area, it did heroic work, including, famously, the discovery of the Rosetta stone, which allowed for the deciphering of Egyptian hieroglyphics.

Unlike earlier European invaders, the French had not come for the greater glory of the Christian god and hoped that a lack of religious conflict would smooth their conquest. Napoleon loudly declared his respect for Islam and hinted, amazingly, at even more. "We Frenchmen," he wrote to the pasha of Aleppo, "are no longer the infidels who . . . came to fight against your faith; we realize how sublime it is; *we profess it ourselves;* and the moment has come for all Frenchmen to . . . become believers like yourselves." He took to reading the Koran and engaged in discussions with Muslim clerics. A piece of Arabic verse published in his newspaper praised him as God's instrument, in terms that would have made even his European panegyrists blush: "Kings bow their proud heads before the invincible BONAPARTE, the lion of battles . . . the heavens of glory bow down before him." But all the reforms and religious flirtation did nothing to prevent an insurrection against his forces in Cairo in October, which they brutally suppressed.

Nor did Napoleon stay in Egypt long enough to bring his ambitious plans to fruition. At the beginning of August 1798, a British fleet under Admiral Nelson decimated the French in Aboukir Bay, cutting Napoleon off from home and making his long-term Egyptian prospects improbable, at best. The next February, fearing an attack by the Ottoman Turks, he marched 10,000 troops east from Egypt, across Sinai, and up what is now the coast of Israel. His troops again bore most of the burden, putting up with brackish water and dogs and camels to eat. Nonetheless, on March 7, they took Jaffa, near the site of present-day Tel Aviv, and continued up the coast toward the Turkish fortress of Acre. But close to 3,000 of his men fell ill with the plague, and marines from a British frigate captured much of the French artillery. Despite several frantic attacks, led by Napoleon in person, Acre — surrounded on three sides by the sea and resupplied by the British — did not fall. The French did manage to secure Egypt temporarily. In April, Napoleon met up with a second French army, under Kléber, and routed a Turkish force at Mount Tabor. Returning to Egypt, he then crushed an attempted Ottoman landing at Aboukir. But as long as the British controlled the Mediterranean, he could not hope for sufficient reinforcements to keep the colony strong enough to survive.

Worse, the letters making it through the British blockade were bringing desperate news from western Europe, where, in part as a result of the Egyptian campaign, a second armed coalition had formed against France. The Turks had declared war, and so had Tsar Paul I of Russia,

aghast at France's ambitions in the east. Austrian and Russian forces under the flamboyant general Suvorov were sweeping back into Italy,
helping to set off huge anti-French insurrections and reducing France's
puppet Italian republics to flotsam on the stream of war. French forces
were falling back in the north as well, while in France itself, the ashes of
the Vendée were reigniting: the rebels even briefly seized Nantes and Le
Mans. Parts of the new Belgian territories rose up as well, in a two-
month-long insurrection. Total French forces had fallen to perhaps
fewer than 200,000 men, a small fraction of their size in 1794, and they
could not initially hold back the flood.

For a brief moment, the dark summer of 1799 in fact looked very
much like the dark summer of 1793, which had brought forth both the
levée en masse and the Terror, and a repetition of both now seemed possible. To remedy the manpower shortage, the Directory implemented
the Jourdan Law, passed the previous year, which established a regular
system of conscription. Unlike the one-time measure of the *levée,* it
made the draft a permanent feature of French life. In July 1799, a Law
of Hostages held relatives of émigrés liable for the émigrés' actions. A
forced loan from the population followed, amid calls for a formal declaration of *la patrie en danger,* which would allow for yet more repressive
measures. Events, in short, were again moving with hurricane speed,
and it was time for Napoleon to return home. Incidentally, he had also
received reports of Joséphine's infidelity and ached to confront her.

The conclusion of the Egyptian expedition did its architect no credit.
At the end of August 1799, Napoleon and nearly all his top commanders embarked on two fast frigates. They slipped through the British
dragnet and reached France in early October. Napoleon left his successor, Kléber, to contend with increasing unrest and renewed Turkish attacks, with little chance of resupply. In 1800, a Muslim zealot would
murder Kléber in Cairo, and a year later, his successor, Menou (the
same man we met as a liberal aristocratic deputy to the 1790 National
Assembly), would finally surrender to the Turks and British, bringing
the brief-lived French colony to a predictable, inglorious end.

Historians often present the fall of French Egypt as a tragic end to
an otherwise glorious adventure. But this episode, which cost tens of
thousands of French lives and many more Muslim ones, was problematic — verging on absurd — from the start. Historians have given too
much credence to the claim that it constituted a serious strategic thrust

against Britain. They have speculated too energetically on Egypt's possible role as a French colony. They have lavished attention on the work of the Egyptian Institute. In fact, there were few rational reasons for the invasion. Egypt could, just possibly, have served as a base against British India. But at a time when most British traffic to India took the long route around Africa (the Suez Canal lay a century in the future), its strategic value remained relatively small — especially given Britain's clear maritime superiority. As French travelers in the region had long reported, the country had only very limited economic potential as a colony, and the work of the Institute, ambitious and interesting as it was, by itself could hardly justify such a massive expenditure of lives and resources.

There is some truth to the notion that Napoleon went to Egypt in part because it suited nearly everyone for him to be out of France. After the 1797 peace with Austria, he had first contemplated an invasion of England, then given it up as impractical. He had far-reaching political ambitions but as yet no realistic hope of achieving them. Remaining in France, though, and taking sides in its increasingly tawdry politics would only tarnish his image. Better to win new laurels elsewhere. As for the five Directors at the head of the government, they too welcomed the chance to be rid of an uncomfortably ambitious and popular general.

But the invasion of Egypt was also about something even less substantial than political convenience: glory. By early 1798, Napoleon's vision of himself as a "superior man" had been confirmed to him time and again by events and by the echo chamber of his own propaganda machine. To judge by the comments he made at the time, he truly believed that he might be another Alexander. Where better to prove the point than in Alexander's own domain — "the east"? Like most educated Europeans of the day, his youthful literary diet had included, amid the novels and history, a good dose of "oriental" exotica. These works provided little reliable information about the chain of civilizations that stretched from North Africa to East Asia, instead depicting the East as a mysterious realm of extremes: of luxury, debauch, and despotism, but also heroic deeds. It was a place where the daring, superior self might express itself more fully than amid the restraints of "civilized" Europe. It was undoubtedly this alluring fantasy that inspired Napoleon when he told his friend and secretary, Bourrienne: "Everything wears out here; my glory has already disappeared. This little Europe does not supply enough of it for me. I must seek it in the East, the fountain of glory." Even after his less than glorious return, he could not abandon these delusions. In a letter he wrote to Madame de Rémusat in the early 1800s, it was already as if the real expedition had never taken place:

> In Egypt, I found myself freed from the obstacles of an irksome civiliza-
> tion. I was full of dreams. I saw myself founding a religion, marching
> into Asia, riding an elephant, a turban on my head and in my hand a
> new Koran that I would have composed to suit my need. In my under-
> taking I would have combined the experience of the two worlds, exploit-
> ing for my own profit the theater of all history . . . The time I spent in
> Egypt was the most beautiful of my life because it was most ideal.

An absurd fantasy, of course, but beguiling, especially to himself. As during the Revolution, fantasy drove military policy to a degree that modern observers might barely think possible — were it not, that is, for the most recent Western invasion of a large Middle Eastern country, under equally implausible pretexts.

Absent from Napoleon's later reveries was any consideration of the actual tactics he had used to conquer, and then keep order in, Egypt. But far from representing any return to the chivalric warfare of times past, the Egyptian campaign fit squarely into the pattern of Revolutionary total warfare. No prince of the Old Regime would have attempted to impose an entirely new political and social order on a conquered state, the way Napoleon imposed his reforms on Egypt. And few princes of the Old Regime would have treated the Egyptian population as he did.

Consider the revolt of Cairo. In late October 1798, insurgents shook the French hold on the city and killed several high-ranking French officers, including Napoleon's own aide-de-camp. In response, the French did not hesitate to use the tactics they had perfected in the Vendée, sacking the neighborhood of Al-Azhar and killing as many as three thousand Egyptians. When the principal group of rebels took refuge in Cairo's grand mosque and asked for quarter, Bonaparte allegedly replied: "the hour of vengeance has sounded. You began and I will finish." Napoleon's official correspondence preserves the chilling order that he then issued to his chief of staff: "Citizen general, give the order to the commander in the square to cut the throats of all prisoners who were taken bearing arms. They will be brought tonight to the banks of the Nile . . . and their headless corpses thrown in the river."

Nor was this the worst atrocity committed. When the French took Jaffa in March 1799, four thousand Ottoman troops surrendered to them. Napoleon ordered all but the officers taken to the beach, lined up, and shot — allegedly over the protests of his own senior staff. Bourrienne later constructed an elaborate justification for this action, insisting that the French had no food or drink to give to the prisoners. It is a spurious argument — if Napoleon cared only about provisions, why would he bother insisting, in his written orders, that "precautions be taken to prevent any of the prisoners from escaping"? Whatever his logistical situation, Napoleon may well also have been trying to impress the allegedly ruthless Turkish governor of Syria. It was the sort of obscenely grand gesture that Alexander might have made.

And it was not the sort of gesture that Napoleon reserved exclusively for "the east," for although not immune from the prevailing racism of the day, he was very much an equal-opportunity killer. From the very start of his significant military exploits, in 1796, he had imposed unprecedented demands on occupied civilian populations. When these populations resisted, he responded with unrestrained violence.

Consider, for instance, what had happened in northern Italy in May 1796. Napoleon's forces had just entered Milan, and the area remained unsettled. Rumors spread of French defeats, and in several areas, thousands of peasants assembled, armed with farm implements, pikes, and fowling pieces, to chase out the occupiers. The city of Pavia rose up as well, trapping its small French garrison. Napoleon quickly sent out mobile columns against the insurgent forces. One of them intercepted a thousand peasants near the small town of Binasco, killed a hundred, and put the rest to flight. Binasco itself had not taken part in the insurrection, but Napoleon, desperate to prevent the troubles from spreading, ordered it put to the torch. "A vast conspiracy was being hatched against us," he wrote to his chief of staff by way of justification. In an official proclamation, he bluntly announced that those who did not demonstrate their loyalty "will be treated as rebels; their villages will be burned. May the terrible example of Binasco open their eyes!" Napoleon then stormed Pavia and held off ordering the city's total destruction only when the besieged French garrison appeared, safe and sound. Instead, he contented himself with letting his soldiers run wild for twenty-four hours, raping and looting. He also arrested several hundred leading citizens from the region and sent them back to France as hostages.

Such scenes repeated themselves throughout the years of the Directory. After Napoleon's forces turned south in the summer of 1796, it was the turn of Lugo, in the Papal States, to suffer the fate of Binasco. When the French moved into Switzerland in 1798, several Catholic cantons resisted, leading French observers to dub them "the Swiss Vendée" and to respond with tactics worthy of Turreau. In and around the Swiss town of Stanz, some six hundred houses were burned, and 1,200 men, women, and children died. Further scenes reminiscent of the Vendée occurred throughout Italy during the massive revolts of 1799, especially in the south, where French general Championnet had attempted to transform the kingdom of Naples into the "Parthenopean Republic."

Some of the worst atrocities, though, occurred outside of Europe, in what had once been the crown jewel of France's sugar colonies: Saint-Domingue, today known as Haiti. In 1790, 50,000 white colonists had ruled with unspeakable cruelty over a largely African-born slave population ten times larger. The French Revolution, however, destabilized this fragile situation and triggered the largest slave rebellion in human history. In 1801, after a decade of terrible but ultimately inconclusive fighting, an expedition arrived to restore French rule, led by Napoleon's brother-in-law Charles-Victor-Emmanuel Leclerc. Initially, it met with some success, and Leclerc even managed to deport to France the charismatic Haitian general Toussaint L'Ouverture. But when he tried to disarm thousands of former slaves, he provoked an insurrection and replied to it with exterminationist tactics. "Here is my opinion on this country," he wrote to Napoleon in the fall of 1802. "We must destroy all negroes of the mountains, men and women, keeping only the children younger than twelve; destroy half of those in the plains and not leave alive in the colony a single man of color who has worn epaulettes. Without this the colony will never be peaceful." Words worthy of General Turreau in the Vendée! Before virulent yellow fever doomed the French force (killing Leclerc in the process), its leaders did their best to live up to this sanguinary promise. They summarily executed captured rebels, engaged in bouts of indiscriminate slaughter, and even imported man-eating dogs from Cuba. Although Haiti's death toll is even harder to calculate than that of the Vendée, it is certain that many tens of thousands died from all causes — and conceivably as much as a third of the prewar population.

We will look more closely at the story of French occupations in Chapter 8, but one basic point is worth making here: the horrors experienced in occupied territories were not simply the result of poor or criminal French leadership. They arose out of the transformed nature of war itself, following the breakdown of Old Regime restraints and the experience of the Revolution. Where the French army arrived as an occupier, bloody insurrections often followed, answered by brutal counterinsurgency. Every territory the French occupied had the potential to become a Vendée.

Why? Start with the fact, most often cited by historians, that unlike the armies of the Old Regime, the French forces tried as much as possible to live off the land — to have "war feed war." In most areas where they took control, they imposed large taxes and fines on the native population. They confiscated artistic treasures and religious properties on a large scale. Napoleon did attempt to repress pillage and theft by individual soldiers, but his men nonetheless saw the campaigns as a literal chance to make their fortunes. Napoleon probably did not promise Italian "honor, glory and riches" to his "naked and hungry" men, to quote words he later claimed to have uttered, but they acted as if he had done so.

But the coming of the French meant more than financial burdens. In European countries, it also meant the end of the Old Regime. Unlike occupations carried out in earlier eighteenth-century wars, which tended to leave traditional institutions in place, at least until a final peace settlement, the Revolutionary forces repeated in the conquered territories what they had already carried out at home. They swept away or modified complex ancient systems of taxation, administration, and justice. They cut back or abolished social privileges. As in France itself, the changes touched the lives of virtually the whole population, threatening established livelihoods and everywhere generating tremendous anxiety. Even where particular groups stood to gain from the occupation — seeing a hated tax lifted, a law court moved closer to home, or coveted land suddenly offered for sale — the sheer uncertainty made it easy for insurgents to gain support. In the areas annexed by France, attempts to introduce conscription in 1798–99 had much the same effect that it had had in the Vendée in 1793: the demands of total war sparked bloody revolt.

As in France itself, religion provided some of the driest, most combustible tinder, and the French sprayed showers of sparks onto it. By 1796, most French officers and men had spent at least three years in an effectively godless army, from which chaplains and religious services had vanished, even if the Republic itself no longer considered Christianity an enemy. So the armies and the occupied populations gazed on each other like strange alien species, even before the French started to ransack local churches and confiscate local lands. In Lugo, the insurrection began when local authorities, acting for the French, tried to confiscate a statue of Saint Ilaro, the town's patron saint. A crowd led by priests and friars forcefully repossessed it, brought it back to its church amid the pealing of bells, and then went on to assault the town citadel "in the name of our holy religion." Napoleon's vigorously anticlerical deputy Augereau, who had served in the Vendée, showed no desire to negotiate with the people he called "these miserable reptiles." Instead, he stormed Lugo, killing hundreds.

Just as in France itself, the war quickly took on the character of a civil war. Wherever the French took power in Europe, significant numbers of people, especially in the cities, welcomed them in the name of Revolutionary values: Dutch "patriots," German "Jakobiner," Italian "Giacobini." These men staffed the governments of the new satellite republics and carried out — gladly, at least to begin with — French-inspired reforms they themselves had often dreamed of for years. Heavily urban and cosmopolitan, they saw the rural and lower-class insurgents much as the French did: as ignorant, superstitious obstacles to the forces of historical progress. As a result, the occupation became the occasion for any number of settling of old scores: between city and countryside, between regions, between competing institutions.

The greatest potential for bloodshed did not occur where French authority was most oppressive but where it appeared most fragile. In 1799, with the Second Coalition driving French armies back throughout Europe, hopeful revolts spread across the continent like streams of flaming gasoline. In the southern Italian province of Calabria, Cardinal Fabrizio Ruffo proclaimed a crusade against the French and raised a popular army that carried out horrible atrocities against captured French soldiers, "Giacobini," and Jews (whom the rebels all too easily associated with the French). Similarly, in Tuscany, thirteen Jews were burned alive and four hundred suspected "Giacobini" massacred. Where the French still could, they responded brutally, in keeping with their own dynamic of total war.

The spread of insurrections would suggest that the distinction between military and civilian populations remained blurry in 1794–99. On the irregular battlefields of French-occupied territories, it certainly did. As in the Vendée, entire populations were treated as combatants. But in France itself, the same period saw something of the opposite phenomenon: a growing cleavage between military and civilian spheres. The political consequences would be immense.

As we have seen, European states in the eighteenth century had already shown some tendencies to segregate their military forces from the rest of society, above all by building permanent camps and barracks for soldiers and by trying to remake officer corps into full-time professional bodies. But in France, these reforms did not go far enough to change the military's essentially aristocratic character, and at the start of the Revolution, it was precisely this aristocratic character that made the army an object of such enormous, almost paranoid, suspicion to radicals. As a result, not only did the Jacobins bloodily purge aristocrats from the officer corps, but also, through the *levée en masse,* they sought to erase the distinction between army and nation entirely. "What is the army?" a deputy asked. "It is France as a whole . . . All French citizens are the army." Most radicals still believed in the coming end of the age of war and did not want to see France transformed into a permanently warring Sparta. But until the final peace, everyone would fight.

After 1794, however, new and far deeper cracks opened up between the military and civilian society. The soldiers recruited in the first two years of the war remained in the field, largely outside of France and isolated from civilian society. Naturally, they began to identify principally with the army itself and with generals like Napoleon, who so ostentatiously looked out for their welfare. The Revolutionary indoctrination through speeches, songs, and newspapers, to which the Jacobins had subjected the rank and file, did not long survive the end of the Terror and its radical enthusiasms. Now, the generals encouraged soldiers to take pride in victory for its own sake and for its extension of French power. "Soldiers!" Napoleon typically proclaimed. "Do once more what we have done so often, and Europe will not challenge us for the title of the bravest and most powerful nation in the world!" The generals forced the weakened central government to do away with the political commissioners who had accompanied the armies under the Terror. Increasingly, like Napoleon in Italy, they behaved like princes.

Most significantly for the future, they also drew a severely unfavorable contrast between the patriotism that allegedly prevailed in the armies and the corruption and partisan bickering back home. Napoleon, with his unmatched talent for spectacle, knew precisely how to impress on his soldiers this sense of their own moral superiority. On July 14, 1797, Bastille Day, he staged a military parade in Milan, in which soldiers marched past a monument bearing the names of the dead of the campaign. "You see before you," he told them, "the names of our companions in arms who died on the field of honor." Then, shifting gears, he turned to a darker theme: "the misfortunes which threaten the *patrie*" — a clear reference to the deteriorating political situation back home. As the parade continued, a well-prompted corporal stepped out of the ranks and shouted to him: "General, you have saved France. Your children, who glory in belonging to this invincible army, will shield you with their own bodies. Now, save the Republic!"

Back in France itself, the remnants of the Jacobins unwittingly helped to widen the cracks, while also accelerating the regime's disintegration. In the elections of 1797, when the resurgent right wing triumphed, the Left looked to the army for rescue. One left-wing paper put the matter as bluntly as possible: "The great deluge was necessary to purge the earth. We now need the armies to purify France." A left-wing Director similarly declared, in a speech, that "the Republic exists almost nowhere but in the armies." Napoleon cast his lot with the conspirators and committed his already huge prestige to their cause. Thus the spectacle on July 14, in which he prepared the army and declared that the Republic had nothing to fear from the royalists. He then dispatched one of his subordinates to Paris, along with troops. With their help, the assemblies and the Directory were purged on September 4 — the 18th Fructidor under the new calendar. The Left had prevailed, but at the huge cost of legitimizing military interference in domestic politics and making the army, in the words of historian Jean-Paul Bertaud, "a counter-power."

As for Napoleon, the episode only confirmed him in the superiority he had felt toward politicians since the start of the Italian campaign. His secretary later remembered him saying: "I ought to overthrow them, and make myself King"; he dismissed the Directors as "a pack of lawyers." A diplomat similarly quoted him calling the Republic "a fancy [that] will pass away . . . The nation must have a chief." But Napoleon added, according to both men: "the time has not yet come." It is difficult not to agree with the royalist newspaper that quipped, even before the 18th Fructidor, that Napoleon fought like Alexander but was a citizen in the manner of Julius Caesar. After the coup, another paper asked: "Is the Rubicon already crossed? Will we avoid a military republic?"

Napoleonic France would never be a true military dictatorship, but the coup of Fructidor nevertheless marked a key stage in the appearance of modern militarism. A separation had taken place between civilian and military, and the leaders of the latter had come to the conclusion that they, more than any politicians, most truly represented the nation. Therefore, they had the right to impose their own, military values of order, discipline, and unquestioned patriotism on civilians. By 1799, some figures in the army were saying so explicitly. "When a people becomes conquering," wrote an army captain that year, "it is indispensable that the military spirit dominate over the other orders." According to General Picauld-Desdorides, "our rarely interrupted wars prove to the French that they should be an entirely military people." Such ideas had been almost literally unthinkable under the Old Regime, when the aristocratically led armed forces were considered an integral part of the social fabric rather than a distinct society of its own. A military coup had been impossible, because at the heart of the aristocratic military code lay the principle of absolute loyalty to the king. But now the code and the king were gone, and the most popular general of the age was waiting for his opportunity.

It came two years later. While Napoleon drank from his Egyptian "fountain of glory," the Directory continued to decompose, and the unscrupulous Sieyès — the early Revolutionary hero turned cynical executive — began his search for a "sword." The military situation had turned dire as well, as the Republic's forces fell back and insurrections ignited across Europe. The need for a "savior" had never been greater.

By the time Napoleon landed back in France, in early October, the military situation, at least, had improved. His former deputy from Italy, André Masséna, had defeated the Russians in a climactic battle near

Zurich, and Russian general Suvorov had been pushed into the Alps, where cold and famine decimated his army. General Brune defeated the Anglo-Russian forces in the Netherlands, and on October 22, the unstable Tsar Paul, frustrated with the defeats and unhappy with his Austrian allies, withdrew from the coalition.

Sieyès, however, remained adamant in his search for a general. A cold, precise man who had once advocated the interbreeding of monkeys and humans to provide a new species of born slaves, he had long lost the political enthusiasm of the early Revolution. When asked what he had done under the Terror, he replied laconically: "I survived." Now he wanted simply to restore order and perhaps enrich himself in the process. Napoleon was not his first choice for the role of man on horseback. Sieyès would have preferred a puppet who would not tower over all other political figures. However, his first choice, General Barthélémy-Catherine Joubert, died at the battle of Novi in August. Sieyès then approached General Jean-Victor Moreau, and the two were reportedly together when they heard the news of Napoleon's return. "There is your man," Moreau supposedly remarked to Sieyès.

News of Napoleon's failures in Egypt had not yet caught up with him. Instead, the expedition had only inflated his legend further, precisely as he had hoped. In workers' districts in Paris, police spies reported that he was now being hailed as the "exiled hero" and as "our father, our savior" in popular songs. When he came to Lyons in October, people danced in the streets, and less than a day after his arrival, a play entitled *The Return of the Hero, or Bonaparte at Lyons* was staged there. When the news of his return was announced in Paris theaters, crowds rose to their feet and cheered. "On every face, in every conversation, was written the hope of salvation and the presentiment of happiness." Napoleon, to these ordinary men and women, represented security, stability — and glory.

Once in Paris, Napoleon met with Sieyès, and a plot was quickly hatched (he also reconciled — stormily — with Joséphine). The regime of the Directory was to be dissolved and replaced by three interim "consuls": Napoleon, Sieyès, and Sieyès's colleague Roger Ducos, a nonentity. On November 9, 1799 — the 18th of Brumaire — the upper chamber of the parliament, meeting in the absence of left-wing deputies, duly declared that with France under threat, both chambers would adjourn the next day to the suburban town of Saint-Cloud. Napoleon, before his troops, let loose a stream of abuse against the government: "What have you done with the France I left you so brilliant? I left you peace, I find war! I left you conquests, I find the enemy at our borders!" True, the renewed war was as much his fault as anyone else's, and the enemy had already been driven back — which was more than he had accomplished at the other end of the Mediterranean. But as always with Napoleon, the legend had a force quite independent of the truth.

The next day, the parliament, under the "protection" of Napoleon's soldiers at Saint-Cloud, met for its appointment to commit institutional suicide. But the event almost failed to transpire, for in the lower chamber, whose members dressed in faintly ludicrous simulacra of Roman togas, a large number of deputies balked. What dangers, they demanded to know, amid much grandiloquent swearing of oaths, were so pressing as to demand their dissolution? When Napoleon appeared before them, he was unprepared for the challenges and stammered out vague threats: "Don't forget, I walk with the God of war and the God of victory!" Loud protests greeted him, and he fled the meeting hall. One deputy even pulled out a dagger. Had a strong figure emerged in the chamber, it is quite possible that the parliament might have declared Napoleon an outlaw then and there and sent him to the guillotine.

But once again — as at Maddalena, Toulon, and Arcola — Napoleon survived, and the history books therefore do not remember him as a glorious Republican general who died in the midst of a squalid failed coup. No Mirabeau emerged to rally the deputies; outside, Lucien Bonaparte encouraged the soldiers by waving a dagger and threatening to plunge it into Napoleon's breast if he ever became a tyrant. The soldiers then marched inside, dispersed most of the deputies, and gathered a small rump (100 out of 750) who obediently voted to dissolve the regime and appoint the three consuls to replace it. This recourse to force ("Citizens, you are dissolved!" General Murat told the deputies) altered the nature of the coup, stamping it with a far more explicitly military character than Sieyès had planned for. And of the three consuls, as Sieyès would quickly discover, only one counted. A soldier had come to power.

To be sure, Napoleon had support that ranged far beyond the ranks of the military, and the Eighteenth Brumaire, as it became known, did not amount to the simple triumph of the army over the civilian population. Napoleon appealed to a broad swath of the French — wealthy property owners, first and foremost — who longed for social and political stability after so many years of turmoil. He generated enthusiasm among influential intellectuals. He soothed his more hesitant supporters with promises that his rise to power would *not* mean the installation of a military regime. However, the bond Napoleon had forged with the French was a bond born out of, and dependent on, military glory. Brumaire happened in the midst of a full-scale, Revolutionary war, with much of France already under military rule. Napoleon's ascent might point to the return of internal strength, but it also promised war without end. In practice, the two were inseparable.

7

Days of Glory

Today . . . no government would dare say to its nation: Let us go conquer the world.
— BENJAMIN CONSTANT, 1813

I wanted to rule the world — who wouldn't have, in my place?
— NAPOLEON BONAPARTE, TO BENJAMIN CONSTANT, 1815

Marengo, northern Italy. June 14, 1800. 5:00 P.M.
The day is turning into a disaster. On the flat, muddy plain of Bormida, forty-five miles north of Genoa, a well-drilled Austrian army is slowly and methodically pushing Napoleon Bonaparte toward defeat. As France's First Consul, he is wearing, under his gray topcoat, a sumptuous dark blue uniform trimmed with gold leaf and is carrying a heavy ceremonial sword with a hilt elegantly sculpted into twin lions' heads. But the splendor cannot distract him from the fact that he has made a dreadful mistake. Thinking that a confrontation with the Austrian army of General Michael Melas was days off, he has spread his army thinly across the plain and dispatched his best subordinate, Louis Desaix, southward with six thousand men to block Melas's escape route. Even after the Austrians came across the Bormida River in force in the morning, it took Napoleon more than an hour to realize that the attack was not a mere feint. Now he is feeling the lack of men with desperate intensity. A note he has scribbled to Desaix reads: "For God's sake, come up if you still can."

His soldiers are exhausted and dangerously demoralized. In the French ninety-sixth demi-brigade, the grenadiers can barely see each other in the smoke. Despite rain the day before, the artillery has set the wheat fields on fire, and cartridge boxes left on the ground are exploding, sending shockwaves of panic through the ranks. No reinforcements have come in hours, and so the ammunition is running out. Worse, the French musket barrels are so hot from repeated firing that they can't be loaded without the risk of exploding in their owners' faces. In desperation, the soldiers are using a classic remedy: opening their trousers and urinating into the guns to cool them. But one powerful Austrian cavalry charge may be all that is needed at this point to break the French lines and turn a measured retreat into a rout.

And what then? Possibly, Napoleon can regroup and beat Melas elsewhere. But at this moment, here at Marengo, with Melas already accepting a round of applause from his staff officers, things look distinctly unpromising. Just ten days ago, the last French satellite state in Italy, the "Ligurian Republic" of Genoa, fell to the Austrians. All Napoleon's earlier gains in the country have been wiped out. If he is decisively beaten at Marengo, he will look dangerously like yesterday's man. Other generals are waiting for news and gently casting exploratory lures into the cloudy and treacherous waters of Parisian politics. Will Napoleon survive any better in these waters than Louis XVI or Robespierre?

But now, with the late spring sun still high, comes the first hint of deliverance. Desaix is back. Indeed, he had turned his troops around even before receiving Napoleon's note, correctly judging from the distant sound of guns that a major battle had begun. Desaix clearly enjoys the attention as he gallops in to consult. At thirty-two, he is something of a dandy, with sharp, delicate features and luxuriant dark hair worn long and loose over the shoulders. "The battle is completely lost," he supposedly remarks, but "we have time to gain another today." Across the wavering French lines, the troops cheer the news of his arrival.

And so the battle begins again. Desaix places his division directly in the path of the principal Austrian column. To his right, the French put together a battery of eighteen cannon, and to the left, there moves up a cavalry unit led by General François-Etienne Kellermann, son of the victor of Valmy. The cannon blast canister into the Austrian vanguard, but the bulk of the enemy column holds fast. Desaix leads a frontal attack on horseback. Then potential catastrophe: almost immediately, a bullet takes the general in the chest, and he slumps off his horse, dead. His corpse will lie on the ground for hours, until someone finally recognizes him by his distinctive hair. His troops pull back in disarray.

But the French have one last chance. The thirty-year-old Kellermann has brought five hundred horsemen around to the right of Desaix's position and now leads another charge, directly into the side of the Austrian column. Whether by skill or good luck, he has chosen exactly the right moment, immediately after another French artillery salvo, and he crashes into the Austrians at a moment of maximum confusion. His men's sabers slice down from their charging, snorting horses with hideous effect, and the Austrian column breaks apart in a sudden splash of fear, as men run or plead for their lives. Within minutes, three thousand are dead or prisoners, and the battle has swiveled decisively in Napoleon's favor. Other Austrian cavalry, exhausted and without orders, remain out of the action, and the Austrian commanders finally have no choice but to order a general retreat back across the Bormida.

General Melas has lost nearly 10,000 men, dead and prisoners. Still, the bulk of his army has survived in one piece, and a more adventurous commander — a more Napoleonic one — might try to roll the dice again. But Melas, a seventy-one-year-old who has spent more than half a century in the Austrian army, is no gambler. A cautious, aristocratic officer in the Old Regime style, he has more than a little in common with his contemporary the Duke of Brunswick, who preferred to march the Prussian army away from Valmy intact in 1792 rather than risk continuing the battle, and thereby handed the French Revolutionaries their most famous victory. Now Melas does something similar. He withdraws, asks to negotiate, and on June 16, finding his troops in a disadvantageous position, signs an armistice under which he agrees to pull Austrian forces out of Lombardy and Genoa. The Prussian military theorist Heinrich Dietrich von Bülow, the keenest contemporary observer of the 1800 campaign, will conclude that Napoleon did not grasp success; Melas threw it away.

But the success is there, nonetheless, and thanks to a Napoleonic propaganda machine now powered by the full resources of the French state, Marengo will soon become nothing short of an epic victory (not to mention a famous chicken recipe, supposedly derived from Napoleon's dinner before the battle). The usual battalion of journalists, poets, orators, sculptors, and painters will magically transform the French

Jacques-Louis David: *Napoleon on the Saint-Bernard Pass*

leader's unusually lackluster campaign performance into near-magical strategic acumen, his battlefield luck into an effusion of pure tactical genius. Kellermann's brilliantly timed charge will be played down or overlooked entirely or attributed to direct orders from the omniscient commander. Desaix will be hailed as a glorious hero, but then, he is conveniently dead. The propagandists will also adroitly steer attention back from the battle itself to Napoleon's decision, at the start of the campaign, to march his army into Italy over the high, treacherous St. Bernard pass in the Alps, in the hope of surprising Melas. The army benefited from favorable weather and even then nearly came to grief in the mountains before emerging into the Italian plains, to the consternation of the Austrians. The crossing will become a key chapter in the Napoleonic legend, suggesting comparisons with Hannibal and Charlemagne. It will also give rise to the single most famous image of Napoleon, painted by the resilient Jacques-Louis David, originally in a commission for the king of Spain. In it, the young leader, shorn of the furs he wore in the mountains, and seated on a bucking charger rather than the mule he actually rode, seems to dominate the very rocks, wind, and sky.

On July 2, Napoleon returns to Paris in triumph. The rumors of his fall have vanished like droplets in bright sun. His power is now ensured, and after General Moreau beats the Austrians again at Hohenlinden a few months later, forcing them out of the war altogether, it will be reinforced. As the historian François Furet has observed, Marengo, "far more than Brumaire," has served as "the true coronation of [Napoleon's] power and his regime." But it is a coronation that has come at a price. It is nothing less than "the result of the most one-sided contract that a nation had ever made with its leader, who was forced into a commitment never to be beaten." Napoleon will do his best to keep this commitment. But over the next fifteen years, France's adversaries will learn to play the game of total war. And as they do, Napoleon will find the large-scale struggle for Europe as difficult to control as the small-scale events on the plain of Bormida.

With hindsight, it is tempting to think of Napoleon's entire career as hurtling irresistibly toward that colossal confrontation. But for many years, even after he took power, this supposedly inevitable final destination was anything but clearly in sight. During the period known as the Consulate (1799–1804), Napoleon himself could still scarcely dream that by the age of forty he would rule the greatest empire Europe had seen since the days of the Caesars, striding as a victor into the royal palaces of Austria and Prussia (with Russia soon to follow). Amazing as his career had been so far, the still more amazing conclusion remained largely unthinkable. The path to the "great empire," and thence to its swift, cataclysmic collapse, was surprisingly tortuous.

The Consulate itself was a period of extraordinary achievements, but also of extraordinary tensions. On the one hand, despite quickly seizing supreme power and grinding down the surviving shards of French democracy, Napoleon ostentatiously reinforced critical elements of the

Revolutionary social order, including equality before the law and religious freedom. He even paid lip service to popular sovereignty by submitting his rule to repeated plebiscites. Such was his genuine popularity ("except for Washington in America, no chief magistrate of any republic has ever been so universally popular," wrote an opponent) that he scored genuine victories in these, although he still cheated, so as to make his support seem even more overwhelming. A few years later, after having executed a Bourbon prince for conspiring against him, he declared, with apparent conviction: "I am the French Revolution. I say it again and stick by it."

Yet even while cementing these elements of the Revolutionary heritage, he moved quickly toward older forms of legitimation as well. In 1802, he signed a "Concordat" with Pope Pius VII, restoring Roman Catholicism to a formal public role in French society, even while subordinating it firmly to the state. The same year, he moved closer to monarchy by making himself "Consul for Life." And in 1804, he finally dispensed with the Republic altogether, proclaiming himself emperor. On December 2, he took a crown from the hands of Pope Pius in the Cathedral of Notre Dame and placed it on his head (inimitably, he turned to his brother Joseph on the occasion and remarked, in Italian: "*si babbù ci vede*" — "if only Dad could see us now"). David's former student Jean-Auguste-Dominique Ingres painted the new emperor in his coronation robes as an eerie medieval icon, flat, pale, and expressionless below his massive robes (one critic called the work an attempt "to push back art four centuries"). Yet significantly, even here Napoleon refused to break with modern constitutional forms. The Empire came into being not with the coronation but with an act of Napoleon's tame Senate.

The Consulate was also torn between the militarism that Napoleon had ridden to power and his sincere ambition to forge an explicitly "civilian" regime. Certainly, there can be no gainsaying the centrality of military glory to his rule. His insistence on leading his armies in person and the adulation heaped on him after Marengo testify amply to it. The handpicked Senators founding the Empire in 1804 invoked his military achievements again and again. "What other glory," asked one in a typical effusion, "does not eclipse and efface itself before that of the incomparable Hero who has conquered them all, who has plucked everything out of chaos and created another universe for us?" But the Consulate

Jean-Auguste-Dominique Ingres: *Napoleon in His Coronation Robes*

was not a military regime. Napoleon did not staff his ministries with soldiers and did not rely on the army to maintain order. In fact, such was his success at "pacifying" French territory that by 1804, the army's role in policing had diminished considerably since the unruly late 1790s. Napoleon told one colleague that "I do not govern as a general, but because the nation believes that I have the civilian qualities required for governing." He devoted much of his time and energy to administrative reform and the new law code and cultivated the support of wealthy property owners at least as much as that of his generals.

Finally, and most important for our story, Napoleon posed not simply as a glorious conqueror but also as a peacemaker. The same propaganda machine that celebrated Marengo's "lightning bolts of war" also insisted that Napoleon had fought in 1800 to bring the wars to an end. In a message to his parliament in 1801, the First Consul explained that the end of the Revolution at home meant an end to it abroad as well. The time of "vain abstractions" was over. France would now respect both old and new forms of government. It could now be hoped that "the nations of the south and north alike . . . have abjured hateful passions and decided to put an end to their quarrels." The echoes of the Enlightenment language of peace and progress were unmistakable, and a year later, one of Napoleon's legislators invoked it even more explicitly:

> Now that, in our day, the furor of war has given way to social ideas, now that France has returned with glory to its proper place in the European family, it should . . . coordinate its intentions with those of other peoples, to preserve that harmony of principles which . . . perpetuates that peace which is so necessary to the happiness of all nations.

This was not the utopian hope for immediate and perpetual peace, which had gripped the left-wing deputies of the National Assembly in 1790 and which Napoleon would later, in exile, unconvincingly assert that he had always kept close to his heart. But neither was it the hysterical yearning for "regeneration through blood," which had gripped the Girondins during their push for war in 1791–92.

In fact, throughout Napoleon's career, the loudest defenses of war as a positive good came not from him, but from France's opponents. In 1797, the oracular Savoyard reactionary Joseph de Maistre published a ferocious, enormously influential book entitled *Considerations on France,* which denounced the French Revolution as the work of Satan. In one chapter, he described nature as inescapably violent, thanks to mankind's original sin. And in words eerily reminiscent of the Girondins (although he would have shuddered at the comparison), he

added: "When the human soul has lost its driving force thanks to soft-
ness, skepticism and the gangrenous vices that stem from an excess of
civilization [!], it can only be reinvigorated by blood." Three years later,
the conservative German publicist Friedrich Gentz reprised the theme
in an essay couched as a reply to Kant's *Perpetual Peace*. Although he
agreed with Kant that human reason drove mankind toward an end to
war, the "law of raw nature," he insisted, pointed in the other direction:
"Animal creation lives and prospers only through war." The echoes of
the earlier, Enlightenment enthusiasts for war, such as Embser and
Humboldt, were clear.

Napoleon, despite striking many as the very epitome of "raw nature," never adopted this sort of language. Instead, his public proclamations on war tended to waver between invocations of the old aristocratic code of honor and Enlightenment concepts of peace. And
between 1800 and 1803, he managed to act the part of peacemaker with
remarkable conviction. In this short period, he reached separate diplomatic agreements with the United States, Spain, Austria, Naples, Bavaria, Portugal, Russia, and the Ottoman Empire. Most important, on
March 25, 1802, he signed the Peace of Amiens with Great Britain, ending hostilities with France's strongest and most determined opponent
and bringing the Revolutionary wars, properly speaking, to an end. His
propaganda choir predictably hailed him as the "angel of peace" and
"pacifier of nations."

But the peace did not last. In fact, scarcely a year elapsed before hostilities resumed between France and Britain, to be followed two years later
by the formation of another great anti-French coalition. From then on,
fighting would continue, uninterrupted, until the collapse of Napoleon's empire in 1814. Historians have debated for two centuries why
the peace did not last and will surely continue to do so for at least another two. The majority follow Napoleon's opponents in placing the
blame primarily on the man himself: his unquenchable ambition and
addiction to conquest. They dismiss the peace rhetoric of 1800–3 as a
feint, and some, such as Paul Schroeder, go so far as to brand Napoleon
a "criminal." In France, though, a few scholars continue to take a more
nuanced view or even to follow Napoleon in arguing that his adversaries forced him into war. The emperor, in his prolix final years, provided

plentiful evidence to both sides, protesting his peaceful intentions at length but also remarking casually to Benjamin Constant: "I wanted to rule the world — who wouldn't have, in my place?"

The Napoleon haters probably have the stronger case, but both sides underestimate the extent to which the wars had a dynamism and logic independent of anyone's intentions. They do not fully recognize just how much the meteor strike of the Revolution and its continuing, violent aftershocks had destabilized European international relations, making any peace settlement even more fragile than earlier ones. After more than a century in which western European borders had changed mostly in small increments, the decade 1792–1802 had seen France annex modern Belgium, the German Rhineland, and parts of northern Italy while turning the Netherlands, Switzerland, and more of northern Italy into satellite states. These large-scale transfers left countless border issues unsettled, while France, simply to guard its newly swollen territory and sphere of influence, now perceived vital strategic interests in areas that had once barely excited its attention. Napoleon also believed that France deserved to regain the colonial empire it had lost during the Seven Years' War of 1756–63 and the Haitian Revolution of 1791. So a very long list of potential flashpoints quickly accumulated, from the Netherlands (where Napoleon insisted on keeping troops, in defiance of the treaty) to Malta (which the British refused to evacuate, in defiance of the treaty) to Egypt (which Napoleon openly spoke of retaking) to Haiti (which, as we saw in the previous chapter, he *did* send an expedition to retake, with disastrous results) to the Louisiana Territory (which he reacquired from Spain before selling it to the United States), and so on. In Italy, he annexed additional territories beyond the "natural frontier" of the Alps. In Germany, he helped bring about a large-scale territorial reorganization (known, in the inimitable German, as the *Reichsdeputationshauptschluss*) that ruthlessly swept up the swarming statelets that had depended for survival on the Hapsburg emperor. Not surprisingly, what Napoleon presented as simple defense of France's new position, his adversaries perceived as naked aggression.

Second, it has not been sufficiently appreciated that for all Napoleon's gestures toward older forms of legitimacy, he never managed to reestablish with his enemies the relationship of "honorable adversaries" that had characterized war before 1789. In Britain in particular, suspicion of him remained enormous. "His hold upon France is the sword, and he has no other," Prime Minister William Pitt had warned in 1800. "Can he afford to let his military renown pass away, to let his laurels wither, to let the memory of his achievements sink in obscurity?" Although Pitt left office in 1801, his views remained widely shared in Britain, in large part because of Napoleon's Jacobin past and his unmistakable loathing of all things British. "If my voice has any influence," he had promised in 1798, "England will never have an hour's respite from us. Yes, yes! War to the death with England! Always! — until she is destroyed!" He dreamed of the islands' becoming "a mere appendix of France" — something like Corsica. So it was hardly surprising that the British, in turn, viewed him largely as a usurper.

Finally, we need to remember that to a large extent, Pitt was right: Napoleon's political survival *did* depend on unceasing military accomplishment. He himself said as much at the time of the Peace of Amiens: "A First Consul is not like kings . . . who see their states as an inheritance; he needs brilliant deeds, and, therefore, war." He might put on the mantle of a peacemaker but only one who *imposed* peace, from a position of strength. He could not afford the appearance of weakness and so stubbornly refused to compromise in one dispute after another. Napoleon's own foreign minister, Talleyrand, would later write of 1802–3 that "this peace had not yet received its complete execution before [Napoleon] was sowing the seeds of new wars." In May 1803, Britain seized all the French ships in British ports, and Napoleon ordered the arrest of several thousand Britons unlucky enough to be caught on French soil. The war had resumed.

It remained total war. For all Napoleon's gestures toward the Old Regime, he could not easily reject the style of large-scale, lightning warfare he had perfected in his two Italian campaigns. Furthermore, the sheer number of possible flashpoints with the allies, the sheer size of the territories he now felt he needed to protect, and the sheer number of troops he needed to raise, equip, and support as a result required mobilization on a scale not even seen during the Revolution. Meanwhile, Britain's refusal to treat him as a legitimate sovereign drove Napoleon back toward fantasies of destroying the "new Carthage" as thoroughly as Rome had destroyed the old one. He cared enormously what the British thought of him, to the point that during the peace, he had demanded that the British government suppress attacks on him and his family in the British press (they appeared in profusion, and with a ferocity that puts even modern British tabloids to shame). When the war started again, not only did he take the radical step of arresting all British subjects in France, but also he hired Bertrand Barère, author of the "take no prisoners" decree of 1794, to recycle the bilious Revolutionary writings that had called for the extermination of treacherous Albion.

When he returned to the battlefield, the resources Napoleon could now draw on did in fact make an overpowering assault on his adversaries a realistic possibility. These resources included France's unmatched wealth, now rebuilt after the Revolutionary turmoil; its large population, now swollen well beyond the 30-million mark by the annexations; the Revolutionary tradition of the nation in arms, which the legislation of 1798 had transformed into a system of regular conscription; his own efficient reforms of the French state; the military experience of his now long-serving soldiers; and, finally, his own extraordinary abilities and energy. Typically, he worked an eighteen-hour day, starting soon after midnight, sleeping for an hour or two before dawn, and then continuing straight through until eight or nine in the evening. He could still keep in his head the relevant details about the position, command, and condition of all the units in the army and exhausted his staff. "What a pity the man wasn't lazy," Talleyrand quipped.

The new war also marked the coming of age of Revolutionary military tactics, which were perfectly suited to delivering the sort of blows Napoleon envisioned. Instead of slow, careful maneuvering and a suspicion of large-scale engagements, the French armies now made forced marches in order to compel decisive battles. Instead of trying to capture enemy cities and fortresses, the French aimed at the complete destruction of the enemy army. Instead of the ballet of column and line, they continued to employ swarms of skirmishers and staked success on massive attacks, followed by relentless pursuit of the broken enemy. Above all, instead of a number of separate armies campaigning with only loose coordination between them, Napoleon now commanded a massive, tightly centralized but flexible *Grande Armée,* divided into distinct corps, each composed in turn of several divisions. It was the perfect vehicle for the implementation of total war.

For two years after the end of the peace, Napoleon kept this weapon of mass destruction in camp on the Channel coast, training the men obsessively for an invasion of England. To take them across the "ditch," as he called it, he ordered the construction of over 2,500 gunboats, barges, and landing craft. Yet the invasion never materialized. For all the emperor's scorn for British "shopkeepers," British sailors very effectively kept the French fleet stuck in the Mediterranean, and without its protection, the planned flotilla could not sail. Admiral Villeneuve finally did manage to bring French ships out into the Atlantic in the fall of 1805 but took shelter in the Spanish port of Cádiz rather than confront the British in the Channel. And when Napoleon ordered Villeneuve back to sea in October, Admiral Nelson caught the French and Spanish fleets off Trafalgar and annihilated them. Nelson himself famously perished in the battle, but his victory ended all hope of France competing with Britain on the seas, let alone invading it.

Even before Trafalgar, however, the *Grande Armée* had acquired a different objective. In the summer of 1805, following Napoleon's continued interference in German politics and his kidnapping and execution of the conspiratorial Bourbon prince d'Enghien ("more than a crime, a blunder," in Fouché's famous apostrophe), Austria and Russia joined Britain in the war. In response, on August 23, Napoleon marched the army, nearly 200,000 strong, out of its Channel coast camps, heading for Germany at a speed that regularly exceeded twenty miles a day and sometimes approached thirty-five, despite the men's heavy equipment. Five weeks later, with remarkably few losses to disease and desertion, the tough, seasoned troops crossed the Rhine. By mid-October, they had reached the Danube and, after some of Napoleon's most brilliant maneuvering, surrounded Austria's General Mack in the Bavarian city of Ulm, which quickly turned into a pestilential, shot-racked hellhole. Mack raged, groaned, came close to being relieved by reason of insanity, and finally surrendered. Less than a month later, the French army entered Vienna.

On December 2, the anniversary of his coronation, Napoleon caught up with the remaining Austrian forces and the Russians, near the Czech village of Austerlitz. The rulers of Austria and Russia were there in person, making Austerlitz "the battle of the three emperors." But a concentration of royalty did the allies no more good at Austerlitz than it had at Valmy. The Russian commander, Kutuzov, urged further withdrawal, but the new tsar, Alexander I, impetuously insisted on battle. The French obliged and won a crushing victory, leaving the tsar literally weeping under a tree over the wreck of his army. When Russian troops fled across frozen lakes, Napoleon ordered cannonballs fired onto the

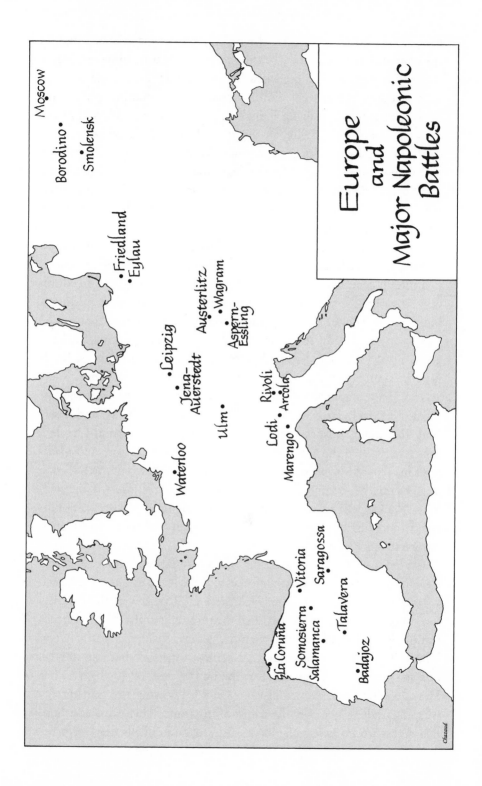

Europe
and
Major Napoleonic
Battles

Moscow

Borodino
Smolensk

Friedland
Eylau

Leipzig

Jena-
Auerstedt

Austerlitz
Wagram

Aspern-
Essling

Waterloo

Ulm

Lodi
Rivoli
Marengo
Arcola

La Coruña
Vitoria
Somosierra
Salamanca
Saragossa
Talavera
Badajoz

Chazaud

ice. As it cracked, a French general remembered, "we saw thousands of Russians with their horses, guns and wagons, slowly settle down into the depths!" A third of the allied force was killed, wounded, or taken prisoner, and hundreds of its cannon became a literal pedestal for Napoleon — or rather, the statue of him erected in the Place Vendôme in Paris. Days later, the demoralized Austrians again sued for peace.

Having delivered this military hammer blow, Napoleon then proceeded to deliver a political one as well. Unlike the Old Regime sovereigns whose company he claimed to have joined, he did not use victory to make moderate adjustments in a relatively static balance of power. Instead, he imposed draconian terms, leading to further large-scale alterations in the map of Europe. In the Treaty of Pressburg, after Austerlitz, the Austrians were forced to surrender Venice and the Dalmatian coast to what had now become Napoleon's Kingdom of Italy (successor to his puppet Cisalpine Republic). They also had no choice but to watch as he continued his reorganization of German territory, cobbling together the midsized German states west of Prussia and Austria into a new, subservient Confederation of the Rhine (between 1792 and 1815, some 60 percent of the German population changed rulers). In the wake of this reorganization, an important symbolic event took place almost as an afterthought. On August 6, 1806, a ceremonial herald blew a trumpet in a Vienna church, and on its plangent note, the long-moribund Holy Roman Empire of the German Nation, once considered the legitimate successor to the realm of Charlemagne, and beyond that, to Rome itself, softly ceased to exist.

But impressive as the Austerlitz campaign had been, Napoleon's most spectacularly crushing victory came a year later, against a different enemy. His defeat of Prussia in 1806 not only eerily foreshadowed the total wars of the twentieth century but also helped bring them about, by lighting a torch of German resentment that would take 140 years to burn out. The philosopher Hegel, who saw the events at rather too close a remove, considered them the hinge on which the history of the world had turned. "The connecting bonds of the world are dissolved and have collapsed like images in a dream," he wrote even before the end of the campaign. He called Napoleon, whom he saw riding near his home in Jena, nothing less than "the world-soul . . . who, sitting here astride a horse, reaches out across the world and dominates it."

Prussia had not fought France for more than a decade. Its young, insecure King Friedrich Wilhelm III had distressing personal memories of Valmy and had long preferred to turn his attention to the east. Since the final partition of Poland in 1795, its richest territories had lain, half-digested, in the maw of the Prussian state (nearly 90 percent of present-day Poland belonged to it). So the Prussians initially had no particular desire to challenge Napoleon. They even entered into a brief alliance with him, prompting an abortive declaration of war against them from Britain. But in the summer of 1806, anxieties about Napoleon's activities on their western borders led the king to switch sides and enter into a new, "Fourth Coalition," which also included Britain and Russia.

It was a disastrous mistake. The Prussian army still lived, to far too great an extent, on the legend of Frederick the Great. Indeed, too many of its generals had personal memories of his days of glory, fifty years before (the historian Gordon Craig once quipped: "it seemed literally true that, in Prussia, old soldiers never died)." The ponderous old Duke of Brunswick, who had lost the battle of Valmy, remained the kingdom's highest commander. Friedrich Wilhelm's army of 235,000 was large and relatively well trained — but only by the standards of the Old Regime. Composed in large part of unwilling peasants, mercenaries, and former prisoners of war, held together by traditionally savage Prussian discipline, it continued to use its conventional order of battle, despite the new tactics Napoleon had perfected.

In late August, not waiting for Russian reinforcements, the Prussians gave Napoleon an ultimatum to withdraw his army beyond the Rhine or fight. In response, Napoleon took part of the *Grande Armée*, already in Germany, and formed it into a powerful square of 180,000 men — the so-called *bataillion carré* — which allowed him to concentrate a huge force quickly on a decisive point. On October 14, it engaged the Prussians in the twin battles of Jena and Auerstadt. Like so many battles, they began with a comedy of errors. As dawn broke, Napoleon, commanding a concentrated detachment of 46,000 on strategic heights near Jena (where Hegel had glimpsed him the day before), found himself facing some 38,000 Prussians under the sixty-year-old Prince of Hohenlohe. Taking them for Brunswick's main force, he quickly summoned reinforcements and by noon had 96,000 men available. Hohenlohe stood no chance against such numbers and compounded his defeat by stubbornly keeping 20,000 infantry standing exposed, in line, as if they were still fighting the Seven Years' War, under merciless fire from French skirmishers hiding behind garden walls. By the end of the day, the French had killed 10,000 of his men and wounded another 15,000. Meanwhile, nearby, Brunswick had been engaged in a characteristic maneuver — withdrawal — but blundered into a French corps under Marshal Louis Davout. In a desperate, brilliant action, Davout beat the larger Prussian force. Brunswick himself fell mortally wounded, and the battles left the Prussian military shattered beyond repair.

But the French triumph did not end there, for Napoleon's forces relentlessly pursued the Prussians. On October 16, Erfurt fell to Marshal Murat, with 6,000 men taken prisoner; the next day, Halle surrendered to Marshal Bernadotte. One by one, the remaining Prussian fortresses passed into French hands, often without offering even token resistance: Hameln, Plassenburg, Stettin, Spandau, Magdeburg. In early November, Napoleon marched triumphantly into Berlin, displaying prisoners from Friedrich Wilhelm's Noble Guard. The king himself had fled to East Prussia. Of the 171,000 soldiers he had sent against Napoleon at the end of the summer, he had lost no less than 96 percent: 25,000 dead or wounded and 140,000 prisoners. Napoleon, meanwhile, issued a bulletin declaring that the defeat of Rossbach — France's epic loss to Frederick the Great in 1757 — had been "expunged." He also paid a visit to Frederick himself, in his tomb at Potsdam. "He stopped at the entrance in a grave, meditative attitude," his aide Ségur recalled. "He remained there nearly ten minutes, motionless and silent." Then he left, although not without first helping himself to Frederick's sword, sash, and Black Eagle decoration, for display in Paris. As the future military strategist Clausewitz, an eyewitness to the campaign, would later write, the Prussian army had been ruined "more completely than any army has ever been ruined on the battlefield."

Despite this epochal defeat, the conflict dragged on for another eight months. The Russians had not yet come to terms, and in February 1807, Napoleon fought them and the remaining Prussians in the ghastly battle of Eylau in Poland, under blinding, stinging snow, without a significant result. But in June, Napoleon crushed the Russians at the battle of Friedland and a month later met Tsar Alexander on a raft in the middle of the Niemen River near Tilsit, at the Russian frontier. In keeping with his monarchical pretensions, Napoleon called the young Russian monarch his "brother," pledged to treat him as an equal, and seduced him into an alliance. He forced Friedrich Wilhelm to wait on the shore, like a naughty child, and the subsequent treaty reduced Prussia to the status of a second-rate power. It lost fully half its territory and subjects (from 10 million to 4.6), was forced to pay massive reparations, saw its army reduced to a token force of 42,000, and as a result of all this, suffered an economic collapse.

In modern European history, only one campaign compares with Napoleon's defeat of Prussia for its sheer, overwhelming speed and force: Hitler's conquest of France in the spring of 1940. Both took less than six weeks (Napoleon, at thirty-three days, was faster, despite his lack of tanks). Both destroyed the adversaries' morale, as well as their physical ability to resist. Both ended with an entire army taken prisoner. At the cessation of hostilities, both losing powers had territory amputated (Prussia far more than France). And both victors described the war as revenge for an earlier defeat — Hitler famously forcing the French to sign the armistice in the same railroad car where the Germans had surrendered at the end of World War I. Even Napoleon's visit to Frederick's tomb eerily foreshadowed the visit that a pensive, silent Hitler would pay in 1940 to the Invalides and the tomb of Napoleon himself. In other words, 1806 was a blitzkrieg. And just like the blitzkrieg of 1940, it left Great Britain alone in the fight:

> Another year! Another deadly blow!
> Another mighty Empire overthrown!
> And we are left, or shall be left, alone;
> The last that dare to struggle with the Foe.

Thus wrote William Wordsworth in November 1806.

The keenest observer of the campaign, however, was Clausewitz. This product of the minor Prussian nobility, then just twenty-six, had already spent half his life in uniform. He was a serious, hardworking man dedicated to the Prussian army, so its massive failure struck him hard both personally (he spent two years as a prisoner in France) and philosophically. And over the next few years, shock congealed into furor, as he watched King Friedrich Wilhelm meekly follow Napoleon's dictates. Finally, in 1812, Clausewitz committed the ultimate apostasy for an officer, abandoning his country in wartime and pledging himself to the Russians, who were now at war with France again. In a passionate justification of his act, which amounted to a military profession of

faith, he bitterly denounced not only his own "dishonored" government but also, significantly, the style of war at which it had once ex-
celled:

> Formerly . . . war was waged in the way that a pair of duellists carried out
> their pedantic struggle. One battled with moderation and consideration,
> according to the conventional proprieties . . . War was caused by nothing
> more than a diplomatic caprice, and the spirit of such a thing could
> hardly prevail over the goal of military honor . . . There is no more talk
> of this sort of war, and one would have to be blind not to be able to per-
> ceive the difference with our wars, that is to say the wars that our age and
> our conditions require . . . The war of the present time is a war of all
> against all. It is not the King who wars on a king, not an army which
> wars on an army, but a people which wars on another, and the king and
> the army are contained in the people.
>   War will only lose this character with much difficulty, and, in truth,
> the return of that old, bloody, yet often boring chess game of soldiers
> fighting is not to be desired.

The passage brilliantly encapsulated the changes that had taken place in
war since 1792, while foreshadowing Clausewitz's great work *On War*.
He now saw the old, aristocratic conventions as mere frippery and
artifice that distorted the true, natural course of war. That true and natural course involved the commitment of every possible resource and all
possible violence, of the sort France had inflicted on his fatherland. No
wonder that he quoted Thomas Hobbes's famous phrase. It felt like a
war of all against all, indeed.

In the summer of 1807, having again defeated all his opponents in continental Europe, Napoleon, at thirty-eight years old, stood at his zenith.
Again, a chance seemed at hand to escape from the unremitting cycle
of war and to establish the Empire on a solid, permanent basis. The
emperor could now boast of having taken his rightful place among
"brother sovereigns" and now aimed to make the Bonapartes into a dynasty to outshine the Hapsburgs or Bourbons. He imperiously placed
his brother Joseph on the throne of the southern Italian kingdom of
Naples (whose Bourbon ruler, with exquisitely poor timing, had declared war on France just after Austerlitz), made his brother Louis king
of Holland, and carved out a new German kingdom, Westphalia, for

his brother Jérôme. He himself was already wearing the crown of the new Kingdom of Italy and installed his stepson Eugène de Beauharnais there as viceroy. His longing for a son of his own was already outweighing his waning adoration for Josephine, and within three years, he would divorce her and marry the Austrian princess Marie-Louise, greatniece of the late, unlamented Marie-Antoinette. In keeping with these grandiose designs, he also created a new nobility, making followers into dukes of Otranto, Rivoli, and Parma; princes of Benevento, PonteCorvo, and Eckmühl; and so forth. A natural authoritarian, he tolerated little opposition from his parliaments and imposed the strictest press censorship in French history, in what amounted in many ways to a return to enlightened despotism. Still, he preferred muzzling his opponents to imprisoning or killing them, and the harshness of his rule cannot compare to that of twentieth-century dictators.

But even after 1807, the Empire did not mark a return to the Old Regime, and the tensions that had riven the regime from the beginning remained strong. The emperor continued to maintain the principles of civil equality and meritocracy, defended the Revolution's redistribution of landed wealth, and kept the top ranks of his administration staffed by former Revolutionaries, such as his long-serving head of internal security, Joseph Fouché, who had spent the Terror overseeing massacres of "traitors," forcing priests to marry, and posting over cemeteries signs that read "death is an eternal sleep." Despite his formal accommodation with the Church, Napoleon remained deeply anticlerical (Pope Pius eventually excommunicated him; he, in turn, kept the pope a prisoner for over six years). The armies, which Napoleon deliberately neglected to supply with chaplains, retained this same hostility to religion.

The Revolutionary heritage manifested itself most powerfully in the lands Napoleon conquered. The territories annexed to the Empire, regardless of their history and traditions, were melted down into standard-issue French *départements,* with administrative structures mirroring those of France itself. And with the French administration came the entire panoply of Revolutionary reforms, enforced, if necessary, at gunpoint. The "satellite kingdoms," although not always forced to swallow such large doses of Jacobin medicine, still underwent profound transformations. Thanks to this process of amalgamation, Napoleon went further than anyone in modern history toward creating a true European superstate (much further than the architects of the current European Union). "I must make all the peoples of Europe one people," he told Fouché, "and Paris the capital of the world." In his last years, he would reminisce fondly about his unfulfilled plans for a single currency, metric system, and law code.

These same plans also testify to Napoleon's continuing hope to forge an explicitly civilian regime. The new administrative machinery of the Empire, from the august State Council in Paris down to the humblest subprefectures of the newly annexed provinces, was civilian in nature. For his principal political support, Napoleon continued to depend, above all, on France's wealthiest landowners, men of business, and *rentiers* — the so-called notables, drawn from the old nobility and bourgeoisie alike — for whom the regime represented stability, prosperity, and progress. He sought insistently to present himself as a civilian patron of the arts and sciences. In keeping with the pattern set under the Consulate, he even continued to protest, in the midst of unending war, of his continuing devotion to an ideal of peace. He cast every campaign as a response to foreign aggression: first and foremost Britain's supposed efforts to strangle France's trade, seduce away its loyal allies, and incite rebellion in its provinces.

Yet these loudly stated intentions had to compete with the thick skein of militarism that had wound its way through the Napoleonic story from the start and that, in a time of repeated, incredible French victories, remained a powerful force shaping imperial society and culture. To begin with, the addition of ermine to Napoleon's wardrobe and Ruritanian titles to his marshals' calling cards brought no return to the aristocratic military ethos of the Old Regime. The French military was still what the Revolution had made it: a world distinct from civilian society. Its continuing commitment to Revolutionary principles of merit only reinforced this distinctiveness, for now over three-quarters of French junior officers had spent years in the ranks, while Napoleon tried to fill the higher ranks with graduates of a new, intensive military school. The officer corps remained very much a full-time profession, to the extent that some of Napoleon's marshals grumbled audibly at having no time to enjoy their new titles and ill-gotten wealth. The days in which a Lauzun could flit languidly from court to campaign and back were long past. As for the ranks, while the machinery of conscription ground away, until the Empire's final years, the stereotypical peasant draftees yearning for family and field constituted only about half its soldiers, the rest being long-serving professionals.

Even without a restoration of the old aristocratic order, Napoleon gave the military overwhelming prestige and privilege, confirming the sense that it was not simply distinct from civilian society but superior to it. Although he might not have ruled *through* the military, he ruled, to a significant extent, *for* it. For example, fully 59 percent of the three-thousand-odd noble titles he created went to high-ranking military officers. As for the Legion of Honor he established as a reward for "merit," it revealed with particular clarity how Napoleon often failed to follow through on his "civilian" rhetoric. "If this honor only went to the military," he insisted at its foundation in 1802, "then the nation would no longer amount to anything." Yet no less than 97 percent of the 48,000 people who earned its coveted red ribbon before 1815 in fact came from the military. In official state ceremonies, marshals of France had the right to walk ahead of even the highest civilian officials.

Even more significantly, the army became, in some ways, a model for civilian society. Many civilian officials wore uniforms, based on military ones, and their clerks worked according to harsh rules that mimicked military discipline. Public festivals and celebrations took on an increasingly military character, and theaters presented an endless stream of plays (at least 143 in France between 1799 and 1815) highlighting the glorious deeds of soldiers. In the forty-five new all-male elite *lycées* (high schools) that the regime created, the boys were organized into "companies" commanded by "sergeants." They wore uniforms, walked to class to the sounds of drumbeats, underwent military training, and listened to endless lectures on honor, patriotism, and duty to the emperor that deliberately tried to adapt the language of the Old Regime to the new world of the First Empire. A typical example, delivered on August 14, 1806, by a rhetorician named Pierre Crouzet, informed his students in no uncertain terms of what might await them after graduation: "fatigue, danger, iron, blood, carnage and death." But they could not flinch, he added, for cowards would bear the brand of dishonor forever. Honor mattered above all. Indeed, "such is a Frenchman's love of honor, that he will sometimes turn it into the cruellest fanaticism . . . and drench his altars in his brothers' blood." Fine stuff, one will agree, for teenage boys gathered together on a summer afternoon. In short,

Napoleon's great opponent the Duke of Wellington did not entirely err when he claimed that the Empire "was constituted upon a military basis. All its institutions were framed for the purpose of forming and maintaining its armies with a view to conquest."

The simple fact that the draft established in 1798 continued to function, pulling in up to 80,000 new recruits a year between 1805 and 1810 and more than six times that figure between 1812 and 1814, had its own effects. Historians of the subject have called attention above all to the way conscription represented an unwelcome, much-resisted imposition on French society. The abundant soldiers' letters that have survived from the period indeed testify eloquently to their homesickness and sheer befuddlement. They did not always know what country they were in, to say nothing of how to spell the place names (Austerlitz became Osterlique, Osterlis, Esterlix, and so on). One soldier marching east toward Russia in 1812 believed that he was on a secret overland route to England! Yet other soldiers felt delight in the opportunities the army brought: for promotion, for enrichment (by pillage), for abundant drink, for education, for simple novelty, for escape from lives of drudgery and toil.

In any case, whether they welcomed it or detested it, the army became their home, with its discipline, its largely all-male camaraderie, its fatigues, its dangers. They had left "civilian" society to join "military" society. And on what we can start to think of as the "home front," families likewise found themselves bound together by the common anxiety of loved ones in peril, far away. All dreaded receiving the visit from the subprefect or other local official bearing horrid news of a death or disappearance, often many months in the past, accompanied by stiff, boilerplate sentiment that hardly consoled them in their agony. "In giving this terrible news to Monsieur Montigny's parents, you can tell them that this young officer, in death, takes with him the grief and the esteem of his commanders and his comrades . . . [He was] a gallant officer who has payed with his life for the fine reputation enjoyed by the 127th regiment." In his brilliant 1808 painting *The Reading of the Bulletin,* Louis-Léopold Boilly gave a sense of just how intently the families of the soldiers now followed the news of distant battles and traced the progress of French armies on the map.

And then there was architecture. Anyone who walks through central Paris today can hardly miss the military stamp that Napoleon put on

Louis-Léopold Boilly: *The Reading of the Bulletin of the Grand Army*

much of his capital. He devised a grandiose building program, centered on monuments to his victories: the Arc de Triomphe, begun under his rule although only finished decades later; the Vendôme Column, in the style of Trajan's column in Rome, cast from the metal of Russian cannon seized at Austerlitz and topped by the emperor's statue; the Arc du Carrousel in the courtyard of the Louvre. Napoleon intended the severely classical structure that is now the Church of the Madeleine to serve as a military Temple of Glory. He renovated the Invalides, built under the Old Regime for disabled veterans, and recast its principal church as a Temple of Mars. In an elaborate ceremony, one of France's greatest military heroes of the Old Regime, Marshal Turenne, was reburied there, in a sarcophagus adorned with the cannonball that had killed him. In the Place des Victoires, statues from the days of the Bourbons gave way to a gigantic bronze nude of Desaix, the hero of Marengo, which shocked the local *bourgeoises* with its anatomical accuracy.

Needless to say, this culture of militarism did not lack a full-grown cult of personality of the supreme commander. The same shameless self-promotion that had characterized Napoleon's rise to power now spewed forth in industrial strength from amply endowed cultural institutions to blanket three-quarters of Europe. For those who preferred their heroes to wear a religious costume, the intimidated pope even obligingly "discovered" an early Christian martyr named Neopolis, rechristened him "Saint Napoleon," and fixed his saint's day on August 15, Napoleon's birthday, which became France's new national holiday (conveniently eclipsing the Catholic Feast of the Assumption). Engravings of the holy man bearing a suspicious resemblance to his modern namesake turned Napoleonic hero worship into a literal cult of the saint. True, Napoleon the Emperor and Napoleon the Saint never succeeded entirely in displacing Napoleon the man of the people. The supreme commander continued to make a point of treating ordinary soldiers — if not ordinary citizens — as equals, and his soldiers avidly repeated the stories of how he took over guard duty from an exhausted recruit or allowed a gruff old veteran to call him "*tu*." But as Napoleon and his empire grew older, his famed popular touch seemed to be felt less and less.

Militarism also inevitably encouraged the same quasi-erotic celebration of violence that had flowed through French culture since the beginning of the Revolutionary wars. Despite the ease with which he slipped into the language of peace, Napoleon still had a tendency to exalt military actions for their sheer grandeur. In conversation in 1810, he defended Louis XIV's "glorious" destruction of the Palatinate, which Enlightenment authors had condemned as the greatest atrocity of the age. During the Russian campaign of 1812, he took delight in the burning of Smolensk and responded to his Grand Equerry's shocked protests with the words "Bah! Gentlemen, remember the words of a Roman emperor: 'A dead enemy always smells sweet!'" The regime exploited General Desaix's heroic sacrifice at Marengo in a long series of portraits, engravings, and statues — including the embarrassing nude in the Place des Victoires — that recalled the sensual beauty of the boy martyr Bara, as painted by Jacques-Louis David. Among the many war paintings shown at the prestigious salons, the largest number — and most popular — gave straightforward overviews of battles. But visitors could also gaze on Anne-Louis Girodet's astonishing 1810 *Revolt of Cairo*, with its seething mass of entwined male bodies. The painting, in the words of one art historian, "makes the moment of death look beguilingly beauti-

Anne-Louis Girodet: *The Revolt of Cairo*

ful." In short, although Napoleon did not explicitly praise war as a positive good in the manner of Humboldt or Gentz, his regime nonetheless continued the reglorification of war that had begun under the Directory.

Toward the end of the First Empire, the keenest liberal thinker of the day, Benjamin Constant, arraigned Napoleon for these militaristic tendencies before the *philosophes'* court of history, in a brilliant essay entitled *The Spirit of Conquest and Usurpation*. Without mentioning the emperor by name, Constant charged him with hypocrisy for speaking the language of peace, even while living by the credo that "military glory is the greatest glory." True, Constant wrote, open celebration of war had become almost unthinkable in the modern age: "no government would dare say to its nation: let us go conquer the World. The nation would respond unanimously: We have no wish to conquer the world" (two years later, Napoleon would in fact confess this very desire to Constant himself, but in private conversation). Nonetheless, Constant charged, conquest was Napoleon's goal, and the writer drew on the historical thought of the Enlightenment to condemn it in the strongest terms. "In some ages of history," he wrote, "war was in the nature of man . . . But the modern world is, in this regard, the opposite of the ancient world . . . We have reached the age of commerce, which must necessarily replace the age of war." Unlike the *philosophes*, Constant described commerce less as a solution to international conflict than its continuation by other means. He also (most likely unwittingly) shared Humboldt's opinion that in the classical age, war had brought out the most noble qualities of the human soul. But unlike Humboldt, he insisted that in modern times, its human and economic costs far outweighed any possible benefit. And so, any modern government that waged wars of conquest was guilty of a "crude and deadly anachronism."

Constant concluded the first part of his essay by suggesting that France had only to abjure this "anachronism" to retake its place among the civilized peoples of the globe. But in doing so, he severely underestimated the extent to which the wars had a logic and inertia of their own and to which Napoleon himself was ultimately trapped by them, reacting to events and struggling to maintain his position rather than simply trying to satisfy his insatiable ambition. Furthermore, as the emperor would discover, despite his repeated triumphs, final, permanent victory proved to be like an asymptote on a graph, impossible to reach. The closer he seemed to approach it, the more powerful the forces he generated against himself until, finally, the Empire itself burst apart under the strain.

Certainly, it proved just as difficult for peace to take hold after Tilsit and the pause that followed the defeat of the Fourth Coalition in 1807 as after the earlier 1802 Peace of Amiens. As before, the seizure of new territory, the creation of new satellite states, and the expansion of spheres of influence created a larger frontier to defend (now far larger than before) and more potential flashpoints. As we will see in the next chapter, it also led to ever more revolts against French authority — a string of new Vendées that ignited wherever French rule seemed fragile, just as had happened in 1798–99.

In fact, after the Fourth Coalition, the entire coastline of continental Europe became a flashpoint of sorts. Despite Napoleon's settlements with the continental powers, Great Britain, again his sole remaining opponent, remained as strong as ever, thanks to its decimation of the French and Spanish fleets at Trafalgar. Unable to invade it or to resist its naval power, and suffering from its strangling of French overseas trade,

Napoleon determined instead to wreck it economically by depriving it of access to European markets. This was the "Continental Blockade" he outlined in decrees issued from Berlin in late 1806, which would eventually expand into an ambitious economic "Continental System." But in the absence of naval power, he could enforce this design only by exerting direct or indirect political control over the coastal states of the Continent — all of them. And in the final analysis, doing so would frequently require armed force.

The deadly risks of this strategy soon became apparent. In July 1807, Napoleon ordered Portugal, a traditional British ally and trading partner, to close its ports to British shipping. When the Portuguese failed to comply, he sent General Junot to seize the country. But the need to move large French forces across Spanish territory further destabilized France's already deteriorating relations with its longtime ally Spain. In early 1808, Napoleon finally decided to replace the Spanish Bourbons with a Bonaparte: Joseph, whom he moved from Naples for the purpose. But this *coup* prompted a large-scale Spanish rebellion, the "Spanish Ulcer" through which the acid of guerrilla war ate away at the vital organs of the Empire. British expeditionary forces under Arthur Wellesley (the future Lord Wellington) and John Moore came to help the Portuguese and Spanish, forcing Napoleon to take personal charge of the campaign in the summer of 1808. But although he won more crushing victories and forced a temporary British evacuation of Spanish territory, the rebellion stubbornly continued.

To make matters worse, in 1809, the Austrian Empire, tempted by the weaknesses that the Spanish war had exposed, renewed the fight against France. Archduke Karl, Austria's most competent commander, forced Napoleon to a terrifyingly costly draw at Aspern-Essling, and it took another strenuous campaign, and French victory at Wagram in July, to bring the Austrians to the table again (it was their fourth defeat at his hands). This time, the peace terms included Napoleon's marriage to princess Marie-Louise, who in 1811 would give him his long-desired son and heir. But where would the next leak in the Continental Blockade spring from? It is difficult not to think of Napoleon in this period as a cartoon Dutch boy frantically sticking finger after finger in a none-too-stable dike.

The logic of total war now began to tell against Napoleon in other ways as well. As the war spread, the sheer scale of combat grew inexorably. It was not simply that, by 1809, France's armies found themselves stretched across theaters of operation that ranged from Iberia to Italy to the north German coast, to say nothing of the major campaign against Austrian regulars. It was not simply that Napoleon had to entrust more and more authority to subordinates who lacked his talent as a commander. The battles themselves were swelling dangerously in size. At Marengo, in 1800, roughly 60,000 soldiers had taken part in the fighting, on both sides. Five years later, at Austerlitz, the number had grown to nearly 165,000. Four years after that, at Wagram, the largest battle yet seen in the gunpowder age, it was 300,000, with some 80,000 dead and wounded. And in 1813, at Leipzig, the total number exceeded 500,000, with fully 150,000 dead and wounded. The front along which Napoleon's armies stretched at the start of a campaign expanded from 80 miles in Italy in 1796 to 130 miles in Germany in 1806 to 240 miles on the Russian border in 1812. Chateaubriand wrote eloquently that "these enormous battles go beyond glory" and contrasted them sharply to the old "civilized warfare . . . which leaves peoples in peace while a small number of soldiers do their duty."

In theory, with its deep reserves of cheap, dispensable conscripts, France could manage such numbers. For every hundred thousand soldiers who lay dead or wounded and desperate to die on the battlefield, there were always another hundred thousand to replace them. It gave Napoleon little pause to send his men to slaughter in such huge numbers, despite his famed rapport with them. The Austrian statesman Metternich claimed that Napoleon told him, in a June 1813 meeting: "I grew up on the battlefield. A man like me does not give a shit about the lives of a million men."

But these oversize battles threatened Napoleon for reasons that had little to do with their gruesome human costs. Napoleon's success as a general had always stemmed from his own tight, centralized control over every aspect of his campaigns, which in turn depended on his amazing memory and agility of mind. But by the time of the 1809 war, the battles were simply growing too large and uncontrollable for one man to oversee in this manner. Worse, just when Napoleon needed his abilities the most, he began to lose them. In 1805, he supposedly remarked to his valet: "One has only a certain time for war. I will be good for six years more; after that even I must cry halt." Well before the six years had elapsed, his associates noticed that his reactions had slowed and that his body had thickened and grown more prone to disease. Napoleon frequently suffered from dysuria, a condition under which urine turns thick and grainy and almost impossible to pass without great pain. At the critical battle of Borodino in 1812, a bout of it induced a violent fever. Napoleon had to manage the battle while suffering from violent fits of shivering, constant pain, and swollen legs. Although the French eked out a victory of sorts, they lost the chance to destroy the Russian army as they had destroyed the Prussians in 1806.

Nonetheless, between 1807 and 1814 the dike held, in large part because of the hesitancy of the allies. True, by 1807, it had become obvious to many observers on the allied side that defeating Napoleon would require painful rebuilding of their armies and governments alike. Even before Napoleon's seizure of power, reformers, such as Prussia's Gerhard von Scharnhorst, had called for the creation of truly national militaries to compete with the army of the *levée en masse.* Yet the governing elites agonized over whether a "revolution from above," as one Prussian official called it, could take place without provoking a French-style revolution from below.

Austria offered the clearest case of this resistance. On June 9, 1808, in a seeming bow to reformers, Emperor Franz established a *Landwehr,* or Home Army, and declared every male between eighteen and forty-five in the hereditary and Bohemian lands of the Austrian crown eligible for service. In theory, something like conscription was now in place, at least for the most trustworthy portion of the Austrian empire's diverse population. Yet it remained largely symbolic. Recruiting during the war of 1809 did not come close to the target of 230,000 men; those who did come into the service, provided with poor weapons and worse leadership, fared from badly to disastrously on the battlefield. The government did not push to expand the experiment and shut it down entirely in 1813.

A far more important reform movement, it is true, got under way in Prussia during these years. The catastrophe of 1806–7 left that kingdom's elite collectively pale, jittering with shock, and humiliated by their army's quick collapse. Following Jena and Tilsit, the king sought the help of longtime reformers, particularly the pragmatic absolutist Karl von Hardenberg and the aristocratic liberal Karl vom Stein, whom later German legend cast as visionary Romantic nationalists. In fact, both were practical men who cared more about modernizing the Prussian state than about the mystical union of all Germans. But in pursuit of their goals, they pushed through changes that indeed amounted to a "revolution from above": an abolition of rural serfdom and urban guilds, the opening up of professions to all comers, an equalization of the tax burden, and a measure of religious toleration (including for Jews). A military committee dominated by Scharnhorst and Neithardt von Gneisenau worked to turn the Prussian military into a professional force in which merit rather than birth or the monarch's favor determined advancement and in which the men obeyed because of genuine loyalty rather than fear of savage punishment. The German historian Friedrich Meinecke concluded approvingly that the reformers managed to change the army "from a mere tool in the hands of the commander-in-chief into a living institution." This meant, of course, that they turned it into a self-contained, noncivilian realm, facilitating the emergence of militarism. In a sign of the desire to separate the realms as thoroughly and visibly as possible, the high command tried to ban women entirely from army life.

Yet although they had immense long-term consequences for German history, the Prussian reforms did not have an immediate impact on the military situation. For more than five years after Tilsit, the cautious, dithering king, all too aware of his shrunken territory and diminished resources, did not dare challenge Napoleon (to the disgust of Clausewitz, as we have seen). The king refused Scharnhorst's call for a Prussian *Landwehr,* declined to join Austria in the war of 1809 (some of his more hot-headed officers led troops out on their own, with disastrous results), and heeded the limits France had imposed on his army. He discouraged anything like nationalist rhetoric: "Nation? That sounds *Jakobinisch.*" Giving in to pressure from Napoleon, he eventually dismissed most of the reformers, including both Stein and Hardenberg. In March 1812, he even entered into a formal alliance with France and committed 30,000 troops to help in the invasion of Russia.

Oddly, as Linda Colley has shown, some of the most significant changes instead took place in Britain, which, well protected by its navy, never resorted to conscription. The British army nonetheless managed to expand sixfold between 1789 and 1814 — although even then it numbered only a quarter of a million men. Part-time and volunteer units at home added half a million men more, although only half of them had weapons. In the first years of the war, Colley writes, the "government was . . . as afraid of its own people as it was of the enemy," but by 1803, voices could be heard urging the government to follow the French example of the people in arms. Even more striking were the actions the British took after 1808 in Portugal, where General William Carr Beresford reorganized and strengthened the army and for a time acted as a virtual dictator. He used traditional Portuguese institutions to impose effective conscription, insisted that the inhabitants evacuate and lay waste to any territory in danger of French occupation, and in general mobilized the entire country for war. By January 1812, he had 110,000 Portuguese serving in the army and militia — a much greater proportion of the population than the French ever managed to call up.

The uneven reform processes among the allies were matched by uneven development in their military strategy and tactics. Napoleon's greatest adversary, the Duke of Wellington, was probably the least Napoleonic of them — an unmistakably aristocratic general who relied on the careful, cautious maneuvering of relatively small bodies of highly trained professional soldiers. "My great object . . . was in general to avoid [fighting] a great battle," he later recalled, in terms reminiscent of Maurice of Saxony. Still, when the occasion demanded it, he had little hesitation ordering lightning attacks. Archduke Karl, brother of the Austrian emperor, who forced Napoleon to the gory draw of Aspern-Essling in 1809, also remained partly loyal to older principles, although he willingly accepted the lessons of the French Revolution as to mobility and open-order fighting. The most Napoleonic figure among the allies, Russia's Alexander Suvorov, had his moment of glory early, even before Napoleon's heyday. A devout believer in rapid mobility and the total destruction of enemy forces, he inspired a Napoleonic cult of personality among his soldiers. But he also had an aristocratic, entirely un-Napoleonic disdain for detail and paperwork, which helped to limit his successes. And his eccentricity was a byword. One English observer wrote of him: "I never saw anything so stark mad." He died in 1800, and his successors — particularly Marshal Mikhail Kutuzov — proved considerably more cautious in their styles of command.

In important ways, then, the wars remained, until 1812, the odd mismatch they had been since the start, with a much-transformed France fighting against adversaries still partially enamored of the aristocratic,

The Devil and His Son

Old Regime ways of war. In only one sense had the allies adopted something like Revolutionary attitudes with real enthusiasm, although also with a more frankly religious twist: their apocalyptic vision of the enemy. For despite Napoleon's acquisition of an imperial title and his marriage to a Hapsburg, he remained anything but an honorable opponent for the powers that fought him. He stood, rather, as the personification of Revolutionary evil — the "Corsican ogre" or "Mediterranean mulatto," as the British press liked to put it — or, indeed, the Antichrist. A much-circulated engraving portrayed him as the literal son of the Devil, and the hugely popular German poet Ernst Moritz Arndt identified him with Satan, in the aptly named 1811 "Song of Revenge":

> *Denn der Satan ist gekommen*
> *Er hat sich Fleisch und Bein genommen*
> *Und will der Herr der Erde sein.*

> For Satan has come
> He has taken on flesh and bone
> And wants to be lord of the Earth.

In November 1806, the Holy Synod of the Russian Orthodox Church formally condemned Napoleon as a false messiah who had conspired with Jews against the Christian faith.

Until 1812, those in the allied camp seeking portents of deliverance from the Napoleonic scourge had as much disappointment as pleasure. They hopefully seized on the 1807 battle of Eylau, Napoleon's least successful since Egypt, as proof of his strategic fallibility. Even the French bulletins, which normally put the needs of morale well before those of the truth ("lying like a bulletin" was a proverbial expression), used "horror" and "massacre" to describe the frozen, hideous aftermath of the battle. But Eylau was followed by victory at Friedland and the summit meeting at Tilsit. The gory draw of Aspern-Essling in 1809 again kindled excitement across Europe. One German newspaper enthusiastically announced Napoleon's death on the battlefield. But Archduke Karl did little to exploit his success, and Napoleon eventually imposed yet another humiliating peace on the Austrian empire.

But the end came quickly — so quickly that Chateaubriand could call the First Empire nothing but "an immense dream, as brief as the fretful night that had engendered it." In 1812, all the tendencies I have already discussed — France's "imperial overstretch," the continual rebellions against French authority, the uncontrollable expansion in the size of armies and battles, Napoleon's own weakening abilities — finally came together in the perfect storm that was Russia. At the start of this campaign, the First Empire was still somewhat unsteady but remained the greatest power ever seen in European history. Six months later, it was a gravely wounded giant, spurting blood under the ravenous gaze of its enemies and allies alike.

Nothing illustrates the implacable logic of total war more than Napoleon's decision to attack Russia. He had good *political* reasons for doing so: by 1812, Tsar Alexander had become a singularly unreliable ally, undermining the Continental System and threatening France's control over Germany and Poland. Yet the campaign made little military sense, and Napoleon went to war with largely undefined military goals, just as the French Revolutionaries had done twenty years earlier. Of course, he hoped to destroy the Russian army, as he had destroyed the Prussians in 1806. But in Russia, he faced an opponent with a population greater than France's and with territory stretching fifteen hundred miles in its European portion alone — and beyond that, five thousand miles farther across Siberia (the tsar insisted that he would retreat to the Pacific before surrendering). Its army, staffed largely by long-serving conscripts, already numbered an intimidating 600,000 men at the start of 1812 and would swell to over 900,000 by September.

Napoleon himself admitted that he did not know precisely what goal he was marching toward. In 1808, he had fancifully proposed to the tsar a joint invasion of British India, and four years later, thoughts of the Orient again ensnared him, as they had done in Egypt. "I do not fear that long road which is bordered by deserts," his aide Narbonne remembered him saying. "After all, that long road is the road to India. Alexander the Great, to reach the Ganges, started from just as distant a point as Moscow." Narbonne claimed Napoleon spoke these lines "as if in a trancelike exaltation." They certainly reflected a trancelike imperviousness to reality, for Napoleon could hardly march the *Grande Armée* four thousand miles into Asia without his Empire exploding behind him (as it was, even the Russian campaign saw dangerous conspiracies against his rule develop in Paris). Napoleon also knew perfectly well of the folly Sweden's King Charles XII had committed a century previously, when he had led his army to destruction, deep inside Russian territory, at Poltava. The emperor had read Voltaire's history of Charles XII closely and even carried it with him during the campaign.

If he needed an excuse not to go, he could have even cited portents. At the very start of the campaign, finding a bridge over the Viliya River destroyed, he scornfully ordered a squadron of Polish cavalry to wade across at a ford. In the middle of the stream, the current swept the horses off their feet, and the heavily equipped riders floundered and drowned. "As they were about to go down," remembered Napoleon's aide Ségur, "they turned towards Napoleon and shouted 'Vive l'Empereur!'" Even before this incident, the heavens themselves seemed to display a warning, in the form of a large comet that had appeared in European skies in the spring of 1811. In Tolstoy's unforgettable words: "Almost in the center of this sky . . . , surrounded and convoyed on every side by stars but distinguished from them all by its nearness to the earth, its white light and long, uplifted tail, shone the huge, brilliant comet of the year 1812 — the comet which was said to portend all manner of horrors and the end of the world."

And yet, he went. In June 1812, the largest army ever assembled in European history approached the Niemen River, Russia's western frontier. It included some 200,000 men from France's pre-1792 borders, another 100,000 from the newly annexed territories, 160,000 Germans, 90,000 Poles and Lithuanians, and a wide smattering of other nationalities — a truly European force. The ongoing war in Spain pinned down an additional 200,000 troops, who otherwise might have accompanied Napoleon. Nonetheless, he counted 450,000 in his main army group and some 655,000 altogether. In the next six months, at least half of them would die.

The popular imagination associates Napoleon's Russian disaster — like Hitler's — with the victories of the famous "General Winter." But another season arguably played just as great a role. Soon after the invasion began, temperatures climbed to as high as 97°F, putting the troops, with their heavy uniforms and packs, into a parched agony that, for the older veterans, must have recalled the Egyptian campaign. But in Egypt, the French initially had to march barely 150 miles. To reach Moscow from the Niemen, they had to go nearly four times that distance. The peasants of the region had largely fled, taking their food supplies along or hiding them in the woods. For the *Grande Armée*, food and water quickly ran short. Jakob Walter, a twenty-four-year-old stonemason from southern Germany, later recalled the march in nausea-inducing detail. So hungry were the men that when they found a hog, they did not even stop to cook it:

> . . . often still living, it would be cut and torn to pieces. Several times I succeeded in cutting off something; but I had to chew it and eat it uncooked, since my hunger could not wait for a chance to boil the meat . . . In order to obtain water for drinking and cooking, holes were dug into the swamps three feet deep in which the water collected. The water was very warm, however, and was reddish-brown with millions of little red worms so that it had to be bound in linen and sucked through with the mouth.

Dysentery quickly followed on this revolting fare, further exacerbating dehydration and turning the Moscow road into the largest, foulest open latrine in human history. Soldiers lay down and held their breath, desperately trying not to vomit. "I am looking forward to getting killed," one conscript wrote home, "for I am dying as I march."

Somehow, the shrinking *Grande Armée* held together and chased the Russians eastward. But rather than risk destruction, the Russians retreated, and the French failed to catch them. Napoleon was operating on a larger scale than ever before and had to rely more than ever on his less-brilliant subordinates (at one point, he chastised his own brother Jérôme for lacking "the most elementary grasp of soldiering"). At several moments, he pondered retreating, but in each case decided to push forward, still hoping to annihilate the Russian army. In mid-August, he almost managed the feat at Smolensk but failed to close his planned trap and gained little but a burned and ruined city. "We passed through the smoking ruins in military formation, with our martial music and customary pomp, triumphant over this desolation, but with no other witness to our glory than ourselves." Thus wrote Ségur. On September 7, with their commander shaking from fever and urinary pain, the French won another pyrrhic victory at Borodino, outside of Moscow, opening the city but losing 28,000 killed and wounded, including 48 generals. And the Russians escaped again.

A week later, the French occupied Moscow (which Saint Petersburg had replaced as Russia's capital a century before). The city had just been evacuated, and the clocks in the Kremlin were still ticking. Finding food and drink, the starving French troops gorged. Then they pillaged, stripping houses of clothing, furniture, tapestries, jewelry, icons: anything that could be carried. But there were scarcely 100,000 of them. Even taking into account the many thousands stationed behind, along the route, or heading toward Saint Petersburg under Marshal Macdonald, the losses had already dwarfed anything yet seen in any European war. It was uncertain whether the remainder of the *Grande Armée* could hold out in the city through the winter or even try. And then, most likely thanks to deliberate Russian acts of arson, the city burned, on a scale not seen in Europe since the great London fire of 1666. Nero-like, Napoleon looked on in fascination. As he later reminisced in exile on Saint Helena:

> It was the spectacle of a sea and billows of fire, a sky and clouds of flame
> — mountains of red rolling flames, like immense waves of the sea, alternately bursting forth and lifting themselves to skies of fire, and then

sinking into the ocean of flame below. Oh, it was the most grand, the most sublime, and the most terrifying sight the world ever beheld!

The one-time aspiring novelist had certainly produced a real-life spectacle that matched any piece of art. But the genre had shifted from heroic epic to Shakespearian tragedy.

The final act came with the retreat. Having lost so much of his army in the march to Moscow, Napoleon now sacrificed nearly all the rest. "Although we are less acclimatized than the Russians, we are fundamentally more robust," he insisted unconvincingly amid Moscow's smoking ruins. "We have not had autumn yet; we shall have plenty of fine days before winter sets in." On October 19, the depleted army, loaded down with the fruits of its pillage, began to leave the city. Nine days later, they staggered past the battlefield of Borodino, where tens of thousands of unburied corpses still lay in the open, half-eaten by animals and vermin, amid a staggering wreck of charred tree trunks and the detritus of war: "battered helmets and breastplates, broken drums, fragments of weapons, shreds of uniforms, and bloodstained flags."

Then, on November 6, the snow began, the thermometer plummeted (eventually reaching as low as −35°F), and the tragedy devolved into a phantasmagorical horror, almost beyond imagining. Jean-Michel Chevalier, a French officer from Versailles:

> We no longer saw French soldiers on the roads, only phantoms covered in rags, pallid figures with long, dirty, ashen beards, their heads a tangle of handkerchiefs, their hands and feet wrapped in lamb skins, with old bedspreads, women's skirts, horse blankets and animal skins covering their heads and bodies, so that one barely saw their dull, gaunt eyes. And all these piles of torn, burned disgusting scraps, all of it marched mechanically, aimlessly, at random, without a shade of hope. Little by little the blood stopped circulating, the feet swelled first, then the blood rose towards the head, the eyes turned haggard, seeing nothing but fantastic phantoms, then blood came out of the nose . . . a satanic and convulsive laugh . . . an unintelligible rattle . . . The wretch went blind, spun about like a drunk, and fell, laughing an infernal laugh.

Jean-Roch Coignet, a long-serving "grognard" of peasant origins who had risen to officer rank in the elite Imperial Guard:

> There was no longer any discipline or any human feeling for one another. Each man looked out for himself. Every sentiment of humanity

was extinguished. No one would have reached out his hand to his father, and that can be easily understood. For he who stooped down to help his fellow would not be able to rise again . . . The men fell frozen stiff all along the road. If, by chance, any of them came upon a bivouac of other unfortunate creatures who were thawing themselves, the newcomers pitilessly pushed them aside, and took possession of their fire. The poor creatures would then lie down to die upon the snow. One must have seen these horrors in order to believe them.

The starving soldiers threw away their pillage or desperately traded precious jewels and icons for the smallest scraps of food. Some ate raw flesh carved out of the sides of live horses, which didn't even notice, because of the cold. Others, finding small supplies of flour, made a foul bread dough with axle grease substituting for fat and gunpowder for salt. The men slept in the open, and in the morning, the living would wake amid a field of snow-covered corpses. Lice and vermin gnawed at them. Toes, fingers, noses, and penises fell victim to frostbite; eyes, to snow blindness. On November 23, the remains of the army reached the Berezina River, to find the other side occupied by the Russians. Over the next few days, heroic soldiers, mostly Dutch, built two makeshift bridges farther north, standing up to their chins in the freezing water. Most of the army passed, but one bridge collapsed under the strain, and as the Russians approached, a mad panic ensued on the other. Thousands of soldiers and civilians rushed onto it, knocking each other into the ice-choked currents. At least nine thousand people died.

Total war ends with an army transformed into a starving, skeletal, lice-ridden, barely human mass, covered in motley rags, its eyes blank and hopeless. This had been the case in the Vendée, at the end of the Northwind Turn, as the huddled remnants of the Catholic and Royal Army staggered to slaughter at the banks of the Loire. It was the case now in western Russia, as the *Grande Armée* limped back across the Niemen. "Assuming that Napoleon's object was to destroy his own army," wrote Tolstoy, "the most expert strategist could hardly conceive of any other series of actions which would so completely and infallibly have accomplished that purpose." Indeed, Napoleon had not simply matched the Russian folly of Charles XII but far exceeded it. According to the historian David Chandler, he lost a total of 370,000 men to death and 200,000 to Russian captivity. The numbers included nearly all of his 50,000-strong elite Imperial Guard, as well as 200,000 horses and 1,050 cannon. "The crusts on my hands, ears and nose had grown like fir-bark, with cracks and coal black scales," recalled Jakob Walter about the end of the retreat. "My face resembled that of a heavily bearded Russian peasant; and, when I looked into the mirror, I astonished myself." Napoleon's empire had likewise changed almost beyond recognition.

Even this almost unimaginable catastrophe, though, did not, by itself, doom Napoleon. He still controlled most of continental Europe and still had Prussia and Austria as at least titular allies. He still had in place an efficient system of conscription and hoped, in 1813, to raise no fewer than 656,000 new troops to carry on the war. He did not come close, but the number still suggests something of the scale of his capacities. But as the survivors of the Russian campaign reached a temporary safe haven in Poland, they had to deal with the consequences of two military disasters, not one. For total war in this period had two faces. One was the mammoth clashing of armies of the sort seen at Austerlitz, Wagram, Borodino, and Leipzig. But there was another, as well, one more reminiscent of the Vendée.

8

War's Red Altar

Millions to fight compell'd, to fight or die
In mangled heaps on War's red altar lie.

— PERCY BYSSHE SHELLEY, 1809

Shall I die in prose?

— THEODOR KÖRNER, 1813

BACK IN THE FALL OF 1806, even as Napoleon Bonaparte's *Grande Armée* was smashing irresistibly across northern Germany, a much smaller detachment of his soldiers was faltering in a seemingly much simpler task nine hundred miles to the south. In the Abruzzi region of southern Italy, Major Joseph-Léopold Hugo was leading some eight hundred men deep into the Appenine Mountains. They were a motley group even by the standards of Napoleon's new multinational empire: mainland French, Corsicans, Italians, and, most strangely, black Haitians — prisoners of war taken in the suppression of Toussaint L'Ouverture's independence struggle, shipped to Europe, and formed into a French unit known as the "Black Pioneers" (later, the "Royal Africans"). All owed nominal allegiance to the Kingdom of Naples, now ruled by Napoleon's brother Joseph, but in practice, they followed orders from Paris. They were chasing a legendary rebel leader, Michele Pezza, who went by the nickname of "Fra Diavolo" (Brother Devil).

It should have been an easy task. The previous year, the French had conquered the Kingdom of Naples, which covered the bottom of the Italian peninsula, and in February, Joseph had arrived to take possession. As in the previous French invasion, in 1799, a brushfire insurrection had quickly erupted, most fiercely in Calabria, the "toe of the boot." This time the French had far more force at their command. But the British fleet controlled Neapolitan waters and repeatedly landed insurgent leaders on the coast to keep the rebellion alive. In late August, they delivered Fra Diavolo to Sperlunga, north of the city of Naples, and he raised a force of 1,500 irregular troops.

Throughout September, Hugo pursued him through the thickly wooded Appenines. In his memoirs, the French officer left a vivid sketch of the expedition: the men struggling to climb steep, treacherous paths; slipping on the rocks; constantly at watch for ambushes. The autumn weather set in early, with repeated downpours that soaked the troops and left their guns almost useless. Once, Hugo saw several men killed by lightning. A strong earthquake had hit the Abruzzi earlier in the year, and the villages were half in ruins, houses wavering precariously on skewed frames. Everywhere, the population knew the legend of Fra Diavolo, a peasant and former mule driver with small, black eyes, who had risen from obscurity in 1799 and now claimed the title of Duke of Cassano, as well as the rank of brigadier in the Neapolitan army.

Fra Diavolo repeatedly slipped through Hugo's hands. On September 24, the French finally cornered his force and dispersed most of it, but he escaped with 150 followers. Throughout October, while Napoleon was chewing the Prussian army into sawdust and making his triumphant visit to the tomb of Frederick the Great, Major Hugo was desperately dividing his men to comb broad stretches of land, hoping to stop Fra Diavolo from reaching the coast and the safety of a British ship. Hugo, the thirty-two-year-old son of a Lorraine carpenter and an eighteen-year veteran of the French army, must have wondered whether failure would bring his military career to a premature end — his mercurial wife had already managed to damage it badly by having an affair with a notorious anti-Napoleonic conspirator. Hugo may well have cast his thoughts back to an earlier, equally frustrating moment in his military life, chasing survivors of the Vendée rebellion through the Breton countryside, at which time he had received a severe wound to the foot.

It was only through a lucky break that, on November 1, an apothecary in the village of Baronissi spotted Fra Diavolo and denounced him to the local constabulary, who handed him over to the French. Ten days later, the insurgent leader died on a scaffold in Naples. Hugo, now forgiven his wife's trespasses, could resume his rise through the ranks, eventually to become a general and a count in Bonapartist Spain. For the rest of his life, he would bore dinner-table companions with the story of the dramatic chase in the Abruzzi. "He would wrinkle up his nose like a rabbit — a characteristic expression of the Hugos — wink as though he had a new joke up his sleeve, and then tell us what we had already heard twenty times before." The evocative description comes from Hugo's son, Victor, born in 1802, who more than inherited his father's capacity for vivid prose.

And yet, for all Hugo's personal satisfaction, his feat made surprisingly little difference. The insurgency in Calabria did not end with the capture of even so important a leader as Fra Diavolo. It would continue for another four years, and the French would need brutal, scorched-earth policies to extinguish it. For every leader they captured and executed, others rose up. Partisan bands would continue to raid French convoys, kill French soldiers, and force the French to divert scarce resources. In short, Calabria remained an open sore on the skin of Napoleon's empire: an unneeded distraction at best, a source of dangerous infection at worst. And it was just one of many.

The story of Hugo's chase therefore illustrates another way that the Napoleonic empire was overwhelmed by forces Napoleon himself had unleashed. As the territory under French control ballooned, a series of fierce, damaging revolts erupted across significant parts of it. From Portugal to the Tyrol to Russia, insurgents declared total war on France. In ironic echoes of the French *levée en masse* itself, they pledged every adult male to the fight, insisted that the entire population contribute in any way possible, and called for the death of every French soldier polluting their soil. The Empire responded much as the Republic had done in the Vendée: it branded the insurgents and their supporters brigands and outlaws who deserved none of the rights of ordinary combatants or even of ordinary criminals. They could, it declared, be summarily put to death, their homes and villages destroyed. In short, there loomed the sort of conflict that Carl Schmitt called "absolute enmity."

In some ways, of course, these merciless brushfire wars resembled a long string of earlier ones: most immediately, the 1798–99 uprisings that had stretched in a broad arc from Belgium and western Germany through France itself to Italy; before that, the Vendée; before that, numerous Old Regime rebellions. One point in common was that the anti-Napoleonic insurgencies retained a strong religious component, with many invoking a Christian cause against the secular Empire, just as their predecessors had done against religious opponents or the "godless" French Republic. Nonetheless, the anti-Napoleonic movements also represented something genuinely different, both in their sheer scale and in the place they came to occupy in the European imagination. In the long, grinding, hate-filled struggles of 1806–14, motley rebel bands were transfigured into a new sort of historical figure: the "guerrilla," or partisan, symbol of a conflict without rules and without mercy, where each side utterly denied the other's right to fight or, indeed, to exist — symbol, in other words, of total war. Even the 1798–99 uprisings, massive as they were, did not last long enough to produce these effects (mostly, the French either restored order with reasonable speed or fled in disarray). Only in the Napoleonic years did a new word — "guerrilla," itself drawn from the Spanish for "little war" — arise to describe what Europeans saw as a very different kind of conflict.

Needless to say, this myth and rhetoric disguised a much more complex reality. The guerrillas did not in fact represent entire populations — in many countries, Napoleon had significant support. They did not always act out of patriotic self-interest and often resembled actual brigands far more than their modern admirers would like to admit. They tended to mobilize and attack where French rule was most precarious, not most oppressive. And they proved most successful where they most closely mimicked regular armed forces, not where anarchic popular enthusiasm bubbled most intensely through their ranks. The French, for their part, did not fight systematic campaigns of extermination. Indeed, they often lost control of their operations, leaving commanders on the ground to operate in conditions of near chaos as had happened in the Vendée. Some of them came to informal or tacit agreements with their "outlaw" opponents. Others resorted to large-scale atrocities out of blind frustration or in a desperate attempt to prove to their superiors that they were doing something, anything, to restore order.

Nonetheless, the myth and rhetoric had real importance and helped give the insurgencies an influence that cascaded beyond their immediate effect of pinning down hundreds of thousands of French soldiers whom the Empire badly needed elsewhere. They reinforced the wide-spread image of Napoleon himself as an "ogre" and outlaw who did not deserve the status of honorable adversary, no matter how many emperors he embraced. And they inspired his opponents to conceive of war in a new way, most importantly in the country where he had marked his greatest triumphs: Germany. For it was there, amid the battlefields that marked the definitive end to Napoleon's imperial ambitions in 1813, that the spectacle of the insurgencies helped turn enthusiasm about war for its own sake, which had previously gripped only a small current of intellectuals, into a movement whose tones resounded deeply among the middle and upper classes and that would have tremendous consequences in the century to come.

It is tempting to think that Napoleon might have avoided all these events simply by showing more restraint. But the logic of total war was impossible to escape. As we saw in the previous chapter, by 1812 France held effective sway over nearly the entire European continent, excluding the British Isles, Scandinavia, Russia, and the Turkish empire. Most of the territory either fell under the direct rule of Paris or belonged to an ally or satellite state (several headed by Bonapartes). No conqueror could have easily kept control over such vast stretches of land, and the nature of Napoleonic imperialism made the task even more difficult. Victors of earlier wars, taking over a peripheral state, such as Naples, might have contented themselves with looting it thoroughly and installing their own satraps at the head of its government, while leaving the bulk of its political and social system intact. But as the scope of the wars grew, Napoleon needed the new lands to provide him with revenues and, increasingly, conscripts to feed his ever-famished military machine.

The result was drastic and hugely unpopular reform. In the Kingdom of Italy, the French doubled personal taxes and excise taxes, imposed an "extraordinary contribution" of 15 million *lire,* and instituted conscription with a four-year term of service. In Naples, despite the simmering rebellions, the government managed to nearly double its tax revenues under Joseph and his successor, Joachim Murat. Throughout Europe, Napoleon sought to tax clerical and noble wealth, which previous regimes had exempted from contributions, and to confiscate the fat land holdings of the Catholic Church, as the Revolutionaries had done in France. These policies implied a radical change in the na-

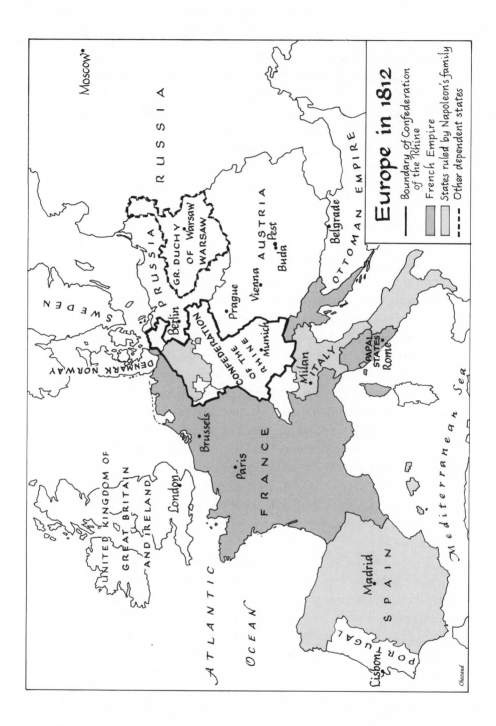

Europe in 1812

— Boundary of Confederation of the Rhine

▨ French Empire

▨ States ruled by Napoleon's family

---- Other dependent states

Moscow

RUSSIA

PRUSSIA

SWEDEN

DENMARK NORWAY

GR. DUCHY OF WARSAW

WARSAW

Berlin

CONFEDERATION OF THE RHINE

Prague

Vienna AUSTRIA

Buda Pest

Munich

Belgrade

OTTOMAN EMPIRE

Brussels

Milan ITALY

PAPAL STATES Rome

Paris

FRANCE

London

UNITED KINGDOM OF GREAT BRITAIN AND IRELAND

ATLANTIC

OCEAN

Madrid SPAIN

PORTUGAL

Lisbon

Mediterranean Sea

Chazaud

ture — and weight — of government influence in daily life. Large areas of Europe discovered a new phenomenon: pervasive bureaucracy, particularly new agencies for tax collection and conscription. With the bureaucracy, most often, came the Napoleonic Law Code and a reorganization of the territory into French-style *départements,* both of which disrupted traditional forms of government and social relations. To implement the new order, there came new police forces, often staffed largely by Frenchmen. In the end, Napoleon often found these complex changes easiest to implement through simple annexations to the Empire itself. By 1812, the high-water mark of Napoleonic imperialism, its borders had washed up over the Netherlands and the German North Sea coast, down across Catalonia, and as far as the eastern coast of the Adriatic, today belonging largely to Slovenia and Croatia. As the historian Stuart Woolf has put it, "annexation became a skilled art," practiced by a trained body of professionals who moved from one territory to the next, managing the absorption of each in turn.

But these dislocations, especially when compounded by attacks on the Catholic Church, fed insurrection. True, the major rebellions broke out only in relatively restricted areas: Calabria, Tyrol, Portugal, and Spain. But lower-level resistance to French rule smoldered throughout much of the rest of Europe, and it often took only small sparks of conflict to ignite high-octane disaffection. In 1809, for instance, the introduction of new taxes and regulations on the milling of wheat in northern Italy led thousands of peasants, armed mostly with scythes and pitchforks, to attack major cities, including Bologna. The peasants held Rovigo, in the Veneto, for four days, robbing wealthy houses and inflicting particular violence on the Jews (who, just as in 1798–99, served as the peninsula's first choice of scapegoat). It took the combined efforts of the Italian gendarmerie, National Guard, and army, backed by French soldiers, to restore order. Drawing on examples from France itself during the Directory, imperial officials established heavy-handed "military commissions" in place of civil courts and gave them the power to mete out death sentences without appeal: 150 by the end of 1809 alone.

Napoleon himself expected such difficulties and, to a certain extent, took them in stride. Soon after he had dispatched his brother Joseph to Naples, in 1806, he warned him: "Include in your calculations the fact that within a fortnight, more or less, you will have an insurrection. It is an event that constantly occurs in occupied countries." As a result, he gave hardened military men a prominent place in the ranks of the annexation "professionals." Jacques-François Menou, the one-time liberal aristocrat who had belonged to the Constituent Assembly, survived the Terror and accompanied Napoleon to Egypt (where he converted to Islam), was one of them. He served effectively in Piedmont, rose to become Governor General of Tuscany, where he gained a reputation for excessive severity, and finally moved to the Veneto, where he oversaw the suppression of the 1809 troubles.

Despite the excesses, men like Menou knew their business, and for a surprisingly long time, the Napoleonic regime did manage to keep a semblance of order. But when the Empire attempted to suppress the large Spanish insurrection that began in 1808, it simply could not do so. Instead, Spain became the famous "ulcer" that ate away at the vitals of the Empire, even before the limbs succumbed to Russian frostbite. In particular, Spain saw the development of a guerrilla war every bit as destructive as — and eerily similar to — the insurgency now under way in early twenty-first-century Iraq.

Before Spain, however, there was southern Italy in 1806–10, where much of the pattern was set. The festering memories of 1799, when French General Championnet had attempted to transform the Kingdom of Naples into the "Parthenopean Republic," primed the inhabitants for later resistance. It was during the collapse of this unstable puppet state that Fra Diavolo had made his name and that Cardinal Fabrizio Ruffo had organized tens of thousands of men from small guerrilla bands known as the *masse* into a Vendéan-style army called the *Santa Fede* (holy faith), which carried out dreadful atrocities against retreating French soldiers. It would take little for these bands, which drew on well-established patterns of smuggling, banditry, and resistance to central authority, to come together again.

At first, the new French conquest seemed to go much more smoothly. In late December 1805, after the Bourbon rulers had unwisely entered the war, Napoleon declared that "the dynasty of Naples has ceased to reign." He backed up his bombast with three French corps, two of which advanced easily down the Italian peninsula. By the end of March, they had brought all the mainland kingdom under French control, and the Bourbon rulers fled across the straits to the protection of the British navy in Sicily. In place of the Bourbons came Joseph Bonaparte, Napoleon's more reflective, pleasure-loving older brother, who shared his literary inclinations and had even, in 1799, published a novel (*Moina, or the Peasant Girl of Mont-Cenis*). Previously, Joseph had often chafed under Napoleon's hectoring, protesting about his "tyranny" and "insatiable ambition," and his tendency to turn even family members into "slaves." But the promise of a kingdom brought about a rapid and predictable change of heart. King "Giuseppe I" was soon holding royal audiences in Naples.

Yet the situation in Calabria — isolated, mountainous, close to Sicily — remained volatile. On March 22, in Soveria, near the Ionian Sea, a brawl over the requisitioning of horses by French soldiers led General Jean-Antoine Verdier to send two hundred troops to restore order. A band of more than a thousand armed peasants ambushed them, killed or wounded forty, and captured twenty-six, whom they tortured and, in some cases, castrated. The French army then returned in force, razing the village and taking hundreds of prisoners. French military commissions tried and shot two hundred of them. Nonetheless, in the next weeks, scores of other towns rose up against the French.

And, for the moment, the French forces were spread too dangerously thin to stamp out each spark of resistance. The corps commanded by Marshal Masséna remained bogged down north of Naples, while General Reynier, in the south, had scarcely 9,000 men, many sick, out of the 20,000 he deemed necessary to bring Calabria under firm control. In the vacuum, the *masse* quickly came back into action, under leaders who operated under colorful, bandit-chieftain nicknames, such as The Executioner (*Il Boia*), The Bizarre (*Il Bizarro*), The Monk (*Il Monacho*), Little Joseph (*Giusipello*), and, of course, Fra Diavolo. The British made matters worse by transporting insurgents by sea and, finally, landing several thousand redcoats in Calabria itself. On July 4, they routed Reynier's corps at the battle of Maida, leaving him with barely four thousand men in fighting shape. In the aftermath, even more villages rose up, and isolated detachments of French troops suffered gruesome fates, along with Italians who had supported Joseph's regime. In Acri, the guerrilla leader Spaccapitta ("The Stonecutter") roasted pro-French office holders alive. An insurgent leader gave a speech in Fiumefreddo, arguing that a "people's war" was different from ordinary fighting: "We must hammer the enemies, ambush them, cut off their communications and supplies, and then, attackers and bystanders alike, withdraw to safe places." Above all, Italians needed to wage a "war of extermination" against those in their ranks who supported King Joseph. The words amounted to a manifesto of guerrilla war.

The insurgents did not fit the model of selfless, nationalist freedom fighters. The French officer Nicolas Desvernois — admittedly not the most impartial of witnesses — claimed that "The Monk" and "The Deacon" devoted more energy to extorting food, arms, money, and even women from wealthy Calabrian property owners than they did to attacking the French. But even the insurgents' ally, British General Sir John Moore, called them "mafia . . . a lawless banditti, enemies to all governments whatever . . . fit to plunder and murder, but much too dastardly to face an enemy." Both the insurgents and Italians who served the new regime frequently pursued long-standing vendettas and rivalries under the mask of their competing patriotic rhetorics. Nonetheless, they inflicted real damage on the French, in what Reynier himself called "the most monstrous of wars."

At the end of June 1806, the French seemed to recover somewhat. Masséna finally moved south with an additional six thousand men. The temporizing British again withdrew to Sicily, allowing Reynier to move freely throughout the region. The French also struggled to raise a local force of Civic Guards and a native cavalry unit. Eventually, they hoped, native Italians would take over responsibility for maintaining order in the kingdom, with French forces left with the sole task of guarding against British invasion. This is a classic response to guerrilla war, from Napoleon down to Richard Nixon's policy of "Vietnamization" and the present-day American attempts to create a new Iraqi army. In the long term, in the Kingdom of Naples, it would have some success.

In the short term, however, Joseph Bonaparte's government mostly preferred a different, more brutal strategy: total suppression, as in the Vendée. On July 24, his Cabinet Council approved a manifesto drawn up by Antoine-Christophe Salicetti, an early Corsican patron of Napoleon's who had now become one of the leading "professionals of annexation." It declared Calabria in a state of rebellion and ordered the confiscation of rebel property, the burning of rebel villages, and the erection of public scaffolds to display the bodies of captured insurgents. "All these measures," commented Joseph's counselor Miot de Melito significantly, "[were] similar to those which had been taken by the Convention during the Vendean War."

Within days, Masséna proved the accuracy of the comparison. On August 8, 1806, the vanguard of his six-thousand-man force, marching south into Calabria, arrived at the town of Lauria, where the *masse* had decided to take a stand. Swathed by steep wooded cliffs, boulders, and ravines; surrounded by thick walls; and boasting an impressive ancient citadel, it made for a strong defensive position. A French officer approached, under a flag of truce, to demand submission and supplies, but the *masse* refused in the most dramatic fashion possible: they sent the man back in pieces, in a basket, along with a letter reading "here is the ration of supplies which the town of Lauria sends to the French, the only one suitable for them." In response, Masséna ordered a general assault without quarter. Jean-Michel Chevalier (who would later accompany Napoleon to Russia) remembered:

> Our enraged soldiers clambered up the rocks all around, and despite the inhabitants' desperate defense, despite a hail of bullets, we reached the main town square. And then, everything was sacrificed to our implacable vengeance. The old men, women and children fired on us from the windows or threw stones down at us . . . We were finally forced to set the entire town on fire. And there then took place under our eyes the most terrible scene: women, old men and children rushed out of the burning houses, and threw themselves at the feet of their conquerors . . . But the maddened and furious soldiers slaughtered them!

In a letter to King Joseph, Masséna insisted that he had been unable to prevent "excesses in the flush of victory" but added: "it cannot be doubted that [Lauria] will have a salutary effect." Joseph himself reported to his brother that "this terrible example appears to have restored order." The French, who went on to sack an additional twenty-five villages in the vicinity, found 734 bodies in Lauria and the surrounding heights. A Neapolitan colonel estimated the dead and wounded together at 3,000.

Over the next months, the French continued to use such tactics, all too reminiscent of the Vendée's "infernal columns." After Reynier dispersed several hundred insurgents near San Giovanni, he hanged the fifty who tried to surrender. In another insurgent village, the French imprisoned all the inhabitants until they denounced the insurgent leaders. Desvernois would recall with pride that he exhibited the heads of 184 insurgents in iron cages along the road south from Lauria. "It was important," he wrote, "to maintain the salutary terror spread by such examples."

Yet, frustratingly, for all these "examples," the most powerful army on earth still could not impose its will. It could seize the major towns, but this success meant little in a region where the two largest, Monteleone and Reggio, had scarcely 27,000 inhabitants between them. The French army corps themselves could move about unmolested, but smaller detachments regularly fell prey to attacks from hundreds, even thousands of peasants and artisans, armed mostly with blunderbusses and pitchforks, who sometimes tortured their prisoners to death. As the guerrilla leader at Fiumefreddo had urged, French communications and supplies were regularly cut off. But no sooner had the attacks, chaotic and terrifying, taken place than the insurgents melted back into the hills.

It took until the winter of 1810–11 for the Empire to prevail, by which point Napoleon had shifted Joseph to Spain. A new French general, Charles-Antoine Manhès, dispatched Civic Guards to areas suspected of supporting the partisans, with orders to shoot anyone leaving their village at night or carrying food outside it during the day. Starved of supplies and increasingly isolated from the peasantry, the partisans turned reckless, and one after another of their leaders fell into French hands. Calabria, for all the occasional ferocity of its resistance, had ultimately proved too weak and too divided to disrupt Napoleon's war machine on a permanent basis. For this reason, theorists, such as Carl Schmitt, generally overlook its role in prefiguring the later, more successful Spanish insurgency. Nonetheless, a crimson thread leads straight from the Vendée to Calabria and from there throughout Europe.

It would take a very long book to discuss in detail all the places this crimson thread touched. It touched Russia in 1812, where "flying detachments" approved by General Kutuzov harassed French stragglers and supply lines and where the hussar officer Denis Davidov, wearing peasant costume and a large cross of St. Anne, led thousands of peasants and irregular troops against units of Napoleon's army. It touched Germany, as we shall see, and it touched the Alpine fastnesses of the Tyrol, a region today divided between Austria and Italy. In 1805, Napoleon had passed the Tyrol from its traditional Austrian rulers to the heavy-handed control of his ally King Max Joseph of Bavaria. But when Bavarian control turned wobbly in 1809, an insurrection broke out, led by the pious, charismatic innkeeper Andreas Hofer. The Bavarians responded with a disastrous mixture of savagery and incompetence, forcing Napoleon to deploy his own, more efficient forces of repression, who eventually overwhelmed Hofer's poorly armed but enthusiastic bands. At one point, the emperor ordered his commander: "Declare that I will put the country to fire and sword if they don't turn in all their guns, . . . Every house in which a gun is found shall be razed, and every Tyrolean on whom a gun is found shall be put to death."

But it was Spain, whose violent resistance began even before the Tyrolean revolt and continued long after, that the crimson thread touched most profoundly and where the ground wave of insurrections grew strong enough to shake Napoleon's rule. As early as the summer of 1807, Napoleon had begun to contemplate overthrowing the Spanish branch of the Bourbon dynasty, which had proved anything but a reliable ally to him. He blamed it for the naval disaster at Trafalgar, and after taking Berlin in 1806, he found evidence that Spain had briefly conspired with Prussia against him. To top things off, the conduct of the Spanish royal family lurched embarrassingly between melodrama and farce. For years, the lumpish, mentally unstable King Carlos IV had effectively surrendered power to a favorite, Manuel Godoy, who was generally known to be the lover of Queen Maria Luisa. Fernando, the royal couple's twenty-three-year-old son and heir, was a vain, ignorant bigot who had conspired against his father and written to Napoleon to enlist his help. In October 1807, these letters came to light, and the king put his son under arrest.

Godoy was meanwhile seeking, with embarrassing servility, to placate his French patron. The very day of Fernando's arrest, Spain and France signed the Treaty of Fontainebleau, under whose secret terms a French army could cross Spanish territory en route to its invasion of Portugal, which had defied the Continental Blockade. The treaty foresaw the partition of Portugal into three parts, with one part destined for Godoy himself. In November, General Jean-Andoche Junot crossed the Pyrenees with 28,000 troops. Despite poor logistics that left his men starving and in large part almost barefoot, they overcame weak Portuguese resistance and stumbled into Lisbon in early December. The Portuguese ruling family fled to its colony of Brazil.

Yet Napoleon did not proceed with the partition plan. Instead, he sounded out his brother, by now relatively secure in Naples, about moving to Spain. Initially, Joseph refused, but Napoleon bided his time and continued to reinforce his army in Spain until, by spring 1808, it had reached a strength of nearly 120,000. Resorting to ruses (including, at one point, distracting Spanish soldiers with a snowball fight), these troops peacefully occupied important Spanish fortresses. Marshal Murat made a flamboyant entrance into Madrid on horseback, accompanied by trumpeters, drummers, lavishly uniformed cavalry, and eighty-seven turbanned Egyptian Mamelukes, a living relic of the Egyptian expedition. Murat, who was Napoleon's brother-in-law, hoped that the emperor might give the crown of Spain to *him,* and his upbeat reports to Paris about Spanish opinion served this ambition. "Your Majesty," he wrote Napoleon at one point, "is awaited here like the Messiah." A *slight* exaggeration, to say the least. But initially, few Spaniards saw the French as invaders.

Even before Murat's arrival, the conspiratorial Fernando, released from parental imprisonment, had given Napoleon his opening for the desired change of dynasty. On March 17, his supporters rioted at the royal residence of Aranjuez, forcing Godoy's dismissal and Carlos's abdication. But Napoleon refused to recognize Fernando's ascension and instead summoned both father and son to meet with him personally. In the meantime, the Spanish population had finally grown anxious about the swelling French presence, and when rumors spread that Murat had abducted a Bourbon prince, an uprising took place in Madrid itself. The French suppressed it amid gory street fighting, and the next day, firing squads summarily executed hundreds of prisoners. The painter Francisco de Goya later devoted two of his most brilliant works to these two days in May. One painting highlighted the small number of Mamelukes in the French force so as to evoke Spain's long struggle against Islam. Another offered a phantasmagorical tableau of implacable soldiers taking cold aim at an illuminated, Christ-like victim. The paintings made the *Dos de Mayo* and *Tres de Mayo* iconic dates of the Spanish War.

Meanwhile, in Bayonne, just over the French border, the most impe-

Francisco de Goya: *Tres de Mayo*

rious man of the age was behaving at his imperious worst. Rather than try to reconcile royal father and royal son, he insisted that they *both* abdicate in *his* favor, alternately cajoling, threatening, and bursting into fits of sheer rage. Napoleon had utter contempt for Fernando in particular. "He is so stupid I have not been able to get a word out of him," he wrote to Talleyrand. "Whether you scold him or praise him, his face remains blank." To Fernando's counselor Escoiquiz, Napoleon boasted that "nations with a lot of friars are easy to subjugate — I've had experience with them." When Escoiquiz protested that all Spain would rise up in rebellion, the emperor answered — as it turned out, prophetically: "even if that happened, even if I had to sacrifice 200,000 men, it would be the same." In the short term, the threats worked. Father and son both surrendered their rights and departed for exile in France. The emperor then played a game of musical thrones, ordering Joseph to trade Naples for Madrid and giving Murat, a former grocer and army private, the lesser but nonetheless royal reward of southern Italy. In Madrid, the Bonapartes at first attempted conciliation, with a moderate new constitution that respected at least some Spanish political traditions.

The confidence and scorn that Napoleon's men felt as they poured into Spain in the late spring of 1808 could not match Napoleon's at Bayonne but was still breathtakingly vast. Surely, they believed, this corrupt and somnolent country could pose no serious resistance to the greatest empire since Rome. To judge from their letters and memoirs, imperial soldiers and administrators mostly seemed to have the same impressions: the dirty, poor, and old-fashioned appearance of Spanish houses, the profusion of monastic robes in the streets, the "dark and wild look of the men," who all seemed lice-ridden. The more literary minded among the French compared crossing the Pyrenees to a journey in time. The financier Ouvrard wrote, eloquently:

> I was leaving a country where all traces of the past had disappeared, where everything dated from the day before . . . In a moment I was finding myself thrown back several centuries . . . The monastic costumes mixed in with the people . . . it was a representation of the seventeenth century; it was history in action.

According to the officer Heinrich von Brandt (one of many Germans who served the Empire in Spain), Spaniards still believed that heretics and Jews had horns and tails. Following the *philosophes* of the Enlightenment, who judged societies by their place on the great ladder of historical progress, and following the Revolutionaries, who had transformed such judgments into political action, Napoleon's men condemned the Spanish as weak and archaic in equal measure.

What the French did not expect was the following: "O happy gothic, barbarian and fanatical Spaniards! Happy with our monks and with our Inquisition, which, according to the ideas of the French Enlightenment, has kept us a century behind other nations. Oh, if we could only go back two centuries more!" These lines, written by Spanish general Manuel Freyre de Castrillon in 1808, formed part of a smoking lava flow of broadsheets and pamphlets that answered Napoleon's actions and helped prompt the uprisings. These writings had little real ideological coherence. Some spoke of liberty and independence in terms that French liberals would have found familiar and even set their words to the tune of the *Marseillaise*. Some adopted a language of national hatred similar to that of Robespierre or Barère, depicting the French as barbaric, even inhuman: "What sort of thing is a Frenchman? A being monstrous and indefinable, a being half-created. There is nobody who does not have the right to kill these ferocious animals." Others, many others, appealed to religious faith: "You [Napoleon] are insulting all of heaven, you are blaspheming God and his very holy Mother, you are . . . trampling the Very Sacred Heart of Jesus-Christ." But what all the writers did, in one way or another, was to sling the invaders' judgments back in their faces and to claim Spain's apparent weaknesses as strengths. And they were accompanied by uprisings across the country that seemed to prove the point: Barcelona, Saragossa, Oviedo, Seville, Valencia, Madrid, and many more. This was not the inevitable "insurrection in a fortnight" against which Napoleon had warned Joseph in Naples. This was rebellion on a massive scale.

The so-called Peninsular War would follow a twisting and complex course for more than five years. In the initial fighting, popular resistance across the country, combined with the action of Spanish regular forces, nearly drove the French back across the Pyrenees. The Spanish even forced an entire French army into the humiliating surrender of Baylen, on July 19, 1808. Soon afterward, the British expeditionary force under the future Lord Wellington compelled Junot to evacuate Portugal. Napoleon, however, personally took charge of the return engagement, crushing the Spanish at Burgos and Somosierra in the fall of 1809 and putting Joseph back in Madrid, with a new, more radical constitution that struck at "feudal" rights and instituted religious toleration. From then until 1813, French, Spanish, Portuguese, and British armies ranged back and forth across the peninsula, while bands of guerrillas grew steadily larger, better organized, and more similar to regular armed forces. Fighting between the regular armies concentrated particularly around the Spanish-Portuguese border, with fortress towns, such as Ciudad Rodrigo and Badajoz, changing hands several times. A legitimist Spanish government, loyal to the "longed-for king" Fernando (*el rey deseado*), challenged King "José" Bonaparte, mostly from the southern city of Cádiz. At times, the French faced little opposition from regular armies, but the guerrillas were a different matter, and the number of troops Napoleon had to maintain in the peninsula testify eloquently to their importance: from 165,000 in June 1808 to more than 300,000 in October and to well over 350,000 in July 1811. Only when the Russian campaign greedily sucked men away did the number shrink, falling below 100,000 by July 1813, with catastrophic consequences. Estimates of total French military deaths in Spain vary widely, but they may have amounted to as many as 180,000 — eerily close to Napoleon's 1808 prediction.

In the meanings it held for its participants, the Peninsular War, like the Calabrian one, stood as the diametrical opposite of the wars of the Old Regime. Far from recognizing each other as honorable adversaries, the French and the Spanish treated each other mostly as criminals who lacked any vestige of legitimacy as combatants. Both sides also insisted on an absolute identification between the fighters and the population in general. "If we had wanted to carry out Marshal Soult's decree against the insurgent Spaniards, we would have had to put almost the entire population of the country to death." Thus the French officer Albert-Jean Rocca. With these elements of absolute enmity in place, the scene was set for total war, and total war quickly materialized, making the peninsula the most merciless conflict in Europe since the Vendée.

Although the guerrilla conflict captured imaginations most enduringly, the excesses and atrocities of the Peninsular War took many different murderous forms. There were the Madrid executions of 1808, scorched into European memory by Goya as deeply as Picasso would later scorch the name of Guernica. There were the ferocious initial reactions to the French — for instance, the massacre of as many as 330 French citizens by a mob in Valencia on June 5, 1808. And there was Napoleon's brutal march on Madrid in the fall of 1809, in which soldiers, eager for revenge and made desperate by a lack of supplies, took to sacking even towns that offered no resistance. "The churches were sacked, the streets were choked with the dead and the dying," wrote Joseph's counselor Miot de Melito about the sack of Burgos. "In fact, we witnessed all the horrors of an assault, although the town had made no defense! . . . We may date from this period the manifest moral change which took place in the French army . . . The soldiers . . . would no longer do anything but fight and plunder; military discipline vanished." In terms that recalled his 1806 words about adopting the "barbarism" of his enemies, Napoleon himself proclaimed that if the Spanish did not submit, he would treat them "as conquered provinces and give my brother another throne. I will then place the crown of Spain on my own head and will know how to make it respected by the wicked."

The most concentrated horror of the war, meanwhile, did not involve the guerrillas at all but uniformed troops involved in that classic form of Old Regime warfare, a siege. Pre-1789 sieges were often horrible things, but they most often ended once the besieger had definitively breached a city's defenses (honor did not demand more). In the Aragonese city of Saragossa, in 1808, a different scenario played itself out.

At the start of the war, Saragossa, on the banks of the Ebro River, was in gentle decline. Its population had fallen from more than 80,000 a hundred years before to barely 43,000, and its most visible industry was Catholic worship, as evidenced in its twenty-five monasteries, sixteen convents, a huge cathedral and basilica, and seventy other churches. The people had particular devotion to the basilica of *el Pilar* — the site where the Virgin Mary had allegedly appeared on a pillar of marble and commanded the apostle James to build a church. In the spring of 1808, Saragossa, like many other Spanish cities, declared itself in revolt against the "intruder king" (*el rey intruso*), and power passed in large part to a charismatic local noble officer, José Palafox (whose subsequent role has been much exaggerated, notably by himself). The city remained badly fortified, with only one thousand regular Spanish troops available to protect it, and on June 15, French general Lefebvre-Desnouettes attempted to storm it. But the population offered unexpectedly fierce resistance, spurred on by the supposed miraculous appearance, a month before, of a palm tree topped by a crown in the sky above the basilica. Thousands of men and women rushed to the walls, aided by peasants from the nearby countryside, eager to serve the "virgin of the pillar." The French retreated in disorder.

On June 28, they tried again, this time under Jean-Antoine Verdier, the same man who had helped carry out the scourging of southern Italy. Once again, Saragossa beat the French off. According to legend, a Catalan girl named Augustina Zaragoza Domenech managed to take over a cannon from her dying lover and fire it point-blank at the advancing French, saving a key strongpoint. Verdier pulled back and began a ferocious bombardment instead. On June 30 alone, his men fired 1,400 explosive shells into the city. The siege continued through mid-August, reaching its height on the last day of July, when shells set the hospital of Nuestra Señora de Gracia on fire, and patients and staff leapt to safety to the accompaniment of inhuman screams from helplessly incarcerated lunatics. One French witness reported that "the city was like a volcano as explosion ceaselessly followed explosion . . . The streets were strewn with corpses." Bombs and grenades knocked whole pieces of buildings into the streets, while cannonballs smashed openings in the walls for French troops. A British witness later reported that virtually every house bore the marks of cannon shot. But when Verdier demanded the city's surrender, its leaders sent back the message *Guerra y cuchillo* — "war to the knife." A lack of troops kept Verdier from mounting a successful assault, and finally he withdrew. The men and women of Saragossa marched in joyful procession, singing: "the Virgin of the Pillar does not want to be French."

Several months later, the French returned with a much larger force commanded by the hardened and competent Marshal Lannes. But the Spanish had many more troops as well and had constructed elaborate fortifications. Once again, the French launched a storm of fire, lobbing as many as 42,000 explosive shells into the city during December. With Saragossa overcrowded by soldiers, civilian defenders, and refugees from the countryside, a typhus epidemic began, killing more than 350 people a day. In January, Lannes's infantry began to penetrate into the city, but despite the truly infernal conditions prevailing there, Palafox again refused to surrender and promised to hang any defenders who abandoned their posts.

There then began some of the worst urban combat ever seen in Europe before the twentieth century. The French advanced literally house by house. "It is necessary to mine them and blow them up one after the other, break down the partition walls and advance over the rubble." Sometimes, the battle even proceeded room by room, with both sides gouging loopholes in the walls, sticking their muskets through and blazing away point-blank at each other. A third of the town became a virtually impassable maze of broken rock through which the French could navigate only by following paths cleared by their engineers and marked with stakes. The French baron Marbot marveled at the courage of the defenders, who refused to leave houses even as they heard mines rammed into place below them: "One could hear them singing litanies," he later remembered, "at the moment when the walls flew into

Francisco de Goya: *The Disasters of War*

the air, and fell back with a crash, crushing the greater part of them."
Those who survived would immediately find cover and start shooting
again.

In the city's religious establishments, phantasmagorical scenes played
themselves out. French troops advanced while shielding themselves
with huge folio volumes recounting the lives of the martyrs, taken from
a convent library. During a rainstorm, the French took shelter under
painted and varnished canvases of the crucifixion. In monastery basements, men drowned in floods of oil and wine from huge, earthen-
ware containers shattered by explosions. Ancient cadavers were literally
blown from their tombs. In the monastery of San Francisco, a French
soldier saw "the livid, fleshless face and half the body of a bishop who
had been buried in his pontifical robes. His bony, dessicated arms
which pointed toward us, the deep and sombre orbits of his eyes, his
frightening mouth all made him appear to us as a phantom."

Finally, in mid-February, Saragossa surrendered. Of Palafox's 34,000 regular soldiers, only 12,000 had survived to go into captivity. The city's total death toll amounted to at least 50,000 — more than its prewar population. Most of the victims had perished of disease. "Under the arches, and in indescribable confusion, there lay children, old people, the dying and the dead . . . There was a mound of corpses, many stark naked, piled in the middle of the street . . . I have, since then, been present at many scenes of slaughter . . . Yet nowhere have I felt the same emotion as I did at that moment." So wrote the German von Brandt.

But in Saragossa, the French could ultimately prevail. In large parts of the Spanish countryside, they could not. Instead, the countryside saw the development of the war of the guerrillas, which gnawed powerfully at French strength and morale and radically disrupted the administration of the country. The guerrilla war was not the pure romantic effusion of national spirit so often evoked by Spanish historians and novelists (to quote one novel: "imagine that the earth takes up arms to defend itself against invasion, that the hills, the streams, the gorges, the grottos are death-dealing machines which come out to meet the regular troops"). It was considerably more complex and less heroic. But, in the long run, it had deadly effects nonetheless.

To grasp the essence of the conflict, we need look little further than the uncannily similar situation that unfolded in Iraq after the American victory in 2003. American and allied forces engaged in a protracted, frustrating attempt to move Iraq toward peace and stability and a part of the Iraqi population, led by the titular government, sided with them. Another part, probably larger, remained aloof, focusing principally on its own safety and well-being. A third part viewed the foreign forces with open hostility, while a fourth part, probably quite small, engaged in active resistance. Since these insurgents had no chance of successfully confronting the American army in pitched battles, they instead engaged in sneak attacks on small detachments or on civilians, after which they immediately melted back into the population at large. Their actions made it nearly impossible for Americans to leave heavily fortified bases except in heavily fortified convoys. American soldiers complained in private about being unable to secure any territory other than that within immediate range of their guns, with the result that they needed, in the words of one Marine, repeatedly to "sweep the same insurgents, or other insurgents, out of these same towns without being able to hold them, to secure them."

In Spain, the equivalent of the new Iraqi government was the fragile regime of Joseph Bonaparte, supported by the self-proclaimed "enlightened" Spaniards known as the *afrancesados* (literally, "the Frenchified"). A large segment of the population remained aloof from the conflict entirely. Another large segment greeted the French with hostility. The guerrillas themselves probably never numbered more than 40,000.

Their effect, however, was far out of proportion to this figure and far greater than that of their counterparts in Calabria. Their preferred method of attack (lacking car bombs and plastic explosives) was to descend without warning, in bands of hundreds, on small, isolated detachments of French troops — stragglers, sentries, scouts, and messengers. They relied on surprise and shock, and generally retreated on meeting any serious resistance. The memoirs and correspondence of French soldiers on the subject are remarkably monotonous: "We were masters of all the towns and villages upon the road, but not of the environs at the distance of one hundred paces"; "we had sentries carried off or disarmed by invisible enemies every night"; there was "fighting on a daily basis against invisible assailants, spread out in their thousands behind bushes, at the bottom of ravines, hidden at the corner over every wall." On a single day, November 20, 1807, 80 of the 719 French soldiers crossing the Sierra de Gata en route to Portugal simply disappeared. As Miot de Melito put it, melodramatically: "An invisible army spread itself over nearly the whole of Spain, like a net from whose meshes there was no escape."

Here is an example. In the spring of 1812, General Louis Brun was traveling through central Spain in the company of several French civilians and with an escort of eighty soldiers. The road passed into a deep ravine cut by the Guadarrama River, not far from Madrid, and as Brun approached the bridge, a musket salvo broke the calm of the day. Thirteen of his soldiers fell, and when Brun looked to flee back out of the ravine, he saw two hundred *guerrilleros* on horseback, blocking his retreat. Fortunately, a stone pen for sheep, with thick three-foot walls, lay nearby. Brun and the other survivors took up positions there and managed to hold out until a French relief force arrived from Segovia, at which point the attackers took flight. Brun recalled that one of the civilians, a French wine merchant, lay on the ground in the pen and refused to take up a gun until Brun kicked him repeatedly. Scenes of this sort repeated themselves hundreds, perhaps thousands, of times during the years of the war, often with cruel results for the French.

The guerrilla forces were no match for French regular troops in a pitched battle. But getting them into a pitched battle was easier said than done. Rather than tracking these small, mobile forces, the French ended up concentrating mostly in relatively few strongpoints, leaving the rest of the country thinly occupied and therefore effectively out of their control. An entire army corps spent its time simply safeguarding the crucial road from Madrid north to France. General Honoré-Charles Reille, the French military governor of Navarre, in northern Spain, put the matter with stark eloquence in a letter of 1810: "Unfortunately, in this region as in many others of Spain, our influence extends only as far as the range of our cannon . . . The Spanish say quite rightly that our troops are plowing furrows in the water."

The guerrillas had a complex profile. Just as in Calabria, their leaders were part military commander, part bandit-chieftain, and they took colorful nicknames: "The Potter" (*El Cantarero*), "The Priest" (*El Cura*), "The Lad" (*El Mozo*), "The Grandfather" (*El Abuelo*), "The Doctor" (*El Medico*), "The Stick-in-the-Mud" (*El Empecinado*). The social composition of the forces varied widely. Often, as Charles Esdaile has stressed, bands preyed as much or more on their fellow countrymen as on the French. By 1810–11, some had set up regular systems of tolls and taxations, through which even French merchants could pass unmolested, as long as they paid. Many bands had their origins in scattered units of the old Spanish army, which had partly crumbled after Napoleon's victories in 1808. And as time went on, others effectively transformed themselves into new units, complete with standard ranks, regimental organization, uniforms, and even artillery (mostly seized from the French). By 1813, Francisco Espoz y Mina ("Uncle Francisco," or "The King of Navarre"), the Basque commander of the single most successful band, had over 6,000 soldiers organized in ten regiments, dressed in blue uniforms with breeches and jackets, armed with muskets and bayonets, and trained to fight in line and column. Yet he also continued to use established guerrilla tactics and managed to pin down as many as 38,000 French soldiers in 1812–13.

Yet despite their resemblance to both bandits and regular soldiers, the guerrillas represented something different from either. From the start, the remnants of the old Spanish state sought to give them official standing, drawing on the language of the "nation in arms." As early as June 1808, Fernando's supporters in the so-called Junta of Seville called on "all Spaniards" to fight the French. In December, orders followed, authorizing the creation of *partidas,* or partisan bands. And on April 17, 1809, there appeared the declaration of the so-called *Corso Terrestre,* roughly translated as "Privateering on Land": "All the inhabitants of the provinces occupied by French troops who are capable of bearing arms are authorized to do so, even to the extent of using forbidden weapons, to attack and despoil French soldiers . . . , to make it hard for them to live in the country, to seize their provisions . . . in short to do all possible harm to them." Newspapers and pamphlets repeated the message, calling for "a novel system of war" in which the large French armies would be countered with "war on a small scale, with guerrillas and more guerrillas." "All men are soldiers," declared the gazette of the Junta of Catalonia: "in the fields, on the roads . . . in the cities occupied by the enemy, wherever the Catalans show profound hatred for the French." These statements eerily echoed the French declaration of the *levée en masse* of 1793. But now, the incarnation of nation at war was not the uniformed volunteer, shouldering his pike and heading for the frontier, but rather the irregular fighter, taking up any weapon at hand to expel invaders from his broken and tormented country.

What confirmed the *guerrillas* in their stance of absolute enmity toward the French was religion. The massive presence of the clergy on Spanish soil noticed by French observers had a very real effect. In 1808, a full quarter of Spanish land revenue went to the Church. The population of 10,000,000 included 30,000 parish priests and another 120,000 monks, nuns, and other clergy. These men and women preached against the invaders without respite and even promised remission from divine punishment for those who fought against them. A much-used "Spanish Catechism" of 1808 called the French "former Christians and modern heretics" and insisted that it was no more a sin to kill them than it would be to kill a wild animal. The liberal Spanish writer José Blanco White later claimed that "it was not love of independence and liberty which had made the people rise against the Bonapartes" but the fear of "reforms" that would weaken the Church. French officials agreed, with General Reille writing to his superior: "We have two classes of men who do us much harm: priests and monks."

Could the French suppress the guerrillas? By 1808–13, they had long experience to draw on. A large proportion of the officers posted in Spain had previously confronted partisans in the Tyrol and Italy. Hundreds had experience in irregular warfare that went all the way back to the Vendée. General François-Pierre-Joseph Amey, accused of some of the worst crimes committed in the Vendée's "hell columns," ended up in Spain. Joseph Hugo, who had begun his career chasing the survivors of the Vendée and then pursued Fra Diavolo in Calabria, came there as well. General Reille, responsible for counterinsurgency in Aragon and then Navarre, had made his reputation in Italy, integrating Italian forces into the imperial service. Not surprisingly, then, the French attempted to use the same tactics that had worked against previous insurgencies: massive deployment of French mobile columns to areas of guerrilla activity, the taking of hostages to ensure tranquility, exemplary punishment of villages suspected of supporting the guerrillas, swift execution of civilians captured bearing arms, and the raising of local auxiliary forces to take on an increasing share of the burden. The orders for summary executions, hostage taking, and arson came straight from the top. "Hang a dozen individuals in Madrid," Napoleon advised his brother. "There's no lack of bad sorts to choose from." "Tell [Reille] to arrest the brigands' relatives and send them to France," he wrote at another moment. "Levy taxes on the towns where the brigands operate, and burn the houses of their relatives."

In a few cases, the tactics showed signs of succeeding. The tough and talented Marshal Louis Suchet, for instance, managed for a time to impose something close to peace and order in areas of the north. He did so in part through co-opting nobles and other large landowners and in part through terror. His mobile columns shot captured guerrillas and priests found with weapons out of hand. They virtually wiped the town of Saliente off the map, much as Marshal Masséna had destroyed Lauria in Calabria. Suchet took hostages and tried to recruit local auxiliaries. But as the historian of his campaign in Aragon concludes: "Suchet's success was deceptive and fleeting. He had not eliminated resistance, only stunned it." It did not help that the French commanders squabbled mightily with each other and that, increasingly, they had to rely on inexperienced conscripts newly arrived from France. Above all, they simply did not have the manpower to make their tactics work — particularly as the guerrillas were killing or capturing an average of twenty-five French soldiers a day. By 1812, the laboriously achieved control simply crumbled in Suchet's hands.

The reports filed by General Reille from the northern city of Pamplona testify with particular eloquence to the Sisyphean nature of guerrilla war for the French. From mid-1810 to mid-1811, Reille vainly struggled against the increasingly professional force of Espoz y Mina. In letter after letter, he complained about the dread influence of priests and monks, about the guerrillas' swelling numbers, and about his inability to force them into pitched battles or to contain them without garrisoning every major town. Bitterly, he chided his superiors for withdrawing troops rather than sending more. He boasted to them of the priests his men shot and the hostages they took. But it made no impression on Paris, and in April 1811, Napoleon himself chided Reille for "showing little energy" and "leaving everything unpunished." This bolt from Olympus left the general almost speechless with shock, and he reacted by turning increasingly vicious in his tactics, until his own reports come to seem like the draft of a bill of indictment against him for war crimes. On July 8, 1811, he had 40 alleged guerrillas, held prisoner in the citadel of Pamplona, summarily shot and warned that the same thing would happen to another 170 unless the guerrillas abandoned their campaign.

Here was "absolute enmity" on the French side as well. And it takes little effort to imagine the sort of war that followed from the respective positions of the guerrillas and the French. Even high-ranking French officers frankly acknowledged in their memoirs the general mercilessness of the conflict. Joseph Hugo called it a *guerre assassine* ("an assassin's war") and explicitly likened it to the Vendée. Albert-Jean Rocca, who served under Marshal Soult in Andalusia, wrote: "The French could only maintain themselves in Spain through terror. They were constantly facing the need to punish the innocent with the guilty, of revenging themselves on the weak instead of the powerful." He later added his words about how Soult's orders literally implied extermination of the entire population. Both officers explained the viciousness as the result of trying to fight against an entire population rather than a regular army. But from the war in Navarre, one fact speaks even more eloquently than these comments. At one point, *both* General Reille and the guerrilla leader Espoz y Mina promised to execute four of the enemy for each of their own men taken prisoner and shot.

"One might fill volumes with the atrocities committed on both sides in this graceless war," wrote French captain Elzéar Blaze years later. Indeed. Blaze himself recorded gruesome stories of soldiers flayed alive by the guerrillas or placed between wooden boards and sawn in two. Belgian soldiers wrote home of seeing victims of the guerrillas with their eyes plucked out, their genitals cut off and stuffed in their mouths. French troops recounted seeing comrades literally nailed to barn doors and left to die. On the French side, General Jean-Marie-Pierre Dorsenne, the governor of Burgos, developed a ghastly reputation for torture. He made a policy of hanging the bodies of three guerrillas permanently on gallows outside his office; when relatives stole away one body in the night, he immediately ordered a prisoner executed to take the man's place. The hundreds of accounts that survive from both sides are generally impossible to confirm and often contradict one another. (Was the French general René sawn in two? Or lowered inch by inch into a cauldron of boiling water? We have both stories.) But overall, the inhuman character of the war is impossible to deny, as is the uncomfortable fact that men often found ghastly, macabre amusement in meting out pain and death.

The treatment dealt out to Lauria was repeated many times in Spain, and one story resembles that of the Calabrian town in eerie detail. Early in 1809, Marshal Victor, operating in central Spain near Talavera, sent a detachment of twenty-five German soldiers through nearby villages to ask for supplies. Four of them stopped in the village of Arenas, where the inhabitants pretended to greet them with hospitality but then fell on them and killed them. According to the account left by their officer Karl Franz von Holzing, the Spanish women, before murdering the soldiers, crushed their bones and testicles and cut off their penises. Holzing himself then led an expedition against Arenas. When the villagers tried to flee, his men shot at them from a distance as if on a hunting expedition, laughing whenever their victims fell into the grass. The French then set the village on fire. Holzing recalled, with horror, how wild and uncontrolled soldiers dragged young women into the streets and raped them and, in one case, dashed a baby's head against a wall before tossing the body into a fire in front of the shrieking mother.

As the French retreated from Portugal in the spring of 1811, after one last attempt to invade that country, their conduct evoked with particular, nauseating force what Shakespeare had called "the filthy and conta-

gious clouds / Of heady murder, spoil and villainy." The command belonged to Marshal Masséna, the same man who had overseen the sack
of Lauria four and a half years before. In the town of Porto da Mos, two
hundred men, women, and children were burned to death in the parish
church. A German in the British service later recalled:

> Every morning at dawn, when we started out, the burning villages, ham-
> lets and woods, which illuminated the sky, told of the progress of the
> French. Murdered peasants lay in all directions. At one place, which
> contained some fine buildings, I halted at a door to beg water of a man
> who was sitting on the threshold of the house staring fixedly before him.
> He proved to be dead, and had only been placed there, as if he were still
> alive, for a joke . . . The corpse of another Portuguese peasant had been
> placed in a ludicrous position in a hole in a garden wall, through which
> the infantry had broken. It had probably been put there in order to make
> fun of us when we came along . . . The villages through which we
> marched were nothing but heaps of debris.

The ability to track French columns by the smoke from burning villages recalls the Vendée, where Turreau's men scarred the sky in the
same manner. One French soldier in Iberia wrote home that his heart
always lifted when he saw plumes of smoke in the air: they were a giant
arrow pointing him toward his compatriots.

The most powerful evocations of the horrors of this war never even
saw the light of day until 1863. During the war, the great painter Goya,
very much an "enlightened" Spaniard with little sympathy for the
Church, had flirted with the new regime. He even painted Joseph
Bonaparte's portrait. But the unceasing cascade of atrocities revolted
him. They led him to paint his great tableaux of the second and third of
May 1808, which became icons of Spanish national sentiment. And
they also drove him to produce a series of blisteringly powerful etchings
entitled *The Disasters of War*, which depicted atrocities committed by
all sides. Their unflinching, deliberately obscene detail exposed the horrors of war in a manner rarely before seen in European art. In fact, they
speak better to later sensibilities, which perhaps explains why Goya
never published them in his lifetime.

The guerrillas, however, did not defeat Napoleon in Spain. Even
when such forces as Espoz y Mina's turned into something closely re-
sembling regular armies (and managed to get the French to end sum-

Francisco de Goya: *The Disasters of War*

mary executions of prisoners), they still could not hope to beat Napoleon's men in battle. They did, however, manage to tie down hundreds
of thousands of French soldiers desperately needed in other theaters of
operations (particularly Russia), while bleeding them badly and destroying their morale. "The Spanish war: death for soldiers, ruin for officers, fortunes for generals," ran a piece of cynical French graffiti found
on a Spanish wall.

The distinction for beating the French in the field, however, belonged above all to the British and their meticulous, stern commander,
Wellington. Commanding his relatively small, well-disciplined professional force but aided by troops from the old Spanish army and the Portuguese one reorganized by his associate Beresford, he carried out a brilliant series of victories: Talavera, Busaco, Badajoz, Salamanca, Vitoria.
In 1809–10, thrown back into Portugal, he constructed massive fortifications and stopped the French advance. Finally, in 1813, with Napoleon withdrawing troops from the peninsula to replace Russian losses,
Wellington forced the French army back toward the Pyrenees, and Joseph Bonaparte's regime collapsed. At the battle of Vitoria on June 21,

1813, a convoy carrying the papers and treasures of "King José" was intercepted and pillaged, leaving trunks, ledgers, books, and silver scattered across the field — an apt symbol for the wreck of French ambitions. The loot enriched many a common British soldier, and the king's silver chamber pot ended up as a loving cup in the mess of a British Hussar regiment. Joseph Bonaparte himself fled to France; after his brother's final defeat, he emigrated to southern New Jersey, where he lived the life of a dissolute country gentleman until the 1840s on land now used by Ocean Spray to raise cranberries. Wellington crossed the Pyrenees and invaded France.

But the story of total war in this period had one more twist to take. The years 1812–14 may have marked the ragged end of France's first experience with the phenomenon, but at the same time, they marked Germany's real introduction to it. Before 1812, the various German powers had certainly felt the force of post-Revolutionary France's aggression, but as we have seen, they adapted only slowly to their enemies' policies and tactics. Prussia, which went furthest in the reform of the state, remained aloof from the fighting. But during Napoleon's convulsive attempt to preserve his empire after the Russian and Spanish defeats, many Prussians, inspired by the Spanish example, finally came to embrace the idea of all-out conflict, with a fervor that matched anything seen in France.

This episode lasted scarcely a year, from the spring of 1813 to that of 1814. During it, Napoleon occasionally fought with a brilliance that recalled his earlier career, and the French army, with the fatherland again in danger, regained something of the *élan* of its Revolutionary days. The machinery of conscription replenished the Russian and Spanish losses with appalling speed. But the French army had not really recovered. The cavalry and artillery remained decimated by the losses of horses and cannon in Russia, and the new troops were young, inexperienced, and largely unwilling. Worse, Napoleon's supposed German allies soon abandoned him. Even before the debacle, large numbers of Prussian officials and officers had, like Clausewitz, angrily abandoned their cautious king and signed on for service with the Russians. In the last days of 1812, Prussia's General Hans David Yorck, commanding a 30,000-man Prussian contingent under the orders of French Marshal Macdonald, met with Russian officers, with Clausewitz as an intermediary, and formally switched sides. "With a bloody heart I rip asunder the bonds of obedience, and wage war on my own account," he declared melodramatically. Although Friedrich Wilhelm angrily branded Yorck an outlaw and traitor, the pressure on the king to follow his general steadily mounted. In March 1813, he belatedly declared war on France. Sweden came in soon afterward. And in August, after fruitless negotiations between Napoleon and his father-in-law, the Austrian empire did as well. The decisive blow came in October, in the massive "Battle of the Nations" around Leipzig, which ended in a massive French defeat. By early 1814, the allies were crossing the Rhine as well as the Pyrenees. In the spring, Napoleon abdicated, in the hope of putting his young son on the throne, and the allies entered his capital.

During what Germans later called this "war of liberation," an enthusiasm for war as a redemptive, regenerative experience, previously found only in the writings of a few intellectuals, such as Humboldt and Gentz, came to pervade German elite culture. Many of the best-known literary figures of the day — Ernst Moritz Arndt, Heinrich von Kleist, Johann Gottlieb Fichte, Theodor Körner — praised the ongoing struggle as a joyous test of the German spirit, through which a divided and lethargic nation would awaken and grow in health and strength. They compared the event to an earlier such awakening — the revolt of the German tribes against the Romans, led by Rome's supposed ally Arminius (Hermann). Kleist, a playwright who had served in the Prussian army in the 1790s, made Hermann the subject of a play that he hoped would spur his fellow countrymen to national unity and the extermination of the enemy: "For the whole world will only achieve peace from this wolf's brood, when the robber nest is completely destroyed and nothing but a black flag waves from its desolate heap of ruins." Arndt, a prolific poet, historian, and former cleric, sounded the same theme of national awakening:

> *Was ist des Deutschen Vaterland? . . .*
> *So weit die deutsche Zunge klingt*
> *Und Gott im Himmel Lieder singt,*
> *Das soll es sein!*
> *Das ganze Deutschland soll es sein!*

> What is the German's Fatherland? . . .

As far as the German tongue sounds
And God in Heaven sings songs
That is what it should be!
It should be all of Germany!

This poem, one of the most popular of the period, practically became a national anthem, six decades before the actual achievement of German unity.

These writers also had a very clear idea of what shape the war should take. It should be a "people's war," involving the entire population. Yet just as in the case of the Girondins and the *sans-culottes,* their fantasy of total engagement involved anything but autonomous, mechanized destruction on a mass scale. To the contrary, it involved a return to the most elemental forms of combat, in which individual strength, virtue, and passion would decide the outcome. "To arms! To arms!" Kleist wrote in verses meant to be sung — rather horrifyingly — to Beethoven's melody for the "Ode to Joy." "With a club, with a staff . . . Strike him dead! The world's court of judgment won't ask for your reasons!"

In an irony the French would not have appreciated, the Germans saw two recent events in particular as exemplars of such noble primitive war: the Vendée and Spain. Clausewitz cited both to prove that if an entire population rose up, the worst tyranny could not prevail against it. Even though the "tiger" of the French Republic had passed through the Vendée "with the sword of devastation, with murder and flame," it had not subdued it. The survivors of Turreau's columns might not have given such a sanguine account of their sanguinary experiences, but by 1812, a new legend of the Vendée had arisen, in which the destruction figured less prominently than the rebels' tenacious heroism. After the start of the Spanish guerrilla war, with its obvious resemblances to the Vendée, the Germans integrated it into their story as well. Kleist wrote an ode to Palafox, the hero of Saragossa, and adapted a Spanish national "catechism" to the German context. Carl Schmitt would later write: "The spark that flew north from Spain in 1808 found theoretical form in Berlin."

A people's war also involved intense hatred of the enemy, and the intellectuals surpassed even the Jacobins of the Year II in their lust to stimulate it. Arndt in particular provided, in his prolific xenophobic invective, an unsavory foretaste of some of Germany's worst subsequent history. Just as Barère had insisted that French infants suck in Anglophobia with their mother's milk, Arndt demanded that German children learn hatred of the French in the cradle. He called France "an empty, hollow, doll-like, formless, contentless Nothing, lacking strength, meaning and character." Identifying Germany's present enemies and future victims, he said they were "refined, bad Jews," "a Jew People." Just as revoltingly, in 1813, he published a tract with the charming title *On National Hatred* (*Über Volkshaß*), because he thought that the overall phenomenon deserved encouragement. "Since He is the God of love, so hatred pleases him too," this former cleric wrote with an impressive lack of logic. "All nature lives and creates solely through eternal war and struggle . . . God created . . . emnity between the nations." And therefore: "I want hatred against the French, not just for this war, but for a long time, forever . . . This hatred glows as the religion of the German people, as a holy mania in every heart." Here were the logical consequences of Humboldt's dispassionate reflections on language and organic growth, placed in the context of real warfare. Arndt expressed it with egregious vulgarity, but overall, he was not untypical. (Incidentally, the north German university attended by this paragon of learning and toleration was renamed for him the year Hitler took power and still bears his name today.)

In early 1813, Prussia's rulers began to take measures to translate this bellicose rhetoric into action. Acting on their own authority in February, the governing estates of East Prussia created a provincial *Landwehr* (Home Army). The next month, the reluctant king followed suit for the entire country, with compulsory service for all men aged eighteen to forty in the middle classes and landed peasantry and dramatically appealed to his people in print for patriotic unity. But the truly decisive step took place on April 21, when Friedrich Wilhelm issued a further edict. First, it supplemented the *Landwehr* with a *Landsturm* (Home Guard) meant to include all remaining adult males under the age of sixty. It also gave the following orders to the entire population: "Every citizen is required to resist the advancing enemy with weapons of all sorts, not to obey his verbal or written orders, and if the enemy attempts to enforce these with violence, to harm him using all available means." A long list of more detailed strictures followed. Notably, any

Prussian caught serving as a guide to the French "will be shot." Echoing Clausewitz, the king cited precedents from the Vendée and Spain and drew explicitly on the Spanish proclamation of the *Corso Terrestre* of April 1809. But his own, royal imprimatur gave the edict an authority these predecessors had lacked. In this sense, its real precedent was the French decree on the *levée en masse,* issued nearly twenty years before. But in the call to universal armed resistance, not simply universal participation in the war effort, the Prussians arguably presented an even more radical vision of war. Schmitt called the document the "Magna Carta of partisan warfare."

True, in some ways, its importance — and that of the entire cultural shift that lay behind it — can be exaggerated. The *Landsturm,* as we have seen, provoked severe criticism from Prussia's elites and, unlike the *levée en masse,* never really came into operation. Even the more limited *Landwehr* met with widespread resistance. Despite all the talk of Spain and the Vendée, Prussian territory in fact saw very little partisan activity in the summer of 1813 — the war remained a duel of uniformed armies. The patriotic enthusiasm did prompt more than twenty thousand men to volunteer, but they still amounted to only around 12 percent of total Prussian forces. As for the widespread German nationalism supposedly born in 1813, there is little evidence that it spread far beyond the literati. Friedrich Wilhelm himself acknowledged the multinational character of Prussia by issuing his March edict not to "Germans" but to "Prussians, Silesians, Pomeranians and Lithuanians." Heinrich Heine later quipped: "We were told to be patriots, and we became patriotic, because we always do what our princes tell us."

Still, the literati did have real importance. Arndt in particular was close to the Prussian statesman Stein, accompanied him on his return from Russian exile in 1812–13, and wrote, in part, on commission from him. Moreover, the vision of war that he and his fellow writers elaborated was shared by some of the most powerful men in the Prussian state and military, including Stein, Scharnhorst, and Gneisenau. The rhetoric of regeneration through war therefore pervaded the highest levels of Prussian society and government. Just as important, although it did not match the reality of the evolving Prussian army, it shaped the dominant meaning that the "war of liberation" would have for subsequent generations. Key symbols of modern German identity, such as the iron cross, were invented in the "Freikorps" of 1813 volunteers commanded by Baron Adolf von Lützow, whose members included a number of young writers. Chateaubriand was not being entirely whimsical when he proposed renaming the 1813 war "the Young Germany campaign, or the Campaign of the Poets."

One figure in particular would quickly come to embody this campaign for educated Germans. Theodor Körner was born in Dresden in 1791, the son of a well-to-do Saxon official who moved in intellectual circles. He had a restless adolescence, studying mining, law, history, and philosophy at several institutions but gave it all up by age twenty and moved to Vienna to try his hand at playwriting. He met with immediate success, particularly for a work called *Zriny,* which celebrated patriotic heroism but in a safely Hungarian context, thereby suiting the moment of swelling anti-Napoleonic public fervor without overtly challenging a government still officially allied with France. In Vienna, Körner also gained the friendship and sponsorship of none other than Wilhelm von Humboldt, the early advocate of regeneration through war.

In March 1813, still just twenty-one, Körner read of Prussia's declaration of war on France and Friedrich Wilhelm's appeal to his people. Overcome with enthusiasm, he signed up with Lützow's Freikorps and quickly became a lieutenant. Despite a severe head wound, he returned to the fighting by midsummer. He wrote poetry almost continuously about his experiences. In Chateaubriand's fanciful description, he was "young, blond and beautiful, an Apollo on horseback."

Much of the poetry was conventionally patriotic, in the Romantic style of the day ("the nation arises, the storm breaks out"), or praised the new form of war in a manner Clausewitz would have approved: "This is not the sort of war that crowns know of / It is a Crusade, a holy war." But it differed strikingly from the bombast of such older poets as Arndt. To begin with, it was intensely personal, describing Körner's own innermost feelings and recounting his own intimate experiences, whether sitting under the branches of an oak tree ("The Oaks") or singing to his sword before a battle ("Song of the Sword"). He treated the war not only as a crusade but also as what one historian calls "a vehicle for self-realization." In fact, just as Napoleon often seemed to cast himself as a character in a novel, so Körner made himself the literal hero of a cycle of poems and songs, posing alternately as a crusader, a hunter galloping to the sounds of "screaming horns" ("Lützow's Wild Hunt"), or a love-struck admirer of Prussia's beautiful, dead Queen Luise. As so often in this period, literary and military ambitions twisted sinuously around each other.

Sometimes, the poetry presented war as a glorious, boyish adventure. But at other moments, it displayed a dark, frankly erotic fascination with death: indeed, a sort of sensual longing for it. The word "bride" appears again and again in Körner's verse. Sometimes, it is his sword; sometimes, "Germania," or the fatherland ("On the Battlefield of Aspern)." In the "Horseman's Song" of 1813, he included the following:

> Die Ehre ist der Hochzeitsgast,
> Das Vaterland die Braut.
> Wer sie recht brünstiglich umfaßt,
> Den hat der Tod getraut.

> Honor is the wedding guest
> And the Fatherland the bride
> He who lustfully embraces her
> Has been married to death.

In a letter to his beloved, he wrote that the Freikorps was marching out and that "in two days we expect our wedding with death." In a poem composed on the eve of the battle of Danneberg, in May 1813, he declared that true happiness could come only by risking sacrificial death. Above all, he feared a banal, unpoetic death. Sitting, frustrated, on riverbank guard duty while listening to the distant sounds of battle, he wrote:

> Soll ich in der Prosa sterben?
> Poesie, du Flammenquell,
> Brich nur los mit leuchtendem Verderben
> Aber schnell!

> Shall I die in prose?
> Poetry, thou source of fire
> Break loose with shining ruin,
> Quickly!

On August 25, 1813, the poet consummated his grisly, longed-for "marriage," receiving a mortal wound in battle, just a few hours after composing his song to his sword. But the bullet that cut short his life simultaneously made his reputation, particularly after his father collected his poems the next year and published them under the title *Lyre and Sword*. It was an immediate sensation, frequently reprinted, and Körner became arguably the most popular German poet of his generation. Thanks to his youth and beauty, he stirred something of the same emotions felt by the French Revolutionary generation contemplating the sacrifice of the young Bara. Today, verses about the beauty of sacrificial death have thankfully lost their popularity in Germany, but until 1945, Körner remained a central figure in the nation's popular poetic canon. In Leni Riefenstahl's film *The Triumph of the Will*, the storm trooper marching band that serenades Adolf Hitler in the Nuremberg rally is playing music composed to accompany Körner's poem "Lützow's Wild Hunt." In 1943, when Joseph Goebbels notoriously shrieked at the crowds at the Berlin Sports Palace, "Do you want total war?" he finished the speech by quoting Körner's poem "Men and Boys."

With Körner, the reglorification of war that began in Revolutionary France reached its fullest, most outlandish form. As I have argued here, this reglorification did not mark a return to the Old Regime culture of war. War remained as much an extraordinary, exceptional experience for Körner as it had for the eighteenth-century *philosophes*. It was, as his friend Humboldt had tellingly written, the "admittedly fearful extreme." But for Körner, and by extension for much of his generation in Germany, it had become an extreme to be welcomed, an extreme through which individuals and societies alike were tested, proven, and steeled. It was a fantasy of creative violence, of total engagement that would end either in glorious victory or in equally glorious self-immolation.

Just seven months after Körner's death, the moment of self-immolation seemed to come for Napoleon as well. Following the failure of Napoleon's desperately brilliant French campaign of early 1814, allied troops entered Paris at the end of March. On April 3, at the instigation of the slithery former foreign minister Talleyrand, the Senate proclaimed that the emperor had forfeited his throne. On April 12, after having wavered over abdication, Napoleon swallowed poison that his doctor had prepared for him two years before. It had lost its potency and only made him sick. So he lived to bring about yet another extraordinary episode and then to fill the sacrificial role of the modern Prometheus, chained to a lonely South Atlantic rock, picked at by British vultures. And in the glare of his legend, it would become impossible to imagine that any other sort of military figure, or any other way of war, had ever been considered natural.

Epilogue

War is divine.

— JOSEPH DE MAISTRE

AT THE END OF THIS BLOODY ODYSSEY, it might be something of a relief to turn away, if only for a moment, from accounts of battles and atrocities. So consider, for a moment, two classic passages from French literature that deal with something apparently completely different: the problem of how to seduce a virtuous married woman. The first comes from Choderlos de Laclos's great novel of 1782, *Dangerous Liaisons*. It is an epistolary novel, and the letter in question is one of its climaxes. The Viscount de Valmont is describing to his correspondent, the Marquise de Merteuil, how he has finally accomplished the seduction of the angelic Madame de Tourvel:

> You will find, my friend, that I used a pure method that will give you pleasure, and that I remained absolutely true to the principles of this war, which, as we have so often remarked, resembles so much the other sort. Judge me, therefore, as you would judge Marshal Turenne or Frederick the Great. The enemy wanted only to delay, but I forced it to do battle. Thanks to skilled manoevering, I was able to choose the terrain and the positions of the opposing forces. I managed to inspire in the en-

emy feelings of security, so as to be able to close with it more easily as it retreated. I managed to sow terror in its ranks before the battle; I left nothing to chance . . . Finally, I only launched my attack after ensuring that I would have a secure line of retreat, so as not to risk everything I had gained up to this point.

The second passage is from a book published some forty-eight years later: Stendhal's *The Red and the Black*. It describes the first steps by which the young hero, Julien Sorel, seduces the mistress of the house where he works as a tutor, Madame de Rênal, taking her hand in his:

His expression, when he saw Madame de Rênal . . . was singular. He looked at her as if she were an enemy he was preparing to fight . . . He cut short the children's lessons, and then, when [her] presence . . . recalled him to the pursuit of his glory, he decided that tonight she absolutely would have to allow her hand to remain in his. As the sun set, and the decisive moment approached, Julien's heart beat in a singular manner . . . The horrible struggle that his duty was waging against his timidity was so painful for him he could not notice anything outside of himself. The clock sounded out nine forty-five and still he had not dared do anything. Outraged at his own cowardice, Julien said to himself: At exactly ten I will do what I have been promising to do all day, or I will go upstairs and blow my brains out.

As should be obvious, the distance between seduction and fighting battles was not, in fact, so great for either of these novelists. But what different sorts of battles! In Laclos, the tone of the seducer is utterly assured and confident. His battle is one in which absolutely nothing is left to chance. Everything is calculated, planned, down to the last detail. The forces are deployed perfectly, and even then, a line of retreat is carefully guarded. The battle as a whole amounts to a grand, and strangely impersonal, performance. Readers will soon learn that Laclos has actually set up a terrific irony, for nothing would be less assured, or predictable, than the outcome of this particular encounter. But the tone of the letter speaks volumes about Valmont's assumptions and expectations at this point, before his "victory" turns in strange directions. Julien Sorel's tone, meanwhile, could not be less confident or more anguished. In *his* battle, nothing is meticulously prepared, and nearly everything is left to chance. The attacker depends on sheer force and luck.

There is no question of any sort of impersonal performance. What is at stake is Julien's very soul.

Short as they are, these passages beautifully illustrate the changing role of war in the European imagination that took place during Napoleon Bonaparte's lifetime and that I have traced in this book. In the character of Valmont, Laclos — himself an experienced soldier — gave his readers a quintessential aristocratic army officer of the Old Regime. Suave, graceful, self-controlled, Valmont was precisely the type who might have taken extra pairs of silk stockings on campaign, had his wig carefully powdered on the eve of battle, and gone into the fray wearing a splendid costume. He and his contemporaries would have seen nothing unwarlike about this behavior. To the contrary, it was precisely what was expected from true aristocratic warriors, who were supposed to pass seamlessly between the twin theaters of aristocratic life that were the court and the battlefield, putting in equally magnificent, controlled performances in each.

As for Stendhal — another author with considerable experience of things military, including accompanying Napoleon's army to Russia — his Julien Sorel illustrated what the profession of arms had come to represent for millions of Europeans by the early nineteenth century. Julien dreams of a military career (it is the "red" of the book title) and briefly embarks on one in the novel, but not in order to perform any sort of preordained social role. The son of a poor sawmill owner, he wants to impose himself on the world; the military is a means for fulfilling his fantasies and ambitions. He longs for heroic, apocalyptic conflicts through which he will pass with flaming glory (or perish in the attempt). Needless to say, his god is Napoleon Bonaparte. In the scene where Julien first appears, he is reading a book instead of keeping watch on a saw, and his brutal, illiterate father angrily knocks the volume into the water. "[Julien] gazed sadly into the stream where his book had fallen; it was the one he was most fond of, [Napoleon's] *Memorial of Saint-Helena.*"

The final years of Napoleon's rule and life had only enhanced the appeal of war as the ultimate redemptive, transformative test — and Napoleon's own ability to embody this appeal. Following the fall of Paris in 1814, the victorious allies banished him to Elba, within sight of Corsica (British journalists joked about the small island's lack of "Elba room"). The dead Louis XVI's younger brother reclaimed the French throne for the Bourbons. But after less than ten months, Napoleon escaped on board a ship called the *Inconstant* and soon landed on France's Mediterranean coast, beginning the episode known as the Hundred Days. There was now little to be seen, in his paunchy and balding person, of the electrically thin, long-haired general painted by Gros eighteen years before. Nor had the French begun to forget his authoritarianism, the millions who had died during his wars, or the national diminishment that accompanied his defeat. Yet the new King Louis XVIII, fat and fussy, had quickly worn out his less than enthusiastic welcome, and Napoleon's sheer audacity had a stunning effect. The local population rallied to him and so, as he marched north, did the army. On several occasions, soldiers simply refused orders to fire on him. Although some of his former generals clung to the new Bourbon regime that had pardoned them, others — most notably the flamboyant Marshal Michel Ney — came back to his side. By the time he approached Paris on March 20, all the great Romantic clichés about him — an irresistible torrent, an overwhelming storm, an all-consuming fire — again seemed to have the ring of truth. Louis XVIII conveniently forgot an oath to die rather than abandon France a second time and scampered to safety in Belgium. Napoleon, having seduced his keenest critic, Benjamin Constant, into collaboration, revised his imperial constitution in a liberal direction. The allies mobilized their armies to crush him once and for all, and he mobilized in turn.

This time, however, he had little chance of success. His armies were depleted, his armories, stables, and supply depots even more so. Frenzied efforts at rearming fell short of the necessary effect. And so, the end came with merciless speed. Napoleon marched his reconstituted armed forces north into Belgium and in mid-June, after a pair of indecisive battles, faced the British and the Prussians at Waterloo. For the first time, he found himself on the same battlefield as his nemesis from Spain, the Duke of Wellington. As at Marengo, in 1800, his forces were divided, with Marshal Grouchy and 33,000 men detached to fight the Prussians under Marshal Blücher. Unlike at Marengo, however, Napoleon's subordinate did not bring his troops back in time, whereas Blücher provided crucial reinforcements for the British. A grindingly bloody day came to a climax when, with the late spring sky still bright at 7:00 P.M., Napoleon threw his legendary Old Guard against Wellington's "thin red line." The redcoats held, the French broke, and with them, Napoleon's hopes. Four days later, back in Paris, he abdicated a second time and after final, frantic political maneuvering, surrendered to the British. This time, the allies took no chances and banished him to Saint Helena, a rocky South Atlantic island scarcely twice the size of the District of Columbia. There, for six years, he sulked, plotted, squabbled with his British jailers (who refused to acknowledge his imperial title), bored his tiny entourage with endless readings of his favorite plays, and reminisced aloud about his campaigns. In 1821, he died, probably of stomach cancer, although a determined band of conspiracy theorists continues to hold out for arsenic poisoning.

It was an undignified end, to say the least. Yet its very poignancy, coming after the final spasm of glory in the Hundred Days, had an irresistible attraction for the Romantic imagination. One of Napoleon's companions on Saint Helena, Count Emmanuel de Las Cases, helped matters along by publishing an account of the exile, complete with extensive transcriptions of the emperor's reminiscences, as *The Memorial of Saint Helena*. Published to extraordinary popular acclaim in 1823 (as Julien Sorel's passion for the book suggests), it put the final seal on the Napoleonic legend. It had an apparently rambling and confused structure, but its quick, repeated shifts between the miserable banality of Saint Helena and Napoleon's greatest moments of glory succeeded in rendering the emperor a figure of immense pathos. In France itself, his image remained ubiquitous. Coins, drawings, cartoons, playing cards, tobacco boxes, and tiny statuettes all circulated despite the best efforts of the (re-) restored Bourbon regime. Rumors of a new return to France circulated as well, reinforced by the regular appearance of impostors claiming the imperial purple — in the 1840s, more French madmen took themselves for Napoleon than for any other figure except Jesus Christ. Many of their sane compatriots expressed hope for his reappearance by wearing violets in their lapels — the flower comes out, as Napoleon came back, in March.

The legend spread well beyond France. In Britain, whose subjects had fought Napoleon at great cost for nearly two decades, one would have expected to find little sympathy for him. Indeed, to celebrate Waterloo, effigies of the emperor burned across the British Isles (in Yarmouth, the townspeople put one on top of a pyramid of tar barrels for a better blaze and admired the flames while sitting at a thousand-yard-long banquet table and gobbling the iconic English dishes of roast beef and plum pudding). But a significant portion of British radicals idealized the emperor and deplored their own government's treatment of him: "Yet how resplendent is thy setting sun;/ Transported to a living tomb," wrote William Cobbett. When the *Bellerophon,* carrying Napoleon to Saint Helena, briefly docked in Plymouth (the closest he ever got to England), the government quickly ordered it out of British territorial waters, fearing that a sympathetic magistrate might issue a writ of habeas corpus to keep him there.

And, of course, the legend has never died. Even today, Napoleon remains quite possibly the most recognizable figure from all European history. He has certainly figured in more works of fiction and film than any other, including some of the greatest (Tolstoy's *War and Peace,* Victor Hugo's "L'Expiation," Abel Gance's film *Napoleon*), as well as some of the worst (e.g., the 1931 Italian stage play *Campo di Maggio,* secretly coauthored by none other than Benito Mussolini). On a less exalted level, his image sells everything from brandy to chocolates to condoms to antacid. His critics continue to group him among history's great villains. Yet despite all the human misery Napoleon bears responsibility for, most of the historically inclined public still instinctively resists putting him in the same class as Hitler, Stalin, or Mao. One reason is the intimate human quality that he himself put so easily on display ("what a novel my life has been"). Another, especially in France itself, relates to those beneficial reforms he carried out: particularly the Civil Code, with its guarantee of civil equality, and the modern French administrative system. But the most important reason is that he continues to symbolize, for better or worse, a certain sort of human possibility, even human greatness — achieved, first and foremost, through war. Julien Sorel stands for millions of real men and women who have breathed in these intoxicating fumes.

Napoleon's legend persisted after 1815, but the sort of war he embodied fell into eclipse. To the leaders of the states that defeated him, his legend and everything it represented seemed less intoxicating than simply toxic, and they were determined to prevent anything like his wars from ever happening again. This did not mean, however, restoring the Old Regime of war. True, the allies remained, for the most part, unreformed monarchies whose societies and militaries, still dominated by hereditary aristocracies, had changed much less than France during the quarter-century of war. The Russian tsar still counted roughly twenty million serfs — virtual slaves — among his subjects. But even as Napoleonic warfare had forced Austria and Prussia to flirt with the idea of their own *levées en masse* and to open their officer corps to talented commoners, it also gave their rulers pause about the wisdom of trying to return to the pre-1789 style of frequent wars and "balance of power" politics. The Revolution and Napoleon had made clear to them that limited, restrained, aristocratic warfare was simply no longer a possibility. War had become a Pandora's box that threatened to release the evil spirits of revolutionary messianism and imperial ambitions. So when the allies gathered at the so-called Congress of Vienna in 1814 to negotiate the shape of a new European order (something they did not initially plan to do but soon fell into), they in fact ended up embracing something closer to the dreams of Enlightenment visionaries than of Old Regime princes.

To be sure, the practical statesmen of the Congress did not hold out much hope that perpetual peace would eventually arise by itself with the spread of commerce and civilization. They had less in common with Montesquieu or Benjamin Constant, who had developed this theory, than with the *abbé* Saint-Pierre and Kant, who, for all their philosophical impracticality, both recognized that peace would come about only through concerted political action and the formation of a federation of states. The state system born in 1814–15 was no federation, but it did rely on the idea that the great powers would act in concert to manage international disagreements and prevent violent conflict. The treaty of the Holy Alliance, signed in September 1815 by Russia, Austria, and Prussia, went even further. Inspired by the idealistic beliefs of Tsar Alexander, it bound the signatories, as Paul Schroeder has put it, "to deal with each other and with their peoples on the basis of the Christian Gospel so that the European alliance would become a fraternal union between rulers and peoples banishing war and conflict from the earth." All in all, the 1814–15 agreements went well beyond earlier European peace settlements in establishing active mechanisms for the avoidance of future war.

And for a time, it proved remarkably successful. Yes, the decades that followed Waterloo had their share of military violence. The armies of France and its rerestored Bourbons went back into action as early as 1823 — in Spain, of all places, so as to support the reinstated Fernando

VII against liberal opposition. But they did so within the broad context of the "Concert of Europe," and the fighting remained mild by the standards of 1808–14. Overall, the major powers managed quite well to limit conflict within western and central Europe and so to quell the threat of total war. None of them fought against each other again until the Crimean War of 1854–56, which pitted Britain and France (and Turkey) against Russia. And measured against the Napoleonic wars, even the Crimea was a minor affair, with battles that never involved more than 100,000 combatants. The Franco-Prussian War of 1870–71, which led to the creation of a united Germany, saw larger-scale battles, but it lasted less than nine months. It might be argued that the major powers did not so much establish peace as move war offshores, to their violent colonial empires. The War of Indian Independence of 1857 against Britain approached the level of total war, with atrocities that dwarfed anything seen in Napoleonic Spain (if not the Vendée). Yet the achievement of a "long peace" in Europe, however imperfect and transient, was still significant. Such a thing had, quite simply, never been done before. The allies therefore managed to keep the first total war from marking the start of an uninterrupted *age* of total war.

Yet they did not exorcise the specter of total war altogether. The very way they treated Napoleon in defeat marked their acceptance of at least some of the beliefs that had made total war possible. For although they did not *formally* label Napoleon a criminal or put him on trial, neither did they grant him the status of honorable adversary. In formal terms, the exile to Saint Helena fell into a conceptual limbo, but in practice, everyone knew that it amounted to the jailing of a prisoner. Napoleon remained, very literally, a criminal disturber of the peace, and against such creatures, extraordinary means were permitted, indeed encouraged. (On the other hand, lower-ranking French commanders, such as Reille or Dorsenne, whom our own century would certainly condemn for war crimes, faced no punishment for their actions in Spain; their names still appear on the Arc de Triomphe in Paris, along with that of General Turreau, the butcher of the Vendée.)

In another continuity with the Enlightenment, the nineteenth century also saw renewed expressions of a crusading pacifism in Europe — indeed, the emergence of something the Enlightenment had lacked: formal pacifist movements. And despite the bloody disillusionment that had shredded earlier hopes, some writers would, soon enough, dredge up the *philosophes'* claim that war was vanishing from the world of its own accord. The prominent British Liberal Richard Cobden wrote in 1835: "commerce is the grand panacea, which . . . will serve to inoculate with the health and saving taste for civilization all the nations of the world." Some seventy-five years later, on the brink of World War I, the same theme was being sounded by the Anglo-American journalist Norman Angell, whose enormously popular book *The Great Illusion* argued that in the modern age, it had become impossible for any country to profit materially from warfare: "Military power is socially and economically futile." The book was translated into twenty-five languages and sold two million copies. Later, Jean Renoir would pointedly borrow its title for his magnificent film about World War I.

In short, large numbers of Europeans in the nineteenth century continued to see war in much the way the *philosophes* had done: as an abhorrent exception to the progress of modern civilization. The relative success of the Congress system, combined with the continuing development of international trade, encouraged them to believe that *this* time, truly, war was on the brink of extinction. And so, when another total war, more destructive even than the Napoleonic ones, started in 1914, the allied powers were fully primed to rediscover the paradoxical Girondin vision of a final, all-consuming war to achieve perpetual peace: "the war to end all wars."

This pacifist vision, however, was not the only legacy of the Enlightenment and the quarter-century of total war to survive into the post-1815 period. There was also its dark twin: the vision of war as the sublime, redemptive, *desirable* exception. Indeed, during the century that followed Waterloo, this vision grew in inebriating power, thanks to such writers as the reactionary Joseph de Maistre, who had already written about the "purifying" powers of war in the late 1790s. In the 1820s, he expanded on the theme in an influential dark reverie about how God's will prescribed not merely an endless cycle of blood and death but also a terrible lust that drives the mildest of men to slaughter:

> The earth cries out and asks for blood . . . Thus is carried out without cease, from maggot to man, the great law of the violent destruction of living things. The entire world, continuously saturated with blood, is nothing but an immense altar where all that lives must be slaughtered

without end, without measure, without slackening, until the devouring
of all things, until the extinction of evil, until the death of death . . . War
is therefore divine in and of itself, because it is a law of the world . . . War
is divine in the mysterious glory which surrounds it, and in the no less
inexplicable attraction which draws us to it.

Later, others would draw on the work of Charles Darwin to give a new,
twisted shape to ideas of this stripe. Races, nations, and even social
classes, it would be said, competed with one another like species in the
wild, and only the fittest survived. War was a vehicle of social evolution.
By the turn of the twentieth century, the concept of redemptive war
had become so commonly accepted that the philosopher William James
felt the human race could achieve peace only if it discovered a "moral
equivalent of war," a peaceful channel into which to divert natural human bellicosity. "History is a bath of blood," James conceded. "Our ancestors have bred pugnacity into our bone and marrow, and thousands
of years of peace won't breed it out of us." "War is the strong life," he
declared, in echo of Humboldt and de Maistre, "it is life *in extremis.*"
    In the years before World War I, many other writers positively em-
braced this supposed law of nature. Believing their societies increasingly materialistic, corrupt, and petty minded, they longed for a terrible
purification, a sublime ordeal. "I almost desire a monstrous war," wrote
the French poet Paul Valéry in 1891 in what was an entirely banal sentiment among many intellectuals of the time. Heinrich von Treitschke,
one of imperial Germany's leading writers on history and politics,
called war "sacred," "the very sphere in which we can most clearly trace
the triumph of human reason." He added that "the ideal of perpetual
peace is not only impossible, but immoral as well." Most insistently,
perhaps, the artists known as the Futurists, in their manifesto of 1909,
proclaimed: "war is the only hygiene of the world . . . we want to glorify
war, the only cure for the world."
    This extreme message had relatively few adherents, but in a broader
sense, the notion of war as a test helped shape, in crucial ways, the way
Europeans understood and experienced things military during the nineteenth and early twentieth centuries. To begin with, it drove the continuing growth of militarism. Throughout much of the period, armies
turned increasingly professional and increasingly set off from civilian
society in barracks and camps. They became societies apart, and socie-

ties often considered superior because of their readiness to sacrifice, their discipline, and, especially, the supposedly purifying effects of war. The pattern of military intervention in political life, which had begun in its modern form in France in 1795–99, became a commonplace of European history. Even where military *coups* did not take place, the military's claim to moral superiority could have devastating effects on political life. In the Dreyfus Affair of turn-of-the-century France, the army's refusal to admit its error in accusing a Jewish officer of treason, lest its sacrosanct honor and prestige be tarnished, tremendously exacerbated the country's social and political divisions.

Europeans also came to think, in a new way, of war as a test of individuals and to fixate on the individual experience of it. Historians know well, and are grateful for the fact, that even before the laying down of arms in 1815, an avalanche of personal memoirs, diaries, and printed correspondence about the wars had begun to tumble from the printing presses (it sometimes feels as if every redcoat at the Battle of Waterloo subsequently penned his reminiscences of the event). But they have rarely reflected on the amazing novelty of the phenomenon. Up until the late eighteenth century, only a relatively few military figures (virtually all officers) composed military memoirs. These men almost never included reflections on their interior lives and had little concern for the flavor and color of particular events. They celebrated deeds that fit stereotyped images of noble valor, making the writing flat and tedious to modern sensibilities. The post-Napoleonic accounts broke dramatically with this tradition, in their vastly greater numbers, their concern for realism, and their frankly personal style. Although few of them discussed war in the fraught, existential manner of Theodor Körner, the mere fact that they were written and found an eager market suggests a deep connection between war and emerging Romantic notions of the self. Needless to say, Napoleon provided the classic case of this connection and as a result became the most obsessively written-about figure in history up to the time.

This same concern with the war and the "inner self" also began to permeate one other, significant genre of writing. Consider that, in the eighteenth century, few works of military strategy had given much consideration to what we would call "psychological" issues. Napoleon's famous statement that in battle, "moral" factors weigh three times as heavily as "physical" ones already pointed to a new approach, as did the reflections of German reformers, such as Scharnhorst. The trends came to fruition with Clausewitz in his great book *On War,* composed largely in the 1820s. Very much unlike such figures as Maurice of Saxony, Clausewitz devoted many pages to the mental basis of courage and presence of mind, and the effects of light, noise, and the sight of comrades being wounded or killed. Commentators too often attribute Clausewitz's acuity to his "genius" alone, but his attention to military psychology, which has shaped the way armies have trained for war ever since, reflected the cultural changes he lived through during the Napoleonic era.

In 1914, exactly a century after Napoleon's first abdication, total war returned to Europe. The dream that a great blast of military fire might cleanse and purify a corrupt continent escaped from literature and art and again helped drive the actions of statesmen and soldiers. Each side spoke of the total mobilization of resources and, by the end of the conflict, of "total war" itself. True, even before the horrors of trench warfare became widely known, relatively few people agreed with the poet Paul Claudel that the bloody dawn of 1914 would bring "the salvation and regeneration of our poor country" (a remark that eerily echoed Madame Roland in 1791). Despite the widespread legend, it is not true that entire populations ecstatically embraced the call to arms. Nonetheless, the language that justified the fighting, including the language of "the war to end all wars," had a real effect. On battlefields changed beyond recognition from the Napoleonic ones by industrial revolution, it encouraged European armies to persist in a slaughter that Napoleon himself, with his easy contempt for "the lives of a million men," could never have imagined.

World War I and the twentieth century's other multiple plunges into the abyss lie beyond the scope of this book, as do the ways in which they changed the place of war in the Western imagination yet again. The changes were undeniably vast, and so it has become all too easy to assume that they amounted to a sort of break in history — that what Niall Ferguson nicely calls the twentieth century's "War of the World" obliterated any possible connection between the wars of 1792–1815, fought with musket and cannon, and the present day.

But as I have argued in these pages, the idea of such an absolute break is false. For all the impact of the twentieth-century wars, there are still continuities. Echoes. Threads. The changes that took place in Napoleon's Europe still have a surprisingly critical bearing on the world in which we live, above all in the idea of war as exceptional, as something apart from and at odds with the ordinary course of modern life, whether horrifically or sublimely so. The threads stretch out from Europe, moreover, and today grip the United States as strongly — perhaps even more strongly — than they do the old continent itself. The United States was in many senses the eldest child of the Enlightenment and from the start has proven receptive to Enlightenment promises of perpetual peace (as in Washington's eager acceptance of Chastellux's ideas about progress overcoming "the waste of war and the rage of conquest"). In the twentieth and twenty-first centuries, as dangers from without increasingly haunted Americans' imaginations, their attitudes toward war have come more and more to resemble those of the Europeans of the Revolutionary and Napoleonic eras.

For a time in the twentieth century, the continuities were admittedly less obvious. This time was the cold war, which put large parts of the world in a situation weirdly reminiscent of the European Old Regime. For over forty years, the balance of terror between the superpowers imposed a limit on the scope of war that, ironically, permitted an almost continual series of low-level conflicts — and that made such conflicts appear normal. But in the immediate post–cold war period, when perpetual peace seemed, for a brief time, so palpable a prospect, only to be snatched back into the shadows like Eurydice on the path out of Hades, the echoes became particularly clear, and the threads seemed particularly strong.

As I write these words, in mid-2006, the connections are still as visible as ever. Immediately after 9/11, it appeared that the prophets of perpetual peace might vanish from the scene. Yet in a surprisingly short time, they have begun to make themselves heard again. Various journalists, political scientists, and institutes report an apparent decline in "major conflict" since the collapse of the Soviet Union. By one estimate, "the number of armed conflicts has decreased by more than 40 percent, and the number of major conflicts . . . by 80 percent." In 2005, the journalist Gregg Easterbrook wrote in *The New Republic:* "Yes, the end of war has been predicted before, prominently by H. G. Wells in

1915, and horrible bloodshed followed. But could the predictions be right this time?"

This question is worth answering. Yes, the predictions could be right. Europe has become too small a region on which to measure such trends, but the achievement of what seems like a real and durable peace between European states is still a reason for hope. But what these journalists and political scientists miss is not simply that such predictions go back long before H. G. Wells and Norman Angell and even Richard Cobden — that they go back nearly three hundred years. And it is not simply that many of the earlier predictions seemed just as empirically compelling as the present ones. (When Joseph Cornish predicted the end of war in 1784, European nations really did seem to be growing less bellicose.) They also miss the fact that war, the most volatile and unpredictable of all human activities, is uniquely unsuitable for the sort of trend analysis they put such faith in. A graph of eighteenth-century combat deaths compiled in 1790 would have given no hint of the hecatomb on the horizon. A similar exercise carried out in 1913 would have been similarly pointless. We may hope that current trends continue, but the nature of war is that steady, predictable trends rarely continue. Of course, the prophets of peace also miss the paradox that such critics as Carl Schmitt saw very clearly: that the hope for lasting peace can itself fatally tempt societies to engage in one, final great paroxysm of violence.

The vision of war as redemptive continues to flourish as well. It may have lost much of its intellectual credibility in the trenches of World War I, but it never disappeared in the West and today seems especially strong in the United States. Whether or not there is a "new American militarism," as Andrew Bacevich has argued, it is difficult to deny the tremendous moral credit routinely accorded to military service in American culture today (again, witness the Democratic Party's selection of its presidential candidate in 2004 essentially on the basis of his record as a war hero). And it is difficult to miss the new wave of arguments — although they are still presented hesitantly, even in conservative circles — that American military interventions abroad may not simply be good for the world; they may be good for *us* as well. "Peaceful times are superficial times," as the influential journalist Robert Kaplan has written. Without "great military struggles . . . we . . . will not be the nation we once were." President Bush has expressed something of the same idea. "War is terrible," he remarked in the spring of 2006. "But it brings out, you know, in some ways it touches the core of Americans who volunteer to go into combat to protect their souls."

The survival of a belief in redemptive war has not yet, thankfully, led to a resumption of real war on an apocalyptic scale. What some commentators insist on calling our new "world war" against Islamist terror has probably had a smaller total body count, as of mid-2006, than just one single Napoleonic battle — the Battle of the Nations fought around Leipzig in 1813 (it had 150,000 casualties) — to say nothing of the real world wars. In Iraq, despite widespread indignation against American misconduct, it remains the case that American and allied forces have, in fact, struggled mightily to avoid civilian casualties (in this sense, they resemble the soldiers of the eighteenth century in surprising ways). It is only the language that is apocalyptic for now: the representation of terrorists who have no real armies and exert no attraction on non-Muslims as "an enemy who will stop at nothing to achieve world domination and force a life devoid of freedom upon all," to quote a recent, hyperbolic contribution to the *Wall Street Journal.*

With luck, the present conflict will never inflict the kind of destruction of the total wars of the past. But as I have tried to show in this book, language matters. A vision of war as utterly exceptional — as a final, cleansing paroxysm of violence — did not simply precede the total war of 1792–1815. It helped, decisively, to bring it about. Leaders convinced that they were fighting "the last war" could not resist committing ever greater resources to it, attempting to harness all their societies' energies to a single purpose, and ultimately sacrificing lives on an industrial scale so as to defeat supposedly demonic enemies. The apocalyptic language of the twenty-first-century terrorists, and the apocalyptic language they have provoked from the West, has not so far translated into violence on an apocalyptic scale. But it has already created the conditions under which the American public came to support the misguided war in Iraq that has drained away American lives, American treasure, and American credibility in the world — and that has arguably left the United States less secure against more serious threats from elsewhere.

Unfortunately, as I have also suggested in this book, a belief in the exceptionality of war, and a resulting tendency to discuss it in apocalyptic language, forms part of the modern condition. There may well be no escaping it. We need to recognize, though, the extent to which it is a romantic delusion. It has brought neither peace nor transcendence, and it has helped to inspire a soul-tearing weight of misery and death. Is war best thought of in these terms? It may be worth settling for the fact that war, far from being divine, is simply an inextricable part of being human. It is something ordinary, whether we like it or not, and it is all too likely to remain so. What therefore matters above all is limiting the human damage, learning restraint, putting bounds on hatred. This was a lesson that Europeans were stumbling toward, hesitatingly, imperfectly, in the eighteenth century, in the heyday of the aristocratic officer, whose mental universe now seems so alien to us. And so, one final thought. If we are still to find things to celebrate and marvel at in European history, we should certainly let our gazes linger on the age of the Enlightenment, of the French Revolution, and of Napoleon. But we should not belittle what they destroyed.

NOTES

BIBLIOGRAPHY

INDEX

Notes

ABBREVIATIONS

AN   Archives Nationales, Paris.

AP   *Archives parlementaires de 1787 à 1860, Recueil complet des débats législatifs &*
            politiques des Chambres françaises, première série (1787–1799), ed. M. J. Mavidal and
            M. E. Laurent, 82 vols. (Paris: Paul Dupont, 1879–1913).

BNF   Bibliothèque Nationale de France, Paris.

CCEHD   *Cahiers du Centre d'Etudes d'Histoire de la Défense*

CN   Napoléon Bonaparte, *Correspondance de Napoléon 1er, publiée par ordre de l'empereur*
            Napoléon III, 32 vols. (Paris: Imprimerie Impériale, 1858–60).

DC   Edna Hindie Lemay, ed., *Dictionnaire des Constituants, 1789–91,* 2 vols. (Paris:
            Universitas, 1991).

CGN   Napoléon Bonaparte, *Correspondance générale,* ed. Thierry Lentz et al., 12 vols.
            (Paris: Fayard, 2004–).

Moniteur   *Réimpression de l'ancien Moniteur: Seule histoire authentique et inaltérée de la*
            révolution française depuis la réunion des États généraux jusqu'au Consulat (mai 1769–
            novembre 1799), ed. A. Ray, 32 vols. (Paris: Plon, 1858–63).

SHAT   Services Historiques de l'Armée de Terre, Vincennes.

INTRODUCTION

page
 1   "'This war'": Charles-François Dumouriez, *AP,* vol. LII, p. 472 (October 12, 1792).
 2   "Some thought that the world": See, for example, Mueller, *Retreat from Dooms-*
     day.
     "democracies supposedly do not fight": See notably Russett.
     "proper form of society": Fukuyama.
     "Prominent supporters of his administration": See, for instance, Podhoretz.

2   "'Among ourselves, we keep the law'": Cooper, "The New Liberal Imperialism."
    "'The time is approaching'": Cornish, p. 24.
    "It promised that France": *AP*, vol. XV, pp. 661–2 (May 22, 1790).
3   "'a war to the death'": Jacques-François, Baron de Menou, *AP*, vol. XXII,
    pp. 526–7 (January 28, 1791).
    "'It has cost us dearly'": Napoleon to the French Senate, November 21, 1806, in
    CN, vol. XIII, p. 680 (no. 11281).
4   "'Americans are from Mars'": Kagan, "Power and Weakness." See also Kagan, *Of
    Paradise and Power.*
    "'This is now a war for peace'": Wells, p. 11.
    "'this war will be the last war'": Charles-François Dumouriez, *AP*, vol. LII, p. 472
    (October 12, 1792).
5   "'performing poodles'": Quoted in Blanning, *Origins*, p. 38.
6   "'It is the admittedly fearful extreme'": Humboldt.
7   "the very concept and experience of the 'self'": See above all Wahrman.
    "More than a fifth": Rothenberg, *The Art of Warfare*, p. 61.
    "in 1809": Gates, p. 139.
    "Four years later": Rothenberg, *The Art of Warfare*, p. 81.
    "During the Napoleonic period": Sutherland, *The French Revolution*, p. 371.
    "many historians have used it": For instance, Guiomar and the works he cites on
    p. 11; Blanning, *Origins*, p. 211.
    "This formulation seems . . . clear enough": See on this subject the work of
    Chickering, especially "Total War"; also Guiomar, p. 13.
8   "should simply be scrapped": Chickering, "Total War," pp. 23–6.
9   "concerted political attempts": See Guiomar, especially pp. 11–26, 300–5. Argu-
    ably, certain forms of organization foreshadowing total war could be found in
    the sixteenth century in parts of the Netherlands during their war against Spain
    and in the Catholic League of Paris. See Koenigsberger.
    "the term 'total war' itself": See Chickering, "Total War," p. 16; Guiomar,
    pp. 12–3.
    "Calls for total engagement": Guiomar, p. 302. See also the superb article of
    Geyer.
    "'It is with an armed doctrine'": Burke, *Two Letters*, pp. 22–3.
10 "'It is not [now] the king'": Clausewitz, "Bekenntnisdenkschrift," vol. I, p. 750.
    "'the continuation of political intercourse'": Clausewitz, *On War*, p. 87.
    "the slogan of a 'war of nations'": See on this subject Bell, *Cult of the Nation*,
    pp. 78–106.
    "they helped the French war effort much less": Mackenzie, pp. 33–50; also Rousset.
    "Similar attempts at general levies": Rothenberg, *Napoleon's Great Adversaries*,
    pp. 118–9; Rothenberg, *The Art of Warfare*, p. 242; Leggiere, pp. 57–8.
    "Napoleon depended on": See Chandler, *The Campaigns of Napoleon*, pp. 333–4;
    Connelly, *Blundering to Glory*, pp. 73–4.
    "As for the Spanish war": See especially Esdaile, *Fighting Napoleon*.
11 "societies that relied on mercenary armies": See, for instance, Niccolò Ma-
    chiavelli's preface to *L'arte della guerra*, which distinguishes between the "vita
    civile" and the "vita militare," with the first roughly meaning "the life of the
    city." Significantly, whereas Machiavelli's 1720 English translator rendered

"civile" as "civil," a later eighteenth-century translator, explicitly trying for a more colloquial English, had far more difficulty with the word, rendering it variously as "civil," "common," "of a Citizen," and avoiding it altogether. See Machiavelli, *Works* (1720), p. 433; Machiavelli, *Works* (1775), vol. IV, p. 7.

"the word 'civilian' itself": See the *Oxford English Dictionary* (http://dictionary.oed.com), s.v. civilian, and the *Trésor de la langue française* (http://atilf.atilf.fr/tlf.htm), s.v. civil. Both Web sites consulted June 26, 2006.

"As early as 1793": Article 109 of the approved but unimplemented French constitution of 1793 reads: "All Frenchmen are soldiers. They are all trained in the use of arms." (http://fr.wikisource.org/wiki/Constitution_du_24_juin_1793. Consulted June 26, 2006.)

12 "a new, military ethos": See on this point Hopkin, p. 350.

"Militarism, as I would define it": See Chapter 6.

"In the United States today": Bacevich.

13 "220,000 books and articles": Esdaile, *The Wars of Napoleon,* p. ix.

14 "More fundamentally": Joas, pp. 29–42; Mann.

"Nor did he ever exalt violence": On this point, see Arendt, pp. 3–31.

"But they lived mostly in Germany": See Joas, pp. 141–62.

"Yet the hatred he felt": For a brief introduction to Schmitt's thought, see Lilla.

"'Such a war is necessarily'": Schmitt, *The Concept of the Political,* p. 36.

"one that Schmitt himself": See especially Schmitt, *Le Nomos de la Terre,* and Schmitt, *Theorie des Partisanen.*

15 "'absolute enmity'": Schmitt, *Theorie des Partisanen,* p. 55.

"'politics is the continuation'": Foucault, *Il faut défendre la société,* p. 16. Cf. Foucault, *Discipline and Punish,* p. 168.

16 "They have concentrated": One classic such work is Corvisier, *L'armée française.*

"'not even the beginnings'": Keegan, *The Face of Battle,* p. 52.

"In Britain and the United States": See especially Armitage; Tuck.

"In France": See notably Belissa, *Fraternité universelle;* Belissa, *Repenser;* Guiomar.

"In Germany": Jeismann; Hagemann, *"Mannlicher Muth";* Kruse. See also the essays collected by Kunisch and Münkler.

17 "'this quarter-century'": Quoted in Casanova, p. 19.

"readers can turn": Bertaud, *La Révolution armée;* Blanning, *Origins;* Blanning, *French Revolutionary Wars;* Chandler, *Campaigns;* Lynn, *Bayonets.*

18 "Most European empires": See on this particularly Colley, *Captives.*

"Episodes like the Fox Wars": See Edmunds and Peyser.

19 "'The Germans'": Hull, p. 353.

"A few years ago": J.-C. Martin, *La Vendée,* p. 149.

"Even before": Blaufarb, p. 8; see also Bertaud, *La Révolution armée.*

I. OFFICERS, GENTLEMEN, AND POETS

21 "'As I pondered'": Whitman, "As I Ponder'd in Silence."

"He is heir": On Lauzun, see Gontaut-Biron; Maugras, *The Duc de Lauzun and the Court of Louis XV;* Maugras, *The Duc de Lauzun and the Court of Marie-Antoinette.* Lauzun's memoirs have been published in many editions. I have used Lauzun, ed. Pilon.

22 "It is Lauzun's first taste": The campaign is described in Lauzun, pp. 87–106. "'Then I've brought him back'": Ibid., p. 90. For details on the Chardon family, see de Maricourt.

23 "The happy couple": Maugras, *The Duc de Lauzun and the Court of Louis XV,* pp. 189–90; de Maricourt, p. 253.
"Along the way": See Darnton, *Mesmerism,* p. 74; Lauzun, p. 85; Lilti, pp. 78, 241.
"He will serve": See Bodinier, *Les officiers,* p. 262.
"compares his own amorous conquests": Choderlos de Laclos, letter 125.

24 "the most concerted feminine resistance": On Richelieu, see Cole; La Barre de Raillicourt. "The great *philosophe*": Voltaire, *Le Poëme.*
"Those famous nineteenth-century aesthetes": Goncourt and Goncourt.

25 "even in Prussia": Büsch.
"in military dress": Black, *European Warfare,* p. 154; Kennett, p. 81.
"Great Northern War": P. Englund, pp. 56–7; "As for the British army": Wilson, *The Island Race,* pp. 97–8.
"While posted": Babeau, vol. II, p. 203.
"'I lived like a bear'": Quoted in N. Bonaparte, *Napoléon inconnu,* vol. II, p. 202n.

26 "half the period": S. Englund, pp. 21–36. "*most* French officers": Babeau, vol. II, pp. 188, 90. "overmanning": Kennett, p. 65. "In 1789": Léonard, p. 290.
"Serving in a series": The notebook of obscure words is reprinted in N. Bonaparte, *Napoléon inconnu,* vol. II, pp. 258–67. *Rhizophage* means a root eater; *cacique* is a Mexican prince, and *tomogun* is Hindu for greed.
"'having awoken'": Napoleon Bonaparte, "Le comte d'Essex," in N. Bonaparte, *Œuvres littéraires,* vol. I, p. 210.
"'Destiny was mute'": Chateaubriand, p. 403. On Napoleon's literary efforts in general, see Andy Martin.
"Laclos . . . started": See Poisson. "The ranks of French soldier-authors": See Schaeffer.

27 "As for Louis de Fénelon": Notes by the Comte d'Argenson, republished in Tuetey, p. 348.
"Saint-Lambert": See Saint-Lambert.
"no fewer than seven men": http://www.academie-francaise.fr/immortels/. Consulted on June 26, 2006.
"Lauzun had a typical career": Gontaut-Biron, p. 5. "Maurice of Saxony": J.-P. Bois, p. 22. "George, Lord Ettrick": Childs, *The British Army,* p. 43.
"The most prestigious French commissions": Motley, p. 173.

28 "Foreign soldiers": Chagniot, vol. II, p. 25.
"'Remember Limerick'": J.-P. Bois, p. 96. The Clare Regiment having been exiled from Ireland since the 1690s, only 40 percent of its members were still Irish in 1745, but the number of French in it was even smaller.
"Lauzun seriously considered": Lauzun, p. 212. "the young Napoleon": S. Englund, p. 77.
"Consider also . . . the . . . *comte* de Saint-Germain": The Marquis de Sade's father described Saint-Germain's career in a 1757 letter as if it were the most ordinary thing in the world. See Lever, vol. I, p. 737.
"While campaigning": P. Englund, pp. 38–9.

"critics complained": Babeau, vol. II, p. 153.

29   "'a society, a family'": Ray, p. 14.

"the Prussian army, though": Starkey, p. 24.

"'filth of the nation'": Duffy, p. 89. "Sheridan's play": Sheridan, act I, scene i. "'No Dogs'": Lynn, *Bayonets*, p. 63.

"a radically distinct 'warrior culture'": Keegan, *A History of Warfare*, pp. 49–50.

30   "'War is the Matter'": Burke, *A Vindication*, p. 20.

"'Everything in the universe'": Quoted in Léonard, p. 154.

"the Prussian state . . . whereas in France": See Rothenberg, *The Art of Warfare*, p. 12.

"During the War of the Spanish Succession": Corvisier, *L'armée française*, vol. I, p. 65.

31   "when still a little boy . . . His son . . .": Cornette, pp. 152–9.

"'The proper, the only, the essential'": Montaigne, p. 277. "'The nobility knows'": Quoted in Tuetey, p. 1.

"In . . . Pomerania": Büsch, p. 62. "In Sweden": P. Englund, p. 32. "In the 1789 elections": Tackett, pp. 32–4.

"Nobles made up the majority": Storrs and Scott, pp. 15–7; see also Forrest, *Soldiers of the French Revolution*, p. 36. "During the Seven Years' War": Kennett, p. 57.

32   "'to think how the sweet fellows'": Sheridan, act I, scene ii.

"French colonels": Babeau, vol. II, p. 167. "Generals had several carriages": Léonard, p. 172. "cumbersome Duke of Cumberland": Duffy, pp. 84–5.

"Richelieu participated": On Richelieu, see Cole, pp. 22–5, 238, and passim; La Barre de Raillicourt, especially pp. 210–17.

33   "Lauzun . . . insisted": Lauzun, p. 88.

"Commanders like Richelieu": Babeau, vol. II, pp. 257–8; Black, *European Warfare*, pp. 214–5. "'Dogs!'": Quoted in James, p. 27.

34   "As the German sociologist Norbert Elias": Elias, *The Court Society*; Elias, *The History of Manners*.

"'Jésus Maria!'": See Duffy, p. 75.

"'dancing is most necessary'": ibid., p. 51. "the royal Military School": Babeau, vol. II, p. 50.

35   *"Messieurs les Anglais"*: See J.-P. Bois, pp. v–ix.

"the story was widely repeated": See ibid.

"early modern authors": See the fundamental work of Billacois, especially pp. 367–70.

"Two captains": See Mercoyrol de Beaulieu, p. 352.

"Lauzun claimed": Lauzun, p. 259. Tarleton was notorious for his mistreatment of American civilians.

"'The point of honor'": Quoted in Duffy, p. 79.

36   "honor was grounded": "The nature of honor," as the French *philosophe* Montesquieu put it, "is to demand preferences and distinctions." Montesquieu, *Spirit of the Laws*, p. 27.

"Our lives and possessions": Blaise de Montluc, *Commentaires* (1592), quoted in Billacois, p. 351.

"'the ranks are filled with the scum'": Dalrymple, p. 8.

36 "They sought to instill": See the works of Bien, J. Smith, and Blaufarb, but also the trenchant criticism of D. O'Brien, "Traditional Virtues."

37 "the Prussia of Frederick the Great": See Büsch; Craig; Schulze; Showalter.
    "'Most states have armies'": Schulze, p. 201.
    "'offered no danger'": Niccolò Machiavelli, quoted in Contamine, p. 258.
    "In the Swedish attack": P. Englund, especially pp. 203–9. On casualty rates in general, see Rothenberg, *The Art of Warfare*, p. 13.

38 "Fontenoy": Most recently on the battle, see J.-P. Bois; Starkey, pp. 69–103. The best single account of an eighteenth-century European battle is P. Englund.

39 "seven extra pairs of silk stockings": Babeau, vol. II, p. 168.
    "by the British physician": Pringle, passim.
    "King Louis and the Dauphin": J.-P. Bois, p. 86.

40 "under battlefield conditions": On eighteenth-century musketry, see Duffy, pp. 207–15.
    "Overall, total casualties": Starkey, p. 125.
    "'now you see what war really means'": Quoted in ibid. "'This terrible spectacle'": Quoted in ibid.

41 "'The corpses stripped naked'": René-Louis de Voyer de Paulmy, marquis d'Argenson, to Voltaire, near Tournai, May 15, 1745. Letter D3118, in Voltaire, *Œuvres complètes,* vol. XCIII, p. 245.
    "'If you could hear'": Owen.
    "'It was the sort of life'": Lauzun, p. 90. "'I marched on the English'": ibid., p. 253.

42 "absolutely typical": on early modern military memoirs, see Harari.
    "'A hundred bronze thunderclaps'": Voltaire, *Le Poëme.*
    "'The French are great'": Ibid.

43 "'How is it that these gentle'": Ibid.
    "investing with military contractors": Pearson, p. 207.
    "'Thus would I fain'": Addison, p. 244.
    "a 330-page anthology": *Recueil général.*
    "The first printing": See Pomeau, vol. I, pp. 458–64.

44 "Paradoxically, to our eyes": This argument owes a great deal to Wahrman.
    "'religion made humanity a crime'": Froude, vol. X, p. 121. "the technology of war": See G. Parker; cf. Black, *A Military Revolution?*

45 "From 1600 to 1648": See Rabb, pp. 122–33; Childs, *Armies and Warfare,* p. 9.
    "'I am not at all for battles'": Quoted in Léonard, pp. 126–7. See Rothenberg, *The Art of Warfare*, p. 12, for further remarks of the sort.
    "'It is not large armies'": Quoted in Léonard, p. 149.
    "18,000 Saxons": Duffy, p. 7.

46 "'It's a great shame to lose a grenadier'": Quoted by Ray, p. 109.
    "when the French returned": Corvisier, *L'armée française,* vol. I, p. 75.
    "went about their business unmolested": see van Houtte, vol. I, pp. 135–7.
    "Adam Smith dubiously claimed": Quoted in Anderson, p. 53.
    "'It became fashionable'": Quoted in Duffy, p. 305.
    "'The destruction was terrible'": Beevor, pp. 187–8.
    "'a lack of restraint in relation to war'": Quoted in Childs, *Armies and Warfare,* p. 24.

47 "Grotius did not believe": see Grotius.

"'War . . . is not a relationship between individual men'": J.-J. Rousseau, *Du contrat social,* in *Œuvres,* vol. III, p. 357.

"By the standards of the earlier seventeenth century": On the campaign, see Lynn, "A Brutal Necessity?"; von Raumer.

"500,000 dead": Starkey, p. 6.

"'they hung the inhabitants'": Hermann, *Geschichte des russischen Staates,* quoted in Sorel, vol. I, pp. 85–6.

"as many as 26,000 Turkish prisoners": Ibid., p. 86; Black, *European Warfare,* p. 231.

48 "Some historians": See particularly Schroeder, *Transformation of European Politics.*

"'There are fewer cannibals'": Quoted in Chagniot, vol. II, p. 4.

"Today war is waged": Quoted in Léonard, p. 154.

"'the Nations of Europe'": Quoted in Best, *Humanity in Warfare,* p. 36. "'Armies slaughter each other'": Quoted in ibid.

"'wars have in general'": Cornish, p. 24.

49 "The French practiced brutal counterinsurgency tactics": On civil wars in the eighteenth century, see Black, *Culloden;* Frey and Frey, *Societies in Upheaval;* Joutard; Prebble.

"'enemies of the human race'": On this concept, see the stimulating essay by Edelstein.

50 "'I should hate to have been'": Quoted in Souleyman, p. 126. On the reaction to the campaign, see Cornette, p. 324.

"one of the greatest cultural heroes": See Bell, *Cult of the Nation,* pp. 111–2, 121.

"as Carl Schmitt has observed": see especially *Le nomos de la terre.*

51 "Vattel judged": Vattel, vol. 3, chp. 3, §34 (p. 245). More generally, see Edelstein.

"'I prefer to see it as a time'": Ray, p. 11.

2. CONSCIENCE, COMMERCE, AND HISTORY

52 "'War is a great'": Joseph de Maistre, quoted in Lebrun, p. 45.

53 "to fight and war against any man": Quoted in Brock, p. 269. In general on Quaker pacifism, see ibid., pp. 255–366.

"when Voltaire visited Britain": Voltaire, *Lettres philosophiques,* p. 24.

"45 percent": Ceadel, p. 151.

"'When it pleases God'": Penn, vol. II, p. 844.

"'Let the Holy Jesus'": Bellers, p. 8.

"who numbered no more than 50,000": See Braithwaite, passim; Ceadel, p. 151.

"and did not even prosecute": Ceadel, p. 155.

54 "François de Salignac de la Mothe Fénelon": On Fénelon, see James Davis; Goré; Janet. For a concise analysis of his politics, see Keohane, pp. 332–42; Patrick Riley's introduction to Fénelon, *Telemachus,* pp. xiii–xxxi. See also Cuche.

"'A tall, thin, handsome man'": Saint-Simon, vol. XI, p. 438.

"'knocked at all the doors'": Ibid., vol. I, p. 284.

"He tried desperately hard": Saint-Simon wrote, at two separate moments, "he tried to please the valet as much as the master." See Saint-Simon, vol. IX, p. 289, and vol. XI, p. 440.

57 "'It is useless to say, Sire'": Fénelon, "Lettre à Louis XIV," in Fénelon, *Œuvres,* vol. III, pp. 426–7.

58 "'to age under the useless weight'": Saint-Simon, vol. IX, p. 288.
"'I cannot resist . . . He knows what I am suffering'": Fénelon to the duc de Chaulnes, March 4, 1712, in Fénelon, *Œuvres,* vol. III, p. 679.

59 "From his arrival at Versailles": See Janet, pp. 46–7.
"He supplemented them": Fénelon, *Dialogues des morts.*
"'War is an evil'": Ibid., p. 102.
"The book caused an immediate sensation": On the reception of *Les aventures de Télémaque,* see Cherel, pp. 24–7, and the catalogue of the French National Library: http://catalogue.bnf.fr. The British editions can be found online in the Eighteenth-Century Collections Online, published by Gale Thomson (http://infotrac.galegroup.com/menu). Web sites consulted June 26, 2006.

61 "'This is my son'": Tennyson.
"'shipwreck and death'": Fénelon, *Les aventures de Télémaque,* p. 124.
"'When you realize that you are not getting something'": Darnton, *The Great Cat Massacre,* p. 78.

62 "'All peoples are brothers'": Fénelon, *Les aventures de Télémaque,* p. 318.
"historians of pacifist thought": See, for instance, Brock; Friedrich.
"Jean de la Bruyère": La Bruyère.
"distinguishing murder from heroism": Pascal, p. 48.

63 "the *abbé* de Saint-Pierre": The most complete biography remains Drouet, but see also Perkins.
"his most important book": Saint-Pierre, *Projet.* This edition is based on the edition of 1713. Saint-Pierre himself republished it in several different forms during his lifetime.
"'the apothecary of all Europe'" and "'Saint-Pierre of Utopia'": Drouet, pp. 138, 334.

64 "'*Telemachus* appeared'": Bernardin de Saint-Pierre, vol. III, p. 489. "'if any poem could engender'": Terrasson, p. x.
"Lauzun read the book": Lauzun, p. 237.
"Massillon had daringly asked": Kaiser, p. 138. "Royal panegyrists": Cherel, p. 301.
"Later in the century": Petitfils, p. 46.
"Jean-Claude Bonnet has shown": Bonnet, *Naissance du Panthéon,* esp. pp. 29–49.

65 "The indefatigable *abbé* de Saint-Pierre": Saint-Pierre, "Discours."
"'the true key'": Bonnet, *Naissance du Panthéon,* p. 48.
"Fénelon himself . . . among the first four subjects": Ibid., pp. 48–9, 395.
"by the later eighteenth century": On the progress of this idea, see, for instance, Belissa, *Fraternité universelle,* p. 9; Fischbach, p. 92; Mathiez, "Pacifisme et nationalisme," p. 1; Silberner, p. 269.
"'War, like murder'": Condorcet, p. 230.
"'one squeezes the orange'": Quoted in Pearson, p. 216.

66 "'A million assassins'": Voltaire, *Candide,* p. 87. On Voltaire's attitudes toward war, see Léonard, pp. 206–37.

"numerous imitations": See bibliography compiled on http://ub-dok.uni-trier.de/ausstellung/candide/candide_fort.htm. Web site consulted June 26, 2006. On d'Holbach, see, above all, Kors, especially pp. 11–4, 158–60.

67 "According to Robert Darnton": Darnton, *The Forbidden Bestsellers*, pp. 63–4.
"he managed to procure": See Kors, p. 150.
"'We were walking'": Quoted in Price, p. 223.
"'Is there anything more contrary'": Holbach, *Système social*, vol. II, p. 117.

68 "'wicked natural state'": Fénelon, *Les aventures de Télémaque*, p. 433.
"Hobbes explicitly and repeatedly": See Tuck, pp. 109–39.
"including on the *abbé* de Saint-Pierre": See Friedrich, p. 29; Tuck, p. 141.
"and to dispute Hobbes's conclusions": See Tuck, pp. 140–96.
"'the state of peace'": Mercier de la Rivière, p. 467.
"'Hobbes claimed'": "Paix," in *Encyclopédie*.

69 "'The state of society'": Holbach, *Système de la nature*, vol. II, pp. 316–7.
"'What is honor?'": Shakespeare, *Henry IV, Part I*, V:i; "'War, he sung'": John Dryden, "Alexander's Feast."
"'What does this *honor* consist of?'": Holbach, *Système social*, vol. II, p. 151. Italics in original.
"'murder, theft, rape and infamy'": Holbach, *La morale universelle*, vol. II, p. 91.
"'the commanders'": Ibid., vol. II, p. 127.
"'the fear of being despised'": Ibid., vol. II, p. 95.

70 "'is visibly a remnant'": Ibid., vol. II, p. 6.
"'a new humanity'": Voltaire, *Essai sur les moeurs*, vol. VIII, p. 196.
"François-Jean de Chastellux": On Chastellux, see Carson; Kors, especially p. 152; Varnum.

71 "'national hatred . . . hath of late established'": Chastellux, vol. II, p. 281.
"could not possibly lead": Ibid., vol. II, p. 294.
"'Barbarians . . . rush into war'": Robertson, p. 10.

72 "'there are no longer any Frenchmen'": J.-J. Rousseau, *Considérations*, in *Œuvres*, vol. III, p. 960.
"'The entire human race'": Holbach, *La morale universelle*, vol. II, p. 2.

73 "Bordeaux alone": Cobban, vol. I, p. 40.
"The development of commerce": See Vardi.
"The *abbé* de Saint-Pierre had made these points": Saint-Pierre, *Projet*, especially pp. 30, 180.
"'The spirit of conquest'": Melon, quoted in Silberner, p. 172. "'the natural effect of commerce'": Montesquieu, *Spirit of the Laws*, p. 338. "'Commerce tends to wear off'": Robertson, p. 95. "It is the *spirit of commerce*": Kant, "Eternal Peace," p. 264. In this chapter, I refer to Kant's essay, "Zum ewigen Frieden," by the more generally accepted English title "Perpetual Peace." The German original can be found online at http://philosophiebuch.de/ewfried.htm, consulted June 26, 2006. See also Hirschman.
"well-meaning projects . . . proliferated": For a useful summary of French plans, see Souleyman; on Britain, see Ceadel, pp. 63–8.

74 "'hopeless . . . visionary and ridiculous'": Bentham, vol. II, pp. 535–60.
"History, wrote Condorcet": Condorcet, pp. 229–30.

74   "'charming in the sound'": For an account of Washington's first military engagement, see Jennings, pp. 67–70.

     "'It is time'": George Washington to François-Jean de Beauvoir de Chastellux, April 25, 1788, in Washington, p. 479.

75   "'be bounded in a nut shell'": Shakespeare, *Hamlet*, II:ii.

     "'We are civilised'": Kant, "Idea." See also discussion in Friedrich, pp. 79–84.

76   "signboard painting," "a state of war": Kant, "Eternal Peace," pp. 245, 259–65.

     "'the negative substitute'": Ibid., p. 257.

     "*Fiat justitia*," "'act in such a way'": Ibid., pp. 274, 272.

77   "'enemies of reason,'" "'oppressors of freedom'": Condorcet, p. 166.

     "*Die Weltgeschichte*": Schiller, "Resignation." G.W.F. Hegel adopted it as a maxim in his 1821 *Philosophy of Right*.

     "'one is tempted'": Robespierre, *Rapport*, p. 4.

     "'would allow perpetual peace'": Kant, "Eternal Peace," pp. 248–9.

79   "he favorably contrasted": J.-J. Rousseau, *Discours.*

     "'Every citizen should be a soldier'": J.-J. Rousseau, *Considérations,* in *Œuvres,* vol. III, p. 1013. The idea owes much to Machiavelli, *Discorsi,* especially chp. 43.

     "Mably argued": Mably, p. 146.

     "'as easily as the north wind'": Guibert, p. 137. On Guibert, see Palmer, "Frederick the Great, Guibert, Bülow"; Gat, pp. 43–53.

     "Its style of war": Guibert, p. 149.

80   "In both countries . . . and their enemies as the modern Carthage": On this subject, see Colley, *Britons;* Wilson, *Sense of the People;* Bell, *Cult of the Nation,* pp. 78–106; Dziembowski, *Un nouveau patriotisme français;* Rowe; Salas.

     "Pirated and put to music": See Bell, "Aux origines de la 'Marseillaise.'"

81   "'men desire harmony'": Quoted in Mori, p. 226.

     "Kant himself": Kant, "Idea of a Universal Cosmopolitical History."

     "'war . . . has something sublime'": Kant, *Critique of Judgment,* ss. 28.

     "necessary phenomenon . . . 'rejuvenates the people' . . . 'The project of perpetual peace'": Johann Valentin Embser, quoted in Janssen, pp. 51, 47n, 43.

     "'machine-like . . . artificial paralysis'": Humboldt, chp. 5.

3. DECLARING PEACE; DECLARING WAR

84   "'The French nation'": French National Assembly, May 22, 1790, in *AP,* vol. XV, p. 662.

     "'It is a cruel thing'": Madame Roland to Bancal, Paris, June 25, 1791, in Roland, vol. II, p. 313.

86   "No monarch will ever live": On the so-called October Days, see Doyle, *Oxford History,* pp. 121–3; Schama, pp. 456–70.

     "'It is now sixteen or seventeen years'": Burke, *Reflections,* pp. 66–7.

87   "An unlikely place": On the Nootka Sound incident, see Cook, pp. 146–249; Foucrier.

88   "Patriotic opinion": See Cook, p. 215.

89   "The king . . . had ordered": *Moniteur,* vol. IV, p. 366; *AP,* vol. XV, p. 510.

     "In its daily business": In general on the work of the National Assembly, now also known as the Constituent Assembly, see Tackett, especially pp. 209–313.

"Montmorin tried to load the deck": On this moment in the debate, see *AP,* vol. XV, p. 311; Bradby, vol. I, pp. 236–9; Godechot, *La Grande Nation,* pp. 70–1; *Moniteur,* vol. IV, p. 367. The most complete analyses of the debate are to be found in Belissa, *Fraternité universelle,* pp. 179–97, and Whiteman, pp. 115–38.

"It consisted of nearly 1,200 men": See Tackett, p. 20.

90 "no fewer than thirty-five deputies": See ibid., pp. 226–34; Aulard, *Les orateurs de la révolution.*

"On hot spring days": See Bradby, vol. I, p. 165. "Félix Faulcon": Faulcon to Béra, May 19, 1790, Faulcon, vol. II, p. 225.

"The Left was further": On the divisions on the Left, see Tackett, p. 277–82.

91 "'Well, *Messieurs'"*: Quoted in Williams, p. 52.

"That evening": *Chronique de Paris,* no. 145 (May 25, 1790), pp. 578–9. See also Bradby, vol. I, p. 238, and Serna.

92 "the danger of social unrest": See especially Scott, "Problems of Law and Order."

"'I see civil war'": André-Boniface-Louis de Riqueti, vicomte de Mirabeau, in *AP,* vol. XV, p. 592; *Moniteur,* vol. IV, p. 408.

"observers had to redefine the word": See Baker, pp. 203–23; cf. Woloch, *The New Regime.*

"'Who would have said,'": Faulcon to Barbier, May 15, 1790, Faulcon, vol. II, p. 222.

93 "'And this, repeated I'": Williams, p. 45.

"During important debates": For descriptions of the Assembly in Paris, see ibid., pp. 42–5; Bradby, vol. I, pp. 164–82; Lameth, especially vol. II, p. 313; Tackett, pp. 200–234.

"Lauzun had joined": On Lauzun in the Assembly, see *DC,* vol. I, pp. 97–8; Tackett, p. 53; Velay.

94 "'one of the most humiliating'": Quoted in Gontaut-Biron, p. 202.

"'Peace can be bought'": Armand-Louis de Gontaut, duc de Lauzun et Biron, in *AP,* XV, pp. 515–6; *Moniteur,* vol. IV, p. 371.

"'This incidental question'": Alexandre de Lameth in *AP,* vol. XV, p. 516; *Moniteur,* vol. IV, p. 372.

"Lameth made": On Lameth, see Bradby, vol. I, pp. 120–24; *DC,* vol. I, pp. 509–12; Tackett, pp. 179–80.

"'sacrificed entire peoples'": Lameth in *AP,* vol. XI, p. 521 (February 9, 1790).

"'the cause of the kings'": Lameth in *AP,* vol. XV, p. 516; *Moniteur,* vol. IV, p. 372.

95 "'be the man of sway'": William Augustus Miles, March 1791, excerpted in Rudé, p. 88. The literature on Robespierre is immense. The most complete biographies remain Thompson, *Robespierre;* and J. Walter, *Robespierre.* For his career in the Constituent Assembly, see *DC,* vol. II, pp. 813–6.

"'For example . . . you could show'": Maximilien Robespierre, in *AP,* vol. XV, p. 517; *Moniteur,* vol. IV, p. 373.

96 "'It is hard to know'": Quoted in Aulard, *Les grands orateurs,* p. 58. On Mirabeau, see Castries ; *DC,* vol. II, pp. 673–5; and Welch, especially pp. 261–70.

"He had recently entered": Welch, p. 261.

"He now argued": Honoré-Gabriel Riqueti, comte de Mirabeau, *AP,* vol. XV, p. 518; *Moniteur,* vol. IV, p. 374.

96   "'a national, not a ministerial war'": Jacques-François, baron de Menou, in *AP,* vol. XV, p. 518; *Moniteur,* vol. IV, p. 374.

97   "'The National Assembly furthermore declares'": Pierre-Marc-Gaston, duc de Lévis, *AP,* vol. XV, p. 519; *Moniteur,* vol. IV, p. 375. On Lévis, see *DC,* vol. II, pp. 593–5.

"'The great question'" . . . "'I think'": see Lévis, pp. 425–44, quote from p. 442.

"In the Manège": see Lameth, vol. II, p. 274.

"'the most important that was ever agitated'": *The Times* (London), no. 1687 (May 21, 1790), p. 3.

"Jacques-Pierre Brissot": On Brissot, see d'Huart and the still serviceable work of Ellery.

"'the dreams of the old politics,'" "'French honor!'": *Le patriote françois,* no. 281 (May 16, 1790), p. 2; no. 280 (May 15, 1790), p. 2

98   "'Are alliances more useful'": Duc de Lévis, in *AP,* vol. XV, pp. 526–7; the *Moniteur,* vol. IV, p. 383, has a much shorter version of the speech. On the question of alliances, see Frey and Frey, "'The Reign of the Charlatans Is Over.'"

"'May all nations'": Jacques Jallet, in *AP,* vol. XV, p. 528; *Moniteur,* vol. IV, pp. 385–6; *The Times* (London), no. 1688, May 22, 1790, p. 3.

"he presented a largely pragmatic case": Belissa is mistaken to write, in *Fraternité,* p. 182, that the Right fell back on the pragmatic case later in the debate. It dominated their arguments from the beginning.

"'It is the people's interest'": Armand-Sigismond-Félicité-Marie, comte de Sérent, in *AP,* vol. XV, pp. 527–8; *Moniteur,* vol. IV, pp. 383–4. On Sérent, see *DC,* vol. II, pp. 858–60.

99   "the old military aristocracy": The military nobility dominated the entire debate, from May 14 to 22, which can be found, in the most complete version, in *AP,* vol. XV, pp. 510–662. On the family backgrounds, see *DC,* vol. I, pp. 6, 254; vol. II, pp. 512, 858.

"Even before 1789": See Chapter 1. These remarks are based on the work of Bien; Blaufarb, especially pp. 12–81; and J. Smith, *The Culture of Merit.*

"Already, a plan": See Blaufarb, pp. 57–60; Edmond-Louis-Alexis Dubois-Crancé, "Observations sur la constitution militaire" in *AP,* vol. X, pp. 595–614 (December 15, 1789).

100 "'We are citizens first'": *Avis aux grenadiers,* p. 3 and passim. In general on this subject, see Bertaud, *La Révolution armée,* pp. 43–6; Scott, *The Response of the Royal Army,* especially pp. 51–69.

"'The army's defection'": Chagniot, vol. II, p. 128. Gilbert Bodinier, in the same volume, p. 195, attributes virtually the same quotation to Miot de Mélito.

"In 1790, far from subsiding": See Bertaud, *La Révolution armée;* pp. 46–54; Blaufarb, pp. 75–81; Scott, "Problems of Law and Order," p. 865; Scott, *Response of the Royal Army,* pp. 81–97.

"'the Constitution will be attacked'": Charles-Malo-François, comte de Lameth, in *AP,* vol. XV, pp. 529–30; *Moniteur,* vol. IV, pp. 386–7.

"'The speaker's platform'": Lameth, *Histoire,* vol. II, p. 275.

101 "Pierre-Victor Malouet": On Malouet, see *DC,* vol. II, pp. 627–30; Griffiths.

"'Commerce has changed the face'": Pierre-Victor Malouet, in *AP,* vol. XV, pp. 533–6. The *Moniteur*, vol. IV, pp. 388–9, has a very abbreviated version of the speech.

102 "a paid agent": For evidence of Pétion's corruption, see Duncker, especially p. 21. Duncker also suggests, less persuasively, that Barnave also took Prussian money. "'This vain, superstitious'": Jérôme Pétion de Villeneuve, in *AP*, vol. XV, pp. 536–8. The *Moniteur*, vol. IV, pp. 389–91, has a very abbreviated version of the speech. On Pétion, see *DC*, vol. II, pp. 746–9.

"'Open the history books'": Pétion, in *AP*, vol. XV, p. 539.

"Pétion even invoked": *AP*, vol. XV, pp. 540–4.

"'hateful monsters'": Pétion, in *AP*, vol. XV, p. 539.

103 "'a shelf of metaphysics'": François-Dominique de Reynaud, chevalier de Montlosier, in *AP*, vol. XV, pp. 544–6, quote from p. 545. The account of the speech in the *Moniteur*, vol. IV, p. 391, is incomplete. On Montlosier, see *DC*, vol. II, pp. 691–3.

"'It is a grand, sublime spectacle'": Montlosier, in *AP*, vol. XV, p. 546.

"Even Brissot": *Le patriote françois*, no. 283 (May 18, 1790), p. 2.

"'a sad object of pity'": Jean-Siffrein Maury, in *AP*, vol. XV, pp. 564–75, quote from p. 575; the *Moniteur* gives a much abbreviated version in vol. IV, pp. 398–400. On Maury, see Beik; *DC*, vol. II, pp. 645–8; Raduget.

"'Until this day'": Constantin-François Chassebeuf de Volney, in *AP*, vol. XV, p. 576; *Moniteur*, vol. IV, pp. 402–3. On Volney, see *DC*, vol. II, pp. 942–3, which also gives the principal bibliography of his works.

104 "'This pacific Congress'": *Le patriote françois*, no. 284 (May 19, 1790), p. 3.

"The morning brought": See especially Augustin-Félix-Elisabeth Barrin, comte de La Galissonière, and Philippe-Jacques de Bengy de Puyvallée, *AP*, vol. XV, pp. 610, 616; *Moniteur*, vol. IV, p. 410, has the first speech but omits the second altogether.

"'I am *spoken for*'": The story is recounted in Lameth, vol. II, pp. 280–2n. Italics in original.

105 "'The French nation renounces'": Mirabeau, in *AP*, vol. XV, pp. 618–26, quote from p. 626; *Moniteur*, vol. IV, pp. 413–20, quote from p. 420. The version given by the *Moniteur*, although somewhat garbled and out of order, is more reliable, because the version in the *AP* is taken from a later, printed version that Mirabeau himself edited to make the speech look more favorable to the Left. See Bradby, vol. I, pp. 253–5.

"He repeated, at great length": *Moniteur*, vol. IV, pp. 416, 420.

"'Many orators'": Jacques-Antoine-Marie de Cazalès, in *AP*, vol. XV, p. 640; *Moniteur*, vol. IV, p. 421. On Cazalès, see *DC*, vol. I, pp. 179–81.

"But in the France of 1790": The entire speech is in *AP*, vol. XV, pp. 639–41; *Moniteur*, vol. IV, pp. 421–2.

106 "On this, as on so many other issues": This point is made with particular strength and cogency by Tackett, especially pp. 302–13.

"Brissot could not help": *Le patriote françois*, no. 288 (May 23, 1790), pp. 1–2. On this moment, see also Faulcon, vol. II, p. 231; Lameth, vol. II, p. 313.

"'You have now brought your crimes and lies'": Quoted in Castries, p. 437. In general on the incident, see ibid., pp. 437–8; Welch, pp. 267–8. The pamphlet is generally attributed to the journalist Sébastien Brumeau de la Croix.

106 "Barnave . . . angrily refuted": Barnave, in *AP,* vol. XV, pp. 641–44; *Moniteur,*
vol. IV, pp. 422–4. See also Bradby, vol. I, pp. 245–9; Castries, p. 438.

"'Hang him from the lamppost!'": Castries, p. 438.

"In an inspired address": Mirabeau, in *AP,* vol. XV, pp. 655–9, quote from p. 655;
Moniteur, vol. IV, pp. 438–42.

107 "Mirabeau's amended proposal": For the text of the final decree, see *AP,* vol. XV,
pp. 661–2, quote from p. 439.

"which would find its way unchanged": See http://mjp.univ-perp.fr/france/
co1791.htm, "Constitution de 1791," Article VI, consulted on June 26, 2006.

"Camille Desmoulins reported": Quoted in Belissa, *Fraternité,* p. 193.

"'Frenchmen, you are still slaves'": *Révolutions de Paris,* no. 46 (May 22–29,
1790), p. 406.

"Jean-Paul Marat agreed": *L'Ami du peuple,* no. 112 (May 24, 1790) and no. 113
(May 25, 1790), in Marat, pp. 749, 752.

"'an assembly of Statesmen'": *The Times* (London), no. 1691 (May 26, 1790), p. 2.

"The Scottish writer": Mackintosh, p. 291.

"the poet Klopstock": Klopstock, "Sie, und nicht Wir."

"'a principle which no one will adopt'": Quoted in Belissa, *Fraternité,* p. 195.

108 "'Platonic proclamation'": Sorel, vol. II, p. 89.

"'The reign of the charlatans'": Guillaume-François-Charles Goupil-Préfelne, in
AP, vol. XV, p. 548; *Moniteur,* vol. IV, p. 392.

109 "On June 19": *AP,* vol. XVI, pp. 374–8. On the abolition of nobility, see
Blaufarb, pp. 60–6; Doyle, "The French Revolution and the Abolition of Nobility"; Tackett, pp. 292–6.

"Spain yielded": See Evans.

110 "thousands of nobles": Scott, *Response of the Royal Army,* p. 106.

"In September 1790": See Blaufarb, pp. 66–74.

"'Any nation'": Quoted in Belissa, *Fraternité universelle,* p. 210.

"'Every day, we asked each other'": Mautort, p. 404.

"over 60 percent": Blaufarb, p. 88.

"numbered only 20,000": See Guiomar, p. 28.

"The apparent weakness": The authoritative work on the origins of the wars is
Blanning, *Origins.*

112 "On October 20": *AP,* vol. XXXIV, October 20, 1791, pp. 309–17, quote from p. 315.

"he calmly wrote": Brissot to François Dupont, October 22, 1791, in Brissot, *J. P.
Brissot: Correspondance,* p. 274.

"'avenge your glory'": Quoted in Schama, p. 593; cf. *AP,* vol. XXXIV, p. 316.

"the evidence makes clear": On Brissot's maneuvering, see Furet, "Les Girondins
et la guerre"; Gueniffey, pp. 132–47.

"'The best way to help us . . . These imbeciles don't see'": Quoted in Michon,
p. 29n.

113 "'prodigious, supernatural efforts'": Brissot, *Discours sur la question de savoir si le
roi peut être jugé,* reprinted in Aulard, *La société des Jacobins,* vol. II, pp. 608–26,
quote from p. 619.

114 "a gimcrack tableau": *AP,* vol. XVI, pp. 372–3; Avenel, pp. 111–7.

"he told the members": Cloots, "Discours à l'Assemblée Législative," December
13, 1791, *AP,* vol. XXXVI, pp. 79–80.

"No sooner would French troops cross the borders": "Extrait de l'histoire de la guerre de 1792," *Chronique de Paris,* January 15, 1792, p. 59.

115   "'from the bosom of natural law'": Ronsin, *La ligue des fanatiques,* p. 23. The play was first performed at the Théâtre Molière on June 18, 1791.

"'hate war'": Pierre-Victurnien Vergniaud, "Projet d'adresse au peuple Français," December 27, 1791, in Vergniaud et al., pp. 113–20, quote from p. 119.

"'It is because I want peace'": Anacharsis Cloots, at the Jacobin Club, January 1, 1792, quoted in Michon, p. 48.

"'This war will be the last war'": Charles-François Dumouriez, in the National Convention, October 12, 1792, *AP,* vol. LII, p. 472.

"'There has been in this Revolution'": Malouet, February 5, 1791, *AP,* vol. XXV, p. 499.

"'War is declared'": Ronsin, *Ligue,* title page.

"'This expiatory war'": *Patriote françois,* no. 857, December 13, 1791, p. 1.

"'Remember those crusades'": Brissot, *Second discour [sic],* p. 27.

116   "'All the nations of Europe'": Menou, January 28, 1791, *AP,* vol. XXII, p. 526–7.

"'The French, like lions'": Anacharsis Cloots, "Discours," *AP,* vol. XXXVI, p. 79.

"'Let us, then, Messieurs'": Marguerite-Élie Guadet, January 14, 1792, *AP,* vol. XXXVII, p. 413.

117   "'the exterminating angel'": Quoted in Michon, p. 38. The French phrase "*ange exterminateur*" comes from the standard French translation of 1 Corinthians 10:10 and is also often used to describe the angel of death who slew the first-born children of Egypt.

"'It is a cruel thing to think'": Madame Roland to Bancal, Paris, June 25, 1791, Roland, vol II, p. 313.

"'dessicated . . . listless'": Brissot, December 29, 1791, *AP,* vol. XXXVI, p. 607. "'I have only one fear'": Brissot, *Second discour,* p. 15.

118   "'passive obedience'": Maximilien Robespierre, in the Jacobin Club, January 2, 1792, in Robespierre, *Discours.*

"'The most extravagant idea'": Ibid.

4. THE LAST CRUSADE

120   "'Revolutionary war'": Mao, chp. 5.

"A full account is impossible": On the historiography of the wars, see Connelly, "Historiography." For the most recent example of the "debunking" approach, see Mackenzie. The most important secondary sources on the period are Bertaud, *La Révolution armée,* and Lynn, *Bayonets.*

121   "the letters mostly expressed": Noël, pp. 135 (March 19, 1792), 12 (January 18, 1792), 19 (January 19, 1792), 105 (February 27, 1792).

"'rain that hardly ever stopped'": Duchet, pp. 58–9 (August 2, 1792).

"'We're always sleeping on the ground'": Quoted in Bertaud, *La Révolution armée,* p. 220.

"'It has now been fourteen days'": Simon, p. 70 (March 12, 1793).

"Louis-Joseph Bricard": Bricard, pp. 35–47.

122   "'suffering unspeakable pains'": Simon, p. 75.

123   "one vivid novelty": See Palmer, *Twelve Who Ruled,* p. 354.

123 "various prominent readers": See particularly Servan, *Le soldat citoyen;* Servan, *Projet de constitution.*

124 "'In France every citizen'": Edmond Dubois-Crancé, "Observations sur la constitution militaire," December 15, 1789, *AP,* vol. X, pp. 595–614, quote from p. 612. On Dubois-Crancé, see Iung. On Revolutionary conscription, see most recently Hippler.
"'cured of the sickness'": Servan, *Projet,* p. 6.

125 "who expressed admiration": See Simon, p. 14.
"It may be going too far to say": Although see the compelling article of Lüsebrink.
"'the military spirit'": *Révolutions de Paris,* 19–26 September, 1789, p. 27.
"'never was there a more ridiculous project'": Quoted in Kruse, p. 40.

126 "But neither the Austrians": On the start of the wars, see Blanning, *The French Revolutionary Wars,* pp. 71–4; Guiomar, pp. 28–30.
"'embrace the cause'": Dumouriez, quoted in Gontaut-Biron, p. 250.
"'I can't conceive'": Quoted in Hublot, p. 120.

127 "'They do not know how to use their weapons'": Lauzun to Joseph Servan, quoted in Gontaut-Biron, p. 261.
"'In the blink of an eye'": Foissac-Latour, quoted in ibid., p. 256.

128 "'The first battle we will fight'": Quoted in Blanning, *The French Revolutionary Wars,* p. 72.

129 "'shit camps'": See Chuquet, *Valmy,* especially pp. 76, 169; Hublot, especially pp. 341, 385. On the Valmy campaign in general, see Bertaud, *Valmy.*
"After the fall": See Chuquet, *Valmy,* pp. 82–6; Massenbach, vol. I, pp. 96–7.

130 "At least 1,100 prisoners": Doyle, *Oxford History,* pp. 191–2.
"'two legged Parisian animals'": *The Times* (London), no. 2408, September 10, 1792, p. 1.
"'The bells that will ring'": Georges Danton, *AP,* vol. XLIX, p. 209.
"'rush at the enemies'": Quoted in Hublot, p. 223.
"15,000 recruits": Bertaud, *La Révolution armée,* p. 80.

131 "'The army marching from Paris'": *The Times* (London), no. 2408, September 10, 1792, p. 1.
"'Most of these soldiers'": Rousset, p. 100.
"Sir Edward Creasy's": Creasy. The book has been reprinted hundreds of times and remains in print today.
"'From this place'": See Suratteau, "Goethe et le 'tournant de Valmy,'" pp. 477–9.
"An astonishing character": The newest biography is by Henry. It does not, however, compare with Chuquet's brilliantly written *Dumouriez.*

134 "The battle lasted all day": See Bertaud, *Valmy,* p. 35. In general on the battle, see the lively accounts of ibid. and Chuquet, *Valmy,* supplemented by Hublot. But on Hublot, see the cautionary review by Rothenberg, "Soldiers and the Revolution."
"the humming of tops": Quoted in Schama, p. 639.
"20,000 cannon shots": Bertaud, *La vie quotidienne,* p. 92.
"a general told a cannoneer": Bertaud, *Valmy,* p. 29.

135 "'*Hier schlagen wir nicht*'": Quoted in Chuquet, *Valmy,* p. 215.

"'Try to decipher my letter'": Quoted in Bertaud, *Valmy,* p. 39.

136 "'the soldiers were . . . simple spectators'": Noël, letter of September 21, 1792, p. 271.

"'Valmy, you do not explain it'": Quoted in Hublot, p. 373.

"'that ought to count for a great deal'": Napoleon, quoted in Las Cases, vol. II, p. 297.

"'They continually risked all'": Quoted in Mathiez, *La victoire en l'an II,* p. 235.

137 "And today, after eighty years": V. Hugo.

138 "This leniency": This is the argument of Lynn, *Bayonets,* p. 24. See also Chuquet, *Valmy,* p. 143; Forrest, *Soldiers,* p. 191.

"'Those who command and those who obey'": Quoted in Lynn, *Bayonets,* p. 94.

"the curious matter of the pike": On this subject, see, above all, Lynn, "French Opinion."

139 "the Girondins had blithely promoted it": See, for instance, Lemny, p. 222.

"Carnot . . . argued": Bertaud, *Valmy,* p. 103; see also Bertaud, *La Révolution armée,* p. 162.

"'do not carry out their assaults . . . If we have not been either Spartans, or Athenians'": *AP,* vol. XLVII, pp. 123–4, July 25, 1792. The exchange was between Laureau and Lecointre-Puyraveau.

"'good for nothing'": General Santerre in J.-J. Savary, vol. II, p. 5.

"key symbols": See Soboul, *The Sans-Culottes,* pp. 227–8.

"the supposedly 'impetuous' nature": Ibid.

"Jean Bon Saint-André": See Bodinier, "La républicanisation de la marine," pp. 249–59, especially p. 257.

"'The *sans-culottes* regard patriotism'": Quoted in H. Brown, *War, Revolution,* p. 79.

141 "'Félix Cabanes'": Quoted in Baecque, p. 288. On the paper, see Julia, pp. 208–13; T. Rousseau.

"The Convention itself": Jeismann, p. 153. "'none of us would refuse glory'": Quoted in Baecque, p. 300.

142 "On cue": Robespierre saw it as an alternative to the quasi-religious cult of the recently murdered Marat. See Baecque, p. 281. On the plays, see Mannucci, pp. 189–256. For one example, see Briois.

"'I think he should be shown'": Quoted in W. Roberts, p. 311.

"'It is beautiful to perish'": Quoted in Bertaud, *Guerre et société,* p. 161.

143 "'National hatred must sound forth . . . [The English] are a people'": Barère, *Rapport,* pp. 13, 18.

"Orators throughout France": See Bell, *Cult of the Nation,* pp. 98–101. Cf. Wahnich, pp. 237–346. The decree also applied to soldiers from the German state of Hanover, ruled by Britain's George III.

"'Only the dead'": Quoted in Reinhard, *Le grand Carnot,* vol. II, pp. 107, 130.

"when another deputy proposed": *AP,* vol. LXX (August 7, 1793), p. 451. The deputy in question was Jacques Garnier des Saintes.

"The story even circulated": Pelzer, p. 196. Pelzer and Wahnich offer the most recent and sophisticated discussions of the "take no prisoners" decree.

"'War is a violent state'": Quoted in Reinhard, *Le grand Carnot,* vol. II, p. 106.

"'Those who make war'": Quoted in Belissa, *Fraternité universelle,* p. 365.

144 "he frostily insisted": Robespierre, June 21, 1794, in Aulard, *La société des Jacobins,* vol. VI, pp. 183–5.

"'a clash of proselytisms'": Robespierre, quoted in Bertaud, *La Révolution armée,* p. 194.

"'Prepare for universal peace'": Quoted in Reinhard, *Le grand Carnot,* vol. II, p. 37.

"'grant fraternity and aid'": Quoted in Belissa, *Fraternité universelle,* p. 322.

"'philanthropic ideas . . . behave towards the enemies'": ibid., p. 396. This evolution is discussed in detail in ibid., pp. 253–408.

145 "'The mode of civilized war'": Burke, *A Letter From Mr. Burke.*

"Lord Auckland had called": William, Lord Auckland, to Morton Eden, August 31, 1792, quoted in Black, *European Warfare,* p. 170.

"Six thousand copies . . . 400,000 copies . . . well over 1,000,000 copies": Lynn, *Bayonets,* pp. 157, 141, 143. See also Bertaud, *La Révolution armée,* pp. 146–7.

"100,000 songbooks": Quoted in Forrest, *Soldiers of the French Revolution,* p. 105. See also Lynn, *Bayonets,* p. 143.

146 "'Let us run en masse'": *La soirée du camp,* no. 2, 3 Thermidor Year II (July 21, 1794), pp. 3–4. It was sung to the tune of the "Carmagnole."

147 "First was Carnot": The definitive biography of Carnot is Reinhard's magnificent *Le grand Carnot.*

"Saint-Just's cold insistence": On Saint-Just, see Vinot.

"it was Carnot and Saint-Just": On the Committee of Public Safety, the best overall study remains Palmer's classic *Twelve Who Ruled.*

148 "As the reformer": Dubois-Crancé, "Observations sur la constitution militaire," December 15, 1789, *AP,* vol. X, pp. 595–614.

"150,000 men": See Bertaud, *La Révolution armée,* pp. 91–104.

"deputies from the Convention": Rousset, p. 235.

"'From this moment'": *AP,* vol. LXXII, August 23, 1793, p. 674. On the *levée,* see above all Forrest, "*La patrie en danger.*"

"Hébert tellingly exhorted": Quoted in Soboul, *Les soldats de l'an II,* p. 117.

"'The young men will fight'": *AP,* vol. LXXII, p. 674.

149 "'well over 750,000'": Forrest, *Soldiers,* p. 82.

"By October 1794": Forrest, "*La patrie en danger,*" p. 18; Rothenberg, "The Art of Warfare," pp. 121–2; and, in general, see Alder.

"it was becoming clear": See on this subject Rousset, notably pp. 225–31.

"Philippe-Henri Grimoard": Grimoard, vol. I, pp. 367–9.

150 "'Fifty thousand savage beasts'": Quoted in Rothenberg, *The Art of Warfare,* p. 115. See also Bertaud, *Atlas,* p. 56.

"'The general rules . . . Stun like lightning'": Committee of Public Safety, February 2, 1794; May 27, 1794; August 21, 1794. Quoted in Bertaud, *La Révolution,* p. 230; Soboul, *Les soldats de l'an II,* p. 209.

"200,000 French soldiers died": Bertaud, *La Révolution,* p. 248.

"'soldiers had been expensive'": Rothenberg, *The Art of Warfare,* p. 61.

"The persistent radical dream": See Ozouf, *L'homme régénéré.*

"'No battle plans'": Gouges, p. 133.

151 "on Ney and Hoche": Files kept by Pierre Celliez of the War Ministry, quoted in Chuquet, *Lettres de 1793,* pp. 258–9. See on this general subject, H. Brown, *War, Revolution.*

"Here is where Saint-Just stood out": On Saint-Just in Strasbourg, see Palmer, *Twelve Who Ruled,* pp. 177–201; Vinot, pp. 213–35.

"'Saint-Just appeared'": Quoted in Vinot, p. 214.

"no fewer than 84 generals": Blanning, *French Revolutionary Wars,* p. 126.

"'We can neither honor you'": Quoted in Palmer, *Twelve Who Ruled,* p. 353.

152 "barely 3 percent": Blaufarb, *The French Army,* p. 126; Lynn, *Bayonets,* p. 67.

"officers of a volunteer battalion": Mathiez, *La Victoire en l'an II,* pp. 67–8.

"some of the most competent actively shunned promotion": Mackenzie, p. 44.

"the Convention began to show": See Blaufarb, pp. 106–32. On the "amalgame," see above all Bertaud, *La Révolution armée,* pp. 165–93.

"The Parisian artilleryman Bricard": Bricard, pp. 126–7.

"Lazare Hoche": See Mathiez, *La Victoire en l'an II,* p. 276.

"Guillaume Brune": Phipps, vol. I, pp. 198–201.

"The average age": Rothenberg, *The Art of Warfare,* p. 104.

153 "the dancing master": Liesse to Louis-Marie-Jacques de Narbonne, January 3, 1792, in Chuquet, *Lettres de 1792,* p. 3.

5. THE EXTERMINATING ANGELS

154 "'The hirelings of despotism'": Georges Danton, quoted in Michon, p. 38.

"'You must decide'": Louis-Marie Turreau, in SHAT B⁵8: Armée de l'Ouest, Correspondence: Janvier-Mars 1794.

"Vincent Chapelain is nervous": This account is based on the affidavit of Chapelain from AN W 22, reprinted in Chassin, *La Vendée patriote,* vol. IV, pp. 272–4. See also Chapelain's letter to the administrators of the Vendée, November 26, 1793, reprinted in Chassin, *La Vendée patriote,* vol. III, pp. 368–9. Chapelain's testimony is corroborated by that of Biraud, the mayor of Boupère, in Chassin, *La Vendée patriote,* vol. IV, pp. 274–5.

155 "'I know there may be a few patriots'": Quoted in Lequinio, p. 66. On Grignon, see Six, *Dictionnaire,* vol. I, p. 527.

156 "'We burned and broke heads'": Grignon's report is in J.-J. Savary, vol. III, p. 89.

"220,000 to 250,000": Hussenet, pp. 237–45; J.-C. Martin, *La Vendée et la France,* pp. 315–6. Martin's book, which focuses on the broader relationship of the Vendée region to France, is the best single account of the war.

157 "'the most horrible civil war'": Turreau, p. 199n.

"In 1939, the Catholic Church": J.-C. Martin and Lardière, p. 16.

"one of the best short books": Petitfrère, *La Vendée.*

"He presented little original research": Secher, *Le génocide.* The statistic is given on p. 253. I am using the title of the English translation, which appeared in 2003.

"Simon Schama and Norman Davies": Schama, pp. 787–90; Davies, pp. 704–7. See my review of the English translation: Bell, "History Robed in Reckless Rhetoric."

158 "no less a figure than Alexander Solzhenitsyn": Le Gendre.

"had not, in fact, taken place": See Martin and Lardière.

"'turning the scythe . . . populicidal'": Babeuf, pp. 110, 9. Secher and other commentators mistakenly credit Babeuf with thereby inventing the noun "genocide." He used the French "populicide" as an adjective.

158　"'measures to exterminate'": Barère, in *AP,* vol. LXX, August 1, 1793, p. 101. On the contemporary meaning of "race," see Bell, *Cult of the Nation,* pp. 101–6.

"To the extent": General Grignon, for instance, insisted to a local official on January 23 that "there are nothing but brigands left in the Vendée." Affidavit of citizen Barrion, in Chassin, *Le Vendée patriote,* vol. IV, p. 267.

159　"'exterminated the royalists'": Michelet, vol. II, p. 578.

"particularly apoplectic": See particularly Barère's report on the "inexplicable Vendée" of October 1, 1793, in *AP,* vol. LXXV, pp. 421–6.

"poisoned brandy or even poison gas": See Secher, *Le génocide,* p. 155.

"The Convention *did* call": Decree of August 1, 1793, in *AP,* vol. LXX, p. 108.

"It also declared": Decree of March 19, 1793, in *AP,* vol. LX, p. 331.

"Some of its agents ordered . . . 'take whatever measures'": Sutherland, *The French Revolution,* pp. 204, 222.

"an ambivalent endorsement": The Committee's response of February 6, 1794, is in J.-J. Savary, vol. III, p. 151.

"'without any authorization'": Louis-Marie Turreau to Committee of Public Safety, 27 Nivôse II (January 15, 1794), in SHAT B⁵8; Turreau to Bourbotte, February 15, 1794, quoted in Secher, p. 159. On the tribunals, see Sutherland, *The French Revolution,* pp. 203–4.

"conflicting orders": See especially Martin and Lardière, pp. 27–36; and J.-C. Martin, "Le cas de Turreau." The thesis of tacit approval, originally advanced by Jean-Julien Savary in the 1820s (see J.-J. Savary, vol. III, p. 201), has been revived by Gueniffey, p. 265.

160　"'There . . . it was said'": Babeuf, p. 40.

161　"'the least refusal'": Turreau, p. 198n.

"Like much of western France": On the origins of the insurrection, see P. Bois; Faucheux; Tilly.

163　"'loud, black cloud'": Germain Bethuis, "Extrait des souvenirs d'un magistrat, fils d'un massacré," in Chassin, *La préparation de la Guerre de Vendée,* vol. III, pp. 335–9.

"For centuries": See Bercé, especially pp. 353–83.

"True, several belonged": On the Breton Association, see Godechot, *The Counter-Revolution,* pp. 207–11.

"The Marquis de Bonchamps": Bonchamps, pp. 38–40.

"'You want to dash'": Sapinaud, p. 3.

"as for the former naval officer": Gras, p. 18.

164　"In some towns": la Championnière, pp. 10–15.

"When the blues recaptured Machecoul": Petitfrère, *La Vendée,* p. 51.

"'Look carefully at this blade!'": Mercier du Rocher, p. 143.

"the Republic did start": See J.-C. Martin, *La Vendée,* pp. 43–51. See also Sutherland, *The Chouans.*

165　"'enchanted . . . teeming'": Mercier du Rocher, p. 43. "'deep, dark'": Kléber, cited in Secher, *Le génocide,* p. 130. "'palisades around a fort'": Turreau, pp. 30–4.

"On March 19": Chassin has collected accounts of this episode in *La préparation de la guerre de Vendée,* vol. III, pp. 473–81. The most reliable, by General Henri-François Boulard, is on pp. 476–9.

166　"As Jean-Clément Martin has argued": See J.-C. Martin, *La Vendée,* pp. 33–51.

"'Invisible battalions'": V. Hugo, chp. III.

167 "'Let us march'": Quoted by Mercier du Rocher, p. 139. On the religious fervor, see also Clémanceau, p. xvii; Tilly, p. 332.

"General Cathelineau": See Clémanceau, pp. 33–4; Godechot, *Counter-Revolution*, p. 219.

"In the town of Cholet": See Sapinaud, p. 25n.

"the strangest episode of all": Clémanceau, pp. xxi, 62.

168 "'I have found . . . all military principles'": Biron (Lauzun) to Bouchotte, Niort, May 31, 1793, cited in Rousset, pp. 281–2.

"'We cannot secure'": Quoted in Maugras, *The Duc de Lauzun and the Court of Marie-Antoinette*, p. 475.

"'the colonial Vendée'": *Extrait du régistre*, p. 2. I owe this citation to Malick Ghachem.

169 "'Nothing would have stopped'": Quoted in Petitfrère, *La Vendée*, p. 37.

170 "over 60,000": See J.-C. Martin, *La Vendée*, pp. 206–10.

"after taking the town of Montaigu": Petitfrère, *La Vendée*, pp. 53–4.

"the blues retaliated": La Bouëre, p. 77.

"'Since this is a war of brigands'": Quoted in Secher, *Le génocide*, p. 143.

"'Fall on them'": Boullault, quote from p. 32. The title page states that the play was performed at the Théâtre des Variétés Amusantes on October 2 and 3, 1793.

171 "In skiffs and makeshift rafts": Chassin, *La Vendée patriote*, vol. III, pp. 220–461.

"Marie-Louise-Victoire Donissan": La Rochejaquelein, pp. 163–9, 183.

"'it was a curious spectacle'": Jean-Claude Benaben in Chassin, *La Vendée patriote*, vol. III, p. 420.

"Among the Vendéan leaders": Secher, *Le génocide*, p. 145.

"In the middle of November": See Chassin, *La Vendée patriote*, vol. III, pp. 276–317.

172 "François-Joseph Westermann": See Six, *Dictionnaire*, vol. II, pp. 569–70.

"'we can only defeat the Vendée'": Quoted in Gras, p. 55. See also Chassin, *La Vendée patriote*, vol. II, pp. 284–320.

"he would make a show": See speech by Antoine Merlin de Thionville in SHAT B⁵8, December 1793; Also La Bouëre, p. 78.

"Witnesses claimed": J.-C. Martin, *La Vendée*, p. 181.

"In the city": Documents from the battle of Le Mans are collected in Chassin, *La Vendée patriote*, vol. III, pp. 412–27.

"'hideous slaughter . . . fifteen hours'": Pierre Bourbotte, Pierre-Louis Prieur (de la Marne), and Louis Marie Turreau-Linière (cousin of the general), in a report to the Convention, read on December 15, 1793, in Chassin, *La Vendée patriote*, p. 416. See also J.-J. Savary, vol. II, p. 430.

173 "'Women, priests, monks'": J. Maignan, December 14, 1793, in Chassin, *La Vendée patriote*, vol. III, p. 417.

"'Without stopping for a moment'": Quoted in Secher, *Le génocide*, p. 145.

"One Republican reported": Quoted in ibid., p. 147.

"'There is no more Vendée'": Westermann to the Committee of Public Safety, December 1793, quoted in ibid., p. 150.

174 "Several women who fought": See the memoirs of one of them: Bordereau.

"'This war does not at all resemble'": Antoine-François Momoro, "Rapport sur l'état politique et la situation actuelle de la Vendée," 22 Vendémiaire, year II, in SHAT B⁵7.

174 "'*All* the present inhabitants'": Pierre-Anselme Garrau, Nicolas Hentz, and Marie-Pierre-Adrien Francastel to the Committee of Public Safety, Nantes, 1 Ventôse, year II, in SHAT B⁵8. Italics are mine.

"'would then do the same'": Joseph-Marie Lequinio, extract from the *Gazette de France*, 3 Nivôse, year II, in SHAT B⁵7.

175 "a principal characteristic": Turreau to Bouchotte, 11 January 1794, in SHAT B⁵8.

"Charles-Philippe Ronsin": On Ronsin, see G. Brown; Cobb, pp. 63–5; Herlaut; J.-C. Martin, *La Vendée*, pp. 160–5.

"'literary underground'": Darnton, *Literary Underground*, especially pp. 1–40.

"a demented pamphlet": Ronsin, *La ligue aristocratique*.

176 "only 1,500": Quoted in Slavin, p. 72. My thanks to David Woodworth for this citation.

"'Here, Frenchmen fall'": Lauzun (Biron), *Compte rendu au Comité de Salut public*, quoted in Gontaut-Biron, p. 309. Even more incredibly, Lauzun wrote the letter after having been relieved of his command and placed in danger of the guillotine.

"'[his] conduct is really appalling'": Quoted in Maugras, *The Duc de Lauzun and the Court of Marie-Antoinette*, p. 453.

"'Born in the caste'": Quoted in an appendix, in Lauzun, p. 307.

"A captain on June 30": Herlaut, p. 102. From captain to brigadier general took Napoleon three months. See Chandler, *The Campaigns of Napoleon*, pp. 22–8.

"In September": See J.-C. Martin, *La Vendée*, pp. 161–6; Six, *Dictionnaire*, vol. II, pp. 110, 376–7, 392–3.

177 "who is not recognized as Republican'": Bouchotte to Turreau, November 28, 1793, in SHAT B⁵7.

"'What did I do?'": Quoted in Chassin, *La Vendée patriote*, vol. III, p. 247. See pp. 247–8 for the tensions between Léchelle and the "Mayençais."

"one of these protégés": Ibid., pp. 244–7.

"It was one of Ronsin's protégés": Secher, *Le génocide*, p. 155, admittedly not the most reliable of sources.

178 "'painstaking discipline . . . It is impossible to cover'": Quoted in Gras, p. 126.

"'military promenade'": Turreau to Committee of Public Safety, 27 Nivôse, year II, in SHAT B⁵8.

"Neither a *sans-culotte*": On Turreau, see Gueniffey, p. 265; Six, *Dictionnaire*, vol. II, pp. 517–8.

179 "All means will be used'": Chassin, *La Vendée patriote*, vol. IV, p. 250.

"'to exterminate this rebel race'": Barère in *AP*, vol. LXX, p. 101 (August 1, 1793). See also J.-C. Martin, *La Vendée*, p. 196.

"Antoinette-Charlotte de La Bouëre": La Bouëre, pp. 126–30, quote from p. 130.

180 "'I am in despair'": Chassin, *La Vendée patriote*, vol. IV, p. 257.

"To him, the steady flow": See J.-C. Martin, *La Vendée*, p. 230.

"Officers under General Nicolas Haxo": See memoirs of Dominique Aubertin, in J.-L.-S. Hugo, vol. I, pp. 106–7; J.-C. Martin, *La Vendée*, pp. 244–5.

"'We are going to be bearing iron and fire'": Letter of January 25, 1794, in Joliclerc, p. 155.

"'Wherever we go'": Quoted in Secher, *Le génocide*, p. 164.

hose to 'write' his novel": S. Englund, p. 426.

What a novel my life has been!'": Napoleon, in Las Cases, vol. I, pp. 859, 403.

he gave her a new name": Napoleon to Désirée Clary, September 10, 1794, CGN, vol. I, p. 201 (no. 244).

to whom my heart entirely belongs'": Napoleon to Joseph Bonaparte, June 24, 95, CGN, vol. I, p. 233 (no. 308).

Sweet and incomparable Joséphine'": Napoleon to Joséphine, December 1795, GN, vol. I, p. 285 (no. 387);

Joséphine! Joséphine!'": Napoleon to Joséphine, March 30, 1796, CGN, vol. I, 311 (no. 439).

kiss lower'": Napoleon to Joséphine, April 7, 1796, CGN, vol. I, p. 327 (no. 7), underlining in original.

our little white breast'": Napoleon to Joséphine, November 21, 1796, CGN, l. I, p. 672 (no. 1068). The editors of the CGN note that the original of the cond of these letters has not been found and that the tone and vocabulary dif-from that of other letters. Nonetheless, they accept it as authentic.

Cruel one'": Napoleon to Joséphine, June 8, 1796, CGN, vol. I, p. 436 (no. 662).

our letters'": Napoleon to Joséphine, October 17, 1796, CGN, vol. I, p. 638 . 1005).

no longer love you'": Napoleon to Joséphine, November 23, 1796, CGN, vol. 675 (no. 1074).

acemaker of this vast universe'": Époques, p. 9.

ose inscription called": Courrier de l'armée d'Italie, no. 1, July 20, 1797, p. 3.

distinguished artists and scholars": Napoleon to Oriani, May 24, 1796, N, vol. I, p. 415 (no. 627).

ostentatiously joined": See Jourdan, Napoléon, p. 81.

was only on the evening of Lodi'": Quoted in Dwyer, "Napoleon Bonaparte ero," p. 382. This remark was made to Montholon. Similar remarks to other bers of the Saint-Helena ménage are quoted in ibid. (to Gourgaud); Boy-Brown, p. 323 (to Bertrand); and Tulard, Napoléon, p. 81 (to uncertain).

we only consulted'": "Réfléxions sur la paix et la guerre, par Leussère, cteur de la Sentinelle et ci-devant collaborateur de l'Orateur Plébéien," rier de l'armée d'Italie, no. 47, October 21, 1797, p. 202.

July 1, 1798": On the Egyptian expedition, see Laurens; Lassius; and mpson, Napoleon, pp. 107–33.

usual, grueling demands": See François-Etienne Damas to Jean-Baptiste r, Boulac, July 27, 1798, in Copies of Original Letters, p. 74.

them die of thirst'": Pierre-François Boyer to his parents, Cairo, July saw them die of thirst'": Pierre-François Boyer to his parents, Cairo, July 98, in ibid., pp. 143–4. The letter is signed "Boyer" and can only be the Pi-rançois Boyer who served on the staff of Napoleon's army.

rançois Boyer look down'": "Allocution avant la bataille des pyra-liers, forty centuries look down'": "Allocution avant la bataille des pyra-, July 21, 1798, in CN, vol. IV, p. 340 (no. 2816).

one likes armed missionaries'": Maximilien Robespierre, in the Jacobin January 2, 1792 in Robespierre, Discours.

stitute of Egypt": See Memoirs Relative to Egypt.

renchmen are no longer'": Quoted in Thompson, Napoleon, p. 120. Em-added.

"'Destroy the watermills'": Pardou (or Pardon — handwriting is unclear) to a friend, February 24, 1794, SHAT B⁵8.

181 "'Everywhere the eye fell'": Declaration of Beaudesson, October 6, 1794, in Chassin, La Vendée patriote, vol. IV, pp. 261–2.

"hundreds of pages of them": Mostly in vol. IV of La Vendée patriote, especially pp. 152–498.

"Historians loyal to the memory": See, for instance, the many works of Elie Fournier, Alain Gérard, Simone Loidreau, and, of course, Reynald Secher.

"They indiscriminately mingle": In Reynald Secher's work, one finds allegations that General Grignon's deputy François-Pierre-Joseph Amey burned women and children alive in bread ovens and that when his troops ran out of rebels to burn, they turned to "patriots"; that women were hung naked from trees by their feet and cut in two with swords; that pregnant women were crushed in wine presses until their bellies burst; that officers wore breeches made of tanned human skin. See Secher, Le génocide, especially pp. 163–73.

"The atrocities committed": On Carrier in Nantes, see especially Dugast-Matifeux; Lallié; J.-C. Martin, La Vendée, pp. 213–25.

"'shooting them takes too long'": Quoted in Secher, Le génocide, p. 152.

"many euphemisms": Lallié, pp. 118, 162–3.

"Carrier sadistically reported": Lallié, p. 84. "General Robert reported": Quoted in Petitfrère, La Vendée, p. 60. "'What a revolutionary torrent'": Quoted in Lallié, p. 126.

182 "It is reliably estimated": See Godechot, The Counter-Revolution, p. 224.

"'It is out of a principle of humanity'": Quoted in Lallié, p. 149.

183 "'What is the cause'": Turreau, p. 198n.

"and gaining notoriety": "Trivia."

"Twenty years later": See the biographical notice in Six, Dictionnaire, vol. II, pp. 517–8.

184 "a dynamic of radicalization": See Furet, Penser la Révolution française.

"'A point worth noting'": J.-L.-S. Hugo, vol. II, p. 263.

185 "'This War of the Ignorant'": V. Hugo, part III, book I, chp. I.

6. THE LURE OF THE EAGLE

186 "'Ambition, like all disordered passions'": N. Bonaparte, Œuvres, vol. II, p. 227.

"During his fifty-one years": On Napoleon's brushes with death, see Chandler, "Napoleon and Death."

"Paoli probably sent": S. Englund, Napoleon, p. 53. Englund's biography is by far the best available in English. See also, as reference, Tulard, Napoléon, ou le mythe du sauveur; Schom.

"Despite the tales": See, for instance, Bourrienne, vol. I, pp. 4–5; Some Account of . . . Buonaparte, p. 24.

187 "'he toyed with enrolling'": See S. Englund, p. 77.

"He did dream": Most recently on this subject, see Dwyer, "From Corsican Na-tionalist."

"He therefore devoted": See the first two volumes of N. Bonaparte, Œuvres; N. Bonaparte, Napoléon inconnu.

187 "'that feeds on blood'": "Discours sur la question proposée par l'académie de Lyon," in N. Bonaparte, *Œuvres,* vol. II, p. 227.

"In the battle": Chandler, *Campaigns,* p. 27. "everything I have learned since'": G. M. Trevelyan, quoted in Johnson, p. 20.

"'General, I was born'": Bonaparte to Pasquale Paoli, June 12, 1789, in *CGN,* vol. I, p. 76 (no. 29).

188 "He rhapsodized in print": Napoleon to Matteo Buttafuoco, January 23, 1791, in *CGN,* vol. I, p. 96 (no. 44). "'that's one fat aristocrat less'": Napoleon, quoted in S. Englund, p. 43.

"He set up a Revolutionary club": See Lyons, *Napoleon,* p. 10.

"'I would add to the list of patriots'": Quoted in S. Englund, p. 67.

"at a crucial moment": On Arcola, see Connolly.

189 "'known only by the Parisians'": Quoted in Boycott-Brown, p. 131.

"'There are no men'": Lucien Bonaparte to Joseph Bonaparte, 24 June 1792, in N. Bonaparte, *Napoléon inconnu,* vol. II, p. 397.

190 "he could still express admiration for Robespierre": See S. Englund, pp. 68–9.

191 "Recent scholarship": See notably Jainchill; Jourdan, *La Révolution;* Livesey; Schechter; Woloch, *The New Regime.*

192 "By the fall of 1799": See H. Brown, "Domestic State Violence," pp. 612–3.

"'I need a sword'": Quoted in S. Englund, p. 157.

193 "'We are not living'": Lieutenant Michel, cited in Bertaud, *La Révoution armée,* p. 284.

"four-fifths of its men": Boycott-Brown, p. 126.

"'Why did we fight?'": Soldier cited in Bertaud, *La Révolution armée,* p. 310.

194 "He established a virtual court": Dwyer, "Napoleon Bonaparte as Hero," pp. 390–2; Miot de Melito, pp. 92–4.

195 "Numerous descriptions": See, for instance, Miot de Melito, p. 51; François Vigo-Roussillon, quoted in Boycott-Brown, p. 232; Paul-Charles Thiébault, quoted in Jourdan, *Napoléon,* p. 62; Laure-Adélaïde, duchesse d'Abrantès, quoted in Tulard, *Napoléon,* pp. 69–70.

"'I can still see him'": Duchesse d'Abrantès, quoted in Tulard, *Napoléon,* p. 69.

"taking charge of matters": See Ordre du jour, 23 Fructidor V, in *CN,* vol. I, p. 373 (no. 2175); Napoleon to Minister of the Interior, 18 Prairial V, in *CN,* vol. III, p. 128 (no. 1873). See also Hazareesingh, "Force for Glory."

"Well before 1789": For a concise description of Napoleon's relationship to the "Gribeauval system," see H. Parker.

196 "the tactics that the French army embraced": On Napoleon's tactics, see Chandler, *Campaigns,* especially pp. 131–201; Connolly, *Blundering to Glory;* Rothenberg, *The Art of Warfare,* especially pp. 95–164.

"'The Emperor has discovered'": Quoted in Chandler, *Campaigns,* p. 148.

"On taking command": See Boycott-Brown, pp. 144–5; Chandler, *Campaigns,* pp. 53–7.

"Much of his correspondence": See Napoleon's letters of 8–10 Germinal, year IV, in *CGN,* vol. I, pp. 302–12 (nos. 423–41).

"'I have given out meat'": Napoleon to Joséphine, Nice, 10 Germinal, year IV, in *CGN,* vol. I, p. 311 (no. 439).

197 "He drew up a list": Napoleon to General Vign[…] VI, in *CGN,* vol. I, pp. 1283–89; *Le courrier de l'a[…]* 1797), p. 161.

"The men in question": The episode is recounted[…] Bourgin and Godechot, p. 2.

"This is not the way'": Napoleon to Lucien Bo[…] I, p. 109 (no. 61).

"'I can't express'": Quoted in Roger, p. 384.

198 "'Soldiers, the fatherland'": "Proclamation à l'[…] vol. I, p. 219 (no. 234).

"'Soldiers, you have rushed'": "A ses frères d'arm[…] pp. 368–9 (no. 461).

"Soldiers, Europe'": "Aux soldats de terre et d[…] rannée," May 10, 1798, in *CN,* vol. IV, p. 128 ([…]

"the world's first 'media general'": The esse[…] Hanley; Jourdan, *Napoléon.*

"he founded newspapers": *Le courrier de l'arm[…]* with 248 issues appearing between July 1797 a[…] thousand pages. The less successful *La Franc[…]* lished in Milan, appeared 18 times between[…] Daline; Hanley, chp. III; Jourdan, *Napoléon[…]* p. 84.

199 "'Today, glory has written'": *Courrier de l'a[…]* 1797, p. 206.

"*Journal of Bonaparte*": *Journal de Bonaparte […]* Paris for forty issues in February and March[…] "Popular engravings . . . popular biograph[…] aparte as Hero," p. 388; Hanley, ch. VI; Tul[…] "Hero, dear to peace'": By the poet Lebrun[…] chy and the Revolution. Quoted in Jourdan[…]

200 "Gros, in particular, immortalized the mor[…] Connolly; Prendergast, pp. 145–9; Vovelle,[…]

201 "his wife had to sit and grasp": See Prender[…] "In their reports": See Aulard, *Paris penda[…]* p. 749 (February 14, 1797); vol. IV, p. 75 (A[…] 1797).

202 "The elites of eighteenth-century France":[…] 39; Bonnet, *Naissance du Panthéon;* Jourda[…] "new perceptions of the individual": On d[…] riod, see Goldstein, and Wahrman, a boo[…] "Napoleon's own literary tastes": On thi[…] pp. 3–4; Tieghem, vol. II, pp. 3–13; Nap[…] his pamplets had an "Ossianic" accent; S[…] "Later in his career": Bourrienne, vol. I, [...]

203 "the genre also seemed to provide": See t[…] "a commonplace of cultural history": Da[…] 56.

"'Kings bow their proud heads'": "Ode arabe sur la Conquête de l'Egypte" in *Décade egyptienne,* vol. I (1798), p. 86.

210 "200,000 men": Blanning, *French Revolutionary Wars,* p. 231.

"the dark summer of 1799": Ibid., pp. 230–56.

211 "his youthful literary diet": See the reading notes in N. Bonaparte, *Œuvres,* vol. I, passim.

212 "'Everything wears out here'": Quoted in Bourrienne, vol. I, p. 125.

"'In Egypt, I found myself'": Quoted in Chandler, *Campaigns,* p. 248.

"In response": Laurens, p. 149–51. "'the hour of vengeance'": François, *From Valmy to Waterloo,* p. 73.

"'Citizen general'": Napoleon to Berthier, Cairo, 2 Brumaire, year VII, *CN,* vol. V, p. 115 (no. 3527).

213 "Napoleon ordered": Napoleon to Berthier, Jaffa, 19 Ventôse, year VII, *CN,* vol. V, p. 451 (no. 4013). See also R. Wilson's 1803 *History of the British Expedition to Egypt,* quoted in Tulard, *L'Anti-Napoléon,* p. 55.

"Bourrienne later constructed": Bourrienne, *Memoirs,* vol. I, pp. 194–7.

"'precautions be taken'": Napoleon to Berthier, Cairo, 2 Brumaire, year VII, *CN,* vol. V, p. 451 (no. 4013).

"what had happened in northern Italy": On the revolt, see Lumbroso; Malacrida.

"'A vast conspiracy'": Napoleon to Berthier, Milan, 6 Prairial, year IV, *CGN,* vol. I, p. 416 (no. 629).

"'will be treated as rebels'": "Proclamation aux Habitants de la Lombardie," 6 prairial, year IV, in *CN,* vol. I, p. 394 (no. 493).

"and held off": Napoleon to the Directory, 13 Prairial, year IV, in *CGN,* vol. I, pp. 421–2 (no. 639).

214 "he contented himself": See Lumbroso, pp. 23–6.

"In and around": See, Rothenberg *The Art of Warfare,* p. 120; Sciout, pp. 2761–5; Suratteau, "Occupation, occupants et occupés."

"the massive revolts of 1799": For a good summary, see Blanning, *The French Revolutionary Wars,* especially pp. 238–48.

"In 1790": On the Haitian Revolution, see Dubois; Dubois and Garrigus. Figures from Dubois and Garrigus, p. 13.

"'Here is my opinion'": quoted in Auguste and Auguste, p. 236. This book remains the authoritative source on the Leclerc Expedition and the atrocities committed during it.

"Although Haiti's death toll": For a careful examination of the available figures, see ibid., pp. 313–6.

215 "'honor, glory and riches'": The supposed proclamation was made in Nice on March 27, 1796. It is in *CN,* vol. I, p. 118 (no. 91), but is taken from Napoleon's reminiscences on Saint Helena.

"the Revolutionary forces repeated": Godechot's *La grande nation* remains the most complete guide to this subject but is now supplemented and updated by Belissa, *Repenser.*

216 "'in the name of our holy religion . . . these miserable reptiles'": Quoted in Zaghi, pp. 175, 180.

217   "'What is the army?'" and "'It is France'": Quoted in Lyons, *France under the Directory,* p. 146.

    "they began to identify": See Bertaud, *La Révolution armée,* pp. 322–43.

    "'Do once more'": Proclamation of 21 Brumaire, year V, in *CN,* vol. II, p. 136 (no. 1180).

218   "'You see before you'": "A l'armée," 26 Messidor, year V, in *CN,* vol. III, p. 239–240 (no. 2010).

    "'General, you have saved France'": *Courrier de l'armée d'Italie,* no. 1 (July 20, 1797), p. 4.

    "'The great deluge . . . the Republic exists'": Quoted in Kruse, pp. 317, 312.

    "in the words of historian Jean-Paul Bertaud": Bertaud, *La Révolution armée,* p. 341.

219   "'I ought to overthrow them'": Bourrienne, vol. I, p. 134.

    "'a pack of lawyers'": Miot de Mélito, p. 94.

    "Napoleon fought like Alexander": *Chronique de Paris, ci-devant Courier Républicain,* no. 5, 3 Germinal year V, p. 3.

    "'Is the Rubicon already crossed?'": *Messager du soir,* quoted in Dwyer, "Napoleon Bonaparte as Hero," p. 389.

    "the appearance of modern militarism": On militarism, see introduction to Jansen, pp. 9–23. My perspective is closer to this than to older studies, such as Finer; Vagts.

    "'When a people becomes'": Quoted in Bertaud, *La Révolution armée,* p. 341.

    "'our rarely interrupted wars'": Kruse, p. 329.

220   "A cold, precise man": See Sewell, especially pp. 153–4. On Sieyès, see also Bredin.

    "'There is your man'": Quoted in Crook, p. 51.

    "police spies reported": See Gotteri.

    "When he came to Lyons . . . 'On every face'": Dwyer, "Napoleon Bonaparte as Hero," pp. 393–5, quote from p. 394.

221   "'What have you done'": Quoted in S. Englund, p. 162.

    "'Don't forget, I walk with the God'": Quoted in ibid., p. 164. See also Chandler, "Napoleon and Death."

    "'Citizens, you are dissolved'": Quoted in Benoît and Chevallier, p. 79.

7. DAYS OF GLORY

223   "'Today . . . no government'": Constant, p. 1004.

    "'I wanted to rule the world'": Napoleon Bonaparte, quoted in Herold, p. 276.

    "The day is turning": On Marengo, see Benoît and Chevallier; Chandler, *Campaigns,* pp. 286–98.

    "As France's First Consul": Benoît and Chevallier, p. 13; *Bataille de Marengo,* p. 139.

    "'For God's sake'": Quoted in S. Englund, p. 174.

224   "the French musket barrels": See the account of the battle in Coignet, pp. 74–9.

    "with Melas already accepting": General Danican in *Bataille de Marengo,* p. 139.

    "Other generals are waiting": See Miot de Mélito, pp. 173–4.

    "'The battle is completely lost'": Quoted by Bourrienne, vol. II, p. 13.

225   "His corpse will lie": Benoît and Chevalier, p. 137.
       "one last chance": See particularly the description by Marmont, vol. II, p. 134.
       "10,000 men": Benoît and Chevalier, p. 122.
       "The Prussian military theorist": Bülow, p. 538.
       "The usual battalion": See, for instance, Boisson de Quency; Desorgues; and
       Lamontagne.
226   "Kellermann's brilliantly timed charge will be played down": Notably in the ac-
       count by Napoleon's chief of staff: Berthier, p. 48.
227   "'far more than Brumaire . . . never to be beaten'": Furet, *Revolutionary France,*
       p. 218.
228   "'except for Washington'": Quoted in S. Englund, p. 217. On the plebiscites, see
       Woloch, *Napoleon and His Collaborators,* pp. 94–6.
       "'I am the French Revolution'": Quoted in S. Englund, p. 227.
       "restoring Roman Catholicism": See Boudon, *Napoléon et les cultes.*
       "'to push back art'": Quoted in Boime, p. 15.
       "with an act": S. Englund, p. 229.
       "'What other glory'": In Lentz and Clot, p. 83.
       "But the Consulate": See Lentz, "Was the Napoleonic Regime?"
229   "'I do not govern'": Quoted in Bluche, p. 26.
       "'lightning bolts'": Boisson de Quency, p. 5.
       "'the nations of the south'": Quoted in Belissa, *Repenser,* pp. 173–4.
230   "'Now that, in our day'": Tribune Adet, May 19, 1802, in *AP,* second series, vol.
       III, p. 729.
       "This was not the utopian hope": But see Jourdan, "Napoléon et la paix uni-
       verselle."
231   "'When the human soul'": Maistre, *Considérations sur la France,* p. 48.
       "'law of raw nature . . . through war'": Gentz, pp. 484–5.
       "'angel of peace'": See, for instance, the pamphlet *Cri de la religion,* title page.
       "some, such as Paul Schroeder": See Schroeder, *Transformation,* pp. 229–30;
       Schroeder, "Napoleon's Foreign Policy: A Criminal Enterprise"; also Johnson.
       For a different view, see Lentz, *Nouvelle histoire.*
232   "'I wanted to rule the world'": Quoted in Herold, p. 276.
       "'His hold upon France'" and "'Can he afford'": Pitt, p. 329.
233   "'If my voice has any influence'" "'a mere appendix'": both quoted in Herold,
       p. 191. Napoleon, like most of the French at the time, routinely conflated Eng-
       land and Britain.
       "'A First Consul is not like kings'": Napoleon, quoted in Tulard, *Napoléon,*
       p. 180. Ten years later, he said much the same thing to Metternich. See Metter-
       nich, vol. I, p. 148.
       "'this peace had not yet received'": Quoted in Esdaile, *The Wars of Napoleon,*
       p. 13. See also Dwyer, "Napoleon and the Drive for Glory."
       "he had demanded that the British": See Tombs and Tombs, p. 242.
234   "to recycle the bilious Revolutionary writings": See particularly Barère's anti-
       British newspaper *Mémorial anti-britannique, journal historique et politique* (1803–4).
       "Typically, he worked": On Napoleon's work habits, see Chandler, *Campaigns,*
       pp. 374–6, 462. "'What a pity'": Talleyrand, quoted in S. Englund, *Napoleon,*
       p. 279.

234 "over 2,500 gunboats": Tombs and Tombs, p. 245.
235 "'more than a crime'": Quoted in Gates, p. 17.
     "Napoleon marched the army": See Rothenberg, *The Art of War,* p. 149.
     "Napoleon caught up": On the Austerlitz campaign, see Chandler, *Campaigns,*
     pp. 381–439; Gates, pp. 21–34. "'we saw thousands of Russians'": Marbot, *Memoirs,* vol. I, p. 200.
237 "some 60 percent": Sheehan, p. 251.
     "on its plangent note": Ibid., p. 235.
     "'The connecting bonds'": Hegel, quoted in ibid., p. 350. "'the world-soul'":
     Hegel to Niethammer, October 13, 1806, in Hegel, vol. I, p. 120.
238 "'it seemed literally true'": Craig, p. 26.
     "In late August": On the War of the Fourth Coalition, see Chandler, *Campaigns,*
     pp. 442–590.
239 "no less than 96 percent": Ibid., pp. 499–502.
     "'He stopped . . . He remained there'": Quoted in ibid., p. 499.
     "'more completely than any army'": Clausewitz, *On War,* pp. 153–4.
240 "It lost fully half its territory": See Hagemann, *"Mannlicher Muth,"* pp. 18–22.
     "Another year!'": Wordsworth.
     "This product": See Peter Paret, "The Genesis of *On War."*
241 "'Formerly . . . war was waged'": Clausewitz, "Bekenntnisdenkschrift," pp. 749–50.
242 "A natural authoritarian": On the internal repression, see Bergeron.
     "neglected to supply with chaplains": See Broers, *Europe Under Napoleon,* p. 37.
243 "'I must make all the peoples of Europe'": Quoted in Zamoyski, p. 9. On the
     process of European integration, see Connelly, *Napoleon's Satellite Kingdoms;* Woolf.
     "In his last years": Las Cases, vol. I, p. 1075 and vol. II, p. 345.
     "For his principal political support": This is the perspective, notably, of
     Bergeron; Soboul, *Le premier empire,* and Tulard, *Napoléon.*
     "He sought insistently": See Jourdan, *Napoléon.*
     "He cast every campaign": See notably Napoleon to the French Senate, Berlin,
     November 21, 1806, *CN,* vol. XIII, pp. 679–81 (no. 11281).
     "The French military was still": See Blaufarb, pp. 164–93. See also Hughes,
     which I became aware of too late to consult fully.
     "some of Napoleon's marshals grumbled": Ségur, p. xii.
244 "the stereotypical peasant draftees": See Chandler, *Campaigns,* pp. 333–4; Connelly, *Blundering to Glory,* pp. 73–4.
     "fully 59 percent": See Bertaud, "Napoleon's Officers," pp. 97–9.
     "'If this honor'": Napoleon, quoted on the Legion of Honor Web site: http://
     www. legiondhonneur.fr/shared/fr/histoire/fhisto.html, consulted June 26, 2006.
     "no less than 97 percent": Forrest, "Military Culture," p. 52.
     "In official state ceremonies": Bertaud, "Napoleon's Officers," p. 97. See also
     Godechot, *Institutions,* p. 699.
     "the army became": Godechot, *Institutions,* p. 690. "Public festivals": Forrest,
     "Military Culture," p. 56. "at least 143 in France": Bertaud, "Théâtre," p. 177.
     "In the forty-five new . . . *lycées"*: Godechot, *Institutions,* p. 739.
     "'fatigue, danger . . . brothers' blood'": Crouzet, pp. 3, 6, 8, 11.
245 "'constituted upon a military basis'": Quoted in Howard, *War in European History,* p. 82.

"80,000 . . . more than six times that figure": Boudon, *Histoire du Consulat et de l'Empire,* p. 266; Connelly, *Blundering,* p. 74.

"Historians of the subject": See particularly Forrest, *Conscripts and Deserters;* Woloch, *The New Regime,* pp. 363–409.

"Osterlique, Osterlis": Fairon and Heuse, pp. 86, 145.

"a secret overland route": Nicolas-Joseph Halleux to his father, Lissa (Poland), April 24, 1812, in ibid., p. 271.

"'In giving this terrible news'": Chrétien-Henri, baron Schoeffer, to the sous-préfet of Périgny, in ibid., p. 287.

246   "a grandiose building program": On this subject, see Jacobson. On the reburial of Turenne, see Lindsay. See also Holtman, pp. 163–4.

247   "'Saint Napoleon'": On the holiday, see Hazareesingh, *The Saint-Napoleon.*

"his soldiers avidly repeated the stories": For instance, Coignet, p. 115; a conscript from Theux, Lémon, 12 Thermidor year VIII, in Fairon and Heuse, p. 82; See also Napoleon, quoted in Lynn, "Toward an Army of Honor," p. 172.

"In conversation in 1810": Napoleon, in Herold, p. 209; "'Bah! Gentlemen, remember'": Caulaincourt, p. 77.

"'makes the moment of death'": Wilson-Smith, p. 176. On Girodet, see Grigsby.

248   "'military glory . . . no government would dare'": Constant, pp. 1024, 1004.

"In some ages of history . . . anachronism": Ibid., pp. 991, 993, 995.

249   "France had only to abjure": Ibid., p. 1025.

"it proved just as difficult": In this analysis, I am indebted to Guiomar.

251   "At Marengo": Benoît and Chevalier, p. 117. "at Austerlitz": Chandler, *Campaigns,* p. 410. "at Wagram": Gates, pp. 139, 207. "at Leipzig": Rothenberg, *Art of Warfare,* p. 81; Hagemann, *"Mannlicher Muth,"* p. 36.

"The front along which": Chandler, *Campaigns,* pp. 151–2.

"Chateaubriand wrote eloquently": Chateaubriand, pp. 206–7.

"'I grew up on the battlefield'": Metternich, vol. I, pp. 151–2. Metternich quoted the phrase as "un homme comme moi se soucie peu de la vie d'un million d'hommes," adding in a note: "Je n'ose pas répéter ici l'expression bien plus crue dont se servit Napoléon." That expression was obviously "un homme comme moi se fout de la vie d'un million d'hommes."

"'One has only a certain time'": Quoted in Chandler, *Campaigns,* p. 733.

252   "At the critical battle": See Zamoyski, p. 257.

"'revolution from above'": Quoted in Levinger, p. 263.

"Austria offered the clearest case": On this subject, see Rothenberg, *Napoleon's Great Adversaries,* pp. 118–9; Rothenberg, *The Art of War,* p. 242.

"A far more important reform movement": On this subject, see Dwyer, "Prussia during the French Revolutionary and Napoleonic Wars"; Gray; Sheehan, pp. 291–310.

253   "Friedrich Meinecke concluded": Meinecke, p. 93.

"In a sign of the desire": Hagemann, *"Mannlicher Muth,"* pp. 81–3.

"'Nation? That sounds *Jakobinisch*'": Quoted in S. Englund, p. 402.

"The British army nonetheless": Colley, *Britons,* p. 287. See also Cookson; Muir, *Britain and the Defeat of Napoleon.*

"Part-time and volunteer units . . . to follow the French example": Colley, *Britons,* pp. 293, 289, 318, quote from p. 289.

254 "Even more striking": On Beresford in Portugal, see Oman, vol. III, pp. 171–87 and vol. V, p. 149; Broers, *Europe Under Napoleon,* p. 217; Glover, "'A Particular Service.'"

"'My great object'": Quoted in Gates, p. 4.

"when the occasion demanded it": See A. Roberts, pp. 41–2.

"also remained partly loyal": See Rothenberg, *Napoleon's Great Adversaries,* especially pp. 106–8.

"Russia's Alexander Suvorov": See Longworth. "'I never saw anything so stark mad'": Quoted in ibid., p. 291.

255 "'For Satan has come'": Arndt, "Lied der Rache" (1811) in *Gedichte.*

256 "the Holy Synod": Zamoyski, p. 27.

"Even the French bulletins": S. England, p. 291. "'lying like a bulletin'": Boudon, "Un outil"; Cabanis, p. 271.

"One German newspaper": Tulard, *Napoleon,* p. 355.

"'an immense dream'": Chateaubriand, p. 93.

"'imperial overstretch'": The phrase is Paul M. Kennedy's. See especially pp. 126–39.

257 "the tsar insisted": Zamoyski, p. 73.

"would swell to over 900,000": Ibid., p. 116.

"'I do not fear that long road'": Napoleon, as related by Narbonne, in Herold, p. 199. On Napoleon's thoughts of India, see also Guiomar, p. 289; Zamoyski, p. 33.

"The emperor had read": Ségur, p. 20.

"'As they were about to go down'": Ibid., p. 9.

"'Almost in the center of this sky'": Tolstoy, p. 711.

258 "he counted 450,000 . . . In the next six months": See Chandler, *Campaigns,* pp. 852–53; Connelly, *Blundering,* p. 159.

"'often still living'": J. Walter pp. 41, 43.

259 "'I am looking forward to getting killed'": Fairon and Heuse, p. 274, quoted in Zamoyski, p. 144.

"'the most elementary grasp'": Quoted in ibid., p. 167.

"'We passed through the smoking ruins'": Ségur, p. 33.

"opening the city but losing 28,000": Zamoyski, p. 288.

"the clocks in the Kremlin": Quoted by Caulaincourt, p. 112.

"'It was the spectacle'": Napoleon, as quoted (in English) by O'Meara, in Herold, p. 205.

260 "'Although we are less acclimatized'": Caulaincourt, p. 155.

"'battered helmets'": Ségur, p. 159.

"'We no longer saw'": Chevalier, p. 221.

"'There was no longer any discipline'": Coignet, p. 238.

261 "Some ate raw flesh": Zamoyski, p. 448. "Others . . . made a foul bread dough": Ibid., p. 401. "the living would wake amid a field": Chevalier, p. 222.

"On November 23": Zamoyski, pp. 458–80, gives a gripping, thorough, and impartial account of the episode.

"'Assuming that Napoleon's object'": Tolstoy, p. 1185.

"According to . . . David Chandler": Chandler, *Campaigns,* p. 853.

262   "'The crusts on my hands'": J. Walter, p. 100.

"He still had in place": Chandler, *Campaigns,* pp. 866–8.

8. WAR'S RED ALTAR

263   "'Millions to fight'": Percy Bysshe Shelley, "Poetical Essay," quoted in Woudhuysen, p. 12.

"Shall I die in prose?": Theodor Körner, "Mißmut," in Körner, *Leier und Schwert.*

"black Haitians": See Elting, pp. 274–5.

264   "In late August": See Finley, p. 77; J.-L.-S. Hugo, vol. I, p. 126 (NB: Page numbers in Hugo, vol. I, refer to second pagination). On the campaign, see also Esdaile, "Patriots."

"Throughout September": See Gachot, pp. 220–1; J.-L.-S. Hugo, vol. I, pp. 125–8.

"Fra Diavolo repeatedly slipped": Finley, p. 77; J.-L.-S. Hugo, vol. I, pp. 139–47.

"Hugo may well have cast his thoughts": J.-L.-S. Hugo, vol. I, pp. 10–61; Robb, pp. 19–20.

"It was only through": Finley, p. 78.

265   "'He would wrinkle'": Quoted in Robb, p. 20.

"'absolute enmity'": Schmitt, *Theorie des Partisanen,* p. 55.

266   "a new word": see Artola, "Guerra."

267   "In the Kingdom of Italy": See Grab, "State Power," p. 43.

"In Naples, despite the simmering rebellions": Talleyrand, vol. II, p. 49.

269   "'annexation became a skilled art'": Woolf, pp. 50, 69.

"In 1809 . . . 150 by the end of 1809": See Grab, "State Power," pp. 58–61; Broers, *Napoleonic Empire,* especially pp. 9, 108.

"'Include in your calculations'": Napoleon to Joseph, Paris, March 2, 1806, in *CN,* vol. XII, p. 147 (no. 9911).

270   "and finally moved to the Veneto": Broers, *Napoleonic Empire,* p. 108.

"Napoleon declared": "Proclamation à l'armée," Schönbrunn, December 27, 1805, in *CN,* vol. XI, p. 620 (no. 9625).

271   "Joseph Bonaparte": On Joseph, see Connelly, *The Gentle Bonaparte;* Ross.

"his 'tyranny' and 'insatiable ambition'": Miot de Melito, p. 288.

"On March 22, in Soveria": See Finley, pp. 26–7.

"General Reynier, in the south . . . under colorful, bandit-chieftain nicknames": Desvernois, pp. 103–4, 108–9; Finley, pp. 123–4; Gachot, p. 139.

"The British made matters worse": See Finley, pp. 36–48.

"In Acri": Ibid., pp. 49–52.

"'We must hammer the enemies'": Quoted in Mozzillo, vol. I, pp. 349–50. Mozzillo notes that the contemporary chronicler may well have put words in the insurgent's mouth.

272   "Desvernois . . . claimed": Desvernois, p. 109.

"'mafia . . . a lawless banditti'": Quoted in Esdaile, "Patriots," p. 9.

"Both the insurgents and Italians": See Finley, p. 73.

"'the most monstrous of wars'": Quoted in ibid., p. x.

272　"Masséna finally moved . . . The French also struggled": Ibid., pp. 64, 69.
　　　"'All these measures'": Miot de Mélito, p. 410.

273　"'here is the ration'": As recounted by Chevalier, p. 74.
　　　"'Our enraged soldiers'": Ibid.
　　　"Masséna insisted": André Masséna to Joseph Bonaparte, in J. Bonaparte, vol.
　　　III, p. 115. "'this terrible example'": Joseph Bonaparte to Napoleon, in ibid., vol.
　　　III, p. 124.
　　　"734 bodies . . . 3,000": See Finley, pp. 65–6; Mozillo, p. 368 foldout.
　　　"he hanged the fifty . . . the French imprisoned": Finley, p. 67.

274　"184 insurgents . . . 'It was important to maintain'": Desvernois, pp. 103–4, 108.
　　　"Charles-Antoine Manhès": See Finley, pp. 121–9.
　　　"the hussar officer Denis Davidov": See Zamoyski, pp. 327–9.

275　"'Declare that I will put the country to fire'": Napoleon to Marshal Lefebvre,
　　　July 30, 1809, in N. Bonaparte, *Lettre inédites,* vol. I, pp. 337–8. On the Tyrolean
　　　revolt, see Eyck.
　　　"But it was Spain": For a general history of Spain in this period, the most com-
　　　prehensive account remains Lovett, *Napoleon.* For military affairs, however, and
　　　particularly the guerrilla war, Lovett has been superceded by Esdaile, *The Penin-
　　　sular War,* and Esdaile, *Fighting Napoleon.* A fundamental reference is Arteche y
　　　Moro.

276　"Yet Napoleon did not proceed": See Connelly, *The Gentle Bonaparte,* p. 87.
　　　"a strength of nearly 120,000": Broers, *Europe under Napoleon,* p. 151.
　　　"Resorting to ruses": Tone, p. 43–4.
　　　"Marshal Murat made a flamboyant entrance": Connelly, *The Gentle Bonaparte,*
　　　p. 95. "'Your Majesty is awaited here'": Quoted in Hocquellet, p. 35.

277　"'He is so stupid'": Napoleon to Talleyrand, Bayonne, May 1, 1808, *CN,* vol.
　　　XVII, p. 76 (no. 13815).
　　　"Napoleon boasted . . . Escoiquiz protested": Escoiquiz, p. 131.

278　"To judge from their letters and memoirs": See, for instance, Coignet, p. 165;
　　　Marcel, p. 7 ("dark and wild look"); Schumacher, pp. 28–9; Thiébault, vol. IV,
　　　p. 313.
　　　"'I was leaving a country'": Quoted in Vilar, p. 242.
　　　"According to . . . Heinrich": Brandt, p. 167.
　　　"'O happy gothic, barbarian'": Manuel Freyre de Castrillon, quoted in Hoc-
　　　quellet, p. 107.
　　　"smoking lava flow": See texts quoted by Mesonero Romanos, especially p. 134.
　　　"'What sort of thing is a Frenchman?'" Junta Central (1808), quoted in Tone,
　　　p. 53.

279　"'You are insulting all of heaven'": Quoted in Hocquellet, p. 113.

280　"From 165,000 . . . as many as 180,000": Artola, "Guerra," pp. 33, 41.
　　　"'If we had wanted'": Rocca, p. 225.
　　　"as many as 330 French citizens": Hocquellet, p. 85.
　　　"'The churches were sacked'": Miot de Mélito, p. 459.
　　　"'as conquered provinces'": "Proclamation aux Espagnols," Madrid, December
　　　7, 1808, in *CN,* vol. XVIII, p. 121 (no. 14537).

281　"In the Aragonese city of Saragossa": On the sieges of Saragossa — in Spanish,

Zaragoza — two of the principal primary sources are Alcaide Ibieca and Ayerbe y Lierta. See also Lafoz Rabaza, and Rudorff.

"the supposed miraculous appearance": See Esdaile, *Fighting Napoleon,* p. 63.

"According to legend": See Esdaile, *The Peninsular War,* p. 75.

"1,400 explosive shells": Alcaide Ibieca, vol. I, p. 120.

282   "patients and staff leaped to safety . . . One French witness reported": Rudorff, pp. 141, 155.

"Bombs and grenades . . . A British witness": Alcaide Ibieca, vol. I, p. 199; Lovett, *Napoleon,* p. 258.

"*Guerra y cuchillo,*" "'the Virgin of the Pillar'": Quoted in Rudorff, pp. 148, 166. On the end of the first siege, see the pertinent remarks of Esdaile, *The Peninsular War,* p. 77.

"as many as 42,000 explosive shells": Ayerbe y Lierta, p. 233.

"Palafox again refused": Lovett, *Napoleon,* pp. 273–4.

"'It is necessary to mine them'": Quoted in ibid., p. 275.

"Sometimes, the battle": See Rudorff, pp. 232–3.

"The French baron Marbot": Marbot, vol. I, p. 361.

283   "French troops advanced": Farias, pp. 162–3.

"In monastery basements": Rudorff, p. 236.

"'the livid, fleshless face'": Quoted in ibid., p. 247.

"Of Palafox's 34,000 regular soldiers": See Lovett, *Napoleon,* p. 281.

284   "'Under the arches'": Brandt, p. 64.

"'imagine that the earth'": Benito Pérez Galdós, quoted in Lovett, "The Spanish Guerrillas," p. 81.

"It was considerably more complex": See particularly the analysis of Esdaile, *Fighting Napoleon,* countering the more traditional interpretation of Artola, "Guerra." Two narrower but illuminating monographs on the guerrillas are Alexander and particularly Tone.

"'sweep the same insurgents'": Corporal Edward Shroeder, as reported by his father in Herbert. On this subject, see also the direct comparison drawn by Trocóniz.

285   "the *afrancesados*": See Artola, *Los afrancesados.*

"never numbered more than 40,000": Esdaile, *The Peninsular War,* p. 268. This figure is for the twenty largest *partidas.*

"'We were masters'": E. Blaze, p. 56. "'we had sentries'": Brandt, p. 72. "'fighting on a daily basis'": Jean Marnier, cited in Forrest, "The Ubiquitous Brigand," p. 35.

"On a single day": Moreno Alonso, p. 53. "An invisible army": Miot de Mélito, p. 557.

"In the spring of 1812": Brun de Villeret, pp. 130–1.

286   "'Unfortunately, in this region'": General Honoré-Charles Reille to General Jean-Baptiste Drouet, Pamplona, August 17, 1810, in SHAT C^{8}268.

"colorful nicknames": Esdaile, *The Peninsular War,* p. 266; Rocca, p. 378.

"as Charles Esdaile has stressed": See Esdaile, *Fighting Napoleon.*

"By 1810–11": As claimed by Miot de Mélito, p. 558.

"as time went on": See Tone, pp. 93–7; Esdaile, *Fighting Napoleon,* pp. 38–41. On Mina's force, see Martín, and Mina's own memoirs: Espoz y Mina.

"38,000 French soldiers": Artola, "Guerra," p. 35.

287 "As early as June 1808": On the various Spanish decrees authorizing guerrilla warfare, see Rigoulet-Roze.

"'All the inhabitants'": Quoted in Lovett, *Napoleon,* p. 675, and Artola, "Guerra," p. 17.

"'a novel system of war'": Quoted in Tone, p. 4.

"'All men are soldiers'": Moliner Prada, p. 101.

"a full quarter . . . another 120,000 monks": Boudon, *Napoléon et les cultes,* p. 245.

"preached . . . even promised remission": See Artola, "Guerra," pp. 22–3; Schumacher, p. 38.

"'former Christians'": *Catecismo Civil.*

"fear of 'reforms'": Quoted in Moreno Alonso, pp. 190–1.

"'We have two classes'": Reille to Marshal Jean-Baptiste Bessières, duke of Istria, Pamplona, February 22, 1811, SHAT C^{8}268.

288 "Hundreds had experience . . . Amey . . . Hugo . . . Reille": Six, *Dictionnaire,* s.v. Amey; J.-L.-S. Hugo*;* Broers, "Center and Periphery," p. 68. The assertion of hundreds of officers with experience in Italy and the Vendée is based on soundings in Six, *Dictionnaire.*

"'Hang a dozen individuals'": Napoleon to Joseph Bonaparte, Valladolid, January 11, 1809, *CN,* vol. XVIII, p. 232 (no. 14684).

"'Tell [Reille] to arrest'": Napoleon to Berthier, April 11, 1811, in N. Bonaparte, *Correspondance inédite,* vol. IV, p. 244 (no. 5377).

"the town of Saliente": Alexander, pp. 24–5.

"'Suchet's success was deceptive'": Ibid., p. 232.

"an average of twenty-five French soldiers": Ibid., pp. 235–7.

289 "The reports filed by General Reille": SHAT C^{8}268: "Registre de Correspondance du Gal Reille, du 12 juillet 1810 au 18 Sept 1811"; SHAT C^{8}269: "Registre de Correspondance du Gal Reille, du 21 7bre 1811 au 24 Mars 1812." See also Tone, pp. 121–2.

"Napoleon himself chided Reille": Napoleon to Berthier, April 11, 1811, N. Bonaparte, *Correspondance inédite,* vol. IV, p. 244 (no. 5377).

"On July 8, 1811": Reille to Vice-Constable, July 11, 1811, SHAT C^{8}268.

"Joseph Hugo called it": J.-L.-S. Hugo, vol. II, pp. 119, 262–3.

"'The French could only maintain themselves'": Rocca, p. 144.

"Both officers explained": J.-L.-S. Hugo, vol. II, p. 263, Rocca, p. 5.

"*both* General Reille and . . . Espoz y Mina": Reille to Berthier, Pamplona, October 13, 1810, SHAT C^{8}268; Tone, p. 129.

290 "'One might fill volumes'": Blaze, pp. 58–9.

"recorded gruesome stories": Ibid., p. 58.

"Belgian soldiers": Ferdinand Chantraine, Madrid, November 3, 1810, in Fairon and Heuse, p. 182.

"a ghastly reputation for torture": Thiébault, vol. IV, p. 404.

"hundreds of accounts": On the Spanish side, see particularly Martín, vol. II, pp. 69–111.

"Was the French general René sawn in two?": François, *From Valmy to Waterloo,* p. 183; Schumacher, quoted by Connelly, *The Gentle Bonaparte,* p. 111.

"one story resembles": Holzing, pp. 93–8.

"'the filthy and contagious clouds'": *Henry V,* III:3.

291 "Porto da Mos": Esdaile, *The Peninsular War,* p. 330.

"'Every morning at dawn'": Schaumann, pp. 290–1.

"One French soldier in Iberia": Quoted in Farias, p. 163.

292 "'The Spanish war: death for soldiers'": Quoted in Lovett, "The Spanish Guerrillas," p. 86.

293 "in the mess of a British Hussar regiment": Glover, *Legacy of Glory,* illustration opposite p. 165.

294 "'With a bloody heart'": Quoted in Weber, *Lyrik,* p. 152. See also Paret, *Yorck.*

"For the whole world'": Kleist, *Die Hermannsschlacht,* pp. 187–8.

"'What is the German's Fatherland?'": Arndt, "Des Deutschen Vaterland," in *Gedichte.*

295 "practically became a national anthem": See Weber, *Lyrik,* p. 166.

"'To arms! To arms!'": Kleist, "Ode."

"'with the sword of devastation'": Clausewitz, "Bekenntnisdenkschrift," p. 734.

"a new legend of the Vendée": A new French history conveying this new legend appeared in German translation in 1808, and Prussian minister vom Stein praised it highly. See Johnston, pp. 7–10.

"After the start of the Spanish guerrilla war": See Rassow.

"Kleist wrote": Johnston, p. 47; Schmitt, *Theorie des Partisanen,* p. 15.

"'The spark that flew'": Schmitt, *Theorie des Partisanen,* p. 52.

296 "He called France . . . 'a Jew People'": Quoted in Hagemann, *"Mannlicher Muth,"* p. 249.

"'Since He is the God of love'": Quoted in Jeismann, p. 93.

"In early 1813": Dwyer, "Prussia," p. 254.

"The next month": Huber, vol. I, pp. 49–50; Leggiere, p. 57.

"'Every citizen'": "Verordnung über den Landsturm," April 21, 1813, in Huber, vol. I, pp. 50–3.

297 "'Magna Carta'": Schmitt, *Theorie des Partisanen,* p. 48.

"Prussian territory in fact saw": On this campaign, see Leggiere.

"twenty thousand men to volunteer": See Hagemann, *"Mannlicher Muth,"* p. 37. On p. 41, the author judges the attempt at mobilization "relatively successful." See also Hagemann, "Of 'Manly Valor.'"

"'Prussians, Silesians, Pomeranians and Lithuanians'"; "'We were told to be patriots'": Quoted in Gates, pp. 230, 231.

"Arndt in particular": See Hagemann, "Of 'Manly Valor,'" p. 209.

"Key symbols": See Moran, "Arms and the Concert," p. 62.

298 "'the Young Germany campaign'": Chateaubriand, p. 278.

"One figure in particular": On Körner, see Zipper.

"young, blond and beautiful'": Chateaubriand, p. 280.

"the nation arises'"; "'This is not the sort of war'": Körner, "Männer und Buben"; "Aufruf," in *Leier und Schwert.* All citations from the book are taken from this source and identified by the name of the poem.

"'self-realization'": Moran, "Arms and the Concert," p. 59.

299 "a dark, frankly erotic fascination": See the analysis of Weber, *Lyrik,* pp. 195–6.

"'in two days'": Cited in Sheehan, p. 384.

"'Shall I die in prose?'": Körner, "Mißmut."

300 "Körner became arguably the most popular": Weber, *Lyrik,* pp. 190–2.
"In Leni Riefenstahl's film": See Johnston, p. 203.
"when Joseph Goebbels": The speech can be found at http://www.stern.de/
politik/historie/351801.html, consulted on July 6, 2006.
"Napoleon swallowed poison": See Tulard, *Napoléon,* p. 419.

EPILOGUE

302 "'War is divine'": Maistre, *Soirées,* vol. II, p. 36.
"'You will find'": Choderlos de Laclos, Letter 125.
303 "'His expression, when he saw'": Stendhal, Book I, Chapter IX.
304 "'[Julien] gazed sadly'": Ibid., Book IV, Chapter IV ("Un père et un fils").
"Following the fall of Paris": On the Hundred Days, see S. Englund, pp. 429–
47. Villepin is to be strictly avoided.
306 "It had an apparently rambling": See Morrissey.
"his image remained ubiquitous": See Hazareesingh, *The Legend of Napoleon,* especially pp. 68–98.
"In Britain": See Semmel, especially pp. 148, 173. "'Yet how resplendent'": Cobbett, quoted in ibid., p. 221.
307 "His critics continue": See Johnson; Ribbe.
308 "The state system born in 1814–15": See Schroeder, *Transformation,* pp. 517–82;
also the perceptive observations of Pagden.
"'to deal with each other'": Schroeder, *Transformation,* p. 558.
309 "the nineteenth century also saw": See, notably, Ceadel; Chickering, *Imperial
Germany*; S. Cooper; Grossi.
310 "'commerce is the grand panacea'": Quoted in Ceadel, p. 42.
"'Military power'": Angell, *The Great Illusion,* p. ix.
"'The earth cries out . . . draws us to it'": Maistre, *Soirées,* vol. II, pp. 33, 34, 36.
311 "others would draw": See, for instance, Steinmetz. "'History is a bath of blood
. . . it is life *in extremis*'": James, pp. 22–3.
"'I almost desire'": Quoted in Stromberg, p. 180.
"'sacred . . . the very sphere . . . the ideal of perpetual peace'": Treitschke, vol. I,
p. 29; vol. II, p. 599.
"'war is the only hygiene'": "The Futurist Manifesto," at http://evans-experien-
tialism.freewebspace.com/marinetti.htm, Web site consulted on June 26, 2006.
312 "an avalanche of personal memoirs": For France, see Tulard, *Nouvelle
Bibliographie.* See also the helpful Web sites http://napoleonic-literature.com/
AgeOfNapoleon/Memoirs.html and http://www.napoleon-series.org/research/
eyewitness/c_british.html. Web sites consulted on June 26, 2006.
"Up until the late eighteenth century": For Renaissance memoirs, see Harari.
"emerging Romantic notions of the self": see Taylor; Wahrman.
"'moral' factors": Quoted in S. Englund, p. 105.
313 "The trends come to fruition": See especially Clausewitz, *On War,* pp. 100–12
(Book I, Chapter III).
"'salvation and regeneration'": Quoted in Stromberg, p. 201n. On the subject,
see Stromberg, passim.
"Despite the widespread legend": See, for instance, Becker.

"the ways in which they changed the place of war": See, on this subject, the classic by Fussell.

"what Niall Ferguson nicely calls": N. Ferguson.

314   "Various journalists, political scientists": See Easterbrook; Marshall and Gurr; Mueller, *Remnants.* "'the number of armed conflicts'": see Rogers.

"'Yes, the end of war'": Easterbrook.

315   "a 'new American militarism'": See Bacevich.

"'Peaceful times are superficial times'": Kaplan, "The New Evils," p. 20. See also Kaplan, *An Empire Wilderness;* Kaplan, "The Dangers of Peace"; Kaplan, *Imperial Grunts;* Lipsky. For views similar to Kaplan's, see Ledeen, pp. 60–87.

316   "'War is terrible'": Bush, interview on *Kudlow and Company.*

"'an enemy who will stop at nothing'": Beamer. It is entirely understandable that the author, who lost his son Todd on United flight 93, should express himself in this way. It is less understandable that the *Wall Street Journal* should print his words.

"and that has arguably": See Benjamin and Simon.

Bibliography

Addison, Joseph, "The Campaign, A Poem," in Joseph Addison, *The Works of the Right Honourable Joseph Addison,* ed. Mr. Tickell, 6 vols. (New York: William Durell, 1811), vol. V, pp. 229–45.

Alcaide Ibieca, Augustin, *Historia de los dos sitios que pusieron a Zaragoza en los años de 1808 y 1809 las tropas de Napoleon,* three vols. (Madrid: D. M. de Burgos, 1830).

Alder, Ken, *Engineering the Revolution: Arms and Enlightenment in France, 1763–1815* (Princeton, N.J.: Princeton University Press, 1997).

Alexander, Don. W., *Rod of Iron: French Counterinsurgency Policy in Aragon During the Peninsular War* (Wilmington, Del.: Scholarly Resources, 1985).

Anderson, M. S., *The War of the Austrian Succession, 1740–1748* (London: Longman, 1995).

Angell, Norman, *The Great Illusion: A Study of the Relation of Military Power to National Advantage* (New York and London: G. P. Putnam, 1913).

——, Nobel Peace Prize speech (1933), at http://nobelprize.org/peace/laureates/1933/angell-bio.html, consulted on June 26, 2006.

Arcq, Philippe-Auguste, chevalier d', *La noblesse militaire, ou le patriote françois,* 3rd ed. (n.p., 1756).

Arendt, Hannah, *On Violence* (New York: Harcourt Brace Jovanovich, 1970).

Armitage, David, "The Fifty Years' Rift: Intellectual History and International Relations," *Modern Intellectual History,* vol. I (2004), pp. 97–109.

Arndt, Ernst Moritz, *Gedichte,* at http://gutenberg.spiegel.de/arndt/gedichte/ohtmldir.htm, consulted on June 26, 2006.

Arnold, Robert F., and Karl Wagner, eds., *Achtzehnhundertneun: Die politische Lyrik des Kriegsjahre* (Vienna: Verlag des Literarischen Vereins, 1909).

Arteche y Moro, Don José Gomez de, *Guerra de la independencia: Historia militar de*

España de 1808 á 1814, 14 vols. (Madrid: Impr. y lit. del Depósito de la guerra, 1868–1903).

Artola, Miguel, *Los afrancesados* (Madrid: Alianza Editorial, 1989).

——, "La guerra de guerrillas (Planteamientos estratégicos en la guerra de la Independencia)," *Reviste de Occidente,* vol. X (1964), pp. 12–43.

Ashton, John, *English Caricature and Satire on Napoleon I* (London: Chatto and Windus, 1888).

Augereau, Pierre-Charles François, "Bataille de Castiglione," in *Mémoires de tous,* 2 vols. (Paris: Levavasseur, 1834), vol. II, pp. 277–315.

Auguste, Claude B., and Marcel B. Auguste, *L'expedition Leclerc, 1801–1803* (Port-au-Prince, Haiti: Imprimerie Henri Deschamps, 1985).

Aulard, Alphonse, *Les grands orateurs de la Révolution* (Paris: Rieder, 1914).

——, *Les orateurs de la révolution: L'Assemblée constituante* (Paris: Cornély, 1905).

——, ed., *Paris pendant la réaction thermidorienne et sous le Directoire,* 5 vols. (Paris: Léopold Cerf et al., 1898–1902).

——, ed., *La société des Jacobins: Recueil de documents,* 6 vols. (Paris: Jouaust and Nollet, 1889–97).

Avenel, Georges, *Anacharsis Cloots, l'Orateur du genre humain* (Paris: Champ Libre, 1976).

Avis aux grenadiers et aux soldats du tiers-état ([Paris, 1789]).

Ayerbe y Lierta, Pedro Jordán María de Urríes, marqués de, *Memorias del Marqués de Ayerbe sobre la estancia de Fernando VII en Valençay y el principio de la guerra de la independencia,* ed. Miguel Artola, in *Biblioteca de Autores Españoles,* vol. XCVII (Madrid: Atlas, 1957), pp. 227–73.

Aymes, Jean-René, *La guerra de la independencia en España, 1808–1814,* trans. Pierre Conrad (Madrid: Siglo XXI, 1974).

Babeau, Albert, *La vie militaire sous l'ancien régime,* 2 vols. (Paris: Firmin-Didot, 1888–90).

Babeuf, Gracchus, *Du système de dépopulation, ou la vie et les crimes de Carrier* (Paris: Franklin, [1795]).

Bacevich, Andrew J., *The New American Militarism: How Americans Are Seduced by War* (New York: Oxford University Press, 2005).

Baecque, Antoine de, *The Body Politic: Corporeal Metaphor in Revolutionary France, 1770–1800,* trans. Charlotte Mandell (Stanford, Calif.: Stanford University Press, 1997).

Baker, Keith Michael, *Inventing the French Revolution: Essays on French Political Culture in the Eighteenth Century* (Cambridge: Cambridge University Press, 1990).

Barère, Bertrand, *Mémoires de B. Barère,* 4 vols. (Paris: Jules Labitte, 1842).

——, *Rapport sur les crimes de l'Angleterre envers le Peuple français, et sur ses attentats contre la liberté des Nations,* 7 Prairial II (Paris: Imprimerie Nationale, 1794).

Bataille de Marengo et ses préliminaires racontés par quatre témoins, La (Paris: F. Teissèdre, 1999).

Beamer, David, "United 93: The Filmmakers Got It Right," *Wall Street Journal,* April 27, 2006.

Becker, Jean-Jacques, *1914: Comment les Français sont entrés dans la guerre: Contribution à étude de l'opinion publique, printemps-été 1914* (Paris: Fondation Nationale des Sciences Politiques, 1977).

Beevor, Antony, *The Fall of Berlin 1945* (New York: Penguin, 2002).

Beik, Paul, "The Abbé Maury and the National Assembly," *Proceedings of the American Philosophical Society,* vol. XCV, no. 5 (1951), pp. 545–55.

Béjarry, Amédée de, *Souvenirs Vendéens* (Nantes, France: Emile Grimaud, 1884, repr. Janzé: Yves Salmon, 1981).

Belissa, Marc, *Fraternité universelle et intérêt national (1713–1795): Les cosmopolitiques du droit des gens* (Paris: Editions Kimé, 1998).

——, *Repenser l'ordre européen (1795–1802): De la société des rois aux droits des nations* (Paris: Editions Kimé, 2006).

Bell, David A., "Aux origines de la 'Marseillaise': L' 'Adresse à la nation angloise' de Claude-Rigobert Lefebvre de Beauvray," *Annales historiques de la Révolution française,* no. 299 (1995), pp. 75–77.

——, *The Cult of the Nation in France: Inventing Nationalism, 1680–1800* (Cambridge, Mass.: Harvard University Press, 2001).

——, "History Robed in Reckless Rhetoric," *Los Angeles Times Book Review,* July 27, 2003.

Bellers, John, *Some Reasons for an European State, Proposed to the Powers of Europe* (London: n.p., 1710).

Benjamin, Daniel, and Steven Simon, *The Next Attack: The Failure of the War on Terror and a Strategy for Getting It Right* (New York: Times Books, 2005).

Benoît, Jérémie, and Bernard Chevallier, *Marengo: Une victoire politique* (Paris: Editions de la Réunion des Musées Nationaux, 2000).

Bentham, Jeremy, *The Works of Jeremy Bentham,* ed. John Bowring, 11 vols. (Edinburgh: W. Tait, 1843).

Bercé, Yves-Marie, *Histoire des Croquants* (Paris: Seuil, 1986).

Bergeron, Louis, *France under Napoleon,* trans. R. R. Palmer (Princeton, N.J.: Princeton University Press, 1981).

Bernardin de Saint-Pierre, Jacques-Henri, *Etudes de la Nature,* 3 vols. (Paris, Deterville, 1804).

Bertaud, Jean-Paul, ed., *Atlas de la Révolution française,* vol. III: *L'armée et la guerre* (Paris: Editions de l'Ecole des Hautes Etudes en Sciences Sociales, 1989).

——, *Guerre et société en France de Louis XIV à Napoléon 1er* (Paris: Armand Colin, 1998).

——, "Napoleon's Officers," *Past and Present,* no. 112 (1986), pp. 91–111.

——, *La Révolution armée: Les soldats-citoyens et la Révolution française* (Paris: Robert Laffont, 1979).

——, *"Le théâtre et la guerre à l'époque de Napoléon,"* in Boudon, *Armée, guerre et société,* pp. 177–88.

——, *Valmy: La démocratie en armes* (Paris: Julliard, 1970).

——, *La vie quotidienne des soldats de la Révolution, 1789–1799* (Paris: Hachette, 1985).

Berthier, Alexandre, *Relation de la bataille de Marengo* (Paris: Imprimerie Impériale, 1805, repr. Courbevoie: Durante, 1998).

Bertrand, Henri-Gratien, *Napoleon at St. Helena: Memoirs of General Bertrand* (London: Cassell, 1953).

Best, Geoffrey, *Humanity in Warfare* (New York: Columbia University Press, 1980).

——, *War and Society in Early Modern Europe* (Cambridge: Cambridge University Press, 1976).

Beulas, Eloi i Ors, and Albert Dresaire i Gaudí, *La guerra del Francès a Mataró* (Mataró, Spain: Patronat Municipal de Cultura, 1989).

Biard, Michel, Annie Crépin, and Bernard Gainot, eds., *La plume et le sabre: Volume d'hommages offerts à Jean-Paul Bertaud* (Paris: Publications de la Sorbonne, 2002).

Bien, David D., "The Army in the French Enlightenment: Reform, Reaction and Revolution," *Past and Present,* no. 85 (1979), pp. 68–98.

Billacois, François, *Le duel dans la société française des XVIe–XVIIe siècles: Essai de psychosociologie historique* (Paris: Ecole des Hautes Etudes en Sciences Sociales, 1986).

Black, Jeremy, *Culloden and the '45* (New York: St. Martin's, 1990).

——, *European Warfare: 1660–1815* (London: UCL Press, 1994).

——, *A Military Revolution? Military Change and European Society 1550–1800* (Houndmills, England: Macmillan, 1991).

Blanning, T.C.W., *The French Revolutionary Wars, 1787–1802* (London: Arnold, 1996).

——, "Liberation or Occupation? Theory and Practice in the French Revolutionaries' Treatment of Civilians Outside France," in Grimsley and Rogers, pp. 111–35.

——, *The Origins of the French Revolutionary Wars* (London and New York: Longman, 1986).

Blaufarb, Rafe, *The French Army 1750–1820: Careers, Talents, Merit* (Manchester, England: University of Manchester Press, 2002).

Blaze, Elzéar, *Life in Napoleon's Army: The Memoirs of Captain Elzéar Blaze* (1837), ed. Philip Haythornthwaite (London: Greenhill Books, 1995).

Blaze, Sébastien, *Mémoires d'un apothicaire sur la guerre d'Espagne pendant les années 1808 à 1814,* 2 vols. (Paris: Ladvocat, 1828).

Bluche, Frederic, *Le bonapartisme: Aux origines de la droite autoritaire (1800–1850)* (Paris: Nouvelles Editions Latines, 1980).

Bodinier, Gilbert, *Les officiers de l'armée royale combattants de la guerre d'Indépendance des Etats-Unis, de Yorktown à l'an II* (Vincennes: SHAT, 1983).

——, "La républicanisation de la marine en l'an I et l'an II," in Biard, Crépin, and Gainot, pp. 249–59.

Bohlender, Matthias, "Die Poetik der Schlacht und die Prosa des Krieges: Nationalverteidigung und Bürgermiliz im moralphilosophischen Diskurs der schottischen Aufklärung," in Kunisch and Münkler, pp. 17–41.

Boime, Albert, *Art in an Age of Bonapartism, 1800–1815* (Chicago: University of Chicago Press, 1990).

Bois, Jean-Pierre, *Fontenoy 1745: Louis XV, arbitre de l'Europe* (Paris: Economica, 1996).

Bois, Paul, *Les paysans de l'Ouest; des structures économiques et sociales aux options politiques depuis l'époque révolutionnaire dans la Sarthe* (Le Mans, France: Vilaire, 1960).

Boisson de Quency, Louis, *Veni, Vidi, Vici. Au Premier Consul. Ode sur la passage du Mont Saint-Bernard, la bataille de Marengo, et l'armistice proposé par le général Mélas* (n.p., 1800).

Bonaparte, Joseph, *Mémoires et correspondance politique et militaire du roi Joseph,* ed. A. du Casse, 10 vols. (Paris: Perrotin, 1854–55).

Bonaparte, Napoléon, *Correspondance inédite de Napoléon 1er, conservée aux archives de la guerre,* ed. Ernest Picard and Louis Tuetey, 5 vols. (Paris: Henri-Charles Lavauzelle, 1912–13).

——, *Lettres inédites de Napoléon 1er (an VIII–1815),* ed. Léon Lecestre, 2 vols. (Paris: Plon, 1897).

——, *Napoléon inconnu: Papiers inédits (1786–1793),* ed. Frédéric Masson and Guido Biagi, 2 vols. (Paris: Paul Ollendorff, 1895).

——, *Œuvres littéraires et écrits militaires,* ed. Jean Tulard, 3 vols. (Paris: Claude Tchou, 2001).

Bonchamps, Marie-Marguerite-Renée de, *Mémoires de Madame la Marquise de Bonchamps, rédigés par Mme. la Comtesse de Genlis* (Paris: Baudouin Frères, 1823).

Bonehill, John, and Geoff Quilley, *Conflicting Visions: War and Visual Culture in Britain and France c. 1700–1830* (Aldershot, England: Ashgate, 2005).

Bonnet, Jean-Claude, "Les morts illustres: Oraison funèbre, éloge académique, nécrologie," in Pierre Nora, ed., *Les lieux de Mémoire: La Nation,* three vols. (Paris: Gallimard, 1986), vol. III, pp. 217–41.

——, *Naissance du Panthéon: Essai sur le culte des grands hommes* (Paris: Fayard, 1998).

Bordereau, Renée, *Mémoires de Renée Bordereau, dite Langevin* (Paris: L. G. Michaud, 1814).

Borner, Wilhelm, *Das Weltstaatsprojekt des Abbé de Saint-Pierre: Ein Beitrag zur Geschichte der Weltfriedensidee* (Berlin and Leipzig: Walter Rothschild, 1913).

Bosséno, Christian-Marc, "'Je mis vis dans l'histoire': Bonaparte, de Lodi à Arcole: généalogie d'une image de légende," *Annales historiques de la Révolution française,* no. 313 (1998), pp. 449–65.

Bouchette, François-Joseph, *Lettres de François-Joseph Bouchette,* ed. Camille Looten (Paris: Honoré Champion, 1909).

Boudon, Jacques-Olivier Boudon, ed., *Armée, guerre et société, à l'époque napoléonienne* (Paris: Editions SPM, 2004).

——, "Le 18 Brumaire dans l'Histoire," in Jacques-Olivier Boudon, ed., *Brumaire: La prise de pouvoir de Bonaparte* (Paris: Editions SPM, 2001), pp. 161–73.

——, *La France et l'Europe de Napoléon* (Paris: Armand Colin, 2006).

——, "Les fondements religieux du pouvoir impérial," in Natalie Petiteau, ed., *Voies nouvelles pour l'histoire du Premier Empire: Territoires, Pouvoirs, Identités* (Paris: La Boutique de l'Histoire, 2003), pp. 195–212.

——, *Histoire du Consulat et de l'Empire* (Paris: Perrin, 2000).

——, *Napoléon et les cultes: Les religions en Europe à l'aube du XIXe siècle, 1800–1815* (Paris: Fayard, 2002).

——, "Un outil de propagande au service de Napoléon: *Les Bulletins de la Grande Armée*" in Boudon, *Armée, guerre et société,* pp. 241–53.

Boullault, Mathurin-Joseph, *Les brigands de la Vendée* (Paris: Toubon, 1793).

Bourgin, Georges, and Jacques Godechot, *L'Italie et Napoléon (1796–1814)* (Paris: Recueil Sirey, 1936).

Bourrienne, Louis-Antoine Fauvelet de, *Memoirs of Napoleon Bonaparte,* ed. R. W. Phipps, 4 vols. (New York: Charles Scribner's Sons, 1918).

Boycott-Brown, Martin, *The Road to Rivoli: Napoleon's First Campaign* (London: Cassell, 2001).

Boyer, Jean-Claude, "Les représentations guerrières et l'évolution des arts plastiques en France au XVIIe siècle," *XVIIe siècle,* no. 148 (1985), pp. 291–303.

Bradby, Eliza Dorothy, *The Life of Barnave,* 2 vols. (Oxford: Clarendon Press, 1915).

Braithwaite, William C., *The Second Period of Quakerism* (Cambridge: Cambridge University Press, 1961).

Brandt, Heinrich von, *In the Legions of Napoleon: The Memoirs of a Polish Officer in Spain and Russia,* ed. and trans. Jonathan North (London: Greenhill Books, 1999).

Braudy, Leo, *The Frenzy of Renown: Fame and Its History* (Oxford: Oxford University Press, 1986).

———, *From Chivalry to Terrorism: War and the Changing Nature of Masculinity* (New York: Knopf, 2003).

Bredin, Jean-Denis, *Sieyès: La clé de la Révolution Française* (Paris: Fallois, 1988).

Bricard, Louis-Joseph, *Journal du canonier Bricard,* ed. Lorédan Larchey (Paris: Hachette, 1894).

Briois, *La mort du jeune Barra, ou une journée de la Vendée* (Paris: Chez Barba, 1793–94).

Brissot, Jacques-Pierre, *Discours de J. P. Brissot, député, Sur les dispositions des Puissances étrangères* (Paris: Assemblée Nationale, 1791).

———, *J. P. Brissot: Correspondance et papiers,* ed. Claude Pernoud (Paris: Alphonse Picard & fils, 1912).

———, *Second discour* [sic] *de J. P. Brissot, député* (Paris: Patriote françois, 1791).

Brock, Peter, *Pacifism in Europe to 1914* (Princeton, N.J.: Princeton University Press, 1972).

Broers, Michael, "Center and Periphery in Napoleonic Italy: The Nature of French Rule in the départements réunis, 1800–1814," in Michael Rowe, ed., *Collaboration and Resistance in Napoleonic Europe: State-Formation in an Age of Upheaval, c. 1800–1815* (Houndmills, England: Palgrave Macmillan, 2003), pp. 55–73.

———, *Europe After Napoleon: Revolution, Reaction, and Romanticism, 1814–1848* (Manchester, England: Manchester University Press, 1996).

———, *Europe Under Napoleon, 1799–1815* (London: Arnold, 1996).

———, "The Myth and Reality of Italian Regionalism: A Historical Geography of Napoleonic Italy, 1801–1814," *American Historical Review,* vol. CVIII, no. 3 (2003), pp. 688–708.

———, *The Napoleonic Empire in Italy, 1796–1814: Cultural Imperialism in a European Context?* (Houndmills, England: Palgrave MacMillan, 2005).

———, *The Politics of Religion in Napoleonic Italy: The War against God, 1801–1814* (London: Routledge, 2002).

Brown, Gregory, *A Field of Honor: Writers, Court Culture and Public Theater in French Literary Life from Racine to the Revolution,* at http://www.gutenberg-e.org, consulted on June 26, 2006.

Brown, Howard G., "Domestic State Violence: Repression from the Croquants to the Commune," *Historical Journal,* vol. 42, no. 3 (1999), pp. 597–622.

———, *War, Revolution and the Bureaucratic State: Politics and Army Administration in France, 1791–1799* (Oxford: Clarendon, 1995).

Brun de Villeret, Louis, *Les cahiers du général Brun,* ed. Louis de Saint-Pierre (Paris: Plon, 1953).

Brunel, Françoise, "L'anti-bellicisme de Billaud-Varenne (October 1791–Janvier 1792): Défiance et paix armée," in Biard, Crépin, and Gainot, pp. 217–26.

Brunner, Otto, Werner Conze, and Reinhardt Koselleck, *Geschichtliche Grundbegriffe:*

Historisches lexicon zur politisch-sozialer Sprache in Deutschland, 8 vols. (Stuttgart: Klett-Cotta, 1972–97).

Bülow, Dietrich von, *Der Feldzug von 1800, militarisch, politisch betrachtet* (Berlin: Heinrich Frölich, 1801).

Burke, Edmund, *A Letter from Mr. Burke to a Member of the National Assembly in Answer to Some Objections to His Book on French Affairs* (1791), at http://www.ourcivilisation.com/smartboard/shop/burkee/tonatass/, consulted on June 26, 2006.

———, *Reflections on the Revolution in France,* ed. J.G.A. Pocock (Indianapolis: Hackett Publishing, 1987).

———, *Two Letters Addressed to a Member of the Present Parliament, on the Proposals for Peace with the Regicide Directory of France* (London: F. and C. Rivington, 1796).

———, *A Vindication of Natural Society,* ed. Frank N. Pagano (Indianapolis: Liberty Classics, 1982), p. 20.

Bury, J. B., *The Idea of Progress: An Inquiry into Its Origins and Growth* (New York: Macmillan, 1932).

Büsch, Otto, *Military System and Social Life in Old Regime Prussia, 1713–1807: The Beginnings of the Social Militarization of Prusso-German Society,* trans. John G. Gagliardo (Atlantic Highlands, N.J.: Humanities Press, 1997).

Bush, George W., interview on *Kudlow and Company,* CNBC, May 5, 2006, at http://video.msn.com/v/us/v.htm?g=3ca3db6f-d555–4e72-a695-f7c13a9f845e&f=rssrssmoney&f=15/64rssmoney, consulted on June 26, 2006.

———, State of the Union Address, January 28, 2003, CNN transcript, at http://www.cnn.com/2003/ALLPOLITICS/01/28/sotu.transcript.8/index.html, consulted on June 26, 2006.

Butterfield, Herbert, *Napoleon* (New York: Macmillan, 1939).

Cabanis, André, *La presse sous le consulat et l'empire (1799–1814)* (Paris: Société des Etudes Robespierristes, 1975).

Caldora, Umberto, *Calabria Napoleonica* (Naples: Fausto Fiorentino, 1960).

Cantal, Pierre, *Études sur l'armée révolutionnaire* (Paris: Henri Charles-Lavauzelle, 1907).

Capmany, Antonio de, *Centinela contra Franceses,* ed. Françoise Etienvre (London: Tamesis, 1988).

Caron, Pierre, ed., *La défense nationale de 1792 à 1795* (Paris: Hachette, 1912).

Carson, George Barr, Jr., *The Chevalier de Chastellux: Soldier and Philosophe* (Chicago: University of Chicago, 1944).

Casanova, Antoine, *Napoléon et la pensée de son temps: Une histoire intellectuelle singulière* (Paris: Boutique de l'Histoire, 2000).

Castries, René de la Croix de, *Mirabeau* (Paris: Fayard, 1960).

Catecismo Civil, y breve compendio de las obligaciones del español, conocimiento práctico de su libertad, y explicación de su enemigo, muy util en las actuales circunstancias, puesto en forma de diálogo (n.p., 1809).

Caulaincourt, Armand-Augustin-Louis de, *With Napoleon in Russia,* ed. Jean Hanoteau, trans. George Libaire (New York: William Morrow, 1955).

Ceadel, Martin, *The Origins of War Prevention: The British Peace Movement and International Relations, 1730–1854* (Oxford: Clarendon Press, 1996).

Chagniot, Jean, chapters 1–5 in André Corvisier, ed., *Histoire militaire de la France,* vol. II (Paris: Quadrige, 1997), pp. 3–128.

Chandler, David G., *The Campaigns of Napoleon: The Mind and Method of History's Greatest Soldier* (New York: Scribner, 1966).

———, "Napoleon and Death," in *Napoleonic Scholarship: Journal of the International Napoleonic Society,* vol. I, no. 1 (1997), at http://www.napoleon-series.org/ins/scholarship97/c_death.html, consulted on June 26, 2006.

———, *On the Napoleonic Wars: Collected Essays* (London: Greenhill Books, 1994).

Chassin, Charles-Louis, ed., *La préparation de la Guerre de Vendée, 1789–1793,* 3 vols. (Paris: Paul Dupont, 1892; repr. Mayenne: Joseph Floch, 1973).

———, ed., *La Vendée patriote, 1793–1795,* 4 vols. (Paris: Paul Dupont, 1895; repr. Mayenne: Joseph Floch, 1973).

Chastellux, François-Jean de, *An Essay on Public Happiness, Investigating the State of Human Nature, Under Each of Its Particular Appearances Through the Several Periods of History, to the Present Times,* 2 vols. (London: T. Cadell, 1774).

Chateaubriand, François-René de, *Napoléon par Chateaubriand,* ed. Christian Melchior-Bonnet (Paris: Albin-Michel, 1969).

Chaussard, P.J.B., *La France régénérée* (Paris: Limodin, 1792).

Cherel, Albert, *Fénelon au XVIIIe siècle en France (1715–1820): Son prestige, son influence* (Paris: Hachette, 1917).

Chevalier, Jean-Michel, *Souvenirs des guerres napoléoniennes,* ed. Jean Mistler and Hélène Michaud (Paris: Hachette, 1970).

Chickering, Roger, *Imperial Germany and a World Without War: The Peace Movement and German Society, 1892–1914* (Princeton, N.J.: Princeton University Press, 1975).

———, "Total War: The Use and Abuse of a Concept," in Manfred F. Boemeke, Roger Chickering, and Stig Förster, eds., *Anticipating Total War: The German and American Experiences, 1871–1914* (Washington, D.C.: German Historical Institute, 1999), pp. 13–28.

Chickering, Roger, and Stig Förster, eds., *Great War, Total War: Combat and Mobilization on the Western Front, 1914–1918* (Washington, D.C.: German Historical Institute, 2000).

Childs, John, *Armies and Warfare in Europe, 1648–1789* (New York: Holmes and Meier, 1982).

———, *The British Army of William III, 1698–1702* (Manchester, England: Manchester University Press, 1987).

Chlapowski, Dezydery, *Memoirs of a Polish Lancer: The Pamietnitci of Dezydery Chlapowski,* ed. and trans. Tim Simmons (Chicago: The Emperor's Press, 1992).

Choderlos de Laclos, Pierre-Ambroise-François, *Les liaisons dangereuses,* ed. Yves Le Hir (1999), at http://gallica.bnf.fr/document?O=N101460, consulted on June 26, 2006.

Choppin, Henri, *Insurrections militaires en 1790* (Paris: Lucien Laveur, n.d.).

Chronique de Paris, ci-devant Courier Républicain, rédigé par Jardin.

Chuquet, Arthur, *Dumouriez* (Paris: Hachette, 1914).

———, *Jemappes et la Conquête de la Belgique* (Paris: Plon-Nourrit, 1892).

———, ed., *Lettres de 1792* (Paris: Honoré Champion, 1911).

——, ed., *Lettres de 1793* (Paris: Honoré Champion, 1911).

——, *Valmy* (Paris: Plon-Nourrit, 1890).

Clausewitz, Carl von, "Bekenntnisdenkschrift," in *Schriften — Aufsätze — Studien — Briefe,* ed. Werner Hahlweg, 2 vols. (Göttingen: Vandenhoek and Ruprecht, 1966), vol. I, pp. 682–751.

——, *On War,* ed. and trans. Michael Howard and Peter Paret (Princeton, N.J.: Princeton University Press, 1976).

Clémanceau, Joseph, *Histoire de la Guerre de la Vendée (1793–1815)* (Paris: Nouvelle Librairie Nationale, 1909).

Clerget, C., *Tableaux des armées françaises pendant les guerres de la Révolution* (Paris: R. Chapelot, 1905).

Cobb, Richard, *The People's Armies,* trans. Marianne Elliott (New Haven, Conn.: Yale University Press, 1987).

Cobban, Alfred, *A History of Modern France,* 3 vols. (Harmondsworth, England: Penguin, 1965).

Coignet, Jean-Roch, *The Note-Books of Captain Coignet, Soldier of the Empire, 1799–1816,* trans. M. Carey (London: Greenhill Books, 1998).

Cole, Hubert, *First Gentleman of the Bedchamber: The Life of Louis-François-Armand, maréchal duc de Richelieu* (New York: Viking, 1965).

Colley, Linda, *Britons: Forging the Nation: 1702–1837* (New Haven, Conn.: Yale University Press, 1992).

——, *Captives: Britain, Empire and the World, 1600–1850* (London: Jonathan Cape, 2002).

Condorcet, Jean-Antoine-Nicolas de Caritat, marquis de, *Esquisse d'un tableau historique des progrès de l'esprit humain,* ed. Oliver Herbert Prior and Yvon Belaval (Paris: Vrin, 1970).

Connelly, Owen, *Blundering to Glory: Napoleon's Military Campaigns,* rev. ed. (Wilmington, Del.: Scholarly Resources, 1999).

——, *The Gentle Bonaparte: A Biography of Joseph, Napoleon's Elder Brother* (New York: Macmillan, 1968).

——, "The Historiography of the *Levée en masse* of 1793," in Moran and Waldron, pp. 33–48.

——, *Napoleon's Satellite Kingdoms* (New York: Free Press, 1965).

Conner, Susan P., *The Age of Napoleon* (Westport, Conn.: Greenwood Press, 2004).

Connolly, J. L., Jr., "Bonaparte on the Bridge: A Note on the Iconography of Passage," *Proceedings of the Consortium on Revolutionary Europe,* vol. XV (1985), pp. 45–65.

Constant, Benjamin, *L'esprit de conquête et de l'usurpation dans leurs rapports avec la civilisation européenne,* in *Œuvres* (Paris: Bibliothèque de la Pléiade, 1957 [1814]), pp. 983–1096.

Contamine, Philippe, *War in the Middle Ages,* trans. Michael Jones (Oxford: Basil Blackwell, 1984).

Cook, Warren L., *Flood Tide of Empire: Spain and the Pacific Northwest, 1543–1819* (New Haven, Conn.: Yale University Press, 1973).

Cookson, John, *The British Armed Nation, 1793–1815* (Oxford: Clarendon Press, 1997).

Cooper, Duff, *Talleyrand: A Biography* (New York: Fromm, 1986).

Cooper, Robert, "The New Liberal Imperialism," *The Observer,* April 7, 2002, at http:/

/observer.guardian.co.uk/worldview/story/0,11581,680095,00.html, consulted on June 26, 2006.

Cooper, Sandi E., *Patriotic Pacifism: Waging War on War in Europe, 1815–1914* (Oxford: Oxford University Press, 1991).

Copies of Original Letters from the Army of General Bonaparte in Egypt, Intercepted by the Fleet . . . of Admiral Lord Nelson (London: J. Wright, 1798).

Cornette, Joël, *Le roi de guerre: Essai sur la souveraineté dans la France du Grand siècle* (Paris: Payot & Rivages, 1993).

Cornish, Joseph, *The Miseries of War, and the Hope of Final and Universal Peace, Set Forth in a Thanksgiving Sermon Preached at Colyton, in the County of Devon, July 29th, 1784* (Taunton, England: T. Norris, 1784).

Corvisier, André, *L'armée française de la fin du XVIIe siècle au ministère de Choiseul: Le soldat*, 2 vols. (Paris: Presses Universitaires de France, 1964).

——, "Clientèles et fidélités dans l'armée française aux XVIIe et XVIIIe siècles," in *Hommage à Roland Mousnier: Clientèles et fidélités en Europe à l'époque moderne* (Paris: Presses Universitaires de France, 1981), pp. 213–36.

Corvisier, André, "Les 'héros subalternesè' dans la littérature du milieu du XVIIIᵉ siècle et la réhabilitation du militaire," *Revue du Nord*, vol. LXVI, no. 261/2 (1984), pp. 827–38.

Corvisier, André, and Jean Jacquart, eds., *Les malheurs de la guerre: De la guerre à l'ancienne à la guerre réglée* (Paris: Éditions du CTHS, 1996).

Craig, Gordon A., *The Politics of the Prussian Army, 1640–1945* (Oxford: Oxford University Press, 1956).

Creasy, Edward Shepherd, *The Fifteen Decisive Battles of the World, from Marathon to Waterloo* (London: R. Bentley, 1851).

Cri de la religion à l'illustre, à l'invincible, à l'immortel Bonaparte, le bras du Tout-Puissant, l'ange de la paix, le sauveur de la France, le pacificateur des nations, les délices du genre humain (Paris, 1802).

Crook, Malcolm, *Napoleon Comes to Power: Democracy and Dictatorship in Revolutionary France, 1795–1804* (Cardiff: University of Wales Press, 1998).

Crouzet, Pierre, *Discours sur l'honneur* (Paris: Firmin Didot, 1806).

Cuche, Francois-Xavier, *Une pensée sociale catholique: Fleury, La Bruyère et Fénelon* (Paris: Éditions du Cerf, 1991).

D'Huart, Suzanne, *Brissot: La Gironde au pouvoir* (Paris: Robert Laffont, 1986).

Daline, V. M., "Marc-Antoine Jullien après le 9 Thermidor," *Annales historiques de la Révolution française*, no. 185 (1966), pp. 390–412.

Dalrymple, Campbell, *A Military Essay, Containing Reflections on the Raising, Arming, Cloathing, and Discipline of the British Infantry and Cavalry* (London: Wilson, 1761).

Darnton, Robert, "The Brissot Dossier," *French Historical Studies*, vol. XVII (1991), pp. 200–18.

——, *The Forbidden Bestsellers of Prerevolutionary France, 1769–1789* (New York: W. W. Norton, 1995).

——, *The Great Cat Massacre and Other Episodes in French Cultural History* (New York: Basic Books, 1984).

——, *The Literary Underground of the Old Regime* (Cambridge, Mass.: Harvard University Press, 1982).

———, *Mesmerism and the End of the Enlightenment in France* (Cambridge, Mass.: Harvard University Press, 1968).

Davies, Norman, *Europe: A History* (Oxford: Oxford University Press, 1996).

Davis, James Herbert, Jr., *Fénelon* (Boston: Twayne Publishers, 1979).

Davis, John A., "The Many Faces of Modernity: French Rule in Southern Italy, 1806–1815," in Michael Rowe, ed., *Collaboration and Resistance in Napoleonic Europe: State-Formation in an Age of Upheaval, c. 1800–1815* (Houndmills, England: Palgrave Macmillan, 2003), pp. 74–89.

Décade egyptienne, Journal littéraire et d'économie politique, le (Cairo, An VII).

Defoe, Daniel, *An Essay Upon Projects* (1697), at http://etext.library.adelaide.edu.au/d/d31es/part16.html), consulted on June 26, 2006.

Delivré, Emilie, "The Pen and the Sword: Political Catechisms and Resistance to Napoleon," in Esdaile, *Popular Resistance,* pp. 161–80.

Déprez, Eugène, *Les volontaires nationaux (1791–1793): Étude sur la formation et l'organisation des bataillons* (Geneva: Slatkine Reprints, 1977).

Derrécagaix, Victor-Bernard, *Nos campagnes au Tyrol: 1797–1799–1805–1809* (Paris: Librairie Militaire R. Chapelot, 1910).

Deschard, Bernard, *L'armée et la Révolution: Du service du roi au service de la nation* (Paris: Desjonquères, 1989).

Desorgues, Théodore, *Chant funèbre en l'honneur des guerriers morts à la bataille de Marengo* (Paris: Chez les Marchands de Nouveautés, 1800).

Desvernois, Nicolas-Philibert, *Souvenirs militaires du baron Desvernois,* ed. Emmanuel Bousson de Mairet (Paris: Charles Tanera, 1858).

Devleeshouwer, Robert, "Le cas de la Belgique," in Robert Devleeshouwer, ed., *Occupants Occupés, 1792–1815* (Brussels: Université libre de Bruxelles, 1969), pp. 43–65.

Dewald, Jonathan, *Aristocratic Experience and the Origins of Modern Culture: France, 1570–1715* (Berkeley: University of California Press, 1993).

Discours des députés par la Convention Nationale du Peuple Rhéno-Germanique (Paris: Imprimerie Nationale, 1793).

Donaldson, Joseph, *Recollections of the Eventful Life of a Soldier* (Philadelphia: G. B. Zieber, 1845).

Dörner, Andreas, "Funktionale Barbarei: Heinrich von Kleists 'Kriegstheater' und die Politik des Zivilisationsabbaus," in Kunisch and Münkler, pp. 327–49.

Doyle, William, "The French Revolution and the Abolition of Nobility," paper presented to the Johns Hopkins University History Department Seminar, March 31, 2004.

———, *The Oxford History of the French Revolution* (Oxford: Oxford University Press, 1989).

Drouet, Joseph, *L'abbé de Saint-Pierre: L'homme et l'œuvre* (Paris: Honoré Champion, 1912).

Dryden, John, "Alexander's Feast," at http://andromeda.rutgers.edu/~jlynch/Texts/alexander.html, consulted July 10, 2006.

Dubois, Laurent, *Avengers of the New World: The Story of the Haitian Revolution* (Cambridge, Mass.: Harvard University Press, 2004).

Dubois, Laurent and John D. Garrigus, *Slave Rebellion in the Caribbean, 1789–1804* (New York: Bedford/St. Martin's, 2006).

Duchet, Lucien, ed., *Deux volontaires de 1791: Les frères Favier de Montluçon, Journal et lettres* (Montluçon, France: A. Herbin, 1909).

Dufay, Pierre, *Les sociétés populaires et l'armée* (Paris: Daragon, 1913).

Duffy, Christopher, *The Military Experience in the Age of Reason* (New York: Atheneum, 1988).

Dugast-Matifeux, Charles, ed., *Carrier à Nantes* (Nantes, France: Vier, 1885).

Duncker, M. Max, "Friedrich Wilhelm II und Graf Hertzberg," *Historische Zeitschrift,* vol. XXXVII (1877), pp. 1–43.

Dwyer, Philip G., "From Corsican Nationalist to French Revolutionary: Problems of Identity in the Writings of the Young Napoleon, 1785–1793," *French History,* vol. XVI, no. 2 (2002), pp. 132–52.

———, "Napoleon Bonaparte as Hero and Saviour: Image, Rhetoric and Behaviour in the Construction of a Legend," *French History,* vol. XVIII, no. 4 (2004), pp. 379–403.

———, "Napoleon and the Drive for Glory: Reflections on the Making of French Foreign Policy," in Dwyer, *Napoleon and Europe,* pp. 118–35.

———, ed., *Napoleon and Europe* (Harlow, England: Longman, 2001).

———, "Prussia During the French Revolutionary and Napoleonic Wars, 1786–1815," in Dwyer, *The Rise of Prussia,* pp. 239–58.

———, ed., *The Rise of Prussia, 1730–1830* (Harlow, England: Longman, 2000).

Dziembowski, Edmond, "Guerre en dentelles ou guerre cruelle? La représentation de la guerre de Sept Ans dans la littérature du XVIIIe siècle," in André Corvisier and Jean Jacquart, eds., *Les malheurs de la guerre: De la Guerre à l'ancienne à la guerre réglée* (Paris: Editions du CTHS, 1996), pp. 313–20.

———, *Un nouveau patriotisme français, 1750–1770: La France face à la puissance anglaise à l'époque de la guerre de Sept Ans* (Oxford: Voltaire Foundation, 1998).

Easterbrook, Gregg, "The End of War?" *New Republic,* no. 4715 (May 30, 2005), pp. 18–21.

Edelstein, Dan, "*Hostis Humani Generis:* Devils, Natural Right, and Terror in the French Revolution," *Telos,* forthcoming.

Edmunds, R. David, and Joseph L. Peyser, *The Fox Wars: The Mesquakie Challenge to New France* (Norman: University of Oklahoma Press, 1993).

Elias, Norbert, *The Court Society,* trans. Edmund Jephcott (New York: Pantheon Books, 1983).

———, *The History of Manners,* trans. Edmund Jephcott (New York: Pantheon Books, 1978).

Ellery, Eloise, *Brissot de Warville: A Study in the History of the French Revolution* (Cambridge, Mass.: Riverside Press, 1915).

Ellis, Geoffrey, *Napoleon* (London: Longman, 1997).

Elting, John R., *Swords around a Throne: Napoleon's Grande Armée* (New York: Da Capo, 1997).

Encyclopédie ou Dictionnaire raisonné des sciences, des arts et des métiers, ed. Denis Diderot and Jean le Rond d'Alembert, 28 vols. (Paris, 1751–72).

Englund, Peter, *The Battle of Poltava: The Birth of the Russian Empire,* trans. Peter Hale (London: Victor Gollancz, 1992).

Englund, Steven, *Napoleon: A Political Life* (New York: Scribner, 2004).

Époques, ou précis des actions mémorables du général Bonaparte, les (Paris: Batilliot, 1799).

Escoiquiz, Juan de, *Memorias de Juan de Escoiquiz,* ed. Miguel Artola, in *Biblioteca de Autores Espanoles,* vol. XCVII (Madrid: Atlas, 1957), pp. 1–152.

Esdaile, Charles J., *Fighting Napoleon: Guerrillas, Bandits and Adventurers in Spain, 1808–1814* (New Haven, Conn.: Yale University Press, 2004).

——, "Patriots, Partisans and Land Pirates in Retrospect," in Esdaile, *Popular Resistance,* pp. 1–24.

——, *The Peninsular War: A New History* (London: Allen Lane, 2002).

——, "Popular Mobilisation in Spain, 1808–1810: A Reassessment," in Michael Rowe, ed., *Collaboration and Resistance in Napoleonic Europe: State-Formation in an Age of Upheaval, c. 1800–1815* (Houndmills, England: Palgrave Macmillan, 2003), pp. 90–106.

——, ed., *Popular Resistance in the French Wars: Patriots, Partisans and Land Pirates* (Houndmills, England: Palgrave Macmillan, 2005).

——, *The Wars of Napoleon* (London: Longman, 1995).

Espoz y Mina, Francisco, *Memorias del general Don Francisco Espoz y Mina,* ed. Miguel Artola, 2 vols. (Madrid: Atlas, 1962).

Evans, Howard V., "The Nootka Sound Controversy in Anglo-French Diplomacy — 1790," *Journal of Modern History,* vol. XLVI, no. 4 (1974), pp. 609–40.

Extrait du régistre des délibérations du Diréctoire exécutif, du 16 prairial, l'an 5 de la République francaise, une et indivisible ([Paris]: n.p., 1797).

Eyck, F. Gunther, *Loyal Rebels: Andreas Hofer and the Tyrolean Uprising of 1809* (Lanham, Md.: University Press of America, 1986).

Faber, *Notices sur l'intérieur de la France, écrites en 1806* (Saint Petersburg: Imprimerie de l'Académie Impériale, 1807).

Fairon, Emile, and Henri Heuse, eds., *Lettres de grognards* (Paris: Bénard and Courville, 1936).

Farias, Rafael, *Memorias de la guerra de la independencia, escritas por soldados franceses* (Madrid: Editorial Hispano-Africana, 1919).

Faucheux, Marcel, *L'insurrection vendéenne de 1793: Aspects économiques et sociaux* (Paris: Imprimerie nationale, 1964).

Faulcon, Félix, *Correspondance de Félix Faulcon,* ed. Gabriel Debien, 2 vols. (Poitiers, France: Société des Archives Historiques du Poitou, 1953).

Fénelon, François de Salignac de la Mothe, *Les aventures de Télémaque,* ed. Jeanne-Lydie Goré (Paris: Garnier, 1987).

——, *Dialogues des morts: composés pour l'éducation d'un prince* (Paris: Didot, 1819).

——, *Œuvres de Fénelon,* ed. Louis Aimé-Martin, 3 vols. (Paris: Firmin Didot, 1845).

——, *Telemachus,* ed. and trans. Patrick Riley (Cambridge: Cambridge University Press, 1994).

Ferguson, Adam, *An Essay on the History of Civil Society* (1767), at http://socserv2. socsci.mcmaster.ca/~econ/ugcm/3ll3/ferguson/civil.html), consulted on June 26, 2006.

Ferguson, Niall, *The War of the World: Twentieth-Century Conflict and the Descent of the West* (New York: Penguin Press, 2006).

Ferrier-Caverivière, Nicole, "La guerre dans la littérature française depuis le traité des Pyrénées jusqu'à la mort de Louis XIV," *XVIIe siècle*, no. 148 (1985), pp. 233–47.

Fierro, Alfred, ed., *Les Français vus par eux-mêmes: Le consulat et l'empire: Anthologie des mémorialistes du consulat et de l'empire* (Paris: Robert Laffont, 1998).

Finer, Samuel E., *The Man on Horseback: The Role of the Military in Politics,* 2nd ed. (Boulder, Colo.: Westview Press, 1988).

Finley, Milton, *The Most Monstrous of Wars: The Napoleonic Guerrilla War in Southern Italy, 1806–11* (Columbia: University of South Carolina Press, 1994).

Fischbach, Claudius R., *Krieg und Frieden in der Französischen Aufklärung* (Münster: Waxmann, 1990).

Forrest, Alan, *Conscripts and Deserters: The Army and French Society during the Revolution and Empire* (New York: Oxford University Press, 1989).

——, "The Military Culture of Napoleonic France," in Dwyer, *Napoleon and Europe,* pp. 43–59.

——, *Napoleon's Men: The Soldiers of the Revolution and Empire* (London: Hambledon and London, 2002).

——, "*La patrie en danger:* The French Revolution and the First *Levée en masse,*" in Moran and Waldron, pp. 8–32.

——, *The Soldiers of the French Revolution* (Durham, N.C.: Duke University Press, 1990).

——, "The Ubiquitous Brigand: The Politics and Language of Repression," in Esdaile, *Popular Resistance,* pp. 25–44.

Foucault, Michel, *Discipline and Punish: The Birth of the Prison,* trans. Alan Sheridan (New York: Vintage, 1977).

——, *Il faut défendre la société: Cours au collège de France (1975–1976),* ed. François Ewald et al. (Paris: Hautes Etudes, 1997).

Foucrier, Annick, "Rivalités européennes dans le pacifique: L'affaire de Nootka Sound (1789–1790)," *Annales historiques de la Révolution française,* no. 307 (January–March 1997), pp. 17–30.

France vue de l'armée d'Italie, la, 18 issues (Thermidor to Brumaire, an VI).

François, Charles, *From Valmy to Waterloo: Extracts from the Diary of Capt. Charles François, a Soldier of the Revolution and the Empire* (1906), ed. Jules Claretie, trans. Robert B. Douglas (Tyne and Wear, Englund: Worley, 1991).

——, *Le journal d'un officier français, ou Les cahiers du capitaine François, 1792–1815* (Tours, France: Maison Alfred Mame et Fils, n.d. [1904]).

Frey, Linda and Marsha Frey, "'The Reign of the Charlatans Is Over': The French Revolutionary Attack on Diplomatic Practice," *Journal of Modern History,* vol. LXV (1993), pp. 706–44.

——, *Societies in Upheaval: Insurrections in France, Hungary and Spain in the Early Eighteenth Century* (Westport, Conn.: Greenwood Press, 1987).

Fricasse, Jacques, *Journal de marche d'un volontaire de 1792,* ed. Lorédan Larchey (Paris: La Librairie, 1911).

Friedrich, Carl Joachim, *Inevitable Peace* (Cambridge, Mass.: Harvard University Press, 1948).

Froude, James Anthony, *History of England from the Fall of Wolsey to the Defeat of the Spanish Armada,* 12 vols. (London: Longmans, 1870).

Fukuyama, Francis, "The End of History?" *National Interest,* no. 16 (Summer 1989), pp. 3–18.

Fuller, J.F.C., *The Conduct of War, 1789–1961: A Study of the Impact of the French, Industrial, and Russian Revolutions on War and Its Conduct* (New Brunswick, N.J.: Rutgers University Press, 1961).

Furet, François, "Les Girondins et la guerre: Les débuts de l'Assemblée législative," in François Furet and Mona Ozouf, eds., *La Gironde et les girondins* (Paris: Payot, 1991).

——, *Penser la Révolution française* (Paris: Gallimard, 1978).

——, *Revolutionary France, 1770–1880,* trans. Antonia Nevill (Oxford: Blackwell, 1992).

Furet, François, and Ran Halévi, *La monarchie républicaine: La Constitution de 1791* (Paris: Fayard, 1996).

Fussell, Paul, *The Great War and Modern Memory* (New York: Oxford University Press, 1975).

Gachot, Édouard, *Histoire militaire de Masséna: La troisième campagne d'Italie, 1805–6* (Paris: Plon, 1911).

Gat, Azar, *The Origins of Military Thought from the Enlightenment to Clausewitz* (Oxford: Clarendon Press, 1999).

Gates, David, *The Napoleonic Wars, 1803–1815* (London: Arnold, 1997).

Gay, Peter, *The Enlightenment: An Interpretation,* 2 vols. (New York: W. W. Norton, 1977).

Gentz, Friedrich, "Über den ewigen Frieden" (1800), repr. in Kurt von Raumer, ed., *Ewiger Friede: Friedensrufe und Friedenspläne seit der Renaissance* (Freiburg: Verlag Karl Alber, 1953), pp. 461–97.

Gervais, Captain, *A la conquête de l'Europe: Souvenirs d'un soldat de la Révolution et de l'Empire,* ed. Mme. L. Henry Coullet (Paris: Calmann-Lévy, 1939).

Geyer, Michael, "People's War: The German Debate about a *Levée en masse* in October 1918," in Moran and Waldron, pp. 124–58.

Geyl, Pieter, *Napoleon: For and Against,* trans. Olive Renier (Harmondsworth, England: Penguin, 1949).

Girault de Coursac, Pierrette, *L'éducation d'un roi: Louis XVI* (Paris: Gallimard, 1972).

Glover, Michael, *Legacy of Glory: The Bonaparte Kingdom of Spain, 1808–1813* (New York: Scribner's, 1971).

——, "A Particular Service: Beresford's Peninsular War," *History Today,* vol. XXXVI, no. 6 (1986), pp. 34–8.

Godechot, Jacques, *The Counter-Revolution: Doctrine and Action 1789–1804,* trans. Salvator Attanasio (New York: Howard Fertig, 1971).

——, *La grande nation: L'expansion révolutionnaire de la France dans le monde de 1789 à 1799* (Paris: Aubier, 1956).

——, *Les institutions de la France sous la Révolution et l'Empire,* 2d. ed. (Paris: Presses Universitaires de France, 1968).

——, "Les insurrections militaires sous le Directoire," *Annales historiques de la Révolution française,* no. 56 (1933), pp. 193–221.

Goetz-Bernstein, H.-A., *La diplomatie de la Gironde: Jacques-Pierre Brissot* (Paris: Hachette, 1912).

Goldstein, Jan, *The Post-Revolutionary Self: Politics and Psyche in France, 1750–1850* (Cambridge, Mass.: Harvard University Press, 2005).

Goncourt, Edmond de, and Jules de Goncourt, *La femme au dix-huitième siècle* (1877), at http://freresgoncourt.free.fr/texfemmeau18e/texte.htm, consulted on June 26, 2006.

Gontaut-Biron, Roger de, *Un célèbre méconnu: Le duc de Lauzun, 1747–1793* (Paris: Plon, 1937).

González Hermoso, Alfredo, *Le Robespierre Español* (Paris: Annales Littéraires de l'Université de Besançon, 1991).

Gordon, Alexander, *At Wellington's Right Hand: The Letters of Lieutenant-Colonel Sir Alexander Gordon, 1808–1815,* ed. Rory Muir (Phoenix Mill, England: Sutton, 2003).

Goré, Jeanne-Lydie, *L'itinéraire de Fénelon: Humanisme et spiritualité* (Grenoble: Allier, 1957).

Gotteri, Nicole, "L'esprit public à Paris avant le coup d'État de Brumaire an VIII," in Jacques-Olivier Boudon, ed., *Brumaire: La prise de pouvoir de Bonaparte* (Paris: Éditions SPM, 2001), pp. 15–25.

Gouges, Olympe de, *L'entrée de Dumourier à Bruxelles, ou les vivandiers* (Paris: Regnaud, 1793).

Gourgaud, Gaspard, *Sainte-Hélène: Journal inédit de 1815 à 1818,* ed. vicomte de Grouchy and Antoine Guillois, 2 vols. (Paris: Flammarion, 1899).

Grab, Alexander, "State Power, Brigandage and Rural Resistance in Napoleonic Italy," *European History Quarterly,* vol. XXV (1995), pp. 39–70.

———, *Napoleon and the Transformation of Europe* (Houndmills, England: Palgrave Macmillan, 2003).

Gras, Yves, *La guerre de Vendée (1793–1796)* (Paris: Economica, 1994).

Gray, Marion W., *Prussia in Transition: Society and Politics under the Stein Reform Ministry of 1808* (Philadelphia: American Philosophical Society, 1986).

Grew, Raymond, "Finding Social Capital: The French Revolution in Italy," *Journal of Interdisciplinary History,* vol. XXIX, no. 3 (1999), pp. 407–33.

Griffith, Paddy, *The Art of War of Revolutionary France, 1789–1802* (London: Greenhill Books, 1998).

Griffiths, Robert, *Le centre perdu: Malouet et les "monarchiens" dans la Révolution française* (Grenoble: Presses universitaires de Grenoble, 1988).

Grigsby, Darcy Grimaldo, *Extremities: Painting Empire in Post-Revolutionary France* (New Haven, Conn.: Yale University Press, 2002).

Grimoard, Philippe-Henri, *Tableau historique de la guerre de la Révolution de France, depuis son commencement en 1792, jusqu'à la fin de 1794,* 3 vols. (Paris: Treuttel and Würtz, 1808).

Grimsley, Mark, and Clifford J. Rogers, eds., *Civilians in the Path of War* (Lincoln and London: University of Nebraska Press, 2002).

Griois, Lubin, *Mémoires du général Griois,* ed. Arthur Chuquet, 2 vols. (Paris: Plon-Nourrit, 1909).

Grossi, Verdiana, *Le Pacifisme européen, 1889–1914* (Brussels: Bruylant, 1994).

Grotius, Hugo, *De Jure Belli ac Pacis Libri Tres* (Paris: Nicolas Buon, 1625).

Gueniffey, Patrice, *La politique de la Terreur: Essai sur la violence révolutionnaire, 1789–1794* (Paris: Fayard, 2000).

Guibert, Jacques-Antoine-Hippolyte, comte de, *Essai général de Tactique, précédé d'un discours sur l'état actuel de la politique et de la science militaire en Europe,* in *Stratégiques,* ed. Jean-Paul Charnay (Paris: L'Herne, 1995).

Guiomar, Jean-Yves, *L'invention de la guerre totale: XVIIIe-XXe siècle* (Paris: Le Félin Kiron, 2004).

Hagemann, Karen, "Francophobia and Patriotism: Anti-French Images and Sentiments in Prussia and Northern Germany During the Anti-Napoleonic Wars," *French History,* vol. XVIII, no. 4 (2004), pp. 404–25.

——, "German Heroes: The Cult of the Death [sic] for the Fatherland in Nineteenth-Century Germany," in Stefan Dudink, Karen Hagemann, and John Tosh, eds., *Masculinities in Politics and War: Gendering Modern History* (Manchester, England: Manchester University Press, 2004), pp. 116–34.

——, *"Mannlicher Muth und Teutsche Ehre": Nation, Militär und Geschlecht zur Zeit der Antinapoleonischen Kriege Preußens* (Paderborn, Germany: Ferdinand Schöningh, 2002).

——, "Of 'Manly Valor' and 'German Honor': Nation, War and Masculinity in the Age of the Prussian Uprising Against Napoleon," *Central European History,* vol. XXX, no. 3 (1997), pp. 187–220.

Hanley, Wayne, *The Genesis of Napoleonic Propaganda, 1796–1799,* at http://www. gutenberg-e.org/haw01/, consulted on June 26, 2006.

Hanson, Victor Davis, *Carnage and Culture: Landmark Battles in the Rise of Western Power* (New York: Doubleday, 2001).

Harari, Yuval Noah, *Renaissance Military Memoirs: War, History, and Identity, 1450–1600* (Rochester, England: Boydell, 2004).

Hardman, John, *Robespierre* (New York: Longman, 1999).

Hazareesingh, Sudhir, "Force for Glory," *Times Literary Supplement,* February 18, 2005.

——, *The Legend of Napoleon* (London: Granta, 2004).

——, *The Saint-Napoleon: Celebrations of Sovereignty in Nineteenth-Century France* (Cambridge, Mass.: Harvard University Press, 2004).

Healey, F. G., *The Literary Culture of Napoleon* (Geneva: Droz, 1959).

Hegel, Georg Wilhem Friedrich, *Briefe von und an Hegel,* ed. Johannes Hoffmeister, 4 vols. (Hamburg: Felix Meier, 1952).

Henry, Isabelle, *Dumouriez, Général de la Révolution* (Paris: L'Harmattan, 2002).

Herbert, Bob, "A Black Hole," *New York Times,* December 5, 2005.

Herlaut, Auguste-Philippe, *Le général rouge Ronsin (1751–1794): La Vendée, l'armée révolutionnaire parisienne* (Paris: Clavreuil, 1956).

Herold, Christopher, trans. and ed., *The Mind of Napoleon: A Selection from His Written and Spoken Words* (New York: Columbia University Press, 1955).

Herr, Richard, "Good, Evil, and Spain's Rising Against Napoleon," in Richard Herr and Harold Parker, eds., *Ideas in History* (Durham, N.C.: Duke University Press, 1965), pp. 157–82.

Hippler, Thomas, "Service militaire et intégration nationale pendant la Révolution française," *Annales historiques de la Révolution française,* 2002, no. 3, pp. 1–16.

Hirschman, Albert O., *The Passions and the Interests: Political Arguments for Capitalism before Its Triumph* (Princeton, N.J.: Princeton University Press, 1977).

Hocquellet, Richard, *Résistance et révolution durant l'occupation napoléonienne en Espagne, 1808–1812* (Paris: La Boutique de l'Histoire, 2001).

Holbach, Paul-Henri Thiry, baron d', *La morale universelle, ou les devoirs de l'homme fondés sur sa nature*, 3 vols. (Amsterdam: M.-M. Rey, 1776).

———, *Système de la nature ou des loix du monde physique et du monde moral*, 2 vols. (London, n.p., 1771).

———, *Système social, ou principes naturels de la morale et de la politique avec un examen de l'influence du gouvernement sur les moeurs*, 3 vols. (London, n.p., 1773).

Holtman, Robert B., *Napoleonic Propaganda* (Baton Rouge: Louisiana State University Press, 1950).

Holzing, Karl Franz von, *Unter Napoleon in Spanien: Denkwürdigkeiten eines badischen Rheinbundoffiziers (1787–1839)*, ed. Max Dufner-Greif (Berlin: Hans von Hugo, 1937).

Hopkin, David M., *Soldier and Peasant in French Popular Culture, 1766–1870* (Woodbridge, England: Royal Historical Society, 2003).

Houtte, Hubert van, *Les occupations étrangères en Belgique sous l'ancien régime*, 2 vols. (Ghent: Van Rysselberghe & Rombaut, 1930).

Howard, Michael, *The Invention of Peace: Reflections on War and International Order* (New Haven, Conn.: Yale University Press, 2000).

———, *War in European History* (Oxford: Oxford University Press, 1976).

Huber, Ernst Rudolf, ed., *Dokumente zur deutschen Verfassungsgeschichte*, 3 vols. (Stuttgart: W. Kohlhammer, 1961).

Hublot, Emmanuel, *Valmy, ou la défense de la nation par les armes* (Paris: Fondation pour les études de défense nationale, 1987).

Hughes, Michael J., *"'Vive la République! Vive l'Empereur!'*: Military Culture and Motivation in the Armies of Napoleon, 1803–1808," Ph.D. dissertation, University of Illinois, Champaign-Urbana, 2005.

Hugo, Joseph-Léopold-Sigisbert, *Mémoires du Général Hugo*, 3 vols. (Paris: Ladvocat, 1823).

Hugo, Victor, *Quatre-vingt-treize* (1873), at http://abu.cnam.fr/cgi-bin/donner_html?quatrevt1, consulted on June 26, 2006.

Hull, Isabel, *Absolute Destruction: Military Culture and the Practices of War in Imperial Germany* (Ithaca, N.Y.: Cornell University Press, 2005).

Humboldt, Wilhelm von, *Ideen zu einem Versuch die Grenzen der Wirksamkeit des Staates zu bestimmen* (1792), at http://gutenberg.spiegel.de/humboldw/wirksam/wirksam.htm, consulted on June 26, 2006.

Hunt, Lynn, "The Paradoxical Origins of Human Rights," in Jeffrey N. Wasserstrom, Lynn Hunt, and Marilyn B. Young, eds., *Human Rights and Revolutions* (Lanham, Md.: Rowman & Littlefield, 2000), pp. 3–17.

Hussenet, Jacques, "Comment dénomber les morts de la Vendée?" in *La Vendée: Après la terreur, la reconstruction* (Paris: Perrin, 1997).

Iung, Théodore, *L'armée et la Révolution: Dubois-Crancé*, 2 vols. (Paris: Charpentier, 1884).

Jacob, Margaret C., "The Crisis of the European Mind: Hazard Revisited," in Phyllis Mack and Margaret C. Jacob, eds., *Politics and Culture in Early Modern Europe: Essays in Honor of H. G. Koenigsberger* (Cambridge: Cambridge University Press, 1987), pp. 251–71.

Jacobson, Andrew, "The Pageant Swift and Free: The State and Public Representation in Paris and London, 1799–1830," Ph.D. dissertation, Yale University, 1998.

Jainchill, Andrew, "The Constitution of the Year III and the Persistence of Classical Republicanism," *French Historical Studies*, vol. XXVI, no. 3 (2003), pp. 399–436.

James, William, "The Moral Equivalent of War" (1910), in Leon Bramson and George W. Goethals, eds., *War: Studies from Psychology, Sociology, Anthropology* (New York: Basic Books, 1964), pp. 21–31.

Janet, Paul, *Fénelon* (Paris: Hachette, 1892).

Jansen, Christian, ed., *Der Bürger als Soldat: Die Militarisierung europäischer Gesellschaften im langen 19. Jahrhundert: ein internationaler Vergleich* (Essen, Germany: Klartext, 2004).

Janssen, Wilhelm, "Friede," in Brunner, Conze, and Koselleck, vol. II, pp. 543–91.

——, "Krieg," in Brunner, Conze, and Koselleck, vol. III, pp. 567–617.

——, "Johann Valentin Embser und der vorrevolutionäre Bellizismus in Deutschland," in Kunisch and Münkler, pp. 44–55.

Jeismann, Michael, *Der Vaterland der Feinde: Studien zum nationalen Feindbegriff und Selbstverständnis in Deutschland und Frankreich, 1792–1918* (Stuttgart: Klett-Cotta, 1992).

Jennings, Francis, *Empire of Fortune: Crowns, Colonies and Tribes in the Seven Years War in America* (New York: W. W. Norton, 1988).

Joas, Hans, *War and Modernity*, trans. Rodney Livingstone (Cambridge: Polity, 2003).

Johnson, Paul, *Napoleon* (New York: Viking, 2002).

Johnston, Otto W., *The Myth of a Nation: Literature and Politics in Prussia under Napoleon* (Columbia, S.C.: Camden House, 1989).

Joliclerc, François-Xavier, *Joliclerc: Volontaire aux armées de la Révolution, ses lettres (1793–1796)*, ed. Étienne Joliclerc, intro. Frantz Funck-Brentano (Paris: Perrin, 1905).

Jordan, David P., *The Revolutionary Career of Maximilien Robespierre* (New York: Free Press, 1985).

Jouanna, Arlette, *L'idée de race en France au XVIème siècle (1498–1614)*, 3 vols. (Lille, France: Université de Lille III, 1976).

Jourdan, Annie, "Du sacre du philosophe au sacre du militaire," *Revue d'histoire moderne et contemporaine*, vol. XXXIV (1992), pp. 403–22.

——, "Napoléon et la paix universelle: Utopie et réalité," in J.-C. Martin, ed., *Napoléon et l'Europe*, pp. 55–69.

——, *Napoléon: Héros, Imperator, Mécène* (Paris: Aubier, 1998).

——, *La Révolution, une exception française?* (Paris: Flammarion, 2004).

Joutard, Philippe, ed., *Les camisards* (Paris: Gallimard, 1994).

Joux, Pierre, *La France sauvée: Discours prononcé le 7 décembre 1806* (Nantes, France: Imprimerie de Brun, 1806).

Julia, Dominique, *Les trois couleurs du tableau noir: La Révolution* (Paris: Belin, 1981).

Kagan, Robert, "Power and Weakness," *Policy Review*, June 2002, at http://www.policyreview.org/jun02/kagan_print.html, consulted on June 26, 2006.

——, *Of Paradise and Power: America and Europe in the New World Order* (New York: Knopf, 2003).

Kaiser, Thomas E., "Louis *le Bien-Aimé* and the Rhetoric of the Royal Body," in Sara E. Melzer and Kathryn Norberg, eds., *From the Royal to the Republican Body: In-*

corporating the Political in Seventeenth- and Eighteenth-Century France (Berkeley: University of California Press, 1998), pp. 131–61.

Kant, Immanuel, *The Critique of Judgment* (1790), at http://philosophy.eserver.org/kant/critique-of-judgment.txt, consulted on June 26, 2006.

——, "Eternal Peace," in Carl Joachim Friedrich, *Inevitable Peace* (Cambridge, Mass.: Harvard University Press, 1948), pp. 241–81.

——, "The Idea of a Universal Cosmopolitical History" (1784), in *Kant's Principles of Politics, including his essay on Perpetual Peace. A Contribution to Political Science,* trans. W. Hastie (Edinburgh: Clark, 1891).

Kaplan, Robert D., "The Dangers of Peace," in *The Coming Anarchy: Shattering the Dreams of the Post Cold War* (New York: Random House, 2000).

——, *An Empire Wilderness: Travels into America's Future* (New York: Random House, 1998), excerpted at http://www.nytimes.com/books/first/k/kaplan-empire.html, consulted on June 26, 2006.

——, *Imperial Grunts: The American Military on the Ground* (New York: Random House, 2005).

——, "The New Evils of the 21st Century," in Charles Hermann, Harold K. Jacobson, and Anne S. Moffat, eds., *Violent Conflict in the 21st Century* (Chicago: American Academy of Arts and Sciences, Midwest Center, 1999).

Keegan, John, *The Face of Battle: A Study of Agincourt, Waterloo and the Somme* (Harmondsworth, England: Penguin, 1978).

——, *A History of Warfare* (New York: Knopf, 1994).

Kennedy, Paul M., *The Rise and Fall of the Great Powers: Economic Change and Military Conflict from 1500 to 2000* (New York: Random House, 1987).

Kennett, Lee, *The French Armies in the Seven Years' War: A Study in Military Organization and Administration* (Durham, N.C.: Duke University Press, 1967).

Keohane, Nannerl O., *Philosophy and the State in France: The Renaissance to the Enlightenment* (Princeton, N.J.: Princeton University Press, 1980).

Kléber, Jean-Baptiste, *Kléber en Vendee (1793–1794),* ed. H. Baguenier Desormeaux (Paris: Picard, 1907).

Kleist, Heinrich von, *Die Hermannsschlacht,* ed. Roland Reuß and Peter Staengle (Brandenburg, Germany: Stroemfeld, 1998).

——, "Ode: Germania an ihre Kinder," at http://klassiker.chadwyck.com/English/all/fulltext?action=byid&id=Z400029053, consulted on June 26, 2006.

Kleßmann, Eckart, ed., *Deutschland unter Napoleon in Augenzeugenberichten* (Düsseldorf: Karl Rauch Verlag, 1965).

Klopstock, Friedrich Gottlieb, "Der Erobrungskrieg" (1793), at http://gutenberg.spiegel.de/klopstoc/gedichte/erobrung.htm, consulted on June 26, 2006.

——, "Sie, und nicht Wir. An La Rochefoucauld" (1790), at http://www.fhaugsburg.de/~harsch/germanica/Chronologie/18Jh/Klopstock/klo_rev1.html, consulted on June 26, 2006.

Koenigsberger, H. G., "The Organization of Revolutionary Parties in France and the Netherlands During the Sixteenth Century," *Journal of Modern History,* vol. XXVII (1955), no. 4, pp. 335–351.

Körner, Theodor, *Leier und Schwert* (1814), http://www.gutenberg.spiegel.de/koerner/leier/leier.htm, consulted on June 26, 2006.

Kors, Alan Charles, *D'Holbach's Coterie: An Enlightenment in Paris* (Princeton, N.J.: Princeton University Press, 1976).

Koselleck, Reinhart, *Critique and Crisis: Enlightenment and the Pathogenesis of Modern Society* (Cambridge, Mass.: MIT Press, 1988).

Kruse, Wolfgang, *Die Erfinding des modernen Militarismus: Krieg, Militär und bürgerliche Gesellschaft im politischen Diskurs der Französischen Revolution 1789–1799* (Munich: Oldenbourg, 2003).

Kunisch, Johannes, "Die Denunzierung des Ewigen Friedens: Der Krieg als moralische Anstalt in der Literatur und Publizistik der Spätaufklärung," in Kunisch and Münkler, pp. 57–73.

Kunisch, Johannes, and Herfried Münkler, eds.: *Die Wiedergeburt des Krieges aus dem Geist der Revolution: Studien zum bellizistischen Diskurs des ausgegehenden 18. und beginninden 19. Jahrhunderts* (Berlin: Dunckler and Humblot, 1999).

La Barre de Raillicourt, Dominique, *Richelieu le maréchal libertin* (Paris: Tallandier, 1991).

La Bouëre, Antoinette-Charlotte Le Duc de, *Souvenirs de la comtesse de la Bouëre* (Paris: Plon, 1890).

La Bruyère, Jean de, *Les caractères, ou les moeurs de ce siècle,* ed. Robert Garapon (Paris: Bordas, 1990).

La Championnière, Pierre-Suzanne Lucas de, *Mémoires sur la Guerre de Vendée (1793–1796)* (Paris: Plon-Nourrit, 1904).

La Harpe, Jean-François de, *Oeuvres de La Harpe,* vol. V (Geneva: Slatkine Reprints, 1968).

La Rochejaquelein, Marie-Louise-Victoire Donissan de, *Mémoires de Madame la Marquise de La Rochejaquelein,* ed. Julien-Gaston du Vergier de la Rochejaquelein (Paris: Bourloton, 1889), at http://www.abive.org, consulted on December 15, 2004.

Lafayette, Marie-Joseph-Paul-Yves-Roch-Gilbert du Motier, marquis de, *Mémoires, correspondance et manuscrits du général Lafayette,* 6 vols. (Paris: H. Fournier, 1837–38).

Lafoz Rabaza, Herminio, *La guerra de la independencia en Aragón: Del Motín de Aranjuez a la capitulación de Zaragoza* (Saragossa, Spain: Institución "Fernando el Católico," 1996).

Lahure, L.-J., *Souvenirs de la vie militaire du Lieutenant-Général Baron L.-J. Lahure, 1787–1815,* ed. P. Lahure, 2 vols. (Paris: A. Lahure, 1895).

Lallié, Alfred, *J.-B. Carrier* (Paris: Perrin, 1901).

Lameth, Alexandre de, *Histoire de l'Assemblée constituante,* 2 vols. (Paris: Moutardier, 1828–29).

Lamontagne, Pierre, *Marengo: Ode* (Bordeaux : Fernel, 1800).

Langendorf, Jean-Jacques, "Rühle von Lillienstern und seine Apologie des Krieges," in Kunisch and Münkler, pp. 211–23.

Las Cases, Emmanuel de, *Le mémorial de Sainte-Hélène,* ed. Gérard Walter, 2 vols. (Paris: Gallimard, 1956–57).

Lassius, Yves, *L'Egypte, une aventure savante: Avec Bonaparte, Kléber, Menou 1798–1801* (Paris: Fayard, 1998).

Latreille, Albert, *L'Armée et la nation à la fin de l'ancien régime: Les derniers ministres de la Guerre de la monarchie* (Paris: Chapelot, 1914).

Laurens, Henry, et al., *L'expédition d'Egypte* (Paris: Armand Colin, 1989).

Lauzun, Armand-Louis de Gontaut de, *Mémoires secrets du beau Lauzun,* ed. Edmond Pilon (Paris: Colbert, 1943).

Le Bouvier-Desmortiers, Urbain, *Vie du général Charette* (Nantes, France: Mellinet-Massis, 1823, repr. Bouère: Dominique Martin Morin, 1996).

Le Gendre, Bertrand, "La Vendée et le Goulag: Alexandre Soljenitsyne rend hommage samedi, aux Lucs-sur-Boulogne, aux victimes de la Terreur," *Le Monde,* September 25, 1993.

Lebrun, Richard A., "Joseph de Maistre's 'Philosophic' View of War," in Joyce Duncan Falk, ed., *Proceedings of the Seventh Annual Meeting of the Western Society for French History, 1–3 November 1979, Omaha, Nebraska* (Santa Barbara, Calif.: Western Society for French History, 1981), pp. 43–52.

Ledeen, Michael, *Machiavelli on Modern Leadership: Why Machiavelli's Iron Rules Are As Timely and Important Today As Five Centuries Ago* (New York: Truman Talley Books, 1999).

Leggiere, Michael V., *Napoleon and Berlin: The Franco-Prussian War in North Germany, 1813* (Norman: University of Oklahoma Press, 2002).

Lemny, Stefan, *Jean-Louis Carra (1742–1793): Parcours d'un révolutionnaire* (Paris: L'Harmattan, 2000).

Lentz, Thierry, *Nouvelle histoire du premier empire,* 3 vols. (Paris: Fayard, 2002–).

——, "Was the Napoleonic Regime a Military Dictatorship?" paper delivered at the Consortium for the Revolutionary Era, Atlanta, March 2006.

Lentz, Thierry, and Nathalie Clot, eds., *La proclamation du premier empire, ou Recueil des pièces et actes relatifs à l'établissement du gouvernement impérial héréditaire* (Paris: Nouveau Monde, 2004).

Léonard, Émile G., *L'armée et ses problèmes au XVIIIe siècle* (Paris: Plon, 1958).

Lequinio, Joseph-Marie, *Guerre de la Vendée et des Chouans* (Paris: Pougin, 1795).

Leuwers, Hervé, "Révolution et guerre de conquête: Les origines d'une nouvelle raison d'État (1789–1795)," *Revue du Nord,* vol. LXXXV, no. 299 (1993), pp. 21–40.

Lever, Maurice, ed., *Bibliothèque Sade,* 7 vols. (Paris: Fayard, 1993–).

Levinger, Matthew, "The Prussian Reform Movement and the Rise of Enlightened Nationalism," in Dwyer, *The Rise of Prussia,* pp. 259–75.

Lévis, Pierre-Marc-Gaston, duc de, "Lettres du duc de Lévis (1784–1795)," *La revue de France* (1929), pp. 425–44.

Lilla, Mark, "Carl Schmitt," in Mark Lilla, *The Reckless Mind: Intellectuals in Politics* (New York: New York Review Books, 2001), pp. 48–76.

Lilti, Antoine, *Le monde des salons: Sociabilité et mondantié à Paris au XVIIIe siècle* (Paris: Fayard, 2005).

Lindsay, Suzanne Glover, "Mummies and Tombs: Turenne, Napoleon, and Death Ritual," *Art Bulletin,* vol. LXXXII, no. 3 (2000), pp. 476–502.

Lipsky, David, "Appropriating the Globe," *New York Times Book Review,* November 27, 2005, pp. 7–8.

Livesey, James, *Making Democracy in the French Revolution* (Cambridge, Mass.: Harvard University Press, 2001).

Lockroy, Édouard, ed., *Une mission en Vendée* (Paris: Paul Ollendorff, 1893).

Lofficial, Louis-Prosper, *Journal d'un conventionnel en Vendée,* ed. C. Leroux-Cesbron (Paris: Flammarion, 1896).

Longworth, Philip, *The Art of Victory: The Life and Achievements of Field Marshal Suvorov* (New York: Holt, Rinehart and Winston, 1966).

Loque, Bertrand de, *Deux traités, l'un de la guerre, l'autre du duel* (Lyon: J. Ratoyre, 1589).

Lorson, Pierre, "Guerre et paix chez Fénelon," *XVIIe siècle,* nos. 12–14 (1951), pp. 207–14.

Lort de Sérignan, Arthur de, *Un duc et pair au service de la Révolution: Le duc de Lauzun (Général Biron), 1791–1792: Correspondence intime* (Paris: Perrin, 1906).

Lovett, Gabriel H., "The Spanish Guerrillas and Napoleon," *Proceedings of the Consortium on Revolutionary Europe, 1750–1850,* vol. V (1975), pp. 80–90.

——, *Napoleon and the Birth of Modern Spain,* 2 vols. (New York: New York University Press, 1965).

Lumbroso, Giacomo, *I moti popolari contro I francesi alla fine del secolo XVIII (1796–1800)* (Florence: Felice Le Monnier, 1932).

Lüsebrink, Hans-Jürgen, "'Die Genese der Grande Nation': Vom *Soldat-Citoyen* zur Idee des *Empire,"* in Ulrich Herrmann, ed., *Volk — Nation — Vaterland* (Hamburg: Felix Meiner Verlag, 1996), pp. 118–30.

Lynch, Deidre Shauna, *The Economy of Character: Novels, Market Culture, and the Business of Inner Meaning* (Chicago: University of Chicago Press, 1998).

Lynn, John A., "A Brutal Necessity? The Devastation of the Palatinate, 1688–1689," in Grimsley and Rogers, pp. 79–110.

——, "French Opinion and the Military Resurrection of the Pike, 1792–1794," *Military Affairs,* vol. 41, no. 1 (1977), pp. 1–7.

——, "Guerre et culture, 'Lumières' et Romantisme dans la pensée militaire," in Biard, Crépin, and Gainot, pp. 327–44.

——, "Toward an Army of Honor: The Moral Evolution of the French Army, 1789–1815," *French Historical Studies,* vol. 16, no. 1 (1989), pp. 152–73.

——, *Giant of the Grand Siècle: The French Army, 1610–1715* (Cambridge: Cambridge University Press, 1997).

——, *The Bayonets of the Republic: Motivation and Tactics in the Army of Revolutionary France, 1791–94* (Urbana: University of Illinois Press, 1984).

Lyons, Martyn, *France under the Directory* (Cambridge: Cambridge University Press, 1975).

——, *Napoleon Bonaparte and the Legacy of the French Revolution* (New York: St. Martin's, 1994).

Mably, Gabriel Bonnot de, *Entretiens de Phocion sur le raport de la morale avec la politique* (The Hague: Daniel Alliaud, 1764).

Machiavelli, Niccolò, *L'arte della guerra* (1520), at http://www.classicitaliani.it/machiav/mac22.htm, consulted on June 26, 2006.

——, *Discorsi sopra la prima deca di Tito Livio,* at http://www.classicitaliani.it/index054.htm, consulted on June 26, 2006.

——, *The Works of the Famous Nicholas Machiavel, Citizen and Secretary of Florence* (London: A. Churchill et al., 1720).

——, *The Works of Nicholas Machiavel, Secretary of State of the Republic of Florence,* 4 vols. (London: T. Davies et al., 1775).

Mackenzie, S. P., *Revolutionary Armies in the Modern Era: A Revisionist Approach* (London: Routledge, 1997).

Mackintosh, James, *Vindiciæ Gallicæ. Defence of the French Revolution and Its English Admirers, Against the Accusations of the Right Hon. Edmund Burke* (London: G.G.J. and J. Robinson, 1791).

Maistre, Joseph de, *Considérations sur la France,* ed. Pierre Manent (Paris: Complexe, 1988).

——, *Les Soirées de Saint-Pétersbourg, ou Entretiens sur le gouvernement temporel de la providence,* 2 vols. (Paris: Janssens and Van Merlen, 1822).

Malacrida, Luigi, *L'incendio di Binasco nella guerra napoleonica* (Pavia, Italy: Cardano, 2001).

Manche, Georges-Frédéric, "L'armée française à l'épreuve de la Calabre (1806–1813)," *CCEHD,* no. 19 (2002), pp. 79–119.

Mann, Michael, "War and Social Theory: Into Battle with Classes, Nations and States," in Martin Shaw and Colin Creighton, eds., *The Sociology of War and Peace* (Houndmills, England: Macmillan, 1987), pp. 54–72.

Mannucci, Erica Joy, *Il patriota e il Vaudeville: Teatro, Pubblico e Potere nella Parigi della Rivoluzione* (Naples: Vivarium, 1998).

Mao Zedong [Mao Tse-tung], *Quotations from Chairman Mao Tse-tung,* at http://art-bin.com/art/omaotoc.html, consulted June 28, 2006.

Marat, Jean-Paul, *Œuvres politiques, 1789–1793,* ed. Jacques de Cock and Charlotte Goëtz, 7 vols. (Brussels: Pole Nord, 1989–1995).

Marbot, Jean-Baptiste-Antoine-Marcelin de, *The Memoirs of Baron de Marbot, Late Lieutenant-General in the French Army,* trans. Arthur John Butler, 2 vols. (London: Longmans, Green & Co., 1982).

Marcel, Nicolas, *Campagnes du Capitaine Marcel du 69e ligne en Espagne et en Portugal (1808–1814)* (Paris: Plon, 1913).

Marchand, Louis-Joseph-Narcisse, *Mémoires de Marchand, premier valet de chambre et exécuteur testamentaire de l'empereur,* 2 vols. (Paris: Plon, 1952–55).

Maréchal, Sylvain, *Le jugement dernier des rois* (Paris: C. F. Patris, 1793–94).

Maricourt, André de, "Un intendant de Corse sous Louis XVI. Daniel-Marc-Antoine Chardon et sa famille (1731–1805)," *Revue des questions historiques,* vol. LXX (1905), pp. 497–542.

Marmont, Auguste-Frédéric-Louis Wiesse de, *Mémoirs du Maréchal Marmont duc de Raguse, de 1792 à 1841,* 9 vols. (Paris: Perrotin, 1857).

Marshall, Monty G., and Ted Robert Gurr, *Peace and Conflict 2005: A Global Survey of Armed Conflicts, Self-Determination Movements, and Democracy* (College Park, Md.: Center for International Development and Conflict Management, University of Maryland, 2005).

Martín, Andrés, *Historia de los sucesos militares de la division de Navarra* (1825), ed. J.-M. Irribarren (Pamplona: El Gallico, 1953).

Martin, Andy, *Napoleon the Novelist* (Cambridge: Polity, 2000).

Martin, Jean-Clément, "Le cas de Turreau et des colonnes infernales: Réflexions sur une historiographie," in Biard, Crépin, and Gainot, pp. 237–48.

——, ed., *Napoléon et l'Europe: Colloque de la Roche-sur-Yon* (Rennes, France: Presses Universitaires de Rennes, 2002).

——, *La Vendée et la France* (Paris: Seuil, 1987).

——, "La Vendée, région-mémoire: Bleus et blancs," in Pierre Nora, ed., *Les lieux de mémoire,* 3 vols. (Paris: Gallimard Quarto, 1997), vol. I, pp. 519–34.

Martin, Jean-Clément, and Xavier Lardière, *Le massacre des Lucs: Vendée 1794* (Vouillé, France: Gesté, 1992).

Martin, Marc, *Les origines de la presse militaire en France à la fin de l'ancien régime et sous la révolution (1770–1799)* (Vincennes, France: Service Historique de l'Armée de Terre, 1975).

Masséna, André, *Mémoires d'André Masséna,* 8 vols., ed. Général Koch (Paris: Bonnot, 1966).

Massenbach, Christian Karl August Ludwig von, *Memoiren zur Geschichte des Preussischen Staats unter den Regierungen Friedrich Wilhelm II. und Friedrich Wilhelm III,* 3 vols. (Amsterdam: Kunst- und Industrie-Comptoir, 1809).

Mathiez, Albert, "Pacifisme et nationalisme au XVIIIe siècle," *Annales historiques de la Révolution française,* vol. XIIII (1936), pp. 1–17.

——, *La victoire en l'an II: Esquisses historiques sur la défense nationale* (Paris: Félix Alcan, 1916).

Maugras, Gaston, *The Duc de Lauzun and the Court of Louis XV* (London: Osgood, McIlvaine, 1895).

——, *The Duc de Lauzun and the Court of Marie-Antoinette* (London: Osgood, McIlvaine, 1896).

Maupetit, Michel-René, "Lettres de Michel-René Maupetit," ed. E. Queruau-Lamerie, part IV, *Bulletin de la commission historique et archéologique de la Mayenne,* 2e série, vol. XX (1904), pp. 446–72.

Mautort, Louis-François de Paule Tillette de, *Mémoires du chevalier de Mautort,* ed. Baron Tillette de Clermont-Tonnerre (Paris: Plon-Nourrit, 1895).

McKay, Derek, and H. M. Scott, *The Rise of the Great Powers: 1648–1815* (London: Longman, 1983).

McManners, John, *The French Revolution and the Church* (New York: Harper & Row, 1969).

Meinecke, Friedrich, *The Age of German Liberation, 1795–1815,* ed. Peter Paret (Berkeley: University of California Press, 1977).

Memoirs relative to Egypt, written in that country during the campaigns of General Bonaparte, in the years 1798 and 1799 (London: T. Gillet, 1800).

Mercier de la Rivière, Pierre-Paul, *L'ordre naturel et essentiel des sociétés politiques* (London: Jean Nourse, 1767).

Mercier du Rocher, André, *Mémoires pour servir à l'histoire de la guerre de Vendée,* ed. Thérèse Rouchette (Loudéac: Yves Salmon, 1989).

Mercoyrol de Beaulieu, Jacques de, *Campagnes de Jacques de Mercoyrol de Beaulieu,* 3 vols. (Paris: Renouard, 1915).

Mermale, François, "Lettres inédites d'un sous-lieutenant de l'armée des Alpes (1792–1793)," *Annales historiques de la Révolution française,* vol. VI (1929), pp. 56–74.

Mesonero Romanos, Ramón de, *Memorias de un setentón,* ed. José Escobar and Joaquín Álvariz Barrientos (Madrid: Editorial Castalia, 1994).

Metternich, Clemens Lothar Wengel, *Mémoires,* 2 vols. (Paris: Plon, 1880).

Meyer, Jean, "'De la guerre' au XVIIe siècle," *XVIIe siècle,* no. 148 (1985), pp. 267–90.

Michelet, Jules, *Histoire de la Révolution française,* ed. Gérard Walter, 2 vols. (Paris: Gallimard, 1952).

Michon, Georges, *Robespierre et la guerre révolutionnaire, 1791–1792* (Paris: Marcel Rivière, 1937).

Miot de Melito, André-François, *Memoirs of Count Miot de Melito*, ed. General Fleischmann, trans. Cashel Hoey and John Lillie (New York: Scribner's, 1881).

Moliner Prada, Antonio, "Popular Resistance in Catalonia: Somatens and Miquelets, 1808–14," in Esdaile, *Popular Resistance*, pp. 91–114.

Montaigne, Michel de, *Complete Essays*, trans. Donald M. Frame (Stanford, Calif.: Stanford University Press, 1957).

Montesquieu, Charles-Louis de Secondat, baron de, *The Spirit of the Laws*, ed. and trans. Anne M. Cohler, Basia Carolyn Miller, and Harold Samuel Stone (Cambridge: Cambridge University Press, 1989), p. 27.

Montholon, Charles-Tristan de, *Mémoires pour servir à l'histoire de France sous Napoléon, écrits à Sainte-Hélène*, 7 vols. (London: M. Bossange, 1823–24).

Moran, Daniel, "Arms and the Concert: The Nation in Arms and the Dilemmas of German Liberalism," in Moran and Waldron, pp. 49–74.

Moran, Daniel, and Arthur Waldron, eds., *The People in Arms: Military Myth and National Mobilization since the French Revolution* (Cambridge: Cambridge University Press, 2003).

Moreno Alonso, Manuel, *Los Españoles durante la ocupación napoleónica: La vida cotidiana en la vorágine* (Málaga, Spain: Editorial Algazara, 1997).

Mori, Massimo, "Das Bild des Krieges bei den deutschen Philosophen," in Kunisch and Münkler, pp. 225–40.

Morrissey, Robert, "The *Mémorial de Sainte-Hélène* and the Poetics of Fusion," *Modern Language Notes*, no. 120 (2005), pp. 716–32.

Motley, Mark, *Becoming a French Aristocrat: The Education of the Court Nobility, 1580–1715* (Princeton, N.J.: Princeton University Press, 1990).

Mozzillo, Atanasio, *Chronache della Calabria in Guerra, 1806–1811*, 3 vols. (Rome: Edizioni Scientifiche Italiane, 1972).

Mueller, John E., *Remnants of War* (Ithaca, N.Y.: Cornell University Press, 2004).

——, *Retreat from Doomsday: The Obsolescence of Major War* (New York: Basic Books, 1989).

Muir, Rory, *Britain and the Defeat of Napoleon, 1807–1815* (New Haven, Conn.: Yale University Press, 1996).

——, *Salamanca 1812* (New Haven, Conn., and London: Yale University Press, 2001).

——, *Tactics and the Experience of Battle in the Age of Napoleon* (New Haven, Conn.: Yale University Press, 1998).

Nef, John U., *War and Human Progress: An Essay on the Rise of Industrial Civilization* (Cambridge, Mass.: Harvard University Press, 1950).

Neff, Stephen C., *War and the Law of Nations: A General History* (Cambridge: Cambridge University Press, 2005).

Newitt, Malyn, and Martin Robson, eds., *Lord Beresford and British Intervention in Portugal, 1807–1820* (Lisbon: Imprensa de Ciências Sociais, 2004).

Noël, Gabriel, *Au temps des volontaires, 1792: Lettres d'un volontaire de 1792* (Paris: Plon-Nourrit, 1912).

O'Brien, David, "Propaganda and the Republic of Arts in Antoine-Jean Gros's *Napoléon Visiting the Battlefield of Eylau the Morning after the Battle*," *French Historical Studies*, vol. XXVI, no. 2 (2003), pp. 281–314.

O'Brien, David C., "Traditional Virtues, Feudal Ties and Royal Guards: The Culture of Service in the Eighteenth-Century *Maison Militaire du Roi*," *French History*, vol. XVII, no. 1 (2003), pp. 19–47.

O'Meara, Barry, *Napoleon in Exile, or A Voice from St. Helena: The Opinions and Reflections of Napoleon on the Most Important Events of His Life and Government in His Own Words* (London: Simpkin, and Marshall, 1822).

Oman, Charles, *A History of the Peninsular War*, 7 vols. (Oxford: Clarendon Press, 1902–30).

Ormsby, James Wilmot, *An Account of the Operations of the British Army, and of the State and Sentiments of the People of Portugal and Spain*, 2 vols. (London: James Carpenter, 1809).

Owen, Wilfrid, "Dulce et Decorum Est," at http://www.warpoetry.co.uk/owen1.html, consulted July 9, 2006.

Ozouf, Mona, *L'homme régénéré: Essais sur la Révolution française* (Paris: Gallimard, 1989).

———, "War and Terror in French Revolutionary Discourse (1792–1794)," *Journal of Modern History*, vol. LVI, no. 4 (1984), pp. 579–97.

Pagden, Anthony, "Fellow Citizens and Imperial Subjects: Conquest and Sovereignty in Europe's Overseas Empires," *History and Theory*, vol. XLIV (2005), pp. 28–46.

Palluel-Guillard, André, "L'idée de nation en France entre 1800 et 1815," in Natalie Petiteau, ed., *Voies nouvelles pour l'histoire du Premier Empire: Territoires, Pouvoirs, Identités* (Paris: La Boutique de l'Histoire, 2003), pp. 27–43.

Palmer, R. R., "Frederick the Great, Guibert, Bülow: From Dynastic to National War," in Peter Paret, ed., *Makers of Modern Strategy: From Machiavelli to the Nuclear Age* (Princeton, N.J.: Princeton University Press, 1986), pp. 91–119.

———, *Twelve Who Ruled: The Year of the Terror in the French Revolution* (Princeton, N.J.: Princeton University Press, 1941, repr. 1969).

Pangaud, Léonce, ed., *L'invasion austro-prussienne (1792–94): Documents* (Paris: Alphonse Picard, 1895).

Paret, Peter, "Clausewitz," in Peter Paret, ed., *Makers of Modern Strategy: From Machiavelli to the Nuclear Age* (Princeton, N.J.: Princeton University Press, 1986), pp. 186–213.

———, "Die Darstellung des Krieges in der Kunst," in Kunisch and Münkler, pp. 93–111.

———, "The Genesis of *On War*," in Clausewitz, *On War*, pp. 3–25.

———, "Napoleon and the Revolution in War," in Peter Paret, ed., *Makers of Modern Strategy: From Machiavelli to the Nuclear Age* (Princeton, N.J.: Princeton University Press, 1986), pp. 123–42.

———, *Yorck and the Era of Prussian Reform* (Princeton, N.J.: Princeton University Press, 1966).

Parker, Geoffrey, *The Military Revolution: Military Innovation and the Rise of the West, 1500–1800*, 2nd ed. (Cambridge: Cambridge University Press, 1996).

Parker, Harold T., "Napoleon's Youth and Rise to Power," in Dwyer, *Napoleon and Europe*, pp. 25–42.

Parquin, Charles, *Napoleon's Army: The Military Memoirs of Charles Parquin*, ed. B. T. Jones (London: Greenhill Books, 1987 [orig. 1845]).

Pascal, Blaise, *Pensées sur la religion et sur quelques autres sujets*, ed. Louis Lafuma (Paris: Editions du Luxembourg, 1952).

nd National Identity in Britain and France during the Seven Years'
). dissertation, Boston College (1997).

d., *Robespierre* (Englewood Cliffs, N.J.: Prentice Hall, 1967).

nd, *War to the Death: The Sieges of Saragossa, 1808–1809* (New York:
, 1974).

"Democracies Don't Fight Democracies," *Peace Magazine,* May-June,
http://www.peacemagazine.org/archive/v15n3p10.htm, consulted on
006.

M., *Grasping the Democratic Peace: Principles for a Post–Cold War World*
, N.J.: Princeton University Press, 1993).

Charles-Augustin, *Causeries du lundi,* 15 vols. (Paris: Garnier, 1869–76).

oine-Louis de, *Œuvres complètes de Saint-Just,* ed. Michèle Duval (Paris:
bovici, 1984).

, Jean-François de, *Œuvres de Saint-Lambert,* 2 vols. (Paris: Didot,

Charles-Irénée Castel de, "Discours sur les différences du grand homme
omme illustre," published as introduction to *Histoire d'Épaminondas*
idot, 1739).

our rendre la paix perpétuelle en Europe* (Paris: Fayard, 1986).

Louis de Rouvroy de, *Mémoires complets et authentiques du duc de Saint-*
r le siècle de Louis XIV et la Régence,* ed. Pierre-Adolphe Chéruel, 20 vols.
achette, 1856–58).

Gevaert, "Punic Wars in France and Britain," Ph.D. dissertation, Clare-
raduate School (1996).

Boishuguet, Jeanne-Ambroise de, *Mémoires de Madame de Sapinaud sur*
(Paris: Audin, 1824).

"Favier's Heirs: The French Revolution and the *Secret du Roi,*" *Historical*
vol. 41, no. 1 (1998), pp. 225–58.

-Jean, *Memoirs of the Duke of Rovigo,* at *War Times Journal,* http://
j.com/archives/savary/, consulted on June 26, 2006.

Julien, ed., *Guerres des Vendéens et des Chouans contre la République fran-*
vols. (Paris: Baudouin Frères, 1824–27).

ce de, *Reveries, or Memoirs Upon the Art of War* (London: J. Nourse,

eil, *The Marquis de Sade: A Life* (Cambridge, Mass.: Harvard University
001).

non, *Citizens: A Chronicle of the French Revolution* (New York: Knopf,

, August Ludolf Friedrich, *On the Road with Wellington: The Diary of*
Commissary in the Peninsuar Campaigns,* ed. and trans. Anthony M.
ici (New York: Knopf, 1925).

Ronald, "Gothic Thermidor: The *Bals des victimes,* the Fantastic, and the
ction of Historical Knowledge in Post-Terror France," *Representations,* no.
08), pp. 52–68.

edrich, *Die Braut von Messina Oder die feindlichen Brüder. Ein Trauerspiel*
hören (1803), at http://gutenberg.spiegel.de/schiller/messina/mess105.htm,
lted on June 26, 2006.

Pearson, Roger, *Voltaire Almighty: A Life in Pursuit of Freedom* (London: Bloomsbury,
2005), p. 207.

Pekarek, Marcel, *Absolutismus als Kriegsursache: Die französische Aufklärung zu Krieg
und Frieden* (Stuttgart: W. Kohlhammer, 1997).

Pelletier and Frédéric, *Le vainqueur d'Austerlitz, ou le retour du héros* (Paris: Théâtre des
Jeunes-Artistes, 1806).

Pelzer, Erich, "'Il ne sera fait aucun prisonnier anglais ou hanovrien': Zur Problematik
der Kriegsgefangenen während der Revolutions- und Empirekriege (1792–1815),"
in Rüdiger Overmans, ed., *In der Hand des Feindes: Kriegsgefangenschaft von der
Antike bis zum Zweiten Weltkrieg* (Cologne: Böhlau Verlag, 1999), pp. 189–210.

Penn, William, "An Essay towards the Present and Future Peace of Europe," in *A Collection of the Works of William Penn,* 2 vols. (London: J. Sowle, 1726), vol. II,
pp. 838–48.

Perkins, Merle I., *The Moral and Political Philosophy of the Abbé de Saint-Pierre* (Geneva: Droz, 1959).

Pétigny, Xavier de, *Un bataillon de Volontaires (3me bataillon de Maine-et-Loire), 1792–
1796* (Angers, France: Germain et G. Grassin, 1908).

Petit, Joseph, *Marengo, ou campagne d'Italie* (Paris: Chez les Marchands de nouveautés,
1801).

Petiteau, Natalie, "Débats historiographiques autour de la politique européenne de
Napoléon," in J.-C. Martin, *Napoléon et l'Europe,* pp. 19–31.

———, *Napoléon de la mythologie à l'histoire* (Paris: Seuil, 1999).

Petitfils, Jean-Christian, *Louis XVI* (Paris: Perrin, 2005).

Petitfrère, Claude, *Blancs et bleus d'Anjou (1789–1793),* 2 vols. (Paris: Honoré Champion, 1979).

———, ed., *Le Général Dupuy et sa Correspondance (1792–1798)* (Paris: Société des
Etudes Robespierristes, 1965).

———, *La Vendée et les Vendéens* (Paris: Gallimard, 1981).

Petre, F. Loraine, *Napoleon's Last Campaign in Germany: 1813* (London: John Lane, 1912).

Phipps, Ramsay Weston, *The Armies of the First French Republic and the Rise of the
Marshals of Napoleon I,* 5 vols. (Oxford: Oxford University Press, 1926).

Picard, Ernest, ed., *Au service de la nation: Lettres de volontaires (1792–1798)* (Paris: Félix
Alcan, 1914).

Pion des Loches, Antoine-Augustin-Flavien, *Mes campagnes, 1792–1815,* ed. Maurice
Chipon and Léonce Pingaud (Paris: Firmin-Didot, 1889).

Pitt, William, *Orations on the French War, to the Peace of Amiens* (London: J. M. Dent,
1912).

Podhoretz, Norman, "World War IV: How It Started, What It Means, and Why
We Have to Win," *Commentary,* September 2004, at http://www.commentary
magazine.com/podhoretz.htm, consulted on June 26, 2006.

Poirier de Beauvais, Bertrand, *Mémoires inédits de Bertrand Poirier de Beauvais* (Paris:
Plon-Nourrit, 1893).

Poisson, Georges, *Choderlos de Laclos, ou l'obstination* (Paris: Grasset, 1985).

Pomeau, René, *Voltaire en son temps,* 2nd ed., 2 vols. (Paris: Fayard and the Voltaire
Foundation, 1995).

Pouget, François-René Cailloux de, *Souvenirs de guerre du général baron Pouget,* ed.
Mme. de Boisdeffre, née Pouget (Paris: Plon, 1895).

Prebble, John, *Culloden* (London: Secker and Warburg, 1961).

Prendergast, Christopher, *Napoleon and History Painting: Antoine-Jean Gros's La Bataille d'Eylau* (Oxford: Oxford University Press, 1997).

Price, Munro, "Politics: Louis XVI," in William Doyle, ed., *Old Regime France: 1648–1788* (Oxford: Oxford University Press, 2001).

Pringle, John, *Observations on the Diseases of the Army* (Philadelphia: Edward Earle, 1810).

Quincy, Joseph Sevin de, *Mémoires du Chevalier de Quincy,* ed. Léon Lecestre, 3 vols. (Paris: Renouard, 1898–1901).

Quintana, Manuel José, *Poesias completas* (Madrid: Clásicos Castalia, 1969).

Rabb, Theodore, *The Struggle for Stability in Early Modern Europe* (New York: Oxford University Press, 1975).

Raduget, Xavier, *La carrière politique de l'abbé Maury, 1786–1791* (Paris: Letouzey and Ané, 1912).

Ramies i Verdaguer, Maties, *Els catalans i el domini napoleònic (Catalunya vista pels oficials de l'exèrcit de Napoleó)* (Barcelona: Publicacions de l'Abadia de Montserrat, 1995).

Rapp, Joseph, *Tirol im Jahre 1809* (Innsbruck: Felizian Rauch, 1852).

Rassow, Peter, "Die Wirkung der Erhebung Spaniens auf die Erhebung gegen Napoleon I," *Historische Zeitschrift,* vol. CLXVII (1943).

Raumer, Kurt von, *Die Zerstörung der Pfalz von 1689: Im Zusammenhang der französischen Rheinpolitik* (Munich and Berlin: R. Oldenbourg, 1930).

Ray, Chevalier de, *Réflexions et souvenirs du Chevalier de Ray,* ed. Lucien Mouillard (Paris: Henri Charles-Lavauzelle, 1895).

Rebhann, Fritz M., *Anno Neun: Von Bergisel zum Schönbrunner Frieden* (Vienna: Herold, 1984).

Recueil général des pièces, chansons et fêtes données à l'occasion de la prise du Port-Mahon ("France," 1757).

Reddy, William M., *The Navigation of Feeling: A Framework for the History of Emotions* (Cambridge: Cambridge University Press, 2001).

Reinhard, Marcel, "Nostalgie et service militaire pendant la Révolution," *Annales historiques de la Révolution française,* vol. 30 (1958), pp. 1–15.

——, *Le grand Carnot,* 2 vols. (Paris: Hachette, 1950–52).

Reynaud, Jean-Louis, *Contre-Guerrilla en Espagne (1808–1814): Suchet pacifie l'Aragon* (Paris: Economica, 1992).

Ribbe, Claude, *Le Crime de Napoléon* (Paris: Editions Privé, 2005).

Rigoulet-Roze, David, "La guérilla espagnole contre l'armée napoléonienne," *CCEHD,* no. 18 (2002), pp. 87–113.

Rivoire, Jean-Alexis, *Le patriotisme dans le théâtre sérieux de la Révolution* (Paris: Gilbert, 1950).

Robb, Graham, *Victor Hugo* (New York: W. W. Norton, 1998).

Roberts, Andrew, *Napoleon and Wellington* (London: Weidenfeld and Nicolson, 2001).

Roberts, Warren, *Revolutionary Artists: Jacques-Louis David and Jean-Louis Prieur: The Public, the Populace, and Images of the French Revolution* (Albany: SUNY Press, 2000).

Robertson, William, *The History of the Reign of the Emperor Charles V* (Boston: Phillips, Sampson, 1857).

Robespierre, Maximilien, *Discours cont[...]* fr/discours/guerre.htm, consulted [...]

——, *Rapport fait au nom du comité de [...] et morales avec les principes républic[...]* Nationale, 1794).

Rocca, Albert-Jean de, *Mémoires sur la [...]* Gide fils, 1814).

Roger, Philippe, "Mars au Parnasse," in [...] *Napoléon, les Arts et les Lettres* (Paris[...]

Rogers, Paul, "A World Becoming More [...]* conflict/report_2927.jsp, consulted [...]

Roland de La Platière, Jeanne-Marie, *Lett[...]* vols. (Paris: Imprimerie Nationale, 1[...]

Ronsin, Charles-Philippe, *Détail circonsta[...] Prise de Mons* (Paris: Pougin, 1792).

——, *La ligue aristocratique, ou les Catilin[...]*

——, *La ligue des fanatiques et des tyrans ([...]*

Rosbottom, Ronald C., *Choderlos de Laclos[...]*

Rose, Jacqueline, *Why War? Psychoanalysis[...]* (Oxford: Blackwell, 1993).

Rosenblatt, Helena, "Commerce et relgio[...]* stant," *Commentaire,* no. 102 (2003), p[...]

Ross, Michael, *The Reluctant King: Joseph B[...]* (New York: Mason/Charter, 1977).

Rothenberg, Gunther E., *The Art of Warfare[...]* diana University Press, 1978).

——, *Napoleon's Great Adversaries: The Arch[...] 1814* (Bloomington: Indiana University [...]

——, "Soldiers and the Revolution: The Fr[...] 1799," *Historical Journal,* vol. XXXIV, n[...]

Rothkrug, Lionel, *Opposition to Louis XIV:[...] French Enlightenment* (Princeton, N.J.: P[...]

Rousseau, Jean-Jacques, *Considérations sur le g[...] plètes,* 4 vols. (Paris: Gallimard, 1964), vol[...]

——, *Du contrat social,* in *Œuvres complètes,* 4[...] pp. 347–470.

——, *Discours qui a remporté le prix à l'Acade[...] Question proposée par la même Académie: Si [...] contribué à épurer les mœurs,* at http://un[...] html, consulted on June 26, 2006.

——, "L'état de guerre," in C. E. Vaughn, ed.,[...] *Rousseau,* 2 vols. (Cambridge: Cambridge U[...] 306.

Rousseau, Thomas, et al., *Recueil des actions h[...] français,* (Paris: Imprimerie Nationale, 1793–[...]

Rousset, Camille, *Les volontaires, 1791–1794* (Paris:[...]

Rowe, Nicholas, "Romans and Carthaginians in[...]

Ideology [...]
War," Ph[...]
Rudé, George, [...]
Rudorff, Rayn[...]
  Macmilla[...]
Rummel, R. J.[...]
  1999, at[...]
  June 26, [...]
Russett, Bruce[...]
  (Princeto[...]
Sainte-Beuve, [...]
Saint-Just, Ar[...]
  Gérard [...]
Saint-Lamber[...]
  1795).
Saint-Pierre, [...]
  et de l'[...]
  (Paris: [...]
——, *Projet* [...]
Saint-Simon, [...]
  Simon s[...]
  (Paris: [...]
Salas, Charle[...]
  mont C[...]
Sapinaud de [...]
  la Ven[...]
Savage, Gar[...]
  Journa[...]
Savary, Ant[...]
  www.v[...]
Savary, Jean[...]
  çaise, [...]
Saxe, Mau[...]
  1757).
Schaeffer, [...]
  Press, [...]
Schama, S[...]
  1989) [...]
Schauman[...]
  a W[...]
  Ludo[...]
Schechter[...]
  Prod[...]
  61 (1[...]
Schiller, [...]
  mit [...]
  cons[...]

——, "Resignation: Eine Phantasie," at http://www.buecherzirkel.de/texte/schiller-resignation.htm, consulted on July 5, 2006.

Schivelbush, Wolfgang, *The Culture of Defeat: On National Trauma, Mourning and Recovery*, trans. Jefferson Chase (New York: Picador/Henry Holt, 2004).

Schmitt, Carl, *The Concept of the Political*, ed. and trans. George Schwab (New Brunswick, N.J.: Rutgers University Press, 1976).

——, *Le nomos de la terre dans le droit des gens du jus publicum europaeum*, ed. Peter Haggenmacher, trans. Lilyane Deroche-Gurcel (Paris: P.U.F., 2001).

——, *Theorie des Partisanen: Zwischenbemerkung zum Begriff des Politischen* (Berlin: Duncker and Humblot, 1963).

——, "Totaler Feind, totaler Krieg, totaler Staat" (1937), in *Positionen und Begriffe: Im Kampf mit Weimar — Genf — Versailles, 1923–1939* (Berlin: Duncker and Humblot, 1988), pp. 235–343.

Schneid, Frederick C., *Soldiers of Napoleon's Kingdon of Italy: Army, State and Society, 1800–1815* (Boulder, Colo.: Westview, 1995).

Schom, Alan, *Napoleon Bonaparte* (New York: HarperCollins, 1997).

Schroeder, Paul W., "Napoleon's Foreign Policy: A Criminal Enterprise," *Journal of Military History*, vol. LIV, no. 2 (1990), pp. 147–62.

——, *The Transformation of European Politics, 1763–1848* (Oxford: Clarendon Press, 1994).

Schulze, Hagen, "The Prussian Military State, 1763–1806," in Dwyer, *The Rise of Prussia*, pp. 201–19.

Schumacher, Gaspard, *Journal et souvenirs de Gaspard Schumacher, capitaine aux suisses de la garde royale*, ed. Pierre d'Hugues (Paris: Arthème Fayard, n.d.).

Sciout, Ludovic, *Le directoire*, 4 vols. (Paris: Firmin-Didot, 1895–97).

Scott, Samuel F., "Problems of Law and Order during 1790, the 'Peaceful' Year of the French Revolution," *American Historical Review*, vol. LXXX, no. 4 (1975), pp. 859–88.

——, *The Response of the Royal Army to the French Revolution: The Role and Development of the Line Army 1787–93* (Oxford: Clarendon Press, 1978).

Secher, Reynald, *La Chapelle-Basse-Mer, Village Vendéen: Révolution et Contre-Révolution* (Paris: Perrin, 1986).

——, *A French Genocide: The Vendée*, trans. George Holoch (Notre Dame: Notre Dame University Press, 2003).

——, *Le génocide franco-français: La Vendée-Vengé* (Paris: PUF, 1986).

Ségur, Philippe-Paul de, *Napoleon's Russian Campaign*, trans. J. David Townsend (New York: Time-Life Books, 1965).

Semmel, Stuart, *Napoleon and the British* (New Haven, Conn.: Yale University Press, 2004).

Serna, Pierre, "Le duel durant la Révolution, de la joute archaïque, au combat politique," *Historical Reflections/Réflexions historiques*, vol. XXIX, no. 3 (2003), pp. 409–31.

Servan, Joseph, *Projet de constitution pour l'armée des François, présenté au Comité Militaire de l'Assemblée Nationale, par l'Auteur du Guide de l'Officier en campagne, et par celui du Soldat Citoyen* (Paris, 1789).

——, *Le soldat citoyen, ou vues patriotiques sur la manière la plus avantageuse de pourvoir à la défense du royaume* ("Dans le Pays de la Liberté," 1780).

Sewell, William, *A Rhetoric of Bourgeois Revolution: The Abbé Sieyes and What Is the Third Estate?* (Durham, N.C.: Duke University Press, 1994).

Sheehan, James J., *German History 1770–1866* (Oxford: Clarendon, 1989).

Sheridan, Richard Brinsley, *Saint Patrick's Day, Or the Scheming Lieutenant* (London, 1775), at http://ibiblio.org/gutenberg/etext04/stptd10.txt, consulted on June 26, 2006.

Shovlin, John, "Toward a Reinterpretation of Revolutionary Antinobilism: The Political Economy of Honor in the Old Regime," *Journal of Modern History*, vol. 72, no. 1 (2000), pp. 35–66.

Showalter, Dennis, "Prussia's Army: Continuity and Change, 1713–1830," in Dwyer, *The Rise of Prussia*, pp. 220–36.

Siegfried, Susan Locke, "Naked History: The Rhetoric of Military Painting in Post-Revolutionary France," *Art Bulletin*, vol. LXXV, no. 2 (1993), pp. 235–58.

Siegler-Pascal, S., *Un contemporain égaré au XVIIIe siècle: les projets de l'abbé de Saint-Pierre, 1658–1743* (Paris: Arthur Rousseau, 1899).

Silberner, Edmond, *La guerre dans la pensée économique du XVIe si XVIIIe siècle* (Paris: Librairie du Recueil Sirey, 1939).

Simmons, George, *A British Rifle Man: Journals and Correspondence during the Peninsular War and the Campaign of Wellington,* ed. Willoughby Verner (London: Greenhill Books, 1986).

Simon, Claude, *Correspondance de Claude Simon,* ed. Emmanuel Delorme (Grenoble: Allier, 1899).

Six, Georges, *Dictionnaire biographique des généraux et amiraux français de la Révolution et de l'Empire (1792–1814),* 2 vols. (Paris: Georges Saffroy, 1934).

———, *Les généraux de la Révolution et de l'Empire* (Paris: Bordas, 1947).

Slavin, Morris, *The Hébertistes to the Guillotine: Anatomy of a "Conspiracy" in Revolutionary France* (Baton Rouge: Louisiana State University Press, 1994).

Smith, Adam, *An Inquiry into the Nature and Causes of the Wealth of Nations* (1776), at http://socserv2.socsci.mcmaster.ca/~econ/ugcm/3ll3/smith/wealth/wealbk05, consulted on June 26, 2006.

Smith, Jay M., *The Culture of Merit: Nobility, Royal Service and the Making of Absolute Monarchy in France, 1600–1789* (Ann Arbor: University of Michigan Press, 1996).

———, "Social Categories, the Language of Patriotism, and the Origins of the French Revolution: The Debate over the Noblesse Commerçante," *Journal of Modern History*, vol. 72, no. 2 (2000), pp. 339–74.

Soboul, Albert, *L'armée nationale sous la Révolution (1789–1794)* (Paris: France d'Abord, 1945).

———, *Le premier empire, 1804–1815* (Paris: Presses Universitaires de France, 1973).

———, *The Sans-Culottes: The Popular Movement and Revolutionary Government 1793–1794,* trans. Remy Inglis Hall (Princeton, N.J.: Princeton University Press, 1980).

———, *Les soldats de l'an II* (Paris: Club français du livre, 1959).

Some Account of the Early Years of Buonaparte, at the Military School of Brienne (London: Hookham and Carpenter, 1797).

Sorel, Albert, *L'Europe et la révolution française,* 8 vols. (Paris: Plon, 1885–1906).

Souleyman, Elizabeth V., *The Vision of World Peace in Seventeenth and Eighteenth-Century France* (New York: G. P. Putnam's Sons, 1941).

Spiquel, Agnès, "La double guerre," in Claude Millet, ed., *Hugo et la Guerre* (Paris: Maisonneuve and Larose, 2002), pp. 227–47.

Starkey, Armstrong, *War in the Age of Enlightenment, 1700–1789* (Westport, Conn.: Praeger, 2003).

Steele, Brent D., and Tamera Dorland, eds., *The Heirs of Archimedes: Science and the Art of War Through the Age of Enlightenment* (Cambridge, Mass.: MIT Press, 2005).

Steinmetz, Sebald Rudolf, *Die Philosophie des Krieges* (Leipzig: J. A. Barth, 1907).

Stendhal, *Le rouge et le noir: Chronique de XIXe siècle,* ed. Pierre-Georges Castex (1999), at http://gallica.bnf.fr/document?O=N101497, consulted on June 26, 2006.

Stone, Bailey, *Reinterpreting the French Revolution: A Global-Historical Perspective* (Cambridge: Cambridge University Press, 2002).

Storrs, Christopher, and H. M. Scott, "The Military Revolution and the European Nobility, c. 1600–1800," *War in History,* vol. III (1996), pp. 1–41.

Stromberg, Ronald N., *Redemption by War: The Intellectuals and 1914* (Lawrence: Regents Press of Kansas, 1982).

Sur Bonaparte: Conversation (n.p., [1799]).

Suratteau, J.-R., "Goethe et le 'tournant de Valmy,'" in *Annales historiques de la Révolution française,* no. 309 (1997), pp. 477–9.

——, "Occupation, occupants et occupés en Suisse de 1792 à 1814," in *Occupants-Occupés, 1792–1815* (Brussels: Université Libre de Bruxelles, 1969), pp. 165–216.

Sutherland, D.M.G., *The Chouans: The Social Origins of Popular Counter-Revolution in Upper Brittany, 1770–1796* (Oxford: Clarendon Press, 1982).

——, *The French Revolution and Empire: The Quest for a Civic Order* (Malden, Mass.: Blackwell, 2003).

Tackett, Timothy, *Becoming a Revolutionary: The Deputies of the French National Assembly and the Emergence of a Revolutionary Culture (1789–1790)* (Princeton, N.J.: Princeton University Press, 1996).

Talleyrand-Périgord, Charles-Maurice de, *Mémoires du prince de Talleyrand,* 2 vols. (Paris: Henri Javal, 1953).

Taylor, Charles, *Sources of the Self: The Making of the Modern Identity* (Cambridge, Mass.: Harvard University Press, 1989).

Tennyson, Alfred, "Ulysses," at http://www.victorianweb.org/authors/tennyson/ulyssestext.htm, consulted July 10, 2006.

Terrasson, Jean, *Sethos* (Paris: H. L. Guerin, 1731).

Thiébault, Paul-Charles-François-Adrien-Henri Dieudonné, *Mémoires du Général-Baron Thiébault,* ed. Fernand Calmettes, 5 vols. (Paris: Plon, 1895).

Thompson, J. M., *Napoleon Bonaparte: His Rise and Fall* (Oxford: Basil Blackwell, 1952).

——, *Robespierre,* 2 vols. (New York: D. Appleton, 1936).

Tieghem, Paul van, *Ossian en France,* 2 vols. (Paris: F. Rieder, 1917).

Tilly, Charles, *The Vendée* (Cambridge, Mass.: Harvard University Press, 1964).

Tolstoy, Leo, *War and Peace,* trans. Rosemary Edmonds (London: Penguin, 1982).

Tombs, Robert, and Isabelle Tombs, *That Sweet Enemy: The French and the British from the Sun King to the Present* (London: Heinemann, 2006).

Tone, John Lawrence, *The Fatal Knot: The Guerilla War in Navarre and the Defeat of*

Napoleon in Spain (Chapel Hill and London: University of North Carolina Press, 1994).

Treitschke, Heinrich von, *Politics,* trans. Blanche Dugdale and Torben de Bille, 2 vols. (New York: Macmillan, 1916).

"Trivia," *William and Mary Quarterly,* 3rd Series, vol. XI, no. 4 (1954), pp. 633–4.

Trocóniz, Fernando F., "El Empecinado en Iraq," *El Siglo,* no. 584 (January 5, 2004), at http://www.elsiglodeuropa.es/siglo/historico/troconiz/2004/584Troconiz.htm, consulted on July 5, 2006.

Tuck, Richard, *The Rights of War and Peace: Political Thought and the International Order from Grotius to Kant* (Oxford: Oxford University Press, 1999).

Tuetey, Louis, *Les officiers sous l'ancien régime: Nobles et roturiers* (Paris: Plon-Nourrit, 1908).

Tulard, Jean, *L'Anti-Napoléon: La légende noire de l'Empereur* (Paris: Julliard, 1965).

——, ed., *Dictionnaire Napoléon,* 2 vols. (Paris: Fayard, 1999).

——, *Murat* (Paris: Hachette, 1983).

——, *Napoléon, ou le mythe du sauveur* (Paris: Fayard, 1987).

——, ed., *Nouvelle bibliographie critique des mémoires sur l'Epoque Napoléonienne écrits ou traduits en français* (Geneva: Droz, 1991).

Turreau, Louis-Marie, *Mémoires pour servir à l'histoire de la guerre de la Vendée* (Évreux, France: Chaumont, 1795).

Vagts, Alfred, *A History of Militarism* (New York: Greenwich Editions, 1959).

Vardi, Liana, *The Land and the Loom: Peasants and Profits in Northern France, 1680–1800* (Durham, N.C.: Duke University Press, 1993).

Varnum, Fanny, *Un philosophe cosmopolite du XVIIIe siècle: Le chevalier de Chastellux* (Paris: Rodstein, 1936).

Vattel, Emeric de, *Le droit des gens,* 3 vols. (Washington, D.C.: Carnegie Endowment, 1916).

Vauvenargues, Luc de Clapiers de, *Œuvres complètes,* ed. Henry Bonnier, 2 vols. (Paris: Hachette, 1968).

Velay, Clément C., *Le duc de Lauzun, 1747–1793: Essai de dialogue entre un homme et son temps* (Paris: Buchet/Chastel, 1983).

Vergniaud, Pierre Victurnien, et al., *Œuvres de Vergniaud, Gensonné, Guadet,* ed. A. Vermorel (Paris: Achille Faure, 1867).

Viallaneix, Paul, and Jean Ehrard, eds., *La bataille, l'armée, la gloire, 1745–1871,* 2 vols. (Clermont-Ferrand: Faculté des Lettres et Sciences Humaines de l'Université de Clermont-Ferrand II, 1985).

Vigny, Alfred, *Servitude and Grandeur of Arms,* trans. Roger Gard (London: Penguin, 1996).

Vilar, Pierre, "Quelques aspects de l'occupation et de la résistance en Espagne en 1794 et au temps de Napoléon," in Robert Devleeshouwer, ed., *Occupants Occupés, 1792–1815* (Brussels: Université Libre de Bruxelles, 1969), pp. 221–52.

Villat, Louis, *La Corse de 1768 à 1789,* 3 vols. (Besançon: Millot, 1924).

Villepin, Dominique de, *Les Cent-Jours, ou l'esprit de sacrifice* (Paris: Perrin, 2001).

Vinot, Bernard, *Saint-Just* (Paris: Fayard, 1985).

Voltaire, *Candide,* ed. Daniel Gordon (New York: Bedford/St. Martin's, 1999).

——, "Guerre," in *Dictionnaire philosophique,* at http://www.voltaire-integral.com/19/guerre.htm, consulted on June 26, 2006.

——, *Essai sur les moeurs et l'esprit des nations, et sur les principaux faits de l'histoire, depuis Charlemagne jusqu'à Louis XIII,* 8 vols. (Paris, 1804).

——, *Lettres philosophiques,* ed. René Pomeau (Paris: Garnier-Flammarion, 1964).

——, *Les œuvres complètes de Voltaire,* ed. Theodore Besterman, 151 vols. (Geneva: Institut et Musée Voltaire, 1970–77).

——, *Le Poème sur la bataille de Fontenoy* (Amsterdam, 1748), at http://un2sg4.unige.ch/athena/voltaire/volt_fon.html, consulted on June 26, 2006.

Vovelle, Michel, *Les Républiques-soeurs sous le regard de la Grande Nation, 1795–1803: De l'Italie aux portes de l'Empire ottoman, l'impact du modèle républicain français* (Paris: L'Harmattan, 2000).

Wahnich, Sophie, *L'impossible citoyen: L'étranger dans le discours de la Révolution française* (Paris: Albin Michel, 1997).

Wahrman, Dror, *The Making of the Modern Self: Culture and Identity in Eighteenth-Century England* (New Haven, Conn.: Yale University Press, 2004).

Wairy, Louis Constant, *Memoirs of Constant, First Valet de Chambre of the Emperor, on the Private Life of Napoleon, His Family and His Court,* trans. Elizabeth Gilbert Martin (New York: Century, 1907).

Walter, Gérard, *Robespierre,* 2 vols. (Paris: Gallimard, 1961).

Walter, Jakob, *The Diary of a Napoleonic Foot Soldier,* trans. and ed. Marc Raeff (New York: Doubleday, 1991).

Washington, George, *George Washington: A Collection,* ed. W. B. Allen (Indianapolis: Liberty Fund, 1988).

Watt, Ian, *The Rise of the Novel: Studies in Defoe, Richardson and Fielding* (Berkeley: University of California Press, 1959).

Weber, Ernst, "Der Krieg und die Poeten: Theodor Körners Kriegsdichtung und ihre Rezeption im Kontext des reformpolitischen Bellizismus der Befreiungskriegslyrik," in Kunisch and Münkler, pp. 285–325.

——, *Lyrik der Befreiungskriege (1812–1815): Gesellschaftspolitische Meinungs- und Willensbildung durch Literatur* (Stuttgart: Metzler, 1991).

Welch, Oliver J. G., *Mirabeau: A Study of a Democratic Monarchist* (London: Jonathan Cape, 1951).

Wells, H. G., *The War That Will End War* (London: Frank & Cecil Palmer, 1914).

Whiteman, Jeremy J., *Reform, Revolution and French Global Policy, 1878–1791* (Aldershot, England: Ashgate, 2003).

Whitman, Walt, "As I Ponder'd in Silence," in *Leaves of Grass,* at http://www.gutenberg.org/dirs/etext98/lvgrs10.txt, consulted July 6, 2006.

Williams, Helen Maria, *Letters Written in France in the Summer 1790* (London: T. Cadell, 1790).

Wilson, Kathleen, *The Island Race: Englishness, Empire and Gender in the Eighteenth Century* (London: Routledge, 2003).

——, *The Sense of the People: Politics, Culture and Imperialism in England, 1715–1785* (Cambridge: Cambridge University Press, 1995).

Wilson-Smith, Timothy, *Napoleon and His Artists* (London: Constable, 1996).

Woloch, Isser, *Jacobin Legacy: The Democratic Movement under the Directory* (Princeton, N.J.: Princeton University Press, 1970).

——, *Napoleon and His Collaborators: The Making of a Dictatorship* (New York: W. W. Norton, 2001).

——, *The New Regime: Transformations of the French Civic Order, 1789–1820s* (New York: W. W. Norton, 1994).

Woolf, Stuart, *Napoleon's Integration of Europe* (London: Routledge, 1991).

Wordsworth, William, "November 1806," at http://rpo.library.utoronto.ca/poem/2348 .htm, consulted on June 26, 2006.

Woudhuysen, H. R., "Shelley's Fantastic Prank," *Times Literary Supplement*, July 14, 2006, p. 12.

Zaghi, Carlo, *La rivoluzione francese e l'Italia: Studi e ricerche* (Naples: Editrice Cymba, 1966).

Zamoyski, Adam, *Moscow 1812: Napoleon's Fatal March* (New York: HarperCollins, 2004).

Zeller, Olivier, "Servir sous Louis XV: Lettres de guerre d'un officier au régiment Royal-Comtois," in Corvisier and Jacquart, pp. 299–311.

Zimmer, Hasko, *Auf dem Altar des Vaterlands: Religion und Patriotismus in der deutschen Kriegslyrik des 19. Jahrhunderts* (Frankfurt: Thesen Verlag, 1971).

Zipper, Albert, *Theodor Körner* (Leipzig: Reclam, 1900).

Index